Social Problems
in American Society

Social Problems in American Society

SECOND EDITION

edited by

James M. Henslin
Southern Illinois University

Larry T. Reynolds
Central Michigan University

HOLBROOK PRESS, INC.   BOSTON

Photographs from *Stock, Boston:* p. 10, Jean-Claude LeJeune; pp. 62 and 98, Peter Southwick; p. 144, Cary Wolinsky; p. 174, Bohdan Hrynewych; p. 218, Nicholas Sapieha; p. 244, Mark Rosenberg; p. 266, Norman Hurst; and p. 328, Daniel S. Brody.

© Copyright 1973 by Holbrook Press, Inc.
470 Atlantic Avenue, Boston

Printed in the United States of America

Library of Congress Cataloging in Publication Data

Henslin, James M   comp.
  Social problems in American society.

  Includes bibliographical references.
  1. United States—Social conditions—1960–
—Addresses, essays, lectures. 2. Social problems.
I. Reynolds, Larry T., joint comp. II. Title.
HN65.H435 1976   309.1′73′092   75–43826
ISBN 0–205–05467–6

For our colleague
Linda
who shares the vision

Contents

Preface

This second edition has been developed with two basic purposes in mind—to examine the interrelationship between social problems and the social structure of American society, and to stimulate the thinking of students in the direction of structural change that can alleviate social problems. Based on these intentions, then, this book is designed for those instructors who recognize that our present society requires basic structural change in order to make life better for its citizens, and for those who see sociology as a relevant social science that can provide analytical, empirical, and theoretical direction for social change.

In maintaining a sociological focus, the authors of these selections emphasize that our social problems are a product of our social structure as it now stands. Many of the selections are policy-oriented and carry a heavy emphasis on the need for social change. The value-criteria by which these selections were chosen and a general theoretical overview of the sociology of social problems are presented in the first section; the remaining sections analyze specific social problems facing contemporary American society.

The second section (Articles 2–5) examines poverty, unemployment, and other problems of structured inequality. Sections 3, 4, and 5 form a unit, focusing on discrimination on the basis of the socio-biological identifiers of sex, race, and age. Sections 6, 7, and 8 form another unit which analyzes the interrelated ecological problems of population, resources, pollution, and energy.

Section 9 examines the subservience of our social institutions to the dominant economic order; Section 10 takes a look at the dire consequences of this subservience to our concentrated economic, political, and military power. The primary focus of Section 10 is on the corporate power structure of the United States. The final section serves to tie together the ideas presented throughout the book.

We have not steered clear of controversy in this second edition, for it is by way of provocative analyses that we hope to stimulate the thinking of students. Our potential for change rests in our youth, where traditional ideas are not so firmly entrenched. If social problems are ever to be solved, the solutions must begin with a clear perception of their root causes. These solutions require structural social change because the problems originate and are maintained by the current social arrangements of American society. It is to this end and for those who share this vision that we dedicate this book.

J. M. HENSLIN

L. T. REYNOLDS

Introduction
to Social Problems

1

James M. Henslin

The Sociologist and the Study of Social Problems

BASIC APPROACHES

Social problems are anything but a unified area of study in sociology. Diverse topics are included under this general term, and there is little agreement among sociologists regarding precisely what the study of social problems should include (Fuller and Myers 1941; Kitsuse and Spector 1973; Westhues 1973; Manis 1974). Just as there is little agreement concerning the proper subject matter of social problems, so there is little agreement among sociologists concerning the proper approach to studying social problems. Current approaches vary widely and cover the spectrum of political opinion, with most texts and anthologies taking a safe middle-of-the-road stance designed to upset as few persons as possible.

There are three basic approaches sociologists take in their study of social problems: systemic, social disorganization, and definitional. In *systemic* analysis, the emphasis is on social structure (the interrelationships between a society's institutions) and on the costs of those structural arrangements. This approach "calls into question the society itself, and asks what one has to forego in order to live in it, and why" (Westhues 1973: 424). The sociologist who approaches social problems from a systemic orientation becomes critical of the existing social order. He assumes that the "costs" he witnesses in society—groups of people being hurt, discriminated against, and generally exploited—are neither necessary nor inevitable, but rather, are due to the social system, that is, to the current structuring of a society's institutions. This approach contains dramatic policy implications, for it focuses on the need

I wish to express my appreciation to John Rodman and the Office of Research and Projects of Southern Illinois University at Edwardsville for help in preparing the manuscript for this book.

for social change—on the need of restructuring social institutions and developing new or alternative forms.

Systemic analysis comes the closest to describing the general orientation of this book. The selections in this volume examine both interrelationships of the institutions of the United States and consequences of these institutional arrangements on those against whom social power is directed. As we focus on the social structure of the United States, we note how American social institutions are arranged and interrelated in such a way that they maintain social problems from one generation to the next. These selections especially emphasize how our social institutions consistently bring the best this society has to offer to the same small groups of people, while they regularly deny access to other groups in our society.

The second major approach to the study of social problems, that of *social disorganization,* was the major framework used by sociologists when courses in social problems first became popular. This approach has been declining in recent years, however, as its basic assumptions increasingly have become untenable. To view social problems from the framework of social disorganization means to take for granted that current social arrangements are good, for, from this orientation, social problems are those areas of social life that threaten the current social order. In this framework, social problems are defined as departures from the norms or standards of society. This approach carries with it a strong commitment to maintain and support the status quo, and its policy implications are directed toward coping, adapting, and adjusting (Westhues 1973: 421–422).

In contrast with the social disorganization perspective, the thrust of the analyses presented here is in a direction far from supporting the status quo. Our current social arrangements, especially the dominance of corporate capitalism and the energies directed toward its perpetuation at all costs, are taken as the root cause underlying the social problems we face in our contemporary society. The policy implications of this book similarly point to an opposite direction, as they are oriented to changing the basic social order, not sustaining it.

The third basic approach in sociology to the study of social problems can be called *definitional.* The emphasis of this approach is analyzing the process by which people define selected aspects of society as social problems, and the process by which people arrive at solutions to those problems. The definitional approach directs attention *away* from the type of society the United States is; this framework places little or no emphasis on social structure, and the student is provided little knowledge regarding how our society is organized such that it produces and maintains social problems. With its emphasis on micro-analysis of sub-aspects of social problems, a focus is commonly placed on such deviant subcultures as prostitution and homosexuality (Westhues 1973:422–4).

This also is *not* the approach of this book. Deviant subcultures are not analyzed in these selections, as it is the opinion of this author that such topics more appropriately belong to the sociology of deviance. Nor does this book focus on the process by which some area of social life comes to be defined as a social problem, although there are sociologists who insist that this is the proper subject matter of social problems analysis. Sociologists who utilize this definitional approach analyze how groups of people actively influence definitions of social problems. Sociologists who carry the definitional approach to an extreme even insist that for something to be a social problem there does not have to be an objective social condition at all; all that is necessary is for people to say that something is a social problem (Kitsuse and Spector 1973).

One can discuss, argue, and even quibble indefinitely regarding what is and is not a social problem, as well as how to best approach the study of social problems. Sociologists have, in fact, been engaged in such "dialogues" for a generation or so, and they still have not come to an agreement. Consequently, it has become popular for authors of texts and editors of anthologies to take an eclectic approach in their presentations of social problems. This matter has never been more succinctly put than this statement by Westhues (1973: 420):

> Without doubt the trend among textbooks to make the sociology of social problems the sociology of approaches (to the study of social problems) is encouraged by the textbook economy. Many authors and publishers seem to believe that the more approaches a textbook reviews and the more eclectic the one it prefers, the higher will be its rate of adoption and thus the more money it will earn. This often leaves the student of social problems struggling to comprehend sociologists' contradictory definitions of the field instead of learning something about the social world.

TOWARD A DEFINITION

At any historical point, certain characteristics of society are viewed as social problems. It is on some of these major areas of current understanding that the selections of this volume focus. Consequently, poverty, sexism, racism, ageism, and crises in population, ecology, and energy are social problems we deal with. Some may dispute whether or not these aspects of our society are social problems, but there appears to be a common consensus that they are, and they certainly fit the definition of social problems which shall be presented shortly.

Other areas of social life that we cover in this book are not yet commonly understood to be social problems. But in analyzing those social problems just listed, these aspects of life in America show up over and over. They prove to be highly related to our major social problems and, indeed, they are the conditions that underlie them—at least according to the approach to sociological understanding that makes the most sense to this author. Consequently, after we have covered some of the commonly agreed upon social problems, we turn to an analysis of the major conditions that both bring them about and maintain their existence. These root causes center on the subservience of our social institutions to the dominant economic-military-political complex that has come to characterize our society (as analyzed in Section 9), and the ascendance of corporate capitalism (as analyzed in Section 10).

The basic definition of social problems used in this book is: *social problems are conditions of society that have negative effects on large numbers of people.* While this definition appears straightforward, as it is meant to be, the terms in the definition deserve some explanation. First, as to "large numbers": there is no absolute number involved, no generally agreed upon minimum number which qualifies a condition as being a social problem. I have in mind, rather, the distinction that C. Wright Mills made (in his book, *The Sociological Imagination*) between "private troubles" and "public issues." If a situation is problematic for an individual or for scattered individuals, this is a "private trouble;" but if a situation is widespread, affecting large numbers of people in a society, then it is a "public issue"—or a "social problem." If a single person in a community is unemployed, for example, or if a few individuals in a few communities are out of work, or if work is hard to find within a particular occupation, this is an example of a private trouble. But if unemployment is fairly common in a society, affecting many communities across the nation, or if unemployment is endemic to a particular economic system, then this is an example of a social problem.

"Negative effects" is a reference to effects upon people that either terminate or impede the development of their human potential. To be somewhat more specific, "negative effects" are people being degraded, harmed, or exploited, especially when this comes about because another group of people is being exalted, favored, or having its interests advanced at the expense of those groups being deprived or injured.

"Conditions of society" refers to the *structural arrangements* within society which produce these negative effects on large numbers of people. This term is meant to emphasize that such things as poverty and racism have their origin in the basic structure of society. It is a particular structuring or interrelating of social institutions that produces those conditions that people usually see as problematic in society.

AND THE SOCIOLOGICAL IMAGINATION

The significance of this definition is that it changes the focus on social problems—*from* symptoms *to* underlying structural causes. Poverty, sexism, racism, pollution, and the other "ills" of society, in other words, are not in and of themselves the problem, but they are instead the surface manifestations of more basic or root causes inherent in our social system.

To make clearer the difference between surface symptoms and root causes, we can use the example of racism. Racial prejudice and discrimination are serious social problems in our society, but to focus on prejudice and discrimination is to miss the underlying characteristics of our society that give rise to them. Our society is structured in such a way that it not only creates racial prejudice and discrimination but it also perpetuates them from one generation to the next. It pits group against group, with whites hating blacks and blacks hating whites. This has the effect of maintaining the current social order by blinding those on the lower end of our social class hierarchy to their *common* situation in life, preventing them from seeing the basic exploitation from which spring their similar life circumstances. They are consequently rendered unable to unite in collective action to remedy their situation. Since structural arrangements in society produce prejudice and discrimination, it is they, the structural arrangements, that are the actual social problem.

The selections in this book are designed to raise the "sociological level of understanding" of introductory students by emphasizing that social problems are not accidents, that they don't simply "happen to be there," but that they are built into and are an essential, integral part of our present social system. Critical to the basic approach of this book is the perspective that it is not as though our social system has a "bind" here and there in its parts, and from time to time certain negative products crop up; it is, rather, that our social system is put together in such a way that it regularly produces negative effects on large numbers of people. Poverty, for example, could be eliminated in the United States. We now possess a vast, efficient technology which has the productive capacity of making poverty but a faint memory of an undesirable past. Yet we do not put our technology to work to eradicate this condition that continually harms so many of our people.

To understand that problems, which we have the capacity to solve but have not done so, are not accidental but are the result of the way our system functions (for example, the priorities we give to production and profits, the decisions our leaders make to further their own class interests, and so on) is to take the focus off the individual and place it squarely where it belongs—on the social system that produces and maintains social problems. Comprehending this perspective is to acquire "the sociological imagination."

VALUE JUDGMENTS AND THE SCIENTIST

It should be apparent from what has been said about the different ways sociologists define social problems that a high level of subjectivity is always involved. For example, the question of what a "negative effect" on people is, is not one which can be scientifically or objectively answered. With objectivity, one can describe, analyze, and predict effects, but to make judgments regarding which of those effects are preferable is to forsake neutrality and objectivity. To say that a particular effect is desirable or undesirable, that it is bad or good, that it harms people or that it helps them, is to make a value judgment.

As a sociologist, I am not simply a "disinterested," "dispassionate" observer of social problems. I am also a member of this society and also have a stake in the outcome of our basic structural arrangements. Consequently, value judgments must be a part of my, or anyone else's, approach to social problems. Even choosing the selections for this book involved making value judgments. I have endeavored to select problems that involve large numbers of people and articles that clearly demonstrate "negative effects" on people. Additionally, I have attempted to include selections in which the structural base of social problems is indicated and analyzed.

Value judgments among scientists are not by any means unique with sociologists, although I am being more frank about this matter than is usually the case. All scientists continually make value judgments as they pursue their work, as they "do their science," although they typically conceal such judgments from others, and perhaps also from themselves, by working under the related myths of "objectivity" and "basic research." Willhelm's article in this volume discusses in more detail how scientific myths and values in science lend support to our social system.

Scientists even make value judgments when they select the problems they study. (To single out one area of social life for research indicates that it is more worthwhile to pursue than another.) They also make value judgments when they turn their research endeavors in the direction of available funding. (Funding of scientific research is primarily provided by public and private elites, who have their own special interests and make use of scientific research to further their own ends.) Scientists make further value judgments when they accept work with one employer rather than another. (Corporations, for example, have vested interests in pursuing only certain problems, ones which are to their benefit to solve.) Scientists continue this judgment-making process as they decide what they will do with the results of their research. (Who will use the results for what purposes? Giving research results to a corporation for use in developing food with higher nutritional content, and giving the results of one's research to the government in order to produce weapons, for example, certainly reflect contrasting value judgments—although even these extremes are frequently hidden under the myth that scientific results are "neutral" and that the scientist is not responsible for what others do with the results of his research.)

When values are not made explicit, they work insidiously. When values are not explicitly stated and clearly examined by scientists, they often go unrecognized. Although they enter into the scientist's work, their effects tend to become invisible, allowing the scientist to presume the myths of objectivity and neutrality. More and more, however, scientists are coming to recognize that their work does indeed regularly involve making value judgments which have far-reaching consequences that directly affect the welfare of the inhabitants of this planet. Indeed, national scientific associations are currently concerned with this issue, making it increasingly difficult for scientists to hide under the myth of value neutrality.

To make my values more explicit, I further want to state that I consider social problems to deal basically with the quality of human life. I strongly feel that social arrangements should contribute to health and life, not sickness and death, and that science, education, and the mass media should disseminate accurate knowledge, not myths. It is also my position that citizens have the inherent and inalienable right to dissent; that they can and should hold ideas which oppose those who occupy the controlling sector of their society. It is also my conviction that actions which are harmful to the well being of humanity are inherently wrong, that exploitation should not be tolerated, and that efforts toward social change for the benefit of the oppressed is a desirable goal for both scientists and other citizens. (Cf., Manis 1974.)

Anyone's values are subjective and certainly can and ought to be questioned. I have no scientific way of demonstrating that these values are, in and of themselves, correct or superior to some other set of values. But I do want to make my values as explicit as possible because they underlie the choice of selections in this volume, as well as being essential to the articles I have written for this book. I also encourage other social scientists to be similarly candid in their approach to the study of social problems.

REFERENCES

Richard Fuller and Richard Myers, "The Natural History of a Social Problem," *American Sociological Review*, 6, June 1941, pp. 320–328.

John I. Kitsuse and Malcolm Spector, "Toward a Sociology of Social Problems: Social Conditions, Value-Judgments, and Social Problems," *Social Problems*, 20, Spring 1973, pp. 407–419.

Jerome G. Manis, "The Concept of Social Problems: Vox Populi and Sociological Analysis," *Social Problems*, 21, 1974, pp. 305–315.

C. Wright Mills, *The Sociological Imagination*, New York: Oxford University Press, 1959.

Kenneth Westhues, "Social Problems as Systemic Costs," *Social Problems, 20,* Spring 1973, pp. 419–431.

Poverty, Inequality, and Unemployment

As indicated in the preface and Article 1, we need to think sociologically as we approach the analysis of social problems. That is, to gain an adequate appraisal, we need to move away from viewing social problems as the manifestation of individual faults and examine how social problems derive from the way society is organized. From the sociological perspective, social problems result not from characteristics of the individual, but from social organization, from the way society is structured. The poverty, inequality, and unemployment that adhere to the American way of life, are built into the institutional framework of our country. They result from our social structure—being some of the many negative consequences derived from the way our social institutions are interrelated. It is to relevant parts of that social structure that we turn in this section—as well as in the following sections of the book.

That poverty is not accidental but is the contrived result of the way our social system is put together, is the thrust of this section. Each author documents this major point in a different way. In Article 2, Lumer analyzes some of the economic and social factors that create and maintain poverty among our people. As he details the effects of these factors on our minorities, the elderly, the underemployed, and the unemployed, he is beginning the theme that shall be emphasized throughout this book—the exploitative nature of our society. Lumer indicates that the profit motive of our economic order lies at the root of our social problem of poverty.

In Article 3, Lundberg examines the extremes in our distribution of material goods. He provides us sharp contrast by focusing on the wealthy in America. As he does so, he also emphasizes the structural nature of the possession and nonpossession of money. He indicates that our present inequitable distribution of income is the *planned* consequence of our social order, that wealth and power join together to

11

form a merged unit of political dominance that is utilized to maintain wealth where it is—and in so doing, to maintain poverty where it is.

But what about our system of progressive taxation? Does not our taxation system greatly equalize income distribution by placing a heavy tax burden on the wealthy in the support of public services? One would certainly think so from the reams of publicity regularly churned out by our government and faithfully reiterated by our mass media, as well as from the ritual teachings in our public school system concerning "progressive" taxation. But that this is not the case is solidly documented by Miller in Article 4. Miller examines the American myth of progressive taxation, and documents the way our taxation system works out in practice. As he does so, he emphasizes how the government uses official statistics to deflate the numbers of poor in America.

It is on this point of deflating or minimizing official figures that Leggett, Cervinka, and Ward focus in the concluding article of this section. They examine the policies of that agency of the United States government which has as its official task the accurate reporting of American employment-unemployment figures. In actuality, however, the Bureau of Labor Statistics operates in quite a different manner. This agency purposely obfuscates unemployment figures, or, to put the matter more baldly, the BLS regularly and directly lies to the American public in order to keep the public from knowing the extent of unemployment in the United States. These authors document the policies adopted by the BLS to systematically decrease the visibility of the unemployed—as though the problem of unemployment can be handled by the sleight of hand manipulation of numbers.

That unemployment and poverty remain with us, there is no doubt; that their extent is regularly minimized in order to stabilize the social system, there can be little doubt. But why must there be poverty in one of the richest nations of the world? It is to this basic question that you can profitably direct your attention as you read this section on poverty, inequality, and unemployment.

As you do so, keep in mind that according to the sociological perspective endemic social problems such as poverty, inequality, and unemployment derive from the structural arrangements of society. Accordingly, to eliminate poverty would require the restructuring of significant parts of our society. That which is so central to our society, the economic sector, would have to undergo profound modification. Those who would stand to benefit the least from such changes are certainly not the poor, the unemployed, or those who find themselves on the "less equal" side of inequality; nor is it the poor who would be threatened with loss by such changes. It is rather, those who are now benefiting the greatest from our present economic arrangement who would be threatened by fundamental and far-reaching changes designed to eradicate poverty.

Keep in mind also that the wealthy have manipulated our political system to consolidate their power and to maintain their wealth. These powerwielders systematically utilize their entrenched and vested political power in order to maintain their privileged position.

2

Hyman Lumer

Why People Are Poor

BLAMING POVERTY ON ITS VICTIMS

The notion has been widely propagated in this country that if anyone is poor or unemployed it is because there is something wrong with him. The great depression of the thirties did much to dispel this fallacy, but it persists nevertheless as the stock-in-trade of reaction.

In its crudest version it takes the form of the slanderous allegation that the poor and the jobless are the lazy and the shiftless. This version is today part of the arsenal of the ultra-Right and its standard-bearer Barry Goldwater. Typical of his views are such pronouncements as these:

"I'm tired of professional chiselers walking up and down the streets who don't work and have no intention of working." (*New York Times,* July 19, 1961.)

"The fact is that most people who have no skills have no education for the same reason—low intelligence or low ambition." (*New York Times,* January 16, 1964.)

There are others who would reject any such openly slanderous characterization of the poor, but who nevertheless ascribe poverty to individual peculiarities or shortcomings. Among these is Galbraith, who maintains that the general poverty of the working class has been abolished, leaving only individual-produced forms. He reduces present-day poverty, therefore, to what he calls "case poverty" and "insular poverty."

The former he defines as poverty related to "some quality peculiar to the individual or family involved—mental deficiency, bad health, inability to adapt to the discipline of modern economic life, excessive

Reprinted from Hyman Lumer, Poverty: Its Roots and Its Future *(New York: International Publishers, 1965), pp. 13–32. Reprinted by permission of International Publishers Co., Inc. Copyright © 1965.*

procreation, alcohol, insufficient education, or perhaps a combination of several of these handicaps. . . ." The latter he defines as a geographical "island" of poverty most of whose inhabitants do not wish to leave it, thus rejecting the solution to their poverty offered by emigration. (*The Affluent Society*, pp. 252–53).

In short, the lazy and incompetent are generally poor; the talented and industrious are generally well off. One may help the poor by means of social welfare measures or private charity, but the divergence in status is inherent in the nature of things. A statistical distribution must have a lower range as well as an upper—in ability as in income. Again, the poor are reduced to a "statistical segment," and as such the category is eternal.

Such an explanation will not stand up. The basic causes of poverty are not individual but social. Individual differences can at most determine who is most apt to be poor, given the existence of poverty. But they cannot explain its existence or its extent. The reasons for these must be sought in economic and social factors beyond the individual's control, ultimately in the character of the processes of production and distribution. True, there are people who suffer poverty because of personal handicaps or just plain misfortune. Such people need special consideration and help. But to take such a social work approach to the overall problem of poverty in our society is only to cover up the real causes.

First of all, the bulk of those in the lowest-paying jobs are not there because of lack of intelligence or other personal deficiencies but for quite other reasons. A large part of them, for example, are Negroes, Puerto Ricans or Mexican-Americans who are victims of discrimination. Others may be workers—particularly older workers—displaced from jobs by automation or the closing down of plants and unable to find anything better.

Secondly, the unemployed Appalachian coal miner or Pittsburgh steelworker is not out of a job because of his "low productivity." On the contrary, it is the multiplication of his productivity by means of new machinery and its utilization by his former employer to reduce the number of workers on his payroll that are responsible. If workers are victims of technological change in our society, this has nothing to do with their personal characteristics. "It was no sloth on the part of the coal miner," writes Bagdikian (*In the Midst of Plenty*, p. 182), "that caused petroleum to emerge as the more versatile fuel. It was no weakness in the railroad engineer that made the car and truck dominate transportation. Nor was it because farmers worked less hard that expensive machinery became more profitable than the simple plow. . . . Yet, the politics and social values of the commercial community, which depend on this versatility and change, assume that poverty and unemployment are casual, self-imposed and self-liquidating."

The Low-Wage Industries

It is noteworthy that half of all families below the $3,000-a-year mark are headed by an employed person earning less than that amount. Some of these are individuals working part time, but in large part they are individuals whose hourly rates are so low that even a full year's work pays them only a poverty-level income.

The main reasons for these shamefully low wages are lack of coverage by the minimum wage law and lack of organization. They are not the result of low productivity. Thus, where the law applies in a section of an industry (as it does in the largest retail units), wages are considerably higher than in the rest of the industry. Moreover, while a janitor in a retail store is no less "productive" than one, say, in an auto plant, the latter is better paid thanks to union organization.

In other words, a large proportion of the poor are in that category simply because they are grossly underpaid. Their poverty is a product of capitalist exploitation; indeed, their condition is the measure of what would be the lot of most workers were it not for union organization and protective legislation.

To this mass of grossly underpaid workers must be added the unemployed and underemployed. At first glance their numbers among the poor may seem insignificant: in addition to the one-half of the poor classified as employed, the Administration figures list only 6 percent as jobless and the remaining 44 percent as unemployable (the aged, the incapacitated, women with children, etc.)

These figures are misleading. For one thing, not all those classified as "unemployable" are necessarily so. The official figures notoriously understate unemployment by omitting those not working but not actively looking for work at the moment. Among the poor this number is especially large, for they experience the greatest difficulty in finding work and are most likely to give up the search as hopeless. There are also the many women with children who do not work simply because no suitable child care facilities are available. And certainly many of the elderly struggling to survive on social security pensions would take work if suitable jobs existed. In short, with greater availability of jobs and child care facilities the number of "unemployables" would dwindle greatly. We need only recall, in this connection, how drastically it shrank during the World War II years.

Further, the official statistics list as employed those working part time, even when this is involuntary. The number of such individuals, who should be considered as at least partially unemployed, is likewise especially high among the poor.

THE "WELFARE STATE" MYTH

Finally, there is the poverty of those unable to work. In a society which is habitually plagued with unsaleable surpluses of goods and which is capable of producing enough of life's necessities for all, there is no valid reason why these should be poor. Indeed few things speak so eloquently of the exploitative character of our society as its failure to maintain its aged and incapacitated at a level of ordinary decency.

The fact is that the widely acclaimed "welfare state" in our country is but a myth. The patchwork of social welfare measures which now exists has been won only in hard struggle against the opposition of big business, and the victories wrested from it have been meager indeed. Present standards are woefully lacking and are considerably behind even those of other capitalist countries. Often they are little advanced beyond the levels of the thirties and more often, in view of the great rise in living costs, they have fallen behind those levels.

Limited and inadequate as they are, these social welfare outlays are a target of unremitting attack. A Goldwater crusades for an end to compulsory social security as an invasion of personal freedom, and attacks the poor as lazy and shiftless parasites on society, deserving of nothing. Others conduct an unending fight to cut relief appropriations and trim relief roles of "chiselers." In state legislatures, unemployment compensation levels, far from being increased, are under constant assault.

Basically, poverty today stems from the drive of the giant corporations for maximum profits, which means not only holding wages down and not only sweating extra profits out of the small farmers, the small businessmen, the Negro people and other groups, but also holding government welfare expenditures to a minimum. As against being taxed for such expenditures, monopoly capital strives rather to use the economic resources of the government for its own benefit with the working people footing the tax bill. The poverty of those without work or unable to work is thus no less a product of capitalist exploitation than that of the masses of underpaid workers. . . .

THE NATURE AND ROOTS OF POVERTY

THE "UNDERCLASS" THEORY

It has become customary to speak of poverty in the United States today as "poverty in affluence." That is, where once the great majority of working people were poor and poverty was the "normal" condition, now most workers are at least reasonably well off and the poor constitute a minority which, for one reason or another, has been bypassed by affluence. As Harrington puts it (*The Other America,* pp. 9–10): "Today's poor, in short, missed the political and social gains of the thirties. They are, as Galbraith rightly points out, the first minority poor in history. . . .

"The first step toward the new poverty was taken when millions of people proved immune to progress."

From this it is but a step to the idea that the poor of today, in contrast to those of the past, constitute a new, distinct class in our society. This is implied in Harrington's phrase "the other America."

The essence of these views, in sum, is that the problem of poverty is no longer that of the working class as a whole but is now the special problem of a minority—an "underclass"—left behind in the accession of the great majority of workers to affluence, and separated from that majority by a widening gap. The task of fighting poverty, therefore, is that of bringing this remnant into the mainstream of a society advancing toward ever greater affluence, meanwhile giving its members every possible form of assistance in their unfortunate plight. We submit, however, that it is also essentially erroneous, no less so than the idea that poverty is the product of individual characteristics. Indeed, the two are not unrelated. To make clear both our objections to this conception and the true status of poverty as we see it, we propose that today poverty and unemployment are not distinct and separate problems.

Unemployment and Poverty

Historically, poverty and unemployment have always gone hand in hand. Layoffs, short work weeks and chronic lack of work have been intertwined with low wages as causes of mass poverty in the ranks of the working class, and in periods of depression the upsurge of unemployment has meant an upsurge of poverty.

Today, however, there is a tendency to separate the two—a tendency growing out of the concept of the "new" poor described above. In support of this view, it is argued that on the one hand only a small part of the poor are unemployed (as distinct from "unemployable") and that on the other hand the unemployed are not usually poor—that their spells of joblessness are not sufficient to reduce their yearly incomes to the poverty level.

More basically, however, the separation is made on the grounds that poverty today is not primarily economic in origin but is very largely the poverty of those by-passed by affluence because of personal characteristics or misfortune. Hence the remedy lies not so much in the economic sphere as in that of social welfare and public assistance. Unemployment, on the other hand, *is* economic in origin and the remedy accordingly lies in the sphere of economic reform.

Furthermore, the exponents of this view maintain, since poverty is static or decreasing whereas unemployment is growing alarmingly, the latter is the more serious problem, as well as one demanding more fundamental solutions. It is therefore the fight against joblessness, not poverty, which is the more basic task today.

With the emphasis placed on the fight for jobs one can fully agree. But the separation of this from the fight against poverty is unwarranted. As already pointed out the coincidence of poverty and unemployment is much greater than the official statistics indicate. Also, as suggested above, the ultimate roots of *all* present-day poverty are economic. The intimate relationship of the two is shown, moreover, by the fact that the slowdown in the decline of poverty largely coincides with the rise of joblessness. Indeed, this rise is one of the main reasons for the renewed concern over poverty today.

Most important, however, is the *nature* of the rise. For it is no transient occurrence, but is associated with an accelerating technological revolution among whose effects is the displacement of workers from their jobs in ever greater numbers. It is this displacement which threatens to swell the ranks of the poor anew and at a growing pace. This new class is made up of workers dispossessed by the machine: their skills, security and status all washed into nothingness by the course of technology."

Added to those fired as a consequence of automation are the growing numbers of young people never hired. Then there are those workers whose jobs are wiped out by the closing down of plants and the shifting of production to other areas—a process which occurs with growing frequency as automation spreads.

These workers are described as inhabiting an "economic underworld of the bypassed." But such a fate is not confined to some special group; it is one which menaces the great mass of American working people. From the threat of displacement by automation and related developments no worker in our capitalist economy is fully immune, whatever his seniority, skill or competence. The great bulk of the working people face a mounting degree of economic insecurity which renders their installment-plan affluence increasingly unstable and uncertain.

The displaced workers are not mere isolated victims of circumstance; they are a harbinger of what the continued advance of automation holds in store for growing numbers. They constitute a bridge between the working class as a whole and the poor—a bridge built of insecurity, displacement, unemployment and low-wage jobs. The poor, therefore, are not a separate class or an "underclass" but are part of the working class and the working people as a whole, the end product of a process of impoverishment in which every worker is in danger of being engulfed. Hence the war on poverty and the war on unemployment are not separate struggles but are parts of one single war.

3

Ferdinand Lundberg

The Elect and the Damned

Most Americans—citizens of the wealthiest, most powerful and most ideal-swathed country in the world—by a very wide margin own nothing more than their household goods, a few glittering gadgets such as automobiles and television sets (usually purchased on the installment plan, many at second hand) and the clothes on their backs. A horde if not a majority of Americans live in shacks, cabins, hovels, shanties, hand-me-down Victorian eyesores, rickety tenements and flaky apartment buildings—as the newspapers from time to time chortle that new Russian apartment-house construction is falling apart. (Conditions abroad, in the standard American view, are everywhere far worse than anywhere in the United States. The French, for example, could learn much about cooking from the Automat and Howard Johnson.)

At the same time, a relative handful of Americans are extravagantly endowed, like princes in the Arabian Nights tales. Their agents deafen a baffled world with a never-ceasing chant about the occult merits of private-property ownership (good for everything that ails man and thoroughly familiar to the rest of the world, not invented in the United States), and the vaulting puissance of the American owners.

A NATION OF EMPLOYEES

Most adult Americans in the quasi-affluent society of today, successors to the resourceful (and wholly imaginative) Americano of Walt Whitman's lush fantasy, are nothing more than employees. For the most part they are precariously situated; nearly all of them are menials. In this particular respect Americans, though illusion-ridden, are like the Russians under Communism, except that the Russians inhabit a less

From Ferdinand Lundberg, The Rich and the Super-Rich: A Study in the Power of Money Today (New York: Lyle Stuart, Inc., 1968). Reprinted by permission.

technologized society and have a single employer. There are, of course, other differences (such as the fact that Americans are allowed a longer civil leash), but not of social position. And this nation of free and equal employees is the reality that underlies and surrounds the wealthy few on the great North American continent.

Those few newspapers that make a practice of printing foreign news occasionally survey Latin American countries. The writers are invariably grieved to find a small oligarchy of big landowners in control, with the remainder of the population consisting of sycophantic hangers-on and landless, poverty-stricken peasants. But I have never seen it remarked that the basic description, with the alteration of a few nouns, applies just as well to the United States, where the position of the landowners is occupied by the financiers, industrialists and big rentiers and that of the peasants by the low-paid employees (all subject to dismissal for one reason or other just like the peasants).

In this table is found one verification of my initial paragraph. It shows that fifty percent of the people, owning 8.3 percent of the wealth, had an average estate of $1,800—enough to cover furniture, clothes, a television set and perhaps a run-down car. Most of these had less; many had nothing at all. Another group of 18.4 percent, adding up to 68.4 percent of the population, was worth $6,000 on the average, which would probably largely represent participation in life insurance or emergency money in the bank. Perhaps this percentage included some of the select company of "people's capitalists" who owned two or three shares of AT&T.

Another 21.89 percent of adults, bringing into view 92.59 percent of the population, had $15,000 average gross estates—just enough to

Gross Estate Size (dollars)	Number of Persons Aged 20 and Over (millions)	Per-cent-age	Average Estate Size (dollars)	Total Gross Estate (billion dollars)	Per-cent-age
0 to 3,500	51.70	50.0	1,800	93.1	8.3
3,500–10,000	19.00	18.4	6,000	114.0	10.2
10,000–20,000	21.89	21.2	15,000	328.4	29.3
20,000–30,000	6.00	5.8	25,000	150.0	13.4
30,000–40,000	2.00	1.9	35,000	70.0	6.3
40,000–50,000	0.80	0.8	45,000	36.0	3.2
50,000–60,000	0.35	0.3	55,000	19.3	1.7
All under 60,000	101.74	98.4	7,900	810.8	72.4
60,000–70,000	0.18	0.1	61,000	10.5	0.9
60,000 and over	1.66	1.6	186,265	309.2	27.6
All estate sizes	103.40	100.0	10,800	1,120.0	100.0
Median estate size			3,500		

cover a serious personal illness. This same 92-plus percent of the population all together owned only 47.8 percent of all assets.

INADEQUATE COUNTER-MEASURES

Not only is poverty in the United States very deep and widespread, Dr. Kolko clearly shows, but the various New Deal measures devised to mitigate it—Social Security, unemployment insurance, disability relief, minimum wage laws and the like—are quite inadequate in their coverage. There is no such thing, as newspapers repeatedly insist, as an embryonic Welfare State in the United States. This is evident in the fact that the average monthly old-age insurance payment in 1963 was $77.03 or $924.36 per year.

As to savings by each income-tenth, the lowest income-tenth has long lived on a deficit. From 1929 to 1950 this deficit varied from 2 to 35 percent, standing at 16 percent in 1950. Not only does this group not own anything but it is deeply in debt. The lower 50 percent of income receivers in 1950 had a net savings deficit of nearly 18.5 percent; the sixth income-tenth from the bottom had only 4 percent of net national savings, with the figures rising thereafter by income-tenths from 10 to 11 to 20 and to 72 percent for the top tenth. During the depression years of 1935–36, the net savings of the top income-tenth amounted to 105 percent, of the next income-tenth 13 percent, of the next income-tenth 6 percent and of the fourth income-tenth 2 percent —adding up to 126 percent. But 60 percent of the lower income receivers incurred debt of 25 percent as an offset.[1] In this numbers game much of what one saves another owes.

To all this some hardy souls respond by saying, "Well, that's the way the ball bounces, that's the way the cookie crumbles." In other words, all this is the consequence of the inevitable interplay of chance factors in which some persons are the lucky winners or the more intelligent players.

PLANNED CONSEQUENCES

But actually the results at both the top and the bottom are contrived. They are the outcome of pertinacious planning. For example, it is known on the basis of other careful studies that the lower income levels are disproportionately populated by Negroes and poor southern whites. They don't account for all of the lowly by any means; but they do account for very many. And the economic plight of both the Negroes and the southern whites is the consequence of a longstanding political power play. Southern Democratic Party gravy-train politicians after the Civil War, seeing a popular local issue in "restoring slavery in all but the name,"[2] asked for and received northern Republican acquiescence that would insure personally lucrative Democratic one-party dictatorial rule in the South. In return they agreed to deliver unbroken congressional support to the Republicans in blocking the rising national clamor, mainly from organized labor, for needed social legislation. For nearly a hundred years the scheme has worked perfectly, and the politically confused southern white in holding the Negro down, culturally and economically, has kept himself down to the same level. The scheme has had wider effects, as it has enabled the wealthy backbone of the Republican Party to keep a good portion of the rest of the country deprived, particularly of needed educational and social measures. The social role of the Republican Party ever since the death of Lincoln has been delay and obstruction, even though off and on there have emerged responsible, forward-looking Republicans.

This isn't to say that the foregoing paragraph accounts for the existence of deep and widespread poverty in the midst of fabulous wealth, but it accounts for some of it.

THE MILD WAR ON POVERTY

President Lyndon B. Johnson in 1964 startled average newspaper readers by suddenly announcing, out of a seemingly cloudless sky, his "war on poverty." This was widely interpreted, cynically, as a pure vote-getting ruse, of no intrinsic merit. For was it not a fact, as newspapers vowed, that there was no genuine poverty in the prosperous, high-living United States? But since then, as a result of official speeches and the passage of an initial anti-poverty measure exceeding $1 billion, the country has been gradually introduced to the strange, even subversive, notion that poverty is prevalent in the United States.

The argument has now shifted, as it is always bound to in the nimble hands of the dialecticians, to what precisely constitutes poverty. Sargent Shriver, director of the Office of Economic Opportunity and former President John F. Kennedy's brother-in-law, suggested that a family of four with a yearly annual income under $3,000 and an individual with an income under $1,500 be classified as poor, which would put more than 30 percent of all families in the poverty-stricken category according to University of Michigan figures. For the University of Michigan *Survey of Consumer Finances* showed for 1962 that, while the figures of the lowest tenth of all spending units (households) were not then available, the figure for the next to the lowest tenth was $1,510 for each household; and for the third from the lowest tenth it was $2,510. For the fourth tenth from the bottom it was only $3,350.[3] Mr. Shriver subsequently raised his figures to $3,130 and $1,540.

The United States Chamber of Commerce predictably challenged Mr. Shriver's first gauge of poverty as too high. "The Chamber of Commerce based its criticism of the old gauge," said the *New York Times,* "on the fact that a small family living in a warm climate and growing most of its own food could live comfortably on $3,000 a year."[4] As the patient could rest easily on this amount of income, why introduce him to luxuries—such as medicine?

Mr. Shriver, himself a wealthy man, more recently indicated that 35 million American families are "poverty stricken," untouched by existing programs for assisting the poor.[5] If one assigns only 3 persons to a poor family, many of which have many more, one obtains 105 million persons out of a population of 180-plus million.

Rather obtusely the Chamber of Commerce people did not recognize that the Administration, in dealing with a serious situation (for whatever motives, humanitarian or self-serving) had produced a deceptive new official yardstick for measuring poverty: income. Down through history poverty has always referred to lack of property. The man who had no property was defined as poor; the more property a man owned the less poor he was. Most people in the United States own little more property than do Russian peasants, and by that standard they are poor.

THE FORTRESS OF INTERLACED WEALTH

What has developed, then, under the operation of inheritance laws handed down from days when property ownership was far more modest to a day when vast properties have been created mainly by technology, is a huge, solid fortress of interlaced wealth against which even clever new wealth-seekers, try as they will, cannot make a tiny dent. About the only way one can get in (and that way isn't always rewarding) is by marriage. If a potential new Henry Ford produces an invention and sets out with friends to market it he generally finds (as did Professor Edwin H. Armstrong, inventor of wideswing radio frequency modulation, the regenerative circuit for vacuum tubes, ultra short-wave super-regeneration and the superheterodyne circuit) that it is boldly infringed by established companies. After he spends the better part of a lifetime in court straining to protect his rights he may win (usually he does not); but if he wins he collects only a percentage royalty. What the infringers can show they have earned through their promotional efforts they may keep, with the blessings of the courts, who are sticklers for equity: All effort must be rewarded. And then the overwrought inventor, as Professor Armstrong did in 1954, can commit suicide.

POLICY-MAKING POWER OF WEALTH

First, the present concentration of wealth confers self-arrogated and defaulted political policy-making power at home and abroad in a grossly disproportionate degree on a small and not especially qualified mainly hereditary group; secondly, this group allocates vast economic resources in narrow-self-serving directions, both at home and abroad, rather than in socially and humanly needed public directions.

When, through its agents, it cannot enlist the government in support of its various plans at home and abroad it can, and does, frustrate the government in various proceedings that have full public endorsement. It involves the nation in cycles of ferocious wars that are to the interest of asset preservation and asset expansion but are contrary to the interest of the nation and the world. It can and does establish connections all over the world that covertly involve American power in all sorts of ways unknown until some last-minute denouement even to Congress and the president.

It doesn't do any of this maliciously, to be sure, any more than an elephant feels malice when it rubs against a sapling and breaks it in two. An elephant must behave like an elephant, beyond any moral stricture. And power of any kind must exert itself. Historically it has invariably exerted itself in its own self-visualized interests.

DEFICIT IN PUBLIC SERVICES

The converse of the great concentration of personal wealth is the deficit in needed public social services. On the corporation front, the country is obviously extremely lusty. But in education and medicine, to cite merely two areas, everything suddenly becomes extremely meager, scrounging and hand-to-mouth. This disparity is curious in a wealthy country and forcefully reminds one of Benjamin Disraeli's allusion to two nations, the rich and the poor. But the deficits in these areas, the dialecticians will be quick to point out, are gradually being met now by government out of taxes. As we shall see later, however, the contribution of the top wealthholders to taxes is disproportionately low.[8] The wealthy, like everyone else, dislike to pay taxes and, unlike most other people, they know how to minimize them through the exercise of political influence. This is one of the nice differences between being wealthy and being poor.

The Constitution of the United States bars the bestowal of titles of nobility. But in many ways it would clear up much that is now obscure if titles were allowed. Not only would they show, automatically, to whom deference was due as a right but they would publicly distinguish those who held continuing hereditary power from people who are merely temporarily voted in or appointed for limited terms. The chroniclers of High Society—that is, the circles of wealth—recognize this need and, in order to show hereditary status and family position, they allude to males in the line of descent by number, as in the case of royal dynasties. Thus in the English branch of the Astor family there is a John Jacob Astor VII.[6] But there are also George F. Baker III, August Belmont IV, William Bird III, Joseph H. Choate III, Irénée and Pierre du Pont III, Marshall Field V, Potter Palmer III, John D. Rockefeller IV, Cornelius Vanderbilt V and so on.[7]

ENDNOTES

1. Gabriel Kolko, *Wealth and Power in America* (New York: Praeger, 1962), p. 48.
2. W. J. Cash, *The Mind of the South* (New York: Knopf, 1954). p. 115.
3. *Statistical Abstract,* 1964, p. 336.
4. *New York Times,* May 3, 1965; 24:3.
5. *New York Times,* May 27, 1965; 4:5.
6. Cleveland Amory, *Who Killed Society?* (New York: Harper, 1960), p. 476.
7. *Ibid.,* index.
8. See the following section (editor's note).

Herman P. Miller

4

Inequality, Poverty, and Taxes

Income distribution in the United States has remained virtually unchanged for one-quarter of a century. According to government figures, the poorest 20 percent of all families received 5 percent of the cash income in 1947 and they receive the same share today. By contrast, the richest 5 percent received 17 percent of the cash income in 1947 and 16 percent today. If the various types of noncash income that are omitted from the official figures are added to the distribution, the share going to the rich is vastly increased.

Except for the select few in the top 1 percent of the income distribution, there is little if any progressivity in the tax structure. According to a recent report by the Brookings Institution, the same proportion of income is paid in taxes by families at the 20 percentile and at the 99th percentile. Because of high taxes and the high cost of living, very little saving is accumulated by the lower and middle income groups. About one-third of all the wealth in the United States is owned by the top 1 percent of the families who have a net worth of $200,000 or more.

Our tax policies are in part responsible for the chronic shortage of the funds that are to deal with many social and economic problems. If we were to tax the rich more, it might be possible to do some of those things we now say we cannot afford to do. Our Federal Income Tax laws show that as a society we have a preference for progressive taxation (i.e., for taxing the rich at higher rates than the poor); yet, in practice we do not adhere to this policy. Why? The answer to this question is by no means clear, but it is worth exploring.

The last major attempt to alter the distribution of income in the United States occurred during the 1960s. At that time, the nation rediscovered the fact that, despite the general affluence, large numbers of Americans lived in abject poverty. Programs were instituted to raise the levels of living for the poor and to change those practices which

Herman P. Miller, "Inequality, Poverty, and Taxes," Dissent, *Winter 1975,* pp. 40–49.

systematically discriminated against ethnic minorities and other disadvantaged groups. Major changes were made in the civil rights laws; training programs were instituted for school dropouts and unskilled workers; and vast expenditures were made to improve the quality of education in low-income areas. Although these changes did not alter the distribution of income very much, they demonstrated widespread awareness and deep concern with the problem at the very highest levels of government.

Today, however, few Americans seem to have much interest in redistributing income. Attention is focused on fuel shortages, inflation, and corruption in government. But even before the onset of these problems, American voters showed strong antagonism to policies designed to alter income distribution. Just a few months prior to the 1972 presidential election, a Harris poll showed that three-fourths of the voters objected to Senator McGovern's proposal "to give each individual in the population $1,000 by sharply increasing taxes on people with incomes of $12,000 and over." There was more objection to McGovern's stand on income redistribution than to any other part of his program, nor is there evidence that attitudes on this subject have changed much since.

The income gap between the rich and the poor in the United States has been narrowed within the lifetime of many who are reading this article. During the depression of the '30s the share of income going to the top 5 percent of the families and individuals dropped sharply; it dropped again during World War II in response to economic forces, which created a great demand for unskilled labor as well as government policies designed to narrow wage differentials between low-paid and high-paid workers. All told, the share of income received by the top 5 percent dropped from nearly one-third of the total income in 1929 to about one-fifth at the end of World War II. Since that time there has been little change in income distribution; however, the average income per family (adjusted to changes in purchasing power) has continued to rise at the rate of 2 percent per year compounded. In other words, the equalization of incomes during the '30s and the early '40s did not diminish the productivity of the economy.

There is no question that equalization of income can be pushed too far. It can destroy incentives to work or invest and thereby become detrimental to the health of the economy. There is little point in changing the percentage of the economic pie received by the poor if it means they will receive a smaller piece. Some socialist countries have found that they have had to widen wage differentials in order to stimulate productivity. But clearly that is not the case in the United States at this time.

All we know from experience is that we had a major redistribution of income 25 years ago and there were no measurable harmful effects. It is entirely possible that we can travel further along the same path without ill effects. We won't know if we don't try; and even if we should try and fail, the action is not irreversible. As a social gamble, such a program is certainly worth serious thought even on the part of the higher income groups who would have to pay the cost. The great majority of the American people have lost faith in their government. They believe that the government serves the interests of the few who are wealthy and powerful rather than the great majority. One way to help change that image would be a major revision of the tax laws, which have long provided a shelter for the rich and have deprived society of the funds needed for income maintenance of the poor, better housing, improved education, and numerous other social and economic programs.

INCOME INEQUALITY AND TAXATION

Incomes in the United States are much more unequally distributed than the official figures show. The Census Bureau reports only cash income. No attempt is made to allocate money income that people receive but fail to report. Also excluded are capital gains, undistributed profits, and imputed income. I have attempted to correct this shortcoming by preparing a revised distribution of families by income levels for 1968, which includes the missing income. The procedures are described in several technical articles that I published jointly with Roger Herriot who is currently in charge of the preparation and analysis of income distribution statistics at the Bureau of the Census.[1]

The official figures for 1968 are based on a total of $543 billion in cash reported in the census survey. But these figures exclude about $260 billion of unreported cash income, capital gains, undistributed profits, and imputed income, all of which accrue disproportionately to the top-income groups. These items are omitted from the official figures primarily because the procedures that have been developed for distributing them by income levels are regarded as too crude to meet government standards. The income is there, nonetheless. Excluding it from the official figures does not change the economic reality.

According to Census statistics, the very small fraction of the consumer units (families of two or more related persons and persons living alone or with nonrelatives) with money incomes over $50,000 in 1968 received 2 percent of the total money income (see Table 1). When the billions of dollars of missing incomes are added, the share going to the top-income group inncreases to 7 percent. According to the census figures, the 2 percent of the units with incomes over $25,000 received 9 percent of the income; according to my best estimate they received 18 percent of the total. Changes of this magnitude are not mere technical adjustments. They basically alter the view of income inequality that exists in our society.

TABLE 1   Percent Distribution of Consumer Units and of Total Income: 1968

Money Income Level	Money Income		Total Income, Before Taxes and Transfer Payments	
	Consumer Units	Income	Consumer Units	Income
Total	100	100	100	100
Under $4,000	27	7	23	4
$4,000 to $25,000	71	84	74	78
$25,000 to $50,000	2	7	3	11
$50,000 and over	*	2	*	7

* Less than one-half of 1 percent.

For some time now, we have been urged by our leaders to tighten our belts and not to embark on new programs of social reform because we cannot afford them. As a result, we have postponed massive efforts to deal with unemployment and underemployment, decaying central cities, poor schools, inadequate medical care, and pollution.

If the rich have considerably more income than we thought they have, it may be possible, through tax reform, to get them to provide the funds we need for new social programs. These funds cannot come from the middle-income groups. After paying their taxes and the inflated costs for food, shelter, clothing, and other necessities, they have very little left. According to figures published by the Survey Research Center of the University of Michigan, about three-fourths of the families with incomes under $3,000 have liquid assets totaling less than $1,000. (Liquid assets include checking and savings accounts and U.S. savings bonds. They represent, as the name implies, resources that are quickly convertible into cash in the event of an emergency.) The picture was not much better for families somewhat higher on the income scale. At the $3,000–$7,500 income level, two-thirds of the families had less than $1,000 to fall back on in case of emergency.

These figures, perhaps better than any others, portray the sense of terror that must strike the breadwinner in the average poor to middle-class family when faced with the loss of a job. Their resources for sustaining emergencies of even short-range duration are meager indeed. Little wonder that the middle-income groups have reacted so strongly in favor of tax reductions and against new government programs that would have to be paid for by higher taxes. They know that as matters stand the brunt of the burden would fall on their shoulders. They now barely manage to get by from one payday to the next without being able to set much aside for a rainy day. This is certainly not true for the higher-income groups. Much as they complain about taxes, they still do most of the saving in this country.

A recent report prepared by Ben Okner and Joseph Pechman of the Brookings Institution shows the proportion of income paid in taxes by each percentile of the population ranged from lowest to highest according to income. This report presents tax rates based on eight different variants regarding the incidence assumptions of the various kinds of taxes. Shown in the chart—Figure 1—are the effective rates of federal, state, and local taxes based on the most progressive and least progressive variants; rates based on the other six variants fall somewhere between these two. It is quite apparent that there is little progressivity in the American tax structure. Using the *most progressive* variant, we find that consumer units at the 20th percentile (i.e., the poorest fifth of the units) pay 21 percent of their income in taxes while consumer units at the 80th percentile (i.e., the wealthiest fifth) pay 23 percent of their income in taxes. The tax rate goes up to 24 percent for the wealthiest 10 percent of the units and to 25 percent for the wealthiest 5 percent. It is only when we go to the very top of the income pyramid, the wealthiest 1 percent, that tax rates become appreciably progressive and reach 38 percent.

We must remember that these results are based on the *most progressive* assumptions. Using the least progressive assumptions, also shown in the chart, we arrive at the remarkable conclusion that consumer units at each income level between the poorest 10 percent and the wealthiest 1 percent pay the same share of their income (25 percent) in taxes. Using these assumptions, the share paid by the wealthiest 1 percent rises just slightly to 29 percent.

Nor are these facts new. They have been known for years. They appear in one form or another in elementary economics textbooks. They are taught to anyone who has taken a good introductory course in economics. Why then do Americans overwhelmingly prefer tax cut and reductions in government spending to tax reforms that would require the rich to pay more? The answer to this question is complicated. For one thing, it takes more than information to change attitudes; it takes a change in feelings. The greatest obstacle to income redistribution and major tax reform is not a lack of evidence that such changes are needed or a lack of knowledge of how to achieve these goals. Rather it is the belief most of us have that such changes are unwise, unfair, and unwarranted, and that some great evil will befall us if they are made. There is little evidence to support these beliefs; they are just ingrained in us by constant repetition in our homes and our schools, on television and in the press. These feelings and attitudes become so much a part of us that we come to assume they are based on facts; but there is no rational basis for such an assumption. Let us look a little closer at the

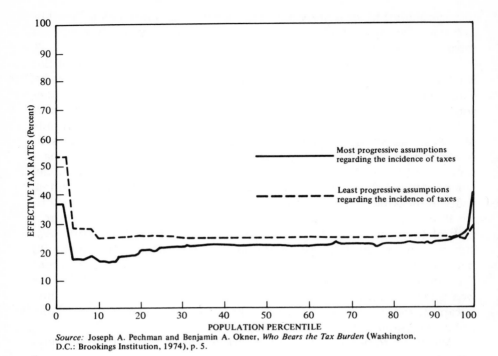

Source: Joseph A. Pechman and Benjamin A. Okner, *Who Bears the Tax Burden* (Washington, D.C.: Brookings Institution, 1974), p. 5.

FIGURE 1.   Effective Rates of Federal, State, and Local Taxes, by Population Percentile, 1966

basis for some of our attitudes regarding income redistribution and tax reform.

For years we have been told by conservative economists that we have little to gain by taxing the wealthy more heavily. Such taxation, we are told, would not bring in much revenue, would lead to a reduction in work effort, and would hurt us all in the end. But these economists only know what they believe in their own hearts to be true, and too often, what they know in their hearts is influenced, one way or another, by those who are putting money into their pockets. There is virtually no scientific evidence to support the view that the incentives of the rich to accumulate more would be destroyed if they were taxed more heavily. The few studies that have been made are small and inconclusive. Professor George Break of the University of California summarized the available empirical evidence for a congressional committee. His conclusion was that "income taxes exert relatively little influence on work incentives and when they do they induce greater effort as frequently as they deter it." He cites one study showing that "higher taxes induced more wives of business executives to enter the labor force and in general led executives themselves to postpone their dates of retirement." It is by no means clear that those among the rich who work would stop working if we taxed them more.

Spokesmen for the rich have long tried to persuade the rest of us that they are being pauperized by heavy taxation. We have been led to believe that the great fortunes such as those created by the Mellons, Carnegies, and the Rockefellers are a thing of the past. Nothing could be further from the truth. The rich among us are still flourishing. During the '50s the number of millionaires doubled, increasing from 27,000 to 53,000. According to the best estimates, the number had grown to 200,000 by the end of the '60s. This represents a fourfold increase from the beginning of the decade.

There is little evidence that taxation has dried up the sources of wealth. Table 2 shows the distribution of consumer units by the total amount of assets owned. These assets include equity in a home or business, checking and savings accounts, savings bonds and other liquid assets, and bonds and stocks. Debts are subtracted from the market value of each of the above assets, and the result is the estimate of net worth for each consumer unit. These figures show that less than one-half of 1 percent of families and individuals with assets of $500,000 or more own 22 percent of all the wealth in the United States; and 1 percent of the units have wealth of $200,000 or more and own over one-third of the wealth. At the bottom end of the distribution we find that 45 percent of the units have net worth totaling less than $5,000; they own only 2 percent of the wealth. It is also important to recognize that most of the assets of this bottom group are in the form of equity in a home or a car, which are not income-producing but are essential for everyday living. An old home or an old car may show up as an asset on the balance sheet, but they can be a real drag on the family budget.

TABLE 2   Cumulative Distribution of Consumer Units by Amount of Wealth: 1962

Amount of Wealth	Percent Distribution	
	Consumer Units	Wealth
Less than $1,000	26	*
Less than $5,000	45	2
Less than $10,000	61	7
More than $200,000	1	35
More than $500,000	*	22

* Less than one-half of 1 percent.

These families have very little, if anything, to fall back on in case of an emergency.

The figures in Table 2 pertain to 1962, when the Federal Reserve Board conducted the most recent comprehensive household survey of the distribution of wealth ownership among families in the United States. More recent data based on the analysis of estate tax returns collected by the Internal Revenue Service suggest that there has been no appreciable change in the distribution of wealth ownership since that time. A paper on this subject, presented at the annual meeting of the American Economic Association in December 1973 by Professor James Smith and Stephen Franklin of the Urban Institute and Pennsylvania State University, concludes that "the distribution of wealth has remained essentially unchanged since 1945."

POVERTY AND INEQUALITY

According to President Nixon's Council of Economic Advisers, "there has been a rapid decline in the number and proportion of families with a cash income below the poverty line." The Council failed to point out that all of this decline took place before Nixon took office. The number of people classified as poor in government statistics dropped from nearly 40 million in 1961 to about 24 million in 1969, or at the rate of about 1.7 million persons per year. Since 1969, the number of poor people has *increased* slightly. The proportion of the population living in poverty dropped regularly from 22 percent in 1961 to 12 percent in 1969; it has not changed since that time. This kind of distortion is typical of the way in which that Administration interpreted statistics. But that is not the point, at the moment. Let us turn our attention to the basic argument, which is true according to the statistics, that the long-term trend in the incidence of poverty in the United States has been downward. What does that mean and how can it be reconciled with the stability of income shares cited above?

It is undeniable that if the economic pie gets bigger each year and the share received by each fifth of the population remains unchanged, all will get more and in that sense they will be better off. The diagram below shows this point quite clearly. Assume that the shaded area represents the national income in a given time period (T_1) and that 5 percent of this income goes to the bottom fifth of the families. Their share of the income is described by the segment OAB. Assume that in a subsequent time period (T_2) the size of the national income grows to the outer circle, but the share received by the bottom fifth remains 5 percent. The amount of their new income is defined by the segment OCD, which is clearly larger than OAB. Using this model, we would say that

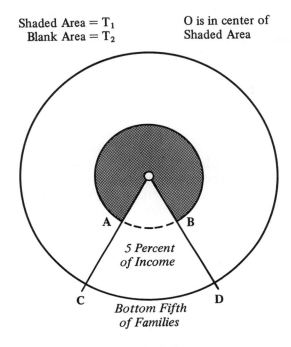

Shaded Area = T_1
Blank Area = T_2

O is in center of
Shaded Area

5 Percent
of Income

Bottom Fifth
of Families

FIGURE 2

the incidence of poverty did not change between T_1 and T_2 (20 percent of the population was poor in both periods), but the *amount* of income received by the bottom income group increased considerably. In other words, the absolute economic well-being of the bottom income groups would have improved even though their income in relation to others would not be changed.

But the fallacy in this model is that the incidence of poverty remains the same whatever the level of income. Every distribution has a bottom 20 percent; if that group is called poor, the incidence of poverty must remain unchanged. Such a definition is a tautology and it is obviously not used in the official statistics. How then is poverty defined in the U.S. and what are the limitations of that definition? According to the Council of Economic Advisers, the principal factor behind the decline in poverty in the U.S. is economic growth. As we shall soon see, there are other reasons.

Few Americans realize that poverty is defined statistically in such a way as to artificially deflate the number of poor and make the problem appear less serious than it really is. The official statistical definition of poverty (or low income as the government now prefers to call it) was adopted a decade ago, when the Kennedy-Johnson War on Poverty was begun. It is based on a food plan (the Economy Budget) designed by the

Department of Agriculture for emergency or temporary use when funds are low. This food plan was priced for a nonfarm family of four in 1963 and it was found to cost $1,042. Assuming that families spend one-third of their income on food, the cost of the total budget was set at $3,128 for a nonfarm family of four. This became the poverty line; families of four with incomes below this amount were statistically classified as poor. Equivalent poverty lines were established for smaller and for larger families. The poverty line was then adjusted back to 1959 on the basis of changes in the cost of living index, and it has been adjusted upward each year since 1963 on the basis of the same index.

It is important to realize that although the numerical value of the poverty line increases each year, it is a fixed standard in terms of the quantity of goods and services that it provides. Under the present definition, no provision is made for the changing of the content of the poverty budget. It is assumed that poor people will maintain the same level of living even though the level of living of everyone else has been rising. A fixed standard may be suitable for measuring changes in poverty for a short period. After 13 years, however, it begins to lose its relevance. In 1959, the poverty line for a family of four was 55 percent of the average family income; by 1972, this rate had dropped to 38 percent. As a result, while many people have been moved above the poverty line, their position relative to others has remained unaltered. They continue to be unable to enjoy the goods and services widely enjoyed by others. Their status in the government figures is changed from poor to nonpoor, but their feelings of deprivation remain unchanged.

The misleading nature of government proclamations heralding the decline of poverty in the United States can be demonstrated with just a few figures. The average income of poor families was $2,178 in 1959 and $2,456 in 1972 (both figures measured in constant dollars of 1972 purchasing power). The average income of families that were not poor was $10,021 in 1959 and $13,672 in 1972 (again, using dollars of constant purchasing power). In other words, the dollar gap between poor and nonpoor families rose from $7,843 in 1959 to $11,216 in 1972. Or, stated differently, the average income of nonpoor families was four and one-half times that of poor families in 1959; by 1972, this ratio had risen to five and one-half times.

When this same comparison is made between the poor and the rich (defined as the top 5 percent of the families ranked from lowest to highest by income), the results are even more striking. The average income of rich families was $27,267 in 1959 and $40,142 in 1972 (in constant dollars). The dollar gap between the rich and the poor, therefore, increased from $25,089 in 1959 to $37,686 in 1972 and the average income of the rich rose from 12.5 times that received by the poor in 1959 to more than 16 times in 1972.

It is of no avail to preach to the American poor that they live better

TABLE 3A

	Average Income	
	1959	*1972*
Poor families	$ 2,178	$ 2,456
Nonpoor families	10,021	13,672
Dollar gap	7,843	11,216
Ratio of nonpoor to poor	4.6	5.6

than most people in most parts of the world or to tell them not to compare their lot with those who are more fortunate. Such admonitions are open invitations to resentment and anger. The fact is that people's feelings about their economic well-being are based, not only on their own incomes, but also on the incomes of those around them and on the income that is considered necessary to get along in this society.

The American experience is not unique in this respect. A recent study by Professor Richard Easterlin of the University of Pennsylvania, based on 30 surveys conducted in 19 different countries where information was collected on the relationship between happiness and income, shows that in all societies, at any given point in time, happiness tends to increase with income (i.e., those who have more income tend to be happier). However, as the income of a society increases, the proportion of

TABLE 3B

	Average Income	
	1959	*1972*
Poor families	$ 2,178	$ 2,456
Rich families (defined as the top 5 percent)	27,267	40,142
Dollar gap	25,089	37,686
Ratio of rich to poor	12.5	16.3

people who say they are happy remains unchanged. On the basis of this and other evidence presented in the report, Professor Easterlin concludes that each person believes he will be happier if his income goes up. And he is happier provided that the income of others does not go up as much as his own. When every income goes up at the same rate, no one is happier; and when the incomes of some people go up, but at a slower rate than the income of others, that becomes a source of discontent. If these studies are valid, our statistical indicators regarding poverty are misleading. We live in a society in which real incomes are going up at the rate of 2 percent per year. If the standard for measuring poverty remains fixed for too long, we may decrease the number of people whom we *call* poor, but we will not change their feeling that they are still poor in relation to others around them.

THE IMPACT OF GOVERNMENT REDISTRIBUTION

The income data described above tell only part of the story. They show how the net national product was distributed before taxes. In 1968, the federal, state, and local governments took one-third of our income in taxes and they gave it back to us in the form of transfer payments, goods, and services. In the reports referred to above, Mr. Herriot and I attempted to distribute the burden of taxation as well as the benefit of government expenditure by income classes. The results are shown in Table 4. The basic procedure required us to make assumptions as to who paid each tax and who benefited from each government service. For many types of services such as education, health, highways, and social welfare it seemed possible to make reasonable assumptions regarding the beneficiaries. The benefits of expenditures on elementary and secondary school education were allocated to families with children in school; benefits from public assistance and social security were allocated to the recipients of these types of income, etc. The big problem was how to allocate the very large fraction of the total that was spent on national defense and related activities. Four different assumptions were used: that the benefits were shared (a) proportionate to income; (b) proportionate to wealth; and (c) equally; (d) one-third according to wealth, one-third to income, and one-third equally.

Presumably the most egalitarian assumption is that we all benefit equally from defense expenditures. This is a valid view if one assumes that we each have one life to save and the same amount of freedom to lose if we should be conquered by an enemy. On this basis the benefits from defense and related activities should be divided equally among all families. Using this assumption we find (from column C in Table 4) that the share of income received by the poorest quarter of the families nearly triples, going from 4 percent to 11 percent; and the share received by the top 3 percent (those making over $25,000) is reduced from 18 percent to 12 percent. This is a sizable reduction of inequality, but it involves a very special and, in my opinion, an unrealistic assumption regarding the distribution of benefits from defense and related expenditures. We spend money for defense to protect our wealth and our income as well as our lives. It is an established principle of law that all lives do not have an equal monetary value. The general rule in wrongful death cases is that the estate can sue for the present value of the expected lifetime earnings of the deceased. According to the Census Bureau reports, for example, the monetary value for an elementary school graduate is about $300,000 and that of a college graduate is over $600,000. These are the amounts that might be asked as payment for damages in wrongful death actions involving persons who had grammar school or college backgrounds. In light of this fact, it seems unreasonable to allocate the benefits of defense expenditures as though we all had an equal share. It would be more reasonable, following the persuasive logic of the law, to make some allowance for the value of our wealth and for our monetary value as human beings.

Table 4 (column B) also shows a distribution based on the assumption that defense expenditures are allocated proportionate to our wealth. This assumption treats defense expenditures as an insurance payment to protect our property. Viewed in this way, the activities of the government cause the share of income going to the bottom quarter of the consumer units to increase at the expense of the middle three-fourths; but the share received by the very small fraction with incomes over $25,000 remains unchanged at about 18 percent. The conclusion based on this interpretation is that the net impact of government intervention on the distribution of income is to transfer income from the middle class to the poor. The rich neither gain nor lose in the process, because most of what

TABLE 4   Percentage Distribution of Income Before and After Government Intervention: 1968

Money Income Level	Total income before *taxes, transfers, and government expenditures*	Total income after *taxes, transfers, and government expenditures**			
		A	*B*	*C*	*D*
Total	100	100	100	100	100
Under $4,000	4	7	8	11	9
$4,000 to $25,000	78	78	75	77	77
$25,000 to $50,000	11	10	10	8	9
$50,000 and over	7	5	7	4	5

* Assumes nonallocatable government expenditures (mostly for national defense) distributed as follows:
  A: total income (each family receives a share proportionate to its income);
  B: total wealth (each family receives a share proportionate to its wealth);
  C: each family receives an equal share;
  D: one-third according to income; one-third according to wealth; and one-third equally.

is taken away from them in taxes is returned in the form of an insurance benefit designed to protect their property.

Column D shows still another, and perhaps more reasonable, way to allocate expenditures for defense and related activities. Since these expenditures are made to protect our freedom, our lives, and our property, why not divide them into three different components and use a different procedure for each? As a starter, we might assume that one-third of the expenditures are made to protect our freedom and that we all get an equal benefit from that component. Assume also that an additional third is spent to protect our lives. These benefits can be allocated proportionate to the present value of the expected lifetime income of each family. We can assume that the final third is spent to protect our property. This share can be distributed proportionate to our wealth. On this basis we find that the share of income going to families with income under $4,000 is more than doubled, going from 4 percent to 9 percent as a result of the intervention of the government; the share going to those with incomes between $4,000 and $25,000 is virtually unchanged; and the share going to those with incomes of $25,000 or more is reduced from 18 percent to 14 percent. The share going to the very wealthy is cut back from 7 percent to 5 percent based on these assumptions.

CONCLUSION

At one time, income distribution was regarded as fixed. Social scientists assumed that an inexorable law determined the distribution of income in a given time and place, and that changes in that distribution could be made only at great peril to the social order. They even gave this law a name, "Pareto's Law," in honor of the Italian economist who was among the first to do empirical work in this field during the latter part of the 19th century. Some economists went so far as to assert that a sharp rise in income inequality would cause a revolution and a sharp drop would cause a civil war. It has been argued that the French and Russian revolutions were caused by undue concentrations of income and wealth whereas the Spanish revolution of the late 1930s was caused by "socialistic trends" that followed the overthrow of the monarchy and "lowered greatly the ratio of concentration from its Pareto norm."

Few economists today believe that there are inexorable laws of income distribution. The fact is that incomes in the United States are more equally distributed today than they were 40 years ago. Most of the redistribution, however, took place during the depression of the '30s and during World War II. There has been little change during the past 25 years. Despite the rhetoric of the Great Society architects, their programs did not change income distribution very much, if at all. But there is no sound economic reason why we should not resume the progress that ended one-quarter of a century ago. We can have a further reduction of inequality and a different distribution of the tax burden without necessarily hurting the economy. Economists who say otherwise are going beyond the limits of the knowledge of their profession. We may not choose to have redistribution as a social goal; but there is no good *economic* reason that requires us to make such a choice. In short, we could decide to raise the incomes of poor people and tax the rich more to help pay for it, if we want to, and not have the feeling that we are violating some natural law or endangering social order.

For the moment, the nation appears to have lost its interest in income redistribution. The rallying cry today is, "Balance the Budget." The economizers are firmly in the saddle. We shall soon see where their policies lead us. It is comforting to know that we have the wealth to create a better world if we become disenchanted with their false economics. All we need is the desire to do so.

ENDNOTES

1. Roger A. Herriot and Herman P. Miller, "The Taxes We Pay," *Conference Board Record,* May 1971; also "Tax Changes Among Income Groups," *Business Horizons* (Indiana University), February 1972.

5

John C. Leggett
Claudette Cervinka
Lila Ward

Let's Count the Unemployed

WHO GETS COUNTED HOW

Official figures on the U.S. "jobless rate" for the month of November, 1974 were stated in the December 7th issue of the New York *Times* to be 6.5% .[1] Are we to believe that figure? Are there just a relatively small number of American jobless while 93.5% have regular paying jobs? If so, what's all this talk about recession? The economy can't be that bad off if so few people are out of work. In fact, the situation is far more serious than the BLS figures suggest. Perhaps four to five times the 6.5% are members of a labor supply willing to work at full time jobs were they to become available.[2] Unemployed but tired of looking for work, housewives ready to go to work, non-working older people (55 and over) and many others are today part of a large and growing army of unemployed, would be-employed and underemployed. Yet the official statistics on unemployment by no means indicate the breadth of this "reserve army." How can this happen?

The Bureau of Labor Statistics (BLS) uses invalid estimates of both unemployed and employed:

1. The BLS does not count the unemployed—instead it presents estimates on hustling job seekers located *within* the labor force.
2. The BLS minimizes the number of persons unemployed by consigning many *would be employed* to the category "not in the labor force."
3. The BLS does not count the employed—it purports to gauge the number attached to various work sites.
4. To arrive at sparingly thin figures on unemployment, the BLS lessens the number of unemployed—the numerator—as it fat-

This article was written for this volume and is printed by permission.

42

tens the frequency of the employed—the vast majority in the denominator—to achieve a quotient percentage comfortably small and politically tolerable.

To make clear the bases for this charge we must observe how the BLS gauges (1) being a member of the labor force, (2) being unemployed, and finally, (3) the employed.

First, who's on the outside and who's on the inside of the labor force?

Persons under 16 years of age are excluded from our count of the labor force, as are all inmates of institutions, regardless of age. All other members of the civilian noninstitutional population are eligible for the labor force by our definitions. Therefore, persons age 16 and over who have no job and are not looking for one are counted as 'not in the labor force'. For many who do not participate in the labor force, going to school is the reason. Family responsibilities keep others out of the labor force. Still others suffer a physical or mental disability which makes them unable to participate in normal labor force activities.

Most of these situations are quite clear: Bob Jones reports that he is attending college; Barbara Green feels that her two young children need her care; or Stephen Smith would like to work, but his doctor told him that he must not because he recently suffered a heart attack. All three of these people are not in the labor force and are classified accordingly, in their respective categories: "in school," "keeping house," and "unable to work."

There is a fourth group of persons who are not in the labor force. They are classified "other," which includes everyone who did not give any of the above reasons for nonparticipation in the labor force. Such persons may be retired and feel that they have made their contribution to the economy throughout the course of their lives, they may want to work only at certain times of the year, or they may believe that no employment is available for workers with their experience or training.[3]

The illustrations are less than wholly inclusive. The category of labor force excludes, for example, inmates who labor in our prisons and asylums. The Attica events of 1971 have brought their labors and their conditions to the forefront of our consciences but not into our statistical analyses where they belong. In addition, the labor force category also excludes millions who are tired of looking for work and have subsequently disappeared from the ranks of the unemployed. Deleted, then, are people who failed to seek work in the last 4 weeks even after they had earlier sought work in vain and later given up.

Prior to 1967, those seeking work in the last 60 days were included as members of the labor force.[4] Today those who have not sought a job in the last four weeks are not in the labor force.[5] In other words, prior to 1967 had a person without work sought a job 5 weeks prior to the BLS interview, he would have been counted as unemployed. After 1967, he would not have been counted as unemployed and hence not part of the labor force. These persons get shoved into the limbo of "not in the labor force."

We do not know the exact number of those who have given up looking for work, but we do know that their numbers are in the millions. Besides those keeping house, going to school or just plain being unable to work, there are the "others" who also fall in the "not in labor force" category. For example, in July, 1972, there were *13,658,000* such persons (See Table 1).[6] Now that is a remarkably large figure. The BLS recently stated that the "others" are . . . people (who) . . . (1) may want to work only at certain times of the year; (2) may believe that no employment is available for workers with their experience or training; or (3) may be financially independent and have no interest in a job."[7]

One might wonder what proportion of that number, plus housewives and older people, would in fact go to work were jobs available. Data from the Second World War strongly suggest that a large proportion of these persons would in fact seek and obtain employment under conditions of full employment opportunity.

Stanley Moses recently observed:

> During the war, between 1940 and 1945, the total labor force, civilian and military, increased by about 10 to 11 million. The military grew from about a few hundred thousand in 1940 to over 12 million by 1945. At the same time, civilian employment increased by about 7 million, most of it war related production.
>
> It is estimated that normal labor force growth would have accounted for about 3 million during the period of 1940 to 1945. Where did the additional 8 million workers come from? They were people who by the existing labor force definition were not part of the labor supply—older and younger males and females of all ages. Youth of school age provided about 4.4 million new workers; older men and women (over 55) provided another 1.6 million; and of the remaining 2 million additional workers, the major part came from women between 25 and 54 who were either new entrants or re-entrants to the labor force.[8]

Who are the unemployed? How does their official count minimize their real size? By 1967, the BLS definition of unemployed had become what it is today:

> Persons are unemployed if they have looked for work, and, of course, do not have a job at the same time. Looking for work

TABLE 1   Employment Status of the Civilian Non-institutional Population, January 1972 and July 1972 (16 years of age and over)

Employment Status	January 1972	July 1972
Total civilian noninstitutional population	142,103,000	143,466,000
Civilian labor force	84,553,000	88,617,000
Employed	79,106,000	83,443,000
At work	75,663,000	72,954,000
Full time	57,678,000	57,844,000
Part time	17,986,000	15,112,000
With a job but not at work	3,443,000	10,489,000
On strike	92,000	124,000
On vacation	681,000	8,400,000
Bad weather	309,000	21,000
Temporary illness	1,704,000	1,125,000
Other	656,000	819,000
Unemployed	5,447,000	5,173,000
Looking for full-time work	4,261,000	4,315,000
Looking for part-time work	1,186,000	859,000
Not in the labor force	57,550,000	54,850,000
Keeping house	35,638,000	36,688,000
In school	9,303,000	1,910,000
Unable to work	2,461,000	2,593,000
Other	10,148,000	13,658,000

Source: Taken from "How the government measures unemployment," Report 418, U.S. Department of Labor, Bureau of Labor Statistics, 1973, p. 7.

may consist of any of the following specific activities:
    Registering at a public or private employment office;
    Meeting with prospective employers;
    Checking with friends or relatives;
    Placing or answering advertisements;
    Writing letters of application;
    Being on a union or professional register.[9]

There are two small groups of people who do not have to meet the test of having engaged in a specific jobseeking activity to be counted as unemployed. Nonetheless, they are people who have hustled either to get or keep a job; (a) persons waiting to start a new job within 30 days, and (b) workers waiting to be recalled from layoff. In all cases, the individual must be currently available for work.[10]
    Finally, who are the employed?

There is a wide range of job arrangements possible in the American economy, and not all of them fit neatly into a given category. For example, people are considered employed if they did any work at all for pay or profit during the survey week. This includes all part-time and temporary work as well as regular full-time year-round employment. Persons are also counted as employed if they have a job at which they did not work during the survey week because they were:

On vacation;

Ill;

Involved in an industrial dispute;

Prevented from working by bad weather;

or

Taking time off for various personal reasons.

These persons are counted among the employed and tabulated separately as "with a job but not at work," because they have a specific job to which they will return.[11]

Let us contemplate this specification. Missing from the unemployed, but counted among the employed, are people who work five, ten, twenty, or thirty, hours a week. In fact, all forms of part-time help count as employed. But that ain't all. Included among the employed are all persons who did at least 15 hours of unpaid work in a family-operated enterprise.[12]

Finding their way into the employed category are short-term strikers, the short and long-term ill (non-institutionalized), plus the two week as well as two month "vacationers." (See Table 1.) To be employed, then, is not the same as to be engaged at work. Stop and think about that one. The distinction between (a) nonwork-employment and (b) work employment is a subtle one that many of us miss even though these millions of the non-working employed fail to earn incomes, as is often the case during a strike, an illness or a vacation. Perhaps we should mention that the category non-working employed suggests the official category of working unemployed—those wretched chiselers on the unemployment rolls who do in fact work but cheat a government dutybound to assess their awful numbers. So much for the employed.

What people sometimes overlook, however, is how both (a) the narrow base for computing who is unemployed and (b) the extraordinarily broad criteria for determining who is beyond the labor force—these two computations—do underestimate the relative importance of the unemployed.

Given these shenanigans, how does this triangular relationship among numerator, denominator, and outcome work? Since many of the objectively unemployed have been secreted by the BLS into the limbo of "not in labor force," where they cannot serve as a sizeable portion of what would otherwise be a fairly large numerator in the overall

"They Count Me As Working"

statistical figure of percentage unemployed, and since neither the not-in-labor force nor unemployed categories include the strikers, the ill, and the vacationers, and furthermore, since these three categories count as employed, the officially unemployed stand as a whittled gnat in statistical ratio to the padded elephant.[13] In effect, we have an unduly puny numerator peering down at a bloated denominator, a total labor force figure consisting of unemployed and employed. What we have is a Kafkaesque situation where a sudden and numerous increase in strikers,[14] hospital patients, and/or vacationers would inadvertently contribute to the immediate minimization of the official figure on unemployment, even when there occurred a trend increase in the number of those officially counted as unemployed, for persons who would normally get laid off and fall in the *unemployed* category become as strikers members of the employed, thereby fattening the denominator. Think about that one, especially in strike-normal communities such as Detroit.

AND THE YOUNG

The BLS underestimates the current seriousness of general unemployment, youth unemployment, and black youth unemployment by sticking with the 1967 decision not to include the 14 and 15 year olds as eligible for labor force status.

Most curious is this deliberate omission. Officially, 14 and 15 year olds are no longer in the labor force. In fact, and strangely enough, they are still counted by the Bureau of Labor Statistics. (See Table 2.) One's curiosity on this matter is whetted by what the findings indicate:

(1) There are proportionately more (officially) unemployed among the 14–15 year olds than in the total labor force;

(2) There are proportionately more blacks than whites unemployed. Indeed the ratio is 3–1 rather than the generally accepted figure of 2–1 for blacks and whites (for all of the black and white labor force participants).

What the data suggest is that dropping out of school to go to work has deleterious consequences for blacks and whites, but especially for blacks. For blacks, dropping out of school quite often means becoming either unemployed or a nonparticipant in the labor force. In the case of whites, what the data suggest is that dropping out of school seldom means dropping out of the labor force, or becoming a long term unemployed seeker of work, although the acquisition of a job may mean short-term employment in a low paying occupation. By contrast, blacks frequently fail to obtain even these low status positions. What Table 2 suggests is that racial discrimination is operative among young dropouts. In a racially comparative sense, dropping out of school is not the problem. Racism apparently is. These facts being what they are, it would appear that we lose a great deal of insight into the operation of our economy when we delete the 14–15 year olds.

The dropping of these young people has accompanied an unadjusted comparison. The Bureau of Labor Statistics has drawn comparisons between the unemployed of the 1970's with those of the early sixties without telling us how if at all the BLS has removed the recently deleted categories from the earlier estimates so as to allow for a fair comparison.

No such statistical control is applied; unadjusted comparisons are made. The BLS has compared oranges without peelings (1974) against oranges with peelings (1961) for example, while forgetting to inform the general public how the comparison has been made. Rather than comparing adjusted figures, the BLS supplies added but separate statistics on dropped groups so that if the researcher wishes, he can compute an adjusted figure.[15] Needless to say, the BLS does not add to our general knowledge of working-class unemployment by suggesting such techniques.

There is no professional excuse for (1) the juggled criteria on unemployed, (2) the unqualified statements on the trend comparisons, and finally, (3) the elementary error of comparing two noncomparable quantities.

A MORE VALID MEASURE

To gauge unemployment over a one year period, the BLS should not only compute but publicize a more valid measure of unemployment, namely, *the aggregate unemployment rate*.

Perhaps more puzzling than the curious ratio of the employed to the unemployed would be the periodicity of the count. Even if we were to assume that monthly reports, corrected for their underestimation, would be useful, we could nonetheless use what would appear to be a more demonstrative measure of unemployment, one in fact computed by the BLS but inadequately publicized by it. From the point of view of at least some unemployed, far more important than a monthly rate is the aggregate unemployment rate. This BLS rate refers to the number of people who are unemployed over a period of one year. Harry Brill makes clear why he thinks this yearly rate is more important:

> If on the average, four million people are jobless each month, that does not necessarily mean that the individuals who are counted as unemployed in one month are the same later. Turnover among the unemployed occurs, and thus the total percentage, or number, of these who have been unemployed during each year must exceed the average monthly count.

TABLE 2   Employment Status of 14–15 year olds by Sex and Color, September, 1974 (in thousands)

Employment Status	Total			White			Negro and Other Races		
	Both Sexes	Males	Females	Both Sexes	Males	Females	Both Sexes	Males	Females
Civilian Noninstitutional Population	8,410	4,275	4,135	7,126	3,632	3,632	1,284	642	642
Civilian Labor Force	1,528	867	661	1,420	803	613	109	64	44
Employed	1,329	744	584	1,260	704	556	68	40	28
Agriculture	194	155	39	183	150	32	11	5	6
Nonagricultural Industries	1,135	589	546	1,078	554	524	57	35	22
Unemployed	200	123	77	159	98	61	40	25	16
Unemployment Rate	13.1	14.2	11.7	11.2	12.2	9.9	36.7	(1)	(1)
Not in Labor Force	6,882	3,407	3,404	5,706	2,830	2,876	1,176	578	598
Keeping House	36	12	24	31	13	18	6	—	—
Going to School	6,622	3,280	3,342	5,492	2,723	2,769	1,130	557	573
Unable to Work	3	3	—	3	3	—	—	—	—
All Other Reasons	220	113	107	179	91	88	41	22	19

Source: Taken From *Employment and Earnings* Vol. 21, No. 4 (October, 1974), p. 41.

This is not news to the Department of Labor. According to the testimony delivered by Secretary of Labor Wirtz before the Senate Committee on Employment and Manpower "approximately fourteen million men and women are unemployed at some time during this year of 1962." Fourteen million individuals are roughly twenty per cent of the total "labor force"! Therefore, the total annual rate (twenty per cent) is 3.77 times the average monthly rate (5.3 per cent) of that year. To that must be added millions of unemployed persons who are not counted by the Department of Labor; and the figure soars to represent eighteen or twenty million individuals.[16]

In other words, average monthly gross figures of four million would contrast with a yearly number of approximately 14 million persons perhaps unemployed for an average duration of time that is rather considerable. Often times average length of time is between eight and ten weeks.[17] The figure of 14 million unemployed for such an average length of time does strongly suggest that something may well be organizationally wrong with such an economy even if one wants to discount later those people moving between jobs, i.e., the frictionally unemployed. In fact, the short term unemployed could be subtracted from the aggregate unemployment rate to give us a better however incomplete picture of the objectively unemployed without detracting from the critical portrait of structural unemployment in the United States.

NEEDED: A BETTER MONTHLY MEASURE

As an accompaniment to the yearly rate, the BLS should gather and publish less contrived figures on *monthly unemployment.*

The BLS has come under considerable criticism because of its slanting of unemployment news. Perhaps in part because of these external criticisms the BLS has experimented with measures which have in fact more clearly indicated the true number of people without work but with the desire to work should a job become available. In 1964, during the rosy days of the Johnson Administration, the Department of Labor published figures which indicated that total monthly unemployment might be considerably higher than the 4.5 million specified in the official figures. The experimental statistical measure did in fact include those not in the official labor force. Specifically, the "unemployed" included (1) those who had worked part-time but wanted a full-time job, (2) those who had given up the search for work plus (3) all the others found beyond the pale of labor force participation, e.g., those who had never searched for work. The BLS appeared to be on its way to evolving a measure of work force (or labor supply), one with a more realistic and human definition than "labor force."

The figures show that among white men aged 45 to 54 with four years of education or less, 221 of every 1000 are not working. Of these, 84 are listed as unemployed and 137 as "not in the labor force."

Among those with college degrees, the corresponding figure shrinks to 39 for those who are not working, including ten unemployed and 29 not in the labor force.[18]

Curiously enough, this more representative measure was dropped by the BLS soon after its innovation. In this sense, the BLS erased its justifiable innovation on work force measurement and opted for continuation of the traditional labor force categorization.

The BLS systematically underestimates the seriousness of black and Spanish speaking unemployment through use of its current techniques by:

    a.   Relegating so many of their numbers to the not in the labor force category;

    b.   Lumping blacks with orientals;

    c.   Placing Spanish speaking people with whites, thereby inflating white unemployment rates and consequently minimizing the gap between "non-white" and "white" unemployed.

Some groups have suffered more than others from the consequences of undercount. Who they are is not too difficult to guess. Blacks, Spanish-speaking people, and women are cases in point. Many of their objectively unemployed fail to get counted. Hence, their cases and their communities cases fail to get the publicity warranted by their circumstances. The case of black youth is truly astonishing, as indicated by the *Wall Street Journal*.

What's more, experts say, the Administration view overlooks what has been happening to the black labor force. As of November, (1970) it has shrunk somewhat despite population growth and the return of more black veterans from Vietnam. In the 16 to 19 age group, for instance, the black male force slumped 12% to 396,000 for the 12 months ended last November; the percentage of eligible blacks in this group working or seeking work dropped to 40.5% from 48.4% a year earlier. (Meantime, the white male teen-age work force was swelling, in both size and participation rate.)

But while fewer black teen-age males were working or seeking work, the group's jobless rate was holding at 21% to 25% of the total work force.

"Some people become so depressed they simply drop out of the labor force," explains Dale Hiestand, associate professor of business at Columbia University's graduate school of business. "But when they do, they aren't counted as unemployed—even though they really are."[19]

Pondering this material, three points come to mind:

1. As of November, 1970, the black labor force was shrinking despite black population growth and the return of black veterans from Vietnam. What this trend indicated was a decrease in the black labor force and an increase in the number of potential black workers. If history repeats itself, a curious and widening gap may well haunt the black community during the mid-1970s.

2. In the case of black late-teenagers found within the labor force, their absolute number dropped by one-eighth over a period of one year. This shrinkage occurred within an overall statistical category that was undoubtedly larger in November, 1970, than a year earlier.

3. In this 16 to 19 age category, the percentage of blacks working or seeking work dropped to approximately 40 percent of their overall number.

The last figure is somewhat shocking, for apparently the employed is considerably less than the 40 percent labor force total, since the group's official unemployment percentage was approximately one-fifth the 40 percent figure. In other words, around one-third of the young blacks were employed; hopefully all of the employed had jobs. But then many of the employed could have been strikers, ill-at-homes, and/or vacationers. Unfortunately, we do not know what these numbers of "employed" might be, although the BLS (or some other governmental bureaus) may perhaps have the data if not the processed tabulations. We do have data on strikers by industry and community, and in the case of Detroit, where many of the strikers are indeed black members of industrial unions, we would not be surprised to discover that thousands of blacks, counted as employed over the average year, have been in fact strikers for one or more periods during the one year interval.

Strikers aside, we do also know that the official number of black unemployed increased sharply during 1970–71 as the economy slid into a recession. Paul Flaim and Paul Schwab's article[20] has documented this point, and we present their data on "employment status by color, sex, and age, 1969 and 1970." (See Table 3.)

What our preceding analysis on blacks suggests is that (a) young blacks found beyond the labor force plus (b) young blacks found in the officially unemployed category, these two groups, together, constitute an overall figure many times greater than the officially employed. Let's not forget, also, that the 16–19 year old employed subsumes part-time employed blacks, including high school students working part-time. They are clearly not in the full-time section of the labor force. Nor will many of them join it soon after their graduation because of the paucity of jobs for blacks with high school degrees.

These figures on persons with and without work should be computed, published, and publicized to indicate the seriousness of the black case. Put in yet another way, when we consider the beyond-the-labor-force category, let us not forget that their numbers are as immense as the *Wall Street Journal* article indicates and by no means near or equal to the official unemployment incidence. We should also keep in mind the real possibility of the current recession duplicating the 1970–71 experience for black youth.[21]

BLACK UNEMPLOYMENT AND SPANISH-SPEAKING PEOPLE

Unknown to many is the way in which black unemployment can be made to appear less serious than it is by the BLS simply counting the Spanish-speaking unemployed as white unemployed even when many Spanish-speaking unemployed define themselves, and are defined, as non-white.

What are the consequences of this inexplicable inclusion? Although ludicrous, this merger of a Spanish-origin statistic into the white category has detrimental consequences not only for Chicanos and Puerto Ricans—who don't even have their own separate and regularly tabulated rates on unemployment—but for blacks who must compare their case with unreal figures on white unemployment. By padding the white rate with Spanish-speaking incidence of officially unemployed, the overall ratio of white-to-nonwhite unemployment is lessened. Indeed, should there be an inordinately large increase in Spanish-speaking unemployed, their increase would so inflate the official number of white

TABLE 3   Race, Employment Status, Sex and Age: 1969–1970 (in thousands)

Employment Status, Sex and Age	Total		White		Negro and Other Races	
	1970	1969	1970	1969	1970	1969
Both sexes, 16–19 years						
Civilian labor force	7,246	6,970	6,439	6,168	807	801
Employment	6,141	6,117	5,568	5,508	573	609
Unemployment	1,105	853	871	660	235	193
Unemployment rate	15.3	12.2	13.5	10.7	29.1	24.0

Source: Taken from Paul O. Flaim and Paul M. Schwab, "Changes in Employment and Unemployment in 1970," *Monthly Labor Review,* 94 (February, 1971), p. 3.

unemployed in certain regions of the United States that the result would startle even the most callous of social scientists. The climbing rate of so-called white unemployed would in fact diminish the percentage gap between white and nonwhite unemployed. Optimistic interpreters could then conceivably argue that the figures strongly suggest that progress is being made in American race relations, for the traditional 2-to-1, black-to-white unemployment differential would be decreasing. Nor is this possibility an impossibility in places such as southern California where the normal incidence of Spanish-speaking unemployed, not to mention voluminous and cyclical increases in their numbers, would seem to be often greater than comparable statistics for the black population.

Again, another statistical uncertainty with very certain results for blacks, this one perhaps of less significance than the Spanish-speaking case because of the relative paucity of cases involved, occurs when the BLS takes people of Asiatic background, at least one group of which (the Japanese-Americans) has an extremely low level of unemployment, and lumps them with blacks inside the nonwhite category. In the case of Japanese-Americans, for example, their leading into the nonwhite category lowers the incidence of unemployment for nonwhites, a category generally perceived as essentially black. And in places such as the Bay Area and Hawaii, where there are numerous Japanese-Americans, their addition would certainly obscure the true incidence of unemployment among blacks.

WOMEN: GROWTH IN THEIR NUMBER OF EMPLOYED AND UNEMPLOYED

During the early 1970's women posted a net gain in the labor force participation. This also meant an increase in their employment. As Flaim and Schwab put it:

> Given the uneven pattern of employment changes by industry, it is not surprising that some labor force groups experienced greater difficulties than others. Adult men, for example, saw their employment growth halted by the sharp job cut-backs in the goods-producing sector. Adult women, on the other hand, being concentrated largely in the less affected service sector, managed to post a relatively sizable employment gain despite the economic slowdown.[22]

But the same article pointed to increased *unemployment* among women as a whole, though some categories of women did post an employment increase:

Traditionally employed in the service-producing industries (which were not severely affected by the recent slowdown) women 20 years and over managed to post an employment gain of about 550,000 in 1970. But even this advance—largely in part-time employment—was considerably below the average job gains achieved by women in recent years. The result was a 350,000 increase in female unemployment and a rise in their jobless rate from 3.7 to 4.8 percent. On balance, however, the year-to-year increase in unemployment among women, although substantial, was relatively less sharp than among males.[23]

This "on balance" view of women having a less serious increase in unemployment may well be accounted for by the real possibility of many women losing their jobs and then dropping out of the labor force by sliding back into the roles of housewives. Once back in the house-wife roles, many do not search for regular jobs and hence do not count as unemployed. Their failure to qualify for the unemployed category would have as a consequence a dampening effect on the growth of female unemployment rates.

The 1974–75 recession has apparently reproduced the same accentuations of unemployment difficulties for blacks, Spanish-speaking and women. As in the early '70's, they are being forced out of the labor force at a rate greater than men. Today many are joining the army of unemployed labor.[24]

The BLS should drop the concept of *labor force* when measuring employment and unemployment. It should opt for a definition of labor supply, one which would include the employed, the unemployed, the partially employed, the underpaid and the would-be-workers.

The employed would consist of those working full-time. The unemployed would consist of those not working, including the old, the housewives, and those too tired to look for work. In all fairness to part-time employed, they would be counted separately from the full-time employed. Nor would we define the underpaid as normally employed. In this way we could use our terms to define a structural problem to be attacked through structural remedies.

Let us not forget the lessons of World War II. The people created full employment and reduced real unemployment by going all out to create work. As Stanley Moses has observed:

In addition to inducements of patriotic ferver and cash, no effort was spared to facilitate working. Elaborate day care programs were for the first time introduced; special training and re-training programs were developed; efforts at counseling and rehabilitation of the handicapped were encouraged; pioneering efforts for scheduling and organizing the work day were experimented with; and extra inducements regarding commuting arrangements and other fringe benefits were preferred. In short, at a time when management and government did everything possible to encourage people to want to work, and the concern was not with devising a methodology which would help understate unemployment data, but rather with stimulating the greatest possible contribution from each person, 8 million additional workers were discovered and absorbed in the labor supply.[25]

History can teach us how to count.

ENDNOTES

1. See "Jobless Rate Up To 6.5 per cent, Highest Since '61," *New York Times*, December 7, 1974, p. 1.
2. Here I am relying upon estimates of unemployment (and subemployment) developed by Bertram Gross and Stanley Moses in their, "Varying Estimates of Aggregate Unemployment, 1973," found in Stanley Moses' "Labor Supply Concepts: The Political Economy of Conceptual Change," 1974, pp. 41–42. Unpublished.
3. "How the Government Measures Unemployment," Bureau of Labor Statistics, Report Number 312 (June, 1967), pp. 7–8. The now-used definition of participation in the labor force is more narrow than it was prior to 1967, when groups such as 14 and 15-year-olds were included. Briefly put, the labor force consists of the employed and the unemployed persistently seeking work. The BLS has evolved certain standard techniques for obtaining information on these groups:

> Statistics on the employment status of the population, the personal, occupational, and other characteristics of the employed, the unemployed, and persons not in the labor force, and related data are compiled for the BLS by the Bureau of the Census and its Current Population Survey (CPS). A detailed description of this survey appears in *"Concepts and Methods Used in Manpower Statistics from the Current Population Survey"* (BLS Report 313). This report is available from BLS on request.
>
> These monthly surveys of the population are conducted with a scientifically selected sample designed to represent the civilian noninstitutional population 16 years and over. Respondents are interviewed to obtain information about the employment status of each member of the household 16 years of age and over. The inquiry relates to activity or status during the calendar week, Sunday through Saturday, which includes the 12th of the month. This is known as the survey week. Actual field interviewing is conducted in the following week.

Inmates of institutions and persons under 16 years of age are not covered in the regular monthly enumerations and are excluded from the population and labor force statistics shown in this report. Data on members of the Armed Forces, who are included as part of the categories "total noninstitutional population" and "total labor force," are obtained from the Department of Defense.

Each month, 50,000 occupied units are designated for interview. About 2,250 of these households are visited but interviews are not obtained because the occupants are not found at home after repeated calls or are unavailable for other reasons. This represents a noninterview rate for the survey of about 4.5 percent. In addition to the 50,000 occupied units, there are 8,500 sample units in an average month which are visited but found to be vacant or otherwise not to be enumerated. Part of the sample is changed each month. The rotation plan provides for three-fourths of the sample to be common from one month to the next, and one-half to be common with the same month a year ago.

See "Labor Force Data," *Employment and Earnings,* 18, No. 3 (September 1971). U.S. Department of Labor, Bureau of Labor Statistics.

A more current discussion on labor force membership basically reiterates the 1971 statement. See *How the Government Measures Unemployment,* Report 418, U.S. Department of Labor, Bureau of Labor Statistics, 1973, pp. 4–7.

4. The job-seeking period specified by the BLS prior to 1967 was in fact 60 days. However, the reference manual specifies one week— *and* 60 days. The U.S. Department of Commerce, Bureau of the Census, published an interviewer's reference manual, and here I refer to a January 1963 copy containing the pre-1967 technique which asked the respondent what he was doing most of last week —working? looking for work? etc. If the respondent was looking for work, how many weeks had he or she been looking? On page CPS-HVS-250 of this manual, the interviewer was instructed on what constituted looking for work. Looking for work included the following kinds of efforts to get a job or start a business:

1. Registration at a public or private employment office.
2. Being on call at a personnel office, a nurses' register or professional register.
3. Meeting with prospective employers.
4. Placing or answering advertisements.
5. Writing letters of application.
6. Working without pay in order to get experience and training.

7. *Awaiting results of any of the above activity undertaken within the preceding 60 days.*

5. In *How The Government Measures Unemployment* (*op. cit.*, p. 6), the report asks "who is counted as unemployed?" and replies:

> Persons are unemployed if they have actively looked for work in the past 4 weeks, are currently available for work, and, of course, do not have a job at the same time. Looking for work may consist of any of the following specific activities:
>> Registering at a public or private employment office;
>> Meeting with prospective employers;
>> Checking with friends or relatives;
>> Placing or answering advertisements;
>> Writing letters of application; or
>> Being on a union or professional register.

6. *Ibid.*, p. 7.
7. *Ibid.*, p. 6.
8. Stanley Moses, *op cit.*, p. 25.
9. See "Labor Force Data," *Employment and Earnings. op. cit.*, p. 140.
10. *Ibid.*
11. *Ibid.* Also see "How The Government Measures Unemployment" (*op. cit.*, p. 4).
12. *Ibid.*, p. 4.
13. I do not wish to suggest that professionals working for the BLS deliberately and maliciously pad statistics. They're just civil servants doing their jobs.
14. In communities such as Detroit, this matter of counting the unemployed strikers as employed involves not a few people. In metropolitan Detroit (1964) there were 95 work stoppages involving 114,000 workers who were idle a total of 2,060,000 work days. Were the BLS to count these workers as unemployed or nonparticipants in the labor force, the overall incidence of unemployment would undoubtedly increase significantly. See U.S. Department of Labor, Bureau of Labor Statistics, *Analysis of Work Stoppages*, Bulletin No. 1460, October 1965, p. 17.
15. One cannot discover these figures (*e.g.*, 14–15 year olds) from the press. Rather one must go to Bureau of Labor Statistics Regional Offices or the occasional library to discover these figures.
16. Harry Brill, "Can We Train Away the Unemployed?" *The Feedback*, 3, (November-December, 1965), pp. 5–12.
17. Paul O. Flaim and Paul M. Schwab have observed that:

> Most of the persons who became unemployed in 1970 managed to find work after a relatively short period of

job hunting. Thus, the average duration of unemployment increases only moderately during the year. At an 8.8 week average, it was only 1 week higher than in 1969, but well below the levels that, in earlier years, had been associated with unemployment rates of the magnitude reached in 1970. Nevertheless, a gradually higher proportion of the unemployed (about one-fifth at year's end had been jobless for at least 15 weeks, while a limited number apparently had left the labor force.

See their "Changes in Employment and Unemployment in 1970," *Monthly Labor Review*, 94 (February 1971), p. 13.

18.   " 'The Hidden' Jobless Figures," *The San Francisco Chronicle*, March 11, 1964, p. 14.

19.   " 'Discouraged' Blacks Leave the Labor Force, Distorting Jobless Rate," *The Wall Street Journal*, January 8, 1971, p. 1.

20.   Flaim and Schwab, *op. cit.*, p. 18. As we indicated earlier, the conditions facing the younger blacks, and here again we consider only the civilian noninstitutional population of 14- and 15-year olds, are even more dire. In September 1971 of those who were black members of the labor force, fifty-four thousand were employed and thirty-four thousand were unemployed. The incidence of unemployment was particularly high among female blacks. Comparable figures for whites were considerably lower. Less than seven percent of that section of the labor force was unemployed. See U.S. Department of Labor, Bureau of Labor Statistics, *Employment and Earnings*, 18 (October 1971), p. 43.

21.   Black youth have been particularly hard-hit by the 1974–75 recession, and the bottom is not in sight. As of September, 1974, the incidence of black, male, 16–19 year olds unemployment was 34.5%, while the figure for comparable black women was 35.2%. For 20–24 year olds, the respective figures were 16.5 % and 20.4%.

For white youth, the figures were males 12.2% (16–19) and 6.3% (20–24), females 16.2% and 8.8%, respectively. Taken from *Employment and Earnings*, Vol. 21, No. 4, October, 1974, p. 25.

Black male "Vietnam Era Veterans" have suffered a very high incidence of unemployment, especially among those 20–24 years of age. In the case of this category, 23.2% are unemployed, according to the BLS. See *ibid.*, p. 62.

22.   Flaim and Schwab, *op. cit.*, p. 16.

23.   *Ibid.*, p. 18.

24.   As indicated in footnote 21, female unemployment for 20–24 year olds was higher than for males. This pattern was common to both whites and blacks. The same female-over male unemployment figures held for other age categories. They have been nationwide as well. In *every* U.S. region, for both white and black, there are cur-

rently more female than male unemployed. The exception is New York-New Jersey, where there are slightly more male than female "Negro" unemployed. See "Geographic Profile of Employment and Unemployment, 1973", Report 431, U.S. Department of Labor, Bureau of Labor Statistics, 1974, pp. 3–4.

25. Stanley Moses, *op. cit.,* p. 25.

The recession has taken a predictable job toll among other oppressed groups as well. In September, 1974, while 5.0% of the *whites* were counted as unemployed, 10.5% of the *"Negroes"* (only) and 8.0% of those of *"Spanish origin"* were without work. In the case of 16–19 year olds (September, 1974), the figures were 11.6%, 33.5% and 20.2%, respectively. (See *Employment and Earnings,* Volume 21, *op. cit.,* p. 60.) (The official policy of the BLS on counting people of Spanish origin is straightforward, however questionable: "Data on persons of Spanish origin are tabulated separately without regard to race/color, which means that they are also included in the data for white and Negro workers. According to the 1970 census, approximately 98 percent of their population is white." *Ibid.,* p. 60.)

As the depression approaches, the objective conditions among women, within black ghettoes, and inside Spanish-American *barrios* assume truly ghastly proportions.

Sexism

In the preceding section we examined how aspects of our society are structured to favor some at the cost of others. We look at a similar situation in this second section. The exploiters here are not the wealthy, but men; those exploited are not the poor, but women. Just as the first articles provided a reconceptualization of our economic order, so these selections provide a reconceptualization of our sexual order.

Sexism pervades our society. It is built into our social institutions. Sexism is not only the consequence of our present social order, but, at the same time, it also aids in the maintenance of that social order. Our social institutions are structured in such a way that women continuously are held under the dominance of men: in the marketplace, at home, in religion, in politics, and in almost every aspect of social life. It is to such discrimination, which is built into our society, that the Women's Liberation Movement has been so forcefully and effectually directing our attention in recent years. In this section, we will examine selected areas of sexual discrimination and their relationship to the maintenance of the status quo.

Sperber's opening article is a scathing denunciation of the form of the family that almost all of us regularly take for granted because it is *the* family type in which we have grown up and to which most of us aspire. Sperber presents us with an appositional view of the nuclear family and romantic love, aspects of our social world that we take for granted as being the right way of ordering our lives. He says that our current socio-economic order needs a servile class of workers to perform the less desirable, but necessary, tasks in life. He then examines the nuclear family as the sifting device that selects males for the more important positions in society while keeping women in subservient positions. The nuclear family helps to maintain the status quo of relationships between the sexes by freeing males from the tasks that require the most drudgery, and by locking females into these same tasks. Moreover, according to this analysis, the nuclear family socializes our young into possessiveness, servility, and insecurity—characteristics which help to maintain the domination and exploitation of the masses by our ruling class.

Mainardi then focuses on the traditional tasks of drudgery assigned to women in our society. Beneath the humor of her presentation lies the seriousness of the political implications of housework. Housework represents the major cleavage between the sexes in our society, where the one sex is "kept in her place," while the other is freed to participate in more creative activities. By her analysis, Mainardi demonstrates that housework is more than trivial. Such a sexual division of labor is designed to perpetuate the traditional inequality of the sexes. Thus, housework and the assigning of a single sex to perform it has large scale political ramifications for maintaining the social order in its status quo.

And if a woman gets "out of place," all sorts of mechanisms can be used to bring her back in line. In what may be a surprise to most readers, Reynolds analyzes rape as one of these mechanisms. Examining the legal procedures surrounding the victim and perpetrator of a rape, she concludes that rape is a socially approved form of social control that restricts the mobility and freedom of women and maintains male prerogative in the erotic sphere of social life. This reconceptualization of rape is startlingly different from analyses of rape that are available elsewhere, and is highly deserving of your careful consideration for a more thorough understanding of how sexism operates in American society.

In the concluding article to this section, Beal turns to an analysis of American women who find themselves in a double bind. Black women are discriminated against on two counts; because they are black and because they are female. Moreover, as Beal indicates, they are discriminated against not only by whites, but also by black males who typically subjugate black females to an inferior position. Our socialization into sexism is so thorough, in other words, that even those males who are actively reacting against their own secondary status respond to black females in a way that they (black males) have rejected as being illegitimate when applied to themselves. So pervasive is our sexism that such prejudicial action is taken unthinkingly—as though it were natural and right.

Since sexism is built into our social institutions and is part of the basic way in which most Americans unthinkingly approach life, it will require a revamping of the social order similar to the requirements for overcoming poverty. It is this message of fundamental change in socio-sexual relations that is the revolutionary aspect of the Women's Liberation Movement. And like attempts to overcome poverty, it is those who have the most to lose by such attempts who most bitterly fear and oppose it. But those in the revolutionary part of this movement ultimately stand against any socio-economic order which perpetuates itself on the exploitation of people. If members of this movement do not sell out for positions of dominance by which they themselves become part of the exploitation of those less powerful than themselves, the fight against sexism can well mean the radical transformation of American society, and perhaps ultimately that of Western civilization.

6

Irwin Sperber

The Marketplace Personality: On Capitalism, Male Chauvinism, and Romantic Love

MALE CHAUVINISM AND SOCIALIZATION IN THE NUCLEAR FAMILY

As an ideology, "male chauvinism" refers to the belief that women are intellectually inferior to men; that their main worth is the extent to which they perform as sexual objects, dutiful mothers and wives, or some combination thereof; that they are inherently prone toward eccentricities, hysteria, gullibility and childishness; that their proper role in government, business, and the academy (to the extent they should have any role here at all) is limited to doing the "crud work" of menial, tedious, unchallenging low wage varieties necessary for the smooth operation of the social machinery but unappealing to men; that women who are openly assertive of their political or intellectual concerns are probably suffering from penis envy, an inferiority complex, or some neurotic need for attention. The modern nuclear family reflects, legitimizes, and reinforces the ideology and the implementation of male chauvinism. The utility of male chauvinism for a capitalist society, the vital service of the nuclear family in promoting male chauvinism, and the consequences of male chauvinism for the socialization of the young are here examined to specify the ways in which the nuclear family is an *inherent* social problem in the capitalist society.

What is the content of this socialization, and how does the structure of the nuclear family impress upon the young a high degree of possessiveness, servility, and insecurity throughout one's life? How are such seemingly psychological defects determined by the characteristic opera-

This article was written for this volume and is printed by permission.

tion of the nuclear family, and how do they directly contribute to the legitimacy of capitalism? How can these attributes of individuals be conceptualized in macroscopic terms as necessary resources for the maintenance of concrete forms of domination and exploitation which serve the interests of a specific ruling class?

The normative patterns of authority in the nuclear family include the husband's domination over the wife and children in regard to the kind of work he is willing to do (if any) around the house, and what he wishes to pursue occupationally for purposes of earning income and achieving vertical mobility. This domination specifically includes the husband's absolute prerogative to relocate the family in accordance with any changes he might wish to make in his career plans. Although usually not openly admitted, the fact that the husband is the breadwinner is the sole basis on which his supreme authority is actually enforced: he who brings in the money shall also be lord of the manor, and this recognition shall be self-evident to all his subjects. The wife's and child's plans can thus be properly disrupted or redefined altogether at the pleasure of the husband in search of a better job in a bigger city or a new home in a more respectable neighborhood; they have no commensurate right to expect him to disrupt or redefine *his* plans at *their* pleasure. Here one sees how a paramount value in capitalism is transmitted not so much as a formally required doctrine but rather as an informally experienced and internalized way of life for all members of the nuclear family.

This *modus operandus*, summarily stated, is that money talks: he who has the most shall be heard the most, and he knows what is good for his loyal subjects (be they wives, sons, daughters, or workers). This lesson is learned early and well by most children in a capitalistic society, regardless of their conscious hostility, indifference, or enthusiasm toward the more explicit moral standards of the adult world. This belief is distinctly useful in promoting the view that wealth, wisdom, domination, and moral legitimacy are virtues which self-evidently hang together, and it obscures any questions about the possible injustices and inequalities of access to the means of obtaining wealth in the first place (e.g., through fraud, military conquest, religious mystification, assassination, and so forth).

One of the essential elements in the maximization of profit and minimization of risk in the investment of capital is the maintenance of a low wage scale and, to the extent that wages determine overall capital expenditures, a low cost of production. Ideally, there must be a class of workers not only docile and servile toward authority in general but also willing to perform menial and tedious duties at low or subsistence wages. Whatever the legalistic merits of "universal suffrage" and "universal compulsory education" in the United States and Canada, the fact remains that women are still expected to be seen and not heard regarding matters of political and intellectual controversy. Buttressed amply from our primary schools through postgraduate studies, this expectation is especially impressed upon wives, mothers, daughters, and sisters in the nuclear family from the cradle to the grave. It is the women who are expected to do the menial housework, spend endless hours with the children, and watch the TV soap operas for cultural enrichment. It is the women who are expected to do the "crud work" at home and in the office. It is they who are paid nothing for housework and subsistence wages for office work, and they who must know their place and refrain from questioning the domination to which they are subjected.

Marlene Dixon, Carol Andreas and other analysts of male chauvinism have forcefully called attention to the insidious discrimination against women in higher education, while several administrators at major universities have declared with unabashed conviction their official view that "a woman's place is in the home." These same authorities are commensurately pleased to have low-paid "chicks" doing the menial tasks in the office and being able to indulge in off-duty (sometimes on-duty) copulation with the hired help. The more "progressive" and "enlightened" of these beneficent authorities even go so far as to mention the fine editorial assistance of their wives while their latest books were being written (often with the unacknowledged help of underpaid female research assistants). Some of the even more liberal men in this vanguard are willing to allow women into graduate school—provided that computer programming, demography, "the family," and similar fields traditionally ensuring 1. *minimal emphasis on historical, political, or theoretical foci* and 2. *cheap labor for academic crud work* are the areas in which the women wish to specialize.

The nuclear family, with its emphasis on an idyllic home in suburbia, promotes the woman's social-psychological isolation from her commonly aggrieved peers and the neutralization of any political concerns that she might have had during her undergraduate years. For the woman who seeks to mitigate some of these atrocities through divorce, a male judge and male-dominated legal system must first be confronted. Even though she might be granted child support or alimony, many subsequently find that the male judge, the male district attorney, and the ex-husband have an infinite list of reasons as to why actual payments are justifiably delayed or avoided altogether. Her options in such cases are then typically as circumscribed as taking a part-time and low-paid job, such as that of waitress or clerk, or going on the welfare rolls (only to face periodic surveillance by investigators and overt or covert "means tests" required by administrators). Given the painful awareness of these degradations typically associated with divorce, many women considering this step decide to remain married (or to go through the motions of conjugal duty) and to live in an encapsulated status effectively similar to that of involuntary servitude. Even many of those who acknowledge the contradiction between such *de facto* servitude and the liberal ethic of freedom of choice have the lingering belief that perhaps they really should perform the traditional duties of *Küche, Kinder, und Kirche,* as well as the part-time clerking, the menial waitressing, and the crud work so necessary to keep the "wheels of industry" turning and to maintain the "high standard of living" to which we are allegedly accustomed.

No one is better suited for the performance of these duties than the woman who has been socialized into the nuclear family, who identifies with its tacit values regarding the second-rate status of women, who transmits her acquired sense of docility and servility to her children in anticipation of their performance of adult roles in the political, economic and academic domains.

ROMANTIC LOVE AND THE MARKETPLACE PERSONALITY

Romantic love is a necessary ideological foundation for monogamy and the nuclear family in advanced capitalist societies. Though some of the tabu against the woman's pursuit of frequent and casual sexual adventures have been eased, the belief that the maintenance of intense simultaneous love affairs is against a woman's "basic nature" still enjoys a lively persistence. Such enterprises are widely regarded as the prerogatives of the man, and some societies explicitly legalize the keeping of mistresses so long as it is done with good taste and a minimum of public scandal. Some writers seek to explain this aspect of romantic love in terms of the allegedly polyerotic and strong libido of the human male and the allegedly monoerotic and weak libido of the human female.[1] Such uncritical and simplistic adaptations of psychoanalysis, in addition to causing understandable disenchantment to those scholars who might otherwise wish to consider a rapprochement between Freud and Marx, ignore the historical evidence of massive exceptions to this seemingly natural doctrine and the great extent to which such seemingly natural sexual traits are culturally conditioned and capable of being reconditioned under suitable conditions. Such vulgarizations do serve such important ideological functions as helping to legitimize *a.* an instrumentalist and manipulative attitude of men toward women, of women toward themselves as serviceable things or commodities, and of men toward one another competing to woo a "chick" away from her "steady"; *b.* the belief that a woman's place is in the home or doing office crud work since females lack the "vitality," "dynamism," and "zip" of men; *c.* the custom that the main task of women is to accommodate the sexual desires and demands of men at home, in the office, and at the annual conventions of professional organizations where the "big action" really unfolds.

In romantic love, the female (whether an adolescent girl or an older woman) is expected to find the one and only true male partner with whom she will be *a.* emotionally, spiritually, sexually, and *permanently* compatible, *b.* ensured of self-fulfillment or self-realization by "living through him" or standing in his shadow, *c.* altogether happy in the sense of giving and receiving undying affection and loyalty, and *d.* eventually the bearer and mother of his children, thus enabling his family name and estate to be carried on. This expectation also applies, though often less strongly, to the male (again, whether an adolescent boy or an older man), and his selection of the "right girl" is generally regarded in the eyes of his peers as well as the adult reference groups toward which he aspires as a bellwether of his probable success in business, politics, or in education. In its most elementary form, this expectation is implemented in what Willard Waller and others have called the "rating and dating complex."

Especially at the formative stage of socialization into the arts and duties of romance, the participants are nurtured into the belief that their problems (whether political, economic, academic, or other) will be solved or rendered unimportant if only the ideal partner is chosen. "Love conquers all." Hence, anxiety one might have over *any* aspect of participation in the larger society is translated into anxiety over finding the "girl of my dreams" or the "boy of my dreams." The achievement of making the "right choice," the achiever is led to believe, will cause his peers to be envious, his community standing to rise tangibly, and his security in the competitive social arena to be consolidated.

Indeed, the rating and dating complex treats the very idea of serious political discussion as boorish, dull, out of place and even self-defeating in the quest for the ideal partner. Serious political action is treated not only as boorish and self-defeating, but also as unthinkable in principle and in practice. This political neutralization of discontent is achieved by making serious public issues (e.g., class conflicts and forms of exploitation) appear subjectively to the victim as though they were only personal problems.[2] To repeat, *the anxiety over one's identity at a given historical period and in a given social class is ideologically and emotionally translated into the question of whether one's partner "really loves me" and whether he or she is really the best of all possible romantic partners.* A perpetual flood of TV programs, comic books, newspaper columns on dating behavior, how-to-do-it guidance manuals, sociology textbooks on marriage and the family, all manner of academic courses on courtship and interpersonal adjustment, commercialized and sexualized glamour products for the "youth market," euphoric folk-rock songs, computer matching services which guarantee satisfaction to lonely customers, and everyday conversational themes at the local high school and university—all contributing to the flourishing and lucrative "youth industries"—is addressed to this very question and often provides concrete "answers" for people of all ages and both sexes. Even if the social self were capable of understanding the paralysis of political and historical consciousness to which this translation of public issues into personal problems leads, even if one were the embodiment of what C. Wright Mills calls the sociological imagination, one could do little as an individual to act over against the ongoing barrage of cultural prescriptions about romantic love and sexual fulfillment. Only through large-scale and well-planned collective struggle can one hope to exert influence against the rating and dating complex or the pervasive myth upon which it is based.

Preoccupation with trying to please one's partner in romantic love becomes virtually an all-consuming obsession, an end-in-itself, leading to the belief that one's self-esteem is determined by how successfully one pleases the other. This orientation is also rewarded in the primary school grades under the rubric of "getting along with others." The social self learns to convey and to take very seriously the posture of the marketplace personality: "I am as you desire me." This posture is extremely useful, if not absolutely imperative, for an economic system in which individuals are expected to perform whatever duties are arbitrarily assigned them by a superordinate authority and to derive their self-esteem from the knowledge that they have successfully done what was expected of them in the eyes of the very same authority.

CONCLUSION: THE NUCLEAR FAMILY VERSUS HUMAN LIBERATION

The constrictions resulting from romantic love and the monogamous relationship to which such love is culturally directed have been discussed in terms of the *de facto* involuntary servitude endured by women as a result of male chauvinism. But the constrictions are far more extensive and insidious than their formal legal and social expressions would appear to indicate. They include the effective stifling of one's capacity for social, intellectual, and sexual transcendence due to ties to a partner which are often originally formed when one had little idea of what one's life-interests or larger responsibilities might encompass. The alleged "solution" to this dilemma, which enables the nuclear family to remain intact, is the recent fashion of "wife-swapping." As its name implies, however, this apparent solution is simply a new version of treating one's wife as a physical commodity that is now *literally* up for grabs.

Those who believe that romantic love, monogamy, or the nuclear family, as we ordinarily understand these terms, can somehow be preserved while struggling for liberation from an exploitive system based on private ownership for private profit or while trying to implement the goals of a socialist society are overlooking the place of this institution in the present social system. The nuclear family is a social problem which has tragically paralyzing consequences for its participants, and it will continue to be a social problem until the economic system for which it performs yeoman's service and the possessiveness which it reinforces and legitimizes are the object of systematic and cooperative reconstruction. The transformation or reconstruction of the nuclear family and of the economic system within which it is sustained can, therefore, be approached as different aspects of the same task, rather than as temporally or philosophically incompatible roads to human self-determination.

ENDNOTES

1. Even some of the more historically informed students of the traditional family accept this belief with little or no critical scrutiny, e.g.: "But for many middle- and upper-class Chinese, concubinage represents a social device for satisfaction of the polyerotic tendencies of the male and, among one's male cohorts at least, as a mode of acquiring prestige." Stuart A. Queen *et al., The Family in Various Cultures* (New York: Lippincott, 1961), p. 91; see also "The Chinese System of Familism," pp. 88–115, in *Ibid.*, which, despite such uncritical moments, does call attention to the role of monogamy in the traditional clan system and economy.

2. For an illustrative description of the symptoms of such an approach to one's problems, though the authors fail to examine the political consequences of it, see Jerome K. Myers and Bertram H. Roberts, *Family and Class Dynamics in Mental Illness* (New York: John Wiley & Sons, 1959), especially "Schizophrenic Patients," pp. 230–240.

Pat Mainardi

7

The Politics of Housework

Though women do not complain of the power of husbands, each complains of her own husband, or of the husbands of her friends. It is the same in all other cases of servitude; at least in the commencement of the emancipatory movement. The serfs did not at first complain of the power of the lords, but only of their tyranny.
John Stuart Mill, *On the Subjection of Women*

Liberated women—very different from women's liberation! The first signals all kinds of goodies, to warm the hearts (not to mention other parts) of the most radical men. The other signals—*housework*. The first brings sex without marriage, sex before marriage, cozy housekeeping arrangements ("You see, I'm living with this chick") and the self-content of knowing that you're not the kind of man who wants a doormat instead of a woman. That will come later. After all, who wants that old commodity anymore, the Standard American Housewife, all husband, home and kids. The New Commodity, the Liberated Woman, has sex a lot and has a Career, preferably something that can be fitted in with the household chores—like dancing, pottery, or painting.

On the other hand is women's liberation—and housework. What? You say this is all trivial? Wonderful! That's what I thought. It seemed perfectly reasonable. We both had careers, both had to work a couple of days a week to earn enough to live on, so why shouldn't we share the housework? So I suggested it to my mate and he agreed—most men are too hip to turn you down flat. "You're right," he said, "It's only fair."

Then an interesting thing happened. I can only explain it by stating that we women have been brainwashed more than even we can imagine. Probably too many years of seeing television women in ecstasy over their shiny waxed floors or breaking down over their dirty shirt collars. Men have no such conditioning. They recognize the essential fact of housework right from the very beginning. Which is that it stinks. Here's my list of dirty chores: buying groceries, carting them home and putting them away; cooking meals and washing dishes and pots; doing the laundry, digging out the place when things get out of control; washing floors. The list could go on but the sheer necessities are bad enough. All of us have to do these things, or get some else to do them for us. The longer my husband contemplated these chores, the more repulsed he became, and so proceeded the change from the normally sweet considerate Dr. Jekyll into the crafty Mr. Hyde who would stop at nothing to avoid the horrors of—*housework*. As he felt himself backed into a corner laden with dirty dishes, brooms, mops, and reeking garbage, his front teeth grew longer and pointier, his fingernails haggled and his eyes grew wild. Housework trivial? Not on your life! Just try to share the burden.

So ensued a dialogue that's been going on for several years. Here are some of the high points:

"I don't mind sharing the housework, but I don't do it very well. We should each do the things we're best at."
MEANING: Unfortunately I'm no good at things like washing dishes or cooking. What I do best is a little light carpentry, changing light bulbs, moving furniture (*how often do you move furniture?*)
ALSO MEANING: Historically the lower classes (black men and us) have had hundreds of years experience doing menial jobs. It would be a waste of manpower to train someone else to do them now.
ALSO MEANING: I don't like the dull stupid boring jobs, so you should do them.

"I don't mind sharing the work, but you'll have to show me how to do it."
MEANING: I ask a lot of questions and you'll have to show me everything everytime I do it because I don't remember so good. Also don't try to sit down and read while I'm doing my jobs because I'm going to annoy hell out of you until it's easier to do them yourself.

"We used to be so happy!" (Said whenever it was his turn to do something.)
MEANING: I used to be so happy.
MEANING: Life without housework is bliss. (*No quarrel here. Perfect agreement.*)

"We have different standards, and why should I have to work to your standards. That's unfair."

MEANING: If I begin to get bugged by the dirt and crap I will say "This place sure is a sty" or "How can anyone live like this?" and wait for your reaction. I know that all women have a sore called "Guilt over a messy house" or "Household work is ultimately my responsibility." I know that men have caused that sore—if anyone visits and the place *is* a sty, they're not going to leave and say, "He sure is a lousy housekeeper." You'll take the rap in any case. I can outwait you.

ALSO MEANING: I can provoke innumerable scenes over the housework issue. Eventually doing all the housework yourself will be less painful to you than trying to get me to do half. Or I'll suggest we get a maid. She will do my share of the work. You will do yours. It's women's work.

"I've got nothing against sharing the housework, but you can't make me do it on your schedule."
MEANING: Passive resistance. I'll do it when I damned well please, if at all. If my job is doing dishes, it's easier to do them once a week. If taking out laundry, once a month. If washing the floors, once a year. If you don't like it, do it yourself oftener, and then I won't do it at all.

"I *hate* it more than you. You don't mind it so much."
MEANING: Housework is garbage work. It's the worst crap I've ever done. It's degrading and humiliating for someone of *my* intelligence to do it. But for someone of *your* intelligence . . .

"Housework is too trivial to even talk about."
MEANING: It's even more trivial to do. Housework is beneath my status. My purpose in life is to deal with matters of significance. Yours is to deal with matters of insignificance. You should do the housework.

"This problem of housework is not a man-woman problem! In any relationship between two people one is going to have a stronger personality and dominate."
MEANING: That stronger personality had better be *me*.

"In animal societies, wolves, for example, the top animal is usually a male even where he is not chosen for brute strength but on the basis of cunning and intelligence. Isn't that interesting?"
MEANING: I have historical, psychological, anthropological, and biological justification for keeping you down. How can you ask the top wolf to be equal?

"Women's liberation isn't really a political movement."
MEANING: The Revolution is coming too close to home.
ALSO MEANING: I am only interested in how *I* am oppressed, not

how I oppress others. Therefore the war, the draft, and the university are political. Womens' liberation is not.

"Man's accomplishments have always depended on getting help from other people, mostly women. What great man would have accomplished what he did if he had to do his own housework?"
MEANING: Oppression is built into the System and I, as the white American male, receive the benefits of this System. I don't want to give them up.

POSTSCRIPT

Participatory democracy begins at home. If you are planning to implement your politics, there are certain things to remember.

1. He *is* feeling it more than you. He's losing some leisure and you're gaining it. The measure of your oppression is his resistance.

2. A great many American men are not accustomed to doing monotonous repetitive work which never ushers in any lasting let alone important achievement. This is why they would rather repair a cabinet than wash dishes. If human endeavors are like a pyramid with man's highest achievements at the top, then keeping onself alive is at the bottom. Men have always had servants (us) to take care of this bottom strata of life while they have confined their efforts to the rarefied upper regions. It is thus ironic when they ask of women—where are your great painters, statesmen, etc? Mme. Matisse ran a millinery shop so he could paint. Mrs. Martin Luther King kept his house and raised his babies.

3. It is a traumatizing experience for someone who has always thought of himself as being against any oppression or exploitation of one human being by another to realize that in his daily life he has been accepting and implementing (and benefiting from) this exploitation; that his rationalization is little different from that of the racist who says "Black people don't feel pain" (women don't mind doing the shitwork); and that the oldest form of oppression in history has been the oppression of 50 percent of the population by the other 50 percent.

4. Arm yourself with some knowledge of the psychology of oppressed peoples everywhere, and a few facts about the animal kingdom. I admit playing top wolf or who runs the gorillas is silly but as a last resort men bring it up all the time. Talk about bees. If you feel really hostile bring up the sex life of spiders. They have sex. She bites off his head.

The psychology of oppressed people is not silly. Jews, immigrants, black men, and all women have employed the same psychological mechanisms to survive: admiring the oppressor, glorifying the oppressor, wanting to be like the oppressor, wanting the oppressor to like them, mostly because the oppressor held all the power.

5. In a sense, all men everywhere are slightly schizoid—divorced from the reality of maintaining life. This makes it easier for them to play games with it. It is almost a cliché that women feel greater grief at sending a son off to war or losing him to that war because they bore him, suckled him, and raised him. The men who foment those wars did none of those things and have a more superficial estimate of the worth of human life. One hour a day is a low estimate of the amount of time one has to spend "keeping" oneself. By foisting this off on others, man gains seven hours a week—one working day more to play with his mind and not his human needs. Over the course of generations it is easy to see whence evolved the horrifying abstractions of modern life.

6. With the death of each form of oppression, life changes and new forms evolve. English aristocrats at the turn of the century were horrified at the idea of enfranchising working men—were sure that it signaled the death of civilization and a return to barbarism. Some working men were even deceived by this line. Similarly with the minimum wage, abolition of slavery, and female suffrage. Life changes but it goes on. Don't fall for any line about the death of everything if men take a turn at the dishes. They will imply that you are holding back the Revolution (their Revolution). But you are advancing it (your Revolution).

7. Keep checking up. Periodically consider who's actually *doing* the jobs. These things have a way of backsliding so that a year later once again the woman is doing everything. After a year make a list of jobs the man has rarely if ever done. You will find cleaning pots, toilets, refrigerators and ovens high on the list. Use time sheets if necessary. He will accuse you of being petty. He is above that sort of thing— (housework). Bear in mind what the worst jobs are, namely the ones that have to be done every day or several times a day. Also the ones that are dirty—it's more pleasant to pick up books, newspapers etc. than to wash dishes. Alternate the bad jobs. It's the daily grind that gets you down. Also make sure that you don't have the responsibility for the housework with occasional help from him. "I'll cook dinner for you tonight" implies it's really your job and isn't he a nice guy to do some of it for you.

8. Most men had a rich and rewarding bachelor life during which they did not starve or become encrusted with crud or buried under the litter. There is a taboo that says that women mustn't strain themselves in the presence of men: we haul around 50 pounds of groceries if we have to but aren't allowed to open a jar if there is someone around to do it for us. The reverse side of the coin is that men aren't supposed to be able to take care of themselves without a woman. Both are excuses for making women do the housework.

9. Beware of the double whammy. He won't do the little things he always did because you're now a "Liberated Woman," right? Of course he won't do anything else either . . .

I was just finishing this when my husband came in and asked what I was doing. Writing a paper on housework. Housework? he said, *Housework?* Oh my god how trivial can you get. A paper on housework.

LITTLE POLITICS OF HOUSEWORK QUIZ

The lowest job in the army, used as punishment is: a) working 9–5 b) kitchen duty (K.P.)

When a man lives with his family, his: a) father b) mother does his housework.

When he lives with a woman, a) he b) she does the housework.

A) his son b) his daughter learns preschool how much fun it is to iron daddy's handkerchief.

From the *New York Times,* 9/21/69: "Former Greek Official George Mylonas pays the penalty for differing with the ruling junta in Athens by performing household chores on the island of Amorgos where he lives in forced exile" (with hilarious photo of a miserable Mylonas carrying his own water). What the *Times* means is that he ought to have a) indoor plumbing b) a maid.

Dr. Spock said (*Redbook* 3/69): "Biologically and temperamentally I believe, women were made to be concerned first and foremost with child care, husband care, and home care." Think about: a) *who* made us b) why? c) what is the effect on their lives d) what is the effect on our lives?

From *Time* 1/5/70, "Like their American counterparts, many housing project housewives are said to suffer from neurosis. And for the first time in Japanese history, many young husbands today complain of being henpecked. Their wives are beginning to demand detailed explanations when they don't come home straight from work and some Japanese males nowadays are even compelled to do housework." According to *Time,* women become neurotic: a) when they are forced to do the maintenance work for the male caste all day every day of their lives or b) when they no longer want to do the maintenance work for the male caste all day every day of their lives.

Janice Reynolds

8

Rape as Social Control

Women do not rape men. In fact, they almost never sexually assault adult males. Why this is so would seem self-evident. But in view of the variety of ways in which men force sexual acts upon women, it appears that women could, rather easily in groups and/or with weapons, do the same to men. Yet they don't.[1] On the other hand, forcible rape and other sexual assaults not legally defined as rapes, on women by men may be the leading crimes against persons in the U.S.

Studies in criminology that might be expected to help explain these facts are less helpful than they might be. Even the most sophisticated of the studies rely so heavily upon contemporary sexist assumptions to guide their inquiry and interpretations, that they have limited utility. First of all, the orienting questions are different from the one that I am interested in here. Psychological and sociological studies often start with the question of why some men rape and other men don't. My question, why men do and women don't is generally assumed. It is assumed that men naturally rape, that most men would if it were not illegal and punishable. In addition, it is assumed that women naturally cannot or would not. The restriction in the legal definitions of forcible rape to sexual acts with forced penetration of the female is simply another manifestation of the cultural assumption that only male sexual aggression exists. Most of the studies incorporate this assumption in that they confine themselves to legally defined forcible rape. Women could sexually assault a man in a highly mechanical way; however it would be no less mechanical than the type of assault men engage in. But the possibility is so far from prevailing assumptions that the law does not even provide for this eventuality. It is not that men cannot be dishonored by sexual attack. They can be if the attacker is a man as in homosexual rape.[2] But men cannot, it is assumed, be dishonored by women in this

This article was written for this volume and is printed by permission.

way; thus no legal retribution is required. (Herschberger, 1948, pp. 15–27).

Criminological studies do effectively destroy one "rape myth," and that is the myth which says that rape is an irrational act committed by psychologically disturbed persons. A number of studies find that men who are charged with rape and attempted rape differ little from their class counterparts on standard personality measures. In addition, rapists frequently plan and make arrangements for the rape, sometimes long in advance of the actual event. Studies also report that from fifteen to twenty percent of rapes involve more than one man and are true social acts in every sense of the word. (Amir 1971; Kaare 1962). All of these characteristics of rape events present an image of rationality as the rule and irrationality as the rare exception.

Susan Griffin (1971), in "Rape: The All-American Crime," argues quite cogently that our cultural definitions of male and female sexuality instruct and encourage men to rape. The equation of virility with strength, the view that a slight man is sexually inadequate, that the ideal couple is one where the male is larger and taller, all of these beliefs support the view that males are sexual aggressors. The socialization of males for a sexually aggressive role begins at a very tender age when little boys are rewarded with the indulgent chuckles of adults as they flip up the skirts of the little girls. And of course the fun of such pranks comes from the screams and chagrin of the little girls. Television, movies and songs all portray the scene of the initially unwilling woman who is overwhelmed by the strength of the male's sexual advances, and they explicitly conclude that she (albeit secretly) prefers this method of sexual interaction. The cultural values are summed up in the words of a song by Oscar Brand: "Seduction is for sissies, but a he-man likes his rape." Such views provide a context of cultural approval for rape.

These cultural definitions seem to be what people are referring to when they insist that "it's a fine line" that distinguishes rape from sexual intercourse. Cultural definitions place them on a fine graduated continuum rather than separating the two into distinct categories. However, the rape victims seem to distinguish quite easily between the two. I would like to expand upon the insights of Griffin and others and draw upon some of the sociological literature to develop a further understanding of the function of rape in a "sexist" society.

Helen Hacker (1951) in a now classic article, "Women as a Minority Group," drew out the parallels between the status of women and Blacks in American society. Since then, much has been written on the various economic, legal and cultural factors which operate to establish and maintain the subordinate status of women in relation to men in much the same way as the subordinate status of Blacks is maintained in relation to whites. However, little attention has been given to the role of physical coercion, violence and the threat of bodily harm in maintaining the subordinate role of women, although the importance of these factors in keeping Black persons down, in the past particularly, is well recognized. In this article, it will be argued that rape is a means of social control aimed at constraining the behavior of women, a way of keeping women in "their place."

Developing this theme requires that we turn conventional categories upside down, because presumably it is the criminal law against rape which is the instrument of social control—not the criminal acts that the law proscribes and punishes. But the contrary view appears more plausible when the laws against rape operate, in practice and application, primarily to punish only those men who do not rape *appropriately*.

Furthermore, some reshifting of the conventional viewpoint is also justified when we compare rape to other extra-legal (in fact, illegal) types of social control that maintain racial subordination. For example, lynching is and was illegal, a type of murder, in the eyes of the law. Yet, it was without doubt a socially acceptable means of controlling Blacks in the not-too-distant past. Thus it is not unheard of for a group of people to maintain laws that proscribe actions which in most cases are supported by popular attitudes.

Such an interpretation of the function of rape is supported further by examination of the unique rituals required of the rape victim if she wishes to have her claim to the victim role tentatively accepted by the prosecutor's office. A medical examination is required to obtain physical evidence, pictures of bruises and injuries may be taken, and injections of antibiotics and hormones to prevent disease and pregnancy are administered. In the state of New York, until quite recently a corroborating witness was required.

The uniqueness of these requirements becomes especially sharp when they are contrasted with those required of a person who alleges robbery. In this case the victim's statements that they actually had goods that were taken is usually sufficient. A witness is not required to corroborate statements that a theft took place or to corroborate their identification of the thief.

The rape victim is also required to demonstrate her good character.[3] Any evidence that suggests that the victim does not adhere to strict moral standards discredits her claim to victim status, and such "evidence" may actually get her labelled as the deviant.[4] However in the case of robbery, juries don't automatically assume that a thief cannot be robbed or that a moral deviant should be robbed. Yet, these assumptions are made in rape cases.

The rape victim has to demonstrate that in no way could her actions be construed as anything but negative to the suggestion of sexual acts.

Even when there is conclusive evidence of brutal treatment, it is not assumed by the court that the victim didn't want this to happen to her. Yet, no one sees the thief as less culpable because his victim didn't struggle with him or because the victim flashed his money around, etc.

It could be that such special care in rape cases is taken to insure that the allegation of rape is not used to harm the guiltless. Since such care is not exercised in handling other allegations which could be used by a fraudulent victim with as much ease as a rape allegation this explanation seems implausible unless one assumes that a woman's perception of sexual events is especially dubious. A more defendable explanation is that police, juries and courts require that a rape victim demonstrate conclusively that she was raped unjustly, the assumption being that rape is normally justified.

A good example that forcible intercourse is categorically viewed as acceptable in some circumstances is that a husband cannot be accused of raping his wife. Similarly, in practice, a man is never convicted of raping a prostitute; and if a woman has had a sexual relationship in the past with a man who later attacks and rapes her, no matter what the level of brutality, her rape allegation is viewed by the court as highly doubtful.

Again it appears that there is a broad category of justifiable rape and that in a criminal case a woman must prove that she was raped unjustifiably. This implies that the courts and juries feel that the safest assumption to make is that, when a man sexually assaults a woman, "she had it coming to her," that she was fair game.

The question then arises regarding what kind of women can be appropriately raped? In answer to this question some of the studies of rape are suggestive, although caution must be used in interpreting their findings. Some of them use samples of convicted rapists, and the most exhaustive study was a sample of persons arrested on the charge of forcible rape. The cases where there are convictions constitute only a small percentage of those where there are arrests, which in turn constitute a small percentage of all reported cases, and these reported cases are an unknown proportion of the total number of all rape incidents.

Griffin (1971, p. 32) maintains that "Like indiscriminate terrorism, rape can happen to any woman." As evidence for this thesis she offers the fact that many rapists assault total strangers. Yet it must be remembered that it is in just these cases where the victim doesn't know the rapist (other things being equal) that the rapist is defined as more culpable (Amir, 1971). In these cases it seems more likely that a long prison term will be meted out to the rapist. This penalty can scarcely be construed as an indication of support for and approval of his actions. In addition, it is difficult to understand how rape and the threat of rape could effectively shape and control the behavior of women, if, no matter what her actions, a man could rape her with impunity.

A more plausible thesis is that rape is viewed as a legitimate punishment for women who give the appearance of violating traditional female role expectations. Rape is defined as legitimate by a broad segment of the society only when a specific type of female is raped.

While no studies of rape have specifically addressed themselves to this hypothesis, a number of findings lend support to it. Kanin's (1957) research on male sex aggression among university students found that men who believe most strongly in the double standard are the most likely to commit rape. Amir's (1971) study of the "planning aspects" of rape suggests that the rapist is selective as to his victim and that the act is not indiscriminately addressed toward any convenient female.

If one looks at the collection of items which studies refer to as "actions of the victim which advertently or inadvertently precipitate rapes," one gets a picture of the kinds of behavior which, from the perspective of the rapist and apparently the authors too, are seen as provocation to rape. A young woman who lives away from her family, a woman who travels alone, or is pleasant to male acquaintances, or acts in an exuberant manner in public, goes out with men unchaperoned, hangs her underwear on a clothesline in public view, gives any appearance of not closely adhering to the double standard, or in general acts on the assumption that carrying on her activities in an instrumental way carries no erotic suggestions, is viewed as giving provocation, wittingly or unwittingly. The authors of some articles seem to suggest that if women only didn't act *freely* they would be spared from humiliation and harm. The important question of why such a lack of freedom and imposition of restraint is required of women in our society and not of men is never raised.

The failure to raise questions of this nature is particularly curious because the present trend in the sociological analysis of deviant behavior, by seeking to understand the social episode as it is shaped by interaction between the participants, opens up the possibility of doing so. When the interactionist perspective which views rape and other deviant behavior as mutually constructed joint action is adopted, the relationship between the rapist and the victim, and the victim's actions, are relevant to the analysis. Such factors are disregarded as irrelevant in studies where rape is viewed as a symptom of individual pathology because the possibility of social forces does not arise.

Apparently the limitation of analysis is interaction studies, of which Amir's (1971) is a good example, is imposed primarily by the interest of the author in lifting some culpability from the rapist by redefining the crime as a victim precipitated crime. Such a redefinition requires that one adopt a sexist standard, a standard which regards actions as sexually provocative when engaged in by women but banal and normal when engaged in by men. In this curious sort of underdog sociology that Amir's (1971) study represents, it is the rapist's side which is chosen.

Instead of leading to questions concerning the sexual politics of our society, Amir's analysis leads him to the conclusion that rape is an expression of a lower class sub-culture of violence and aggression. He bases his conclusion on the fact that fully ninety percent of the rapists in his sample were lower class. Logically extended, this explanation of rape is analogous to the explanation of lynching given by many "respectable" southerners in the past: that only the lower classes, the riff-raff of the society, participate in such actions, and that therefore respectable people need take no responsibility for it.

If rape is simply an expression of generalized violence and aggression, the selectivity exercised as to appropriate objects for aggression would still have to be explained. In addition, the fact that middle class males are seldom brought before the courts (Amir, 1971; Kaare, 1962) should be interpreted with extreme caution. Kirkpatrick's (1957, p. 53) study reports that 6.2% of the coeds in his sample reported attempted forcible rapes by college males, accompanied by threats of bodily harm and infliction of pain. The previous description of the assumptions made by juries and courts indicates that the belief that rape is a justifiable response in certain social situations is widespread in American society and not limited to the lower classes of the population.

In particular, it appears that rape is a punitive action directed toward females who usurp or appear to usurp the culturally defined perogatives of the dominant male role. In order to explore this area further, a number of males were questioned regarding their opinion as to what kind of woman, if any, deserved to be raped. Rather uniformly the males replied that if anyone deserved rape it was the so-called "prick-tease." The majority of those questioned could recall incidents of sexual assaults on young girls which they had either observed or participated in as adolescents. Sometimes the actions described would constitute legally defined forcible rape, but more often there was no penetration. Public exposure of the girl's body or attacks on her genitals with instruments or other bodily violations were the actions most frequently engaged in. When pressed as to what actions on her part were the basis of the informant's judgment that "she got what she deserved," they cited various behaviors, all the way from a "snotty" demeanor to verbal derision of the male's sexual capabilities. Especially infuriating was the girl who was believed to have "put out" for some but would not for others and seemed proud of her ability to be selective. Rape and other kinds of sexual assaults were seen as particularly appropriate ways of showing such women "their place." From the descriptions, it appeared that the girls were behaving in ways that violated the traditional double standard of sexual morality, but were applying a rigorous standard of their own in selecting and rejecting sexual partners. The fact that they seemed to do so with glee added insult to injury from the males' perspectives. This parallels the case of lynching where a frequent basis for the lynching was the alleged violation of sexual codes.

One has to be cautious in interpreting responses gathered in an unsystematic exploratory inquiry, but when these informants' responses are placed in the context of the assumptions concerning rape revealed by court processes and those made by the studies of rape and rapists together with the images of rape projected in the media, a clear pattern emerges. It is that rape and the threat of rape operate in our society to maintain the dominant position of males. It does this by restricting the mobility and freedom of movement of women, by limiting their casual interaction with the opposite sex, and in particular by maintaining the males' perogatives in the erotic sphere. When there is evidence that the victim was or gave the appearance of being out of her place, she can be raped and the rapist will be supported by the cultural values, by the institutions that embody these values, and by the people shaped by these values—this is, by the police, the courts, members of juries, and sometimes the victims themselves.

ENDNOTES

1. In discussing this point with others it was often pointed out about the man in Houston, Amsterdam, etc. who claimed to have been raped. Rumors are rife but I was unable to find documentation of any such cases.
2. In 1974, Michigan revised its rape laws by enacting a new sexual assault law which changes some of the requirements for proof in sexual assault cases. It covers sexual assaults on men as well as women and defines four classes of sexual assault.
3. A new California law designed to deal with this situation prohibits questions about the woman's previous sexual experience.
4. In the case of statutory rape, the wheels of justice can turn against the victim, as she may be prosecuted for violations of the "juvenile code."

REFERENCES

Amir, Menachem, *Patterns in Forcible Rape,* Chicago: University of Chicago Press, 1971.

Gebhard, Paul H., *et al.*, *Sex Offenders: An Analysis of Types*, New York: Harper and Row, 1965.

Griffin, Susan, "Rape: The All-American Crime," *Ramparts, 10,* (September 1971): pp. 26–35.

Hacker, Helen M., "Women as a Minority Group," *Social Forces, 30,* (October 1951): pp. 60–69.

Herschberger, Ruth, *Adam's Rib,* New York: Pellegrini and Cadahy, 1948.

Kanin, E. J., "Male Aggression in Dating-courtship Relations," *American Journal of Sociology, 63,* (1957), pp. 197–204.

Kirkpatrick, Clifford, and Kanin, Eugene, "Male Sex Aggression On a University Campus," *American Sociological Review, 22,* (February 1957): pp. 52–58.

Svalastoga, Kaare, "Rape and Social Structure," *The Pacific Sociological Review, V,* (1962), pp. 48–53.

Weis, Kurt, and Sandra S. Borges, "Victimology and Rape: The Case of the Legitimate Victim," *Issues in Criminology, 8,* (Fall 1973): pp. 71–115.

Frances M. Beal

9

Double Jeopardy:
To Be Black and Female

In attempting to analyze the situation of the black woman in America, one crashes abruptly into a solid wall of grave misconceptions, outright distortions of fact, and defensive attitudes on the part of many. The System of capitalism (and its afterbirth—racism) under which we all live, has attempted by many devious ways and means to destroy the humanity of all people, and particularly the humanity of black people. This has meant an outrageous assault on every black man, woman, and child who resides in the United States.

In keeping with its goal of destroying the black race's will to resist its subjugation, capitalism found it necessary to create a situation where the black man found it impossible to find meaningful or productive employment. More often than not, he couldn't find work of any kind. And the black woman, likewise, was manipulated by the System, economically exploited and physically assaulted. She could often find work in the white man's kitchen, however, and sometimes became the sole breadwinner of the family. This predicament has led to many psychological problems on the part of both man and woman and has contributed to the turmoil in the black family structure.

Unfortunately, neither the black man nor the black woman understood the true nature of the forces working upon them. Many black women tended to accept the capitalist evaluation of manhood and womanhood and believed, in fact, that black men were shiftless and lazy; otherwise they would get a job and support their families as they ought to. Personal relationships between black men and women were thus torn asunder and one result has been the separation of man from wife, mother from child, etc.

America has defined the roles to which each individual should subscribe. It has defined "manhood" in terms of its own interests and "femininity" likewise. Therefore, an individual who has a good job, makes a lot of money, and drives a Cadillac is a real "man," and conversely, an individual who is lacking in these "qualities" is less of a man. The advertising media in this country continuously informs the American male of his need for indispensable signs of his virility—the brand of cigarettes that cowboys prefer, the whisky that has a masculine tang, or the label of the jock strap that athletes wear.

The ideal model that is projected for a woman is to be surrounded by hypocritical homage and estranged from all real work, spending idle hours primping and preening, obsessed with conspicuous consumption, and limiting life's functions to simply a sex role. We unqualitatively reject these respective models. A woman who stays at home, caring for children and the house, leads an extremely sterile existence. She must lead her entire life as a satellite to her mate. He goes out into society and brings back a little piece of the world for her. His interests and his understanding of the world become her own and she cannot develop herself as an individual, having been reduced to only a biological function. This kind of woman leads a parasitic existence that can aptly be described as "legalized prostitution."

Furthermore, it is idle dreaming to think of black women simply caring for their homes and children like the middle-class white model. Most black women have to work to help house, feed, and clothe their families. Black women make up a substantial percentage of the black working force and this is true for the poorest black family as well as the so-called "middle-class" family.

Black women were never afforded any such phony luxuries. Though we have been browbeaten with this white image, the reality of the degrading and dehumanizing jobs that were relegated to us quickly dissipated this mirage of womanhood. The following excerpts from a speech that Sojourner Truth made at a Women's Rights Convention in the nineteenth century show us how misleading and incomplete a life this model represents for us:

> . . . Well, chilern whar dar is so much racket dar must be something out o'kilter. I tink dat 'twixt de niggers of de Souf and de women at de Norf all a talkin' 'bout right, de white men will be in a fix pretty soon. But what's all dis here talkin' 'bout? Dat man ober dar say dat women needs to be helped into carriages, and lifted ober ditches, and to have de best place every whar. Nobody ever help me into carriages, or ober mud puddles, or gives me any best places . . . and ar'nt I a woman? Look at me! Look at my arm! . . . I have plowed, and planted, and gathered into barns, and no man could head me—and ar'nt I a woman? I could work as much as a man (when I could get it), and bear de lash as well

—and ar'nt I a woman? I have borne five chilern and I seen 'em mos' all sold off into slavery, and when I cried out with a mother's grief, none but Jesus heard—and ar'nt I a woman?

Unfortunately, there seems to be some confusion in the Movement today as to who has been oppressing whom. Since the advent of Black Power, the black male has exerted a more prominent leadership role in our struggle for justice in this country. He sees the System for what it really is, for the most part, put where he rejects its values and mores on many issues, when it comes to women, he seems to take his guidelines from the pages of the *Ladies' Home Journal*. Certain black men are maintaining that they have been castrated by society but that black women somehow escaped this persecution and even contributed to this emasculation.

Let me state here and now that the black woman in America can justly be described as a "slave of a slave." When the black man in America was reduced to such an abject state, the black woman had no protector and was used and is still being used in some cases as the scapegoat for the evils that this horrendous System has perpetrated on black men. Her physical image has been maliciously maligned; she has been sexually assaulted and abused by the white colonizer; she has suffered the worst kind of economic exploitation, having been forced to serve as the white woman's maid and wet nurse for white offspring while her own children were starving and neglected. It is the depth of degradation to be socially manipulated, physically raped, used to undermine your own household—and to be powerless to reverse this syndrome.

It is true that our husbands, fathers, brothers, and sons have been emasculated, lynched, and brutalized. They have suffered from the cruellest assault of mankind that the world has ever known. However, it is a gross distortion of fact to state that black women have oppressed black men. The capitalist System found it expedient to oppress them and proceeded to do so without consultation or the signing of any agreements with black women.

It must also be pointed out at this time, that black women are not resentful of the rise to power of black men. We welcome it. We see in it the eventual liberation of all black people from this oppressive System of capitalism. Nevertheless, this does not mean that you have to negate one for the other. This kind of thinking is a product of miseducation; that it's either X or it's Y. It is fallacious reasoning that in order for the black man to be strong, the black woman has to be weak.

Those who are exerting their "manhood" by telling black women to step back into a submissive role are assuming a counterrevolutionary position. Black women likewise have been abused by the System and we must begin talking about the elimination of all kinds of oppression. If we are talking about building a strong nation, capable of throwing off the yoke of capitalist oppression, then we are talking about the total involvement of every man, woman, and child, each with a highly developed political consciousness. We need our whole army out there dealing with the enemy, and not half an army.

There are also some black women who feel that there is no more productive role in life than having and raising children. This attitude often reflects the conditioning of the society in which we live and is adopted from a bourgeois white model. Some young sisters who have never had to maintain a household and accept the confining role which this entails, tend to romanticize (along with the help of a number of brothers) this role of housewife and mother. Black women who have had to endure this kind of function are less apt to have these utopian visions. Those who project in an intellectual manner how great and rewarding this role will be and who feel that the most important thing that they can contribute to the black nation is children, are doing themselves a great injustice. This line of reasoning completely negates the contributions that black women have historically made to our struggle for liberation. These black women include Sojourner Truth, Harriet Tubman, Mary McLeod Bethune, and Fannie Lou Hamer, to name but a few.

We live in a highly industrialized society and every member of the black nation must be as academically and technologically developed as possible. To wage a revolution, we need competent teachers, doctors, nurses, electronics experts, chemists, biologists, physicists, political scientists, and so on and so forth. Black women sitting at home reading bedtime stories to their children are just not going to make it.

ECONOMIC EXPLOITATION OF BLACK WOMEN

The economic System of capitalism finds it expedient to reduce women to a state of enslavement. They oftentimes serve as a scapegoat for the evils of this system. Much in the same way that the poor white cracker of the South, who is equally victimized, looks down upon blacks and contributes to the oppression of blacks—so, by giving to men a false feeling of superiority (at least in their own home or in their relationships with women)—the oppression of women acts as an escape valve for capitalism. Men may be cruelly exploited and subjected to all sorts of dehumanizing tactics on the part of the ruling class, but they have someone who is below them—at least they're not women.

Women also represent a surplus labor supply, the control of which is absolutely necessary to the profitable functioning of capitalism. Women are consistently exploited by the System. They are often paid less for the same work that men do and jobs that are specifically relegated to women are lowpaying and without the possibility of advancement. Statistics from the Women's Bureau of the United States Department of Labor show that in 1967, the wage scale for white women was even below that of black men; and the wage scale for non-white women was the lowest of all:

White Males	$6704
Non-White Males	4277
White Females	3991
Non-White Females	2861

Those industries that employ mainly black women are the most exploitative in the country. The hospital workers are a good example of this oppression; the garment workers in New York City provide us with another view of this economic slavery. The International Ladies Garment Workers Union (ILGWU) whose overwhelming membership consists of black and Puerto Rican women has a leadership that is nearly all lily-white and male. This leadership has been working in collusion with the ruling class and has completely sold its soul to the corporate structure.

To add insult to injury, ILGWU has invested heavily in business enterprises in racist, apartheid South Africa—with union funds. Not only does this bought-off leadership contribute to our continued exploitation in this country by not truly representing the best interests of its membership, but it audaciously uses funds that black and Puerto Rican women have provided to support the economy of a vicious government that is engaged in the exploitation and murder of our black brothers and sisters in our motherland, Africa.

The entire labor movement in the United States has suffered as a result of the superexploitation of black workers and women. The unions have historically been racist and male chauvinistic. They have upheld racism in this country and have failed to fight the white-skin privileges of white workers. They have failed to struggle against inequities in the hiring and pay of women workers. There has been virtually no struggle against either the racism of the white worker or the economic exploitation of the working woman, two factors which have consistently impeded the advancement of the real struggle against the ruling class.

The racist, chauvinistic, and manipulative use of black workers and women, especially black women, has been a severe cancer on the American labor scene. It therefore becomes essential for those who understand the workings of capitalism and imperialism to realize that the exploitation of black people and women works to everyone's disadvantage and that the liberation of these two minority groups is a stepping stone to the liberation of all oppressed people in this country and around the world.

BEDROOM POLITICS

I have briefly discussed the economic and psychological manipulation of black women, but perhaps the most outlandish act of oppression in modern times is the current campaign to promote sterilization of non-white women, in an attempt to maintain the population and power imbalance between the white "haves" and the non-white "have nots."

These tactics are but another example of the many devious schemes that the ruling class elite attempts to perpetrate on the black population in order to keep itself in control. It has recently come to our attention that a massive campaign for so-called "birth control" is presently being promoted not only in the underdeveloped non-white areas of the world, but also in black communities here in the United States. However, what the authorities in charge of these programs refer to as "birth control" is in fact nothing but a method of outright surgical genocide.

The United States has been sponsoring sterilization clinics in non-white countries, especially in India where already some three million young men and boys in and around New Delhi have been sterilized in makeshift operating rooms set up by the American Peace Corps workers. Under these circumstances, it is understandable why certain countries view the Peace Corps not as a benevolent project, not as evidence of America's concern for underdeveloped areas, but rather as a threat to their very existence. This program could more aptly be named the "Death Corps."

The vasectomy, which is performed on males and takes only six or seven minutes, is a relatively simple operation. The sterilization of a woman, on the other hand, is admittedly major surgery. This operation (salpingectomy) must be performed in a hospital under general anesthesia.[1] This method of "birth control" is a common procedure in Puerto Rico. Puerto Rico has long been used by the colonialist exploiter, the United States, as a huge experimental laboratory for medical research before allowing certain practices to be imported and used here. When the birth control pill was first being perfected, it was tried out on Puerto Rican women and selected black women (poor), as if they were guinea pigs to see what its effect would be and how efficient the Pill was.

The salpingectomy has now become the commonest operation in Puerto Rico, commoner than an appendectomy or a tonsilectomy. It is so widespread that it is referred to simply as *la operación. On the Island, 20 percent of the women between the ages of fifteen and forty-five have already been sterilized.*

And now, as previously occurred with the Pill, this method has been imported into the United States. These sterilization clinics are cropping up around the country in the black and Puerto Rican communities.

These so-called "Maternity Clinics," specifically outfitted to purge black women or men of their reproductive possibilities, are appearing more and more in hospitals and clinics across the country.

A number of organizations have recently been formed to popularize the idea of sterilization, such as The Association for Voluntary Sterilization, and the Human Betterment (! ! ! ?) Association for Voluntary Sterilization, Inc., which has its headquarters in New York City. Front Royal, Virginia, has one such "Maternity Clinic" in Warren Memorial Hospital. The tactics used in the clinic in Fauquier County, Virginia, where poor and helpless black mothers and young girls are pressured into undergoing sterilization, are certainly not confined to that clinic alone.

Threatened with the cut-off of relief funds, some black welfare women have been forced to undergo this sterilization procedure in exchange for a continuation of welfare benefits. Mt. Sinai Hospital in New York City performs these operations on its ward patients whenever it can convince the women to undergo this surgery. Mississippi and some of the other Southern states are notorious for this act. Black women are often afraid to permit any kind of necessary surgery because they know from bitter experience that they are more likely than not to come out without their insides. (Both salpingectomies and hysterectomies are performed.)

We condemn this use of the black woman as a medical testing ground for the white middle class. Reports of the ill effects, including deaths, from the use of the birth-control pill only started to come to light when the white privileged class began to be affected. These outrageous Nazi-like procedures on the part of medical researchers are but another manifestation of the totally amoral and brutal behavior that the capitalist System perpetrates on black women. The sterilization experiments carried on in concentration camps some twenty-five years ago have been denounced the world over, but no one seems to get upset by the repetition of these same racist practices today in the United States of America—land of the free and home of the brave.

The rigid laws concerning abortions in this country are another means of subjugation and, indirectly, of outright murder. Rich white women somehow manage to obtain these operations with little or no difficulty. It is the poor black and Puerto Rican woman who is at the mercy of the local butcher. Statistics show us that the non-white death rate at the hands of the unqualified abortionist is substantially higher than for white women. Nearly half of the child-bearing deaths in New York City are attributed to abortion alone and out of these, 79 percent are among non-whites and Puerto Rican women.

We are not saying that black women should not practice birth control. Black women have the right and the responsibility to determine when it is in *the interest of the struggle to have children or not to have them and this right must not be relinquished to anyone.* It is also her right and responsibility to determine when it is in *her own best interests* to have children, how many she will have, and how far apart. The lack of the availability of safe birth-control methods, the forced sterilization practices, and the inability to obtain legal abortions are all symptoms of a sick society that jeopardizes the health of black women (and thereby the entire black race) in its attempt to control the very life processes of human beings. This is a symptom of a society that is attempting to bring economic and political factors into the privacy of the bedchamber. The elimination of these horrendous conditions will free black women for full participation in the revolution, and thereafter in the building of the new society.

RELATIONSHIP TO WHITE MOVEMENT

Much has been written recently about the white women's liberation movement in the United States and the question arises whether there are any parallels between this struggle and the movement on the part of black women for total emancipation. While there are certain comparisons that one can make because we both live under the same exploitative System, there are certain differences, some of which are quite basic.

The white woman's movement is far from being monolithic. Any white woman's group that does not have an anti-imperialistic and antiracist ideology has absolutely nothing in common with the black woman's struggle. In fact, some groups come to the incorrect conclusion that their oppression is due simply to male chauvinism. They therefore have an extremely antimale tone to their dissertations. Black people are engaged in a life-and-death struggle and the main emphasis of black women must be to combat the capitalist, racist exploitation of black people. While it is true that male chauvinism has become institutionalized in American society, one must always look for the main enemy —the fundamental cause of the female condition.

Another major differentiation is that the white women's movement is basically middle class. Very few of these women suffer the extreme economic exploitation that most black women are subjected to day by day. This is the factor that is most crucial for us. It is not an intellectual persecution alone; it is not an intellectual outburst for us; it is quite real. We as black women have got to deal with the problems that the black masses deal with, for our problems in reality are one and the same.

If the white groups do not realize that they are in fact fighting capitalism and racism, we do not have common bonds. If they do not realize that the reasons for their condition lie in the System and not simply that men get a vicarious pleasure out of "consuming their bodies for exploitative reasons" (this kind of reasoning seems to be quite prevalent in certain white women's groups), then we cannot unite with them around common grievances or even discuss these groups in a serious manner because they're completely irrelevant to the black struggle.

THE NEW WORLD

The black community and black women especially must begin raising questions about the kind of society we wish to see established. We must note the ways in which capitalism oppresses us and then move to create institutions that will eliminate these destructive influences.

The new world that we are attempting to create must destroy oppression of any type. The value of this new system will be determined by the status of the person who was low man on the totem pole. Unless women in any enslaved nation are completely liberated, the change cannot really be called a revolution. If the black woman has to retreat to the position she occupied before the armed struggle, the whole movement and the whole struggle will have retreated in terms of truly freeing the colonized population.

A people's revolution that engages the participation of every member of the community, including man, woman, and child, brings about a certain transformation in the participants as a result of this participation. Once you have caught a glimpse of freedom or experienced a bit of self-determination, you can't go back to old routines that were established under the racist, capitalist regime. We must begin to understand that a revolution entails not only the willingness to lay our lives on the firing line and get killed. In some ways, this is an easy commitment to make. To die for the revolution is a one-shot deal; to live for the revolution means taking on the more difficult commitment of changing our day-to-day life patterns.

This will mean changing the routines that we have established as a result of living in a totally corrupting society. It means changing how you relate to your wife, your husband, your parents, and your co-workers. If we are going to liberate ourselves as a people, it must be recognized that black women have very specific problems that have to be spoken to. We must be liberated along with the rest of the population. We cannot wait to start working on those problems until that great day in the future when the revolution, somehow, miraculously, is accomplished.

To assign women the role of housekeeper and mother while men go forth into battle is a highly questionable doctrine for a revolutionary to maintain. Each individual must develop a high political consciousness in order to understand how this System enslaves us all and what actions we must take to bring about its total destruction. Those who consider themselves revolutionary must begin to deal with other revolutionaries as equals. And, so far as I know, revolutionaries are not determined by sex.

Old people, young people, men, and women must take part in the struggle. To relegate women to purely supportive roles or purely cultural considerations is dangerous doctrine to project. Unless black men who are preparing themselves for armed struggle understand that the society which we are trying to create is one in which the oppression of *all* members of that society is eliminated, then the revolution will have failed in its avowed purpose.

Given the mutual commitment of black men and black women alike to the liberation of our people and other oppressed peoples around the world, the total involvement of each individual is necessary. A revolutionary has the responsibility of not only toppling those who are now in a position of power, but creating new institutions that will eliminate all forms of oppression. We must begin to rewrite our understanding of traditional personal relationships between man and woman.

All the resources that the black community can muster up must be channeled into the struggle. Black women must take an active part in bringing about the kind of society where our children, our loved ones, and each citizen can grow up and live as decent human beings, free from the pressures of racism and capitalist exploitation.

ENDNOTE

1. Salpingectomy: through an abdominal incision, the surgeon cuts both fallopian tubes and ties off the separated ends, after which there is no way for the egg to pass from the ovary to the womb.

Racism

As sexism is a method of maintaining social control over a large subservient group, so also is racism. Racism, also like sexism, is not simply a matter of individualistic orientation; it is far more than a matter of psychology. Racism is an endemic part of the American social scene, a form of social control that buttresses the status quo of social arrangements. Racism not only keeps minority groups in line, but it pervasively exerts pernicious effects on those against whom it is directed. Racism is a powerful force in American life, as the introductory essay documents so well.

Willhelm opens this section with a powerful article that reports on and analyzes current racism as it affects American blacks. This opening essay explodes common myths about the black situation in contemporary American life—myths designed to conceal the severity of American racism. Contrary to the popular opinion so carefully manipulated by our mass media, racial discrimination directed against blacks is not decreasing, but is increasing. The popular imagery has it that blacks may not be as well off as whites, but things are getting better for them. As Willhelm documents, however, the situation is becoming progressively worse, not better, with racial discrimination increasing in the major areas of education, income, housing, and health. In education, we find that many of the effects of the Supreme Court's 1954 decision have been wiped out and that racial segregation in our school system is now on the upswing. And, in spite of so much publicity to the contrary, the gap between black and white income is increasing, with automation hitting blacks much harder than whites. Additionally, housing for blacks is continuing to get worse, and as a general reflection of the effects of racism on health, this opening essay notes that the black infant mortality rate is increasing.

Following this provocative opening essay, Collier presents an analysis of racism directed against American Indians. After following a policy of genocide in which Indians were systematically slaughtered by troops of the United States government, we turned to a containment policy, confining the survivors of our carnage to the most useless land we could find. When some of this land was later discovered to be valuable, treaties were systematically broken by "The Great White Father" who wanted to keep valuable land in the hands of whites. Note some of the consequences of our containment policy. The Indian infant mortality rate after the first month of life is three times higher than the national average, while the suicide rate of young Indians is more than three times the national average. Unemployment among some Indian groups runs to 60 percent, while in some areas the educational drop-out rate goes to 75 percent. Many lawyers, supposedly working for the benefit of Indians, refuse to file claims on their behalf, while white businessmen follow their "business as usual" policy on the reservations and regularly exploit welfare recipients. The Bureau of Indian Affairs was supposedly set up to protect Indian rights, but it has, instead, been an arm of the government used to oppress Indians and deny them their rights. White society is the burden Indians must bear, and it is this that is the focus of Collier's article.

Just as the United States government took Indian lands by force, we similarly fought an imperialistic war with Mexico which netted our Southwest: California, New Mexico, Arizona, and Texas. Spanish-speaking Americans represent another conquered people, and again theirs is a history of discrimination. Mexican-Americans, or Chicanos, regularly and systematically come into conflict with the dominant white culture. The Chicanos' traditional ways of life represent a basic orientation to the world that differs from the "Anglos'." They are faced with the dilemma of leaving behind their ways and abandoning their culture, or perishing in obsolescence. It is this theme of culture conflict, along with the nostalgia of days gone by and a way of life no longer viable, that are discussed by Galarza.

Racism pervades our society. It is not simply a matter of individuals here and there being hostile to members of other races. Rather, our social institutions discriminate against minority racial groups and favor "Anglos." Americans are taught to be racist from the time they are born. They quickly learn who is dominant—and they do not have to guess for very long whether it is blacks, Chicanos, Indians, or whites who are in the ruling position. Positive traits are assigned those with wealth and power, while negative traits are assigned those who are left out of the stream of influence. Since not many ever enter this stream, but most are predestined to be poor or close to it (as documented by Lundberg in Article 3), poor whites frequently take comfort in looking down on blacks and other minorities. Though they might be poor, they at least have the satisfaction of knowing that their skin color matches those in control. Such an orientation directly benefits those in power, as Reich demonstrates in the concluding selection, for by keeping the working class divided along racial lines, each views the other as the enemy. Whites fearfully hold on to their precarious jobs, while blacks are resentful of those who have better paying jobs. Each remains blind to their common "have-not" plight, with neither seeing that they are both economically exploited and that the same people directly benefit from their exploitation. It is this economic base that perpetuates American racism and serves to stabilize the present social order that Reich analyzes.

Again, in this section we look beyond individuals in order to examine some of the sociological underpinnings and consequences of racism. We see that racism is not simply a manifestation of individual sentiment, but that it is built into the American social system. To realize that racism is part and parcel of the ordinary way of life in our society is to be directed to questions such as: Who benefits from racism? What mechanisms are used to maintain racism? Is a social system without racism possible? What would such a social system look like? How could one go about changing our social system in order to eliminate racism? How extensive would such changes have to be?

10

Sidney M. Willhelm

Black Obsolescence in a
White America

The civil rights struggles that emerged during the 'fifties and blossomed so conspicuously in the 'sixties supposedly brought forth substantial social improvements and economic gains for America's Black minority;[1] when progress was not immediately apparent, the assurance was given that it would be "right around the corner." Most commentators on the racial scene present an American society which has acted vigorously to eliminate racism and to enhance equal opportunities regardless of race, indicating that Blacks have already attained remarkable gains in the important areas of housing, income, education, health, and employment. With few exceptions, the claim of inevitable racial progress persists as the dominant theme within the reports and surveys that assess contemporary Black-White relations in America.

A closer and more careful evaluation of the evidence, however, reveals just the opposite; the notion of progress itself cannot be sustained so as to demonstrate a lessening of White hostility toward Blacks. "In their optimism and eagerness to prove that assimilation could proceed rapidly—given laws against discrimination and vigorous enforcement of these laws—," writes Lewis Killian, "sociologists have failed to take due and realistic account of the depth of white prejudice and the short-sightedness of white self interest. . . ."[2] Regardless of perspective, virtually all schools of thought among professional, orthodox sociologists have been racist by presenting interpretations that detect some specific quality among Blacks themselves, rather than suggesting any responsibility among Whites, for any difficulty that might impede further progress.[3] As a consequence, most observers concerned with the fate of Black people fail to realize the rapid deterioration in living standards Blacks are now experiencing, and, in addition, the persistence of White

This article was written for this volume and is printed by permission.

racism which accounts for the downward thrusts. America's Black population is increasingly isolated from Whites and therefore becomes much more vulnerable to White oppression; Whites are compelling Blacks to reside within the urban ghettos where conditions deteriorate in the typical manner of slum-living and, in the event Blacks resort to violent uprisings, as during the 'sixties, Whites will retaliate militarily with the intent to exterminate, rather than tolerate, the Black minority. White wrath is so great that not only can we expect greater hardships for Blacks with the passing of each decade but also the possibility of a greater calamity as well: Whites may very well resort to genocide and liquidate Black people as a final solution to any further Black demand for social justice.

EDUCATING FOR "INCOMPETENCE"

Nowhere is the acclaim for Black advancement in a White America greater than in respect to educational achievements. In 1960, 200,000 Blacks enrolled in colleges and universities; 65% attended "Black" colleges. Ten years later, in 1970, the enrollment more than doubled, reaching 470,000, and also shifted so that 66% attended "White" colleges.[4] Nonetheless, a study published in March, 1971 found that "Blacks make up only 3 per cent of the enrollment at predominantly white colleges. . . . The impression has sometimes been created that colleges are over-committed to minorities,' said Frank Newman [author of the study]. 'Blacks [nevertheless] as a per cent of total enrollment are barely holding their own.' "[5] Furthermore, in a most significant article, Ellen Kay Trimberger analyzed how the "open admissions" policy instituted by the City University of New York, a massive university system, has resulted in a tracking device where Blacks are directed so as to enroll in the less prestigious colleges within this city-wide university.[6]

If one takes the percentage of Blacks upon the formerly all-White campus as a mark of improvement, it would seem that Blacks scored a measure of educational attainment in 1970, however modest, relative to 1960. This slight gain, nevertheless, generated not collegiate approval but rather animosities from the ivy halls and towers of the White academy. The academic response to the Black presence assumes the identical avenues of White retaliation found in the society at large: demands for economic reforms, which will reverse the Black enrollment, are now being made and, simultaneously, a resurgence of manifest racism in the form of a scholarly theory, namely, the "I.Q. Argument." The Carnegie Foundation now insists upon doubling tuition, while the Committee for Economic Development, a powerful business organization, calls for the same.[7] It has been estimated that for every $100-increase in tuition, at least 2.5% of the enrolled students will have to stop going to college.[8] Undoubtedly, the higher tuition will result in reduced numbers for both White and Black, but, more significantly, the impact will be proportionately greater for Blacks inasmuch as more Black students come from lower-income families than do Whites. So that such proposals will not constitute economic discrimination against the qualified poor, the plans also call for more scholarships. Yet for Black youths with a college ambition it is simply catch-22 all over again. What good is a scholarship program which tests intelligence for the purpose of compensating for economic hardships while all along academicians declare the inherent mental inferiority of Black-to-White according to the I.Q. Argument?[9] If Blacks supposedly lack a genetic capacity to compete against Whites in taking intelligence tests, then it is rather pointless to claim that scholarships will be color-blind. We are being told, on the one hand, that anyone who is "college material" will secure funding through scholarships, and, on the other hand, scholars —the very ones composing the tests that must be passed—increasingly maintain the innate biological inferiority for Black people.

Already, the administration of standardized tests reveals an ever-accelerating gap between the races with each increment in formal education; as both Black and White students attain an additional grade level prior to high school graduation, standardized tests project greater disparity along racial lines. In 1965, the black-white difference in average grade-level performance stood at 2.4; by the 12th grade, the figure expanded to 3.5.[10] The longer Blacks remain in school the less qualified they become according to the tests being administered for establishing educational accomplishments. Indeed, the Coleman Report found almost 85% of Black students scoring *below* the White average.[11] By manipulating the economic costs so that getting a college education goes up during the 'seventies and, simultaneously, compelling poverty-stricken students to compete for scholarships through written examinations, Blacks are destined to elimination. Why discriminate when one can eliminate? Such a conclusion becomes all the more unassailable when we realize, according to a four-year testing program administered by the Department of Health, Education, and Welfare, that, taking the fourth-grade reading level as the standard, 22.1% of all Blacks and 9.8% of all White youths between 12 and 17 years of age whose families had incomes of less than $3,000 per year were *illiterate*.[12]

Although the percentage of Black schoolchildren attending integrated classrooms increased from 18% to 38% within the South between 1969–1971, the figure remained constant at 27% for the North and West,[13] and no region of the country went beyond the halfway mark. By 1972—18 years after the famous Equality decision by the 1954 Supreme Court—"The percentage of minority group pupils in schools with enrollment more than half Black . . . was," according to the Department of Health, Education, and Welfare, "53.7 per cent for public schools in the 11 states of the old Confederacy. The figure for Northern public schools was 71.7 per cent, and it was 68.2 per cent for the Border states and the District of Columbia."[14] When a metropolitan school district with a substantial Black population initiates affirmative policies to integrate or to end segregation, the White population quickly nullifies the efforts either by fleeing the city proper for the all-white suburbs or by sending their children to private schools. Blacks constitute 36.6% of the public school pupils in New York City, yet, "more than four-fifths of New York's [City] Black pupils attend schools with Black enrollments of 50 per cent or more. And nearly half attend schools that are virtually all-black."[15] In 1970, 119,000 Whites attended Houston's public schools, but two years later there were only 98,000—an 18% reduction; the percentage of minority students increased from 51 to 57 while the White figure dropped from 49 to 43.[16] In December, 1970, Chicago's Board of Education reported that only 40,000 of the city's 270,000 Black pupils attended integrated schools so that 77% of the Black high school students and 90% of the Black elementary school children went to schools with at least a 90% Black enrollment;[17] four years later, in 1974, 86% of the Black students were in schools with 90–100% Black enrollment and 42.8% of the White students were in a school with 90 to 100% Whites.[18]

A report released by the U.S. Office of Education in September, 1972, shows a substantial expansion for private education throughout the nation. The rise was particularly apparent in the South where private, non-church schools mounted by 242%, and church-related protestant schools by 168%.[19] The Federal Office of Education claims that the South's enrollment in nonpublic schools went from 580,000 in the fall of 1968 to an estimated 700,000 by the fall of 1972; "Some observers consider that figure low."[20] During the 'sixties, 2.5 million Whites abandoned the central cities for the suburbs as 3.4 million Blacks entered so that the suburbs went from 95% to 96% White while most metropolitan cities were going Black.[21]

To preserve this intense racial separation, the Supreme Court ruled, in 1974, that busing across city and/or county lines for purposes of racial integration in public schools is unconstitutional. Thus, just as the judicial system upheld state legislation that segregated the schools on the basis of race, so, too, today the Courts extend legal approval to a dual school system that is already predicated upon the Black-White racial distinction. A United Press International newswire dated December 5, 1973, carried this exact message in stating:

> The United States Court of Appeals for the sixth circuit [in Cincinnati, Ohio] said yesterday that one-race schools were a fact of life in some cities and refused a request to expand school busing in Memphis, Tenn.

The three-judge panel declined to overthrow an order by United States District Judge Robert McRae, Jr. in Memphis, which has bused about 25,000 students—and left 25 all-black schools—this year.[22]

This ruling can only mean increasing isolation of Blacks within America's educational system. And this, in turn, can only mean a worsening of educational qualifications for the on-coming Black student generation in terms of White educational expectations for acceptance into American colleges. In Detroit, a city where plans for busing across the school district will not be tolerated by the Supreme Court, 2/3 of the 1971 enrollment of 300,000 students were Black, and the suburban schools were virtually all White; the massive Detroit school district allocated about $650 per student, while the suburbs spent over $1,000 for each of its students.[23] The combination of racism and economics clearly compels us to conclude, beyond all reasonable doubt, that this nation now endorses an educational system that will not only be divided along racial lines but also will be economically debilitating for Black education. White America will not allow any substantial educational gains for Black people; it is therefore not the lack of educational achievements preventing Blacks from securing well-paying jobs,[24] but a White determination to prevent Blacks from gaining educational qualifications in appreciable numbers.

EXPANDING BLACK POVERTY

Key economic indicators also portend serious difficulties for Blacks. In 1949, the difference in Black-White median family income was less than $1,600; by 1964, it was more than $3,000; in 1969, the difference expanded to just over $3,600; in 1972, it stood at $4,585.[25] In 1968, Black income, according to a Bureau of the Census release, was 60% of White; the figure climbed to 61% in 1970, but by 1972 it dropped to 59%.[26] If equality is taken as the measure for success, it is clear that a downward course for income is, as in the case for education, taking place for Blacks during the 'seventies.

There is, moreover, a resurgence of poverty-stricken households among Black families. The number of poor Blacks increased 600,000 between 1969 and 1972, while White poverty declined 500,000.[27] Although more Whites (17.5 million and 67% of the total) than Blacks (7.7 million and 33% of the total) were in poverty in 1970, only 1 out of 10 Whites were so classified while one out of three Blacks persisted in poverty,[28] although the total poverty figure dropped from 40 million in 1959 to 25.5 million in 1970, *the proportion of Blacks among the poor expanded.* In 1959, 28% of those among the poor were Black, in

1970 the figure rose to 33% .[29] In 1972, 1.1 million persons pulled out of the poverty category—and all of these were White; during the same year, 300,000 Blacks dropped into the poverty ranks.[30]

SLUM LIVING

Housing for Blacks is destined to greater debilatation and increased density for the 'seventies than was the case for the 'sixties. The need for the entire nation is overwhelming: according to 1968 estimates, the country must build more new housing by the year 2000 than is now in existence in order to sustain prevailing standards; another 65 million units must be constructed in addition to the present 60 million. Yet, according to Walter Hoadley, executive vice-president of California's Bank of America, "We are facing the worst housing shortage that we have had since the end of World War II. The crisis," he projects, "is going to get worse."[31] Between 1966 and 1969, inflation pushed the cost of new housing up 22% and, as a result, half of all Americans could no longer afford to buy.[32] In 1973, the average cost for a new home stood at $31,500—and it continues to rise.[33] Moreover, the substantial advances in interest rates over the last decade more than doubled the 1960 rate for home mortgages. The National Association of Home Builders claims that "each one point boost in interest drives 3.4 million families out of the housing market."[34] Moreover, metropolitan areas of the East and West commonly require most White suburbanites to pay at least $100 per month in property taxes; in the ghetto of Newark, N.J., the Black homeowner will, within 11 years at prevailing rates, pay $20,000 in property taxes for a $20,000 house purchased in the late 1960s. Such economic extravagances as in the housing market can only mean a much higher percentage of Blacks will become excluded from home ownership during the 'seventies than during the 'sixties; more overcrowding will surely occur in rented quarters as Black families are compelled to cram into smaller living areas to survive skyrocketing rents.

MACHINE PRODUCTION-BLACK REMOVAL

Black unemployment has risen dramatically throughout the nation. Official statistics show that the Black rate still persists at twice the pace for Whites. Yet, as is now very common knowledge, the official rates on unemployment are designed explicitly to conceal more than to reveal; changes have been purposefully introduced so as to reduce the basis for computing what would otherwise be higher rates,[35] while those employed part-time and the dropouts from the labor force who no longer seek employment get excluded from consideration. Such distortions particularly undercount the full extent of joblessness for the Black minority since Blacks are far more likely than Whites to experience long-term unemployment and thus become so discouraged as to give up job-seeking, and proportionately more are forced into part-time work than are Whites. Further, what must not be overlooked is that Black unemployment would still be substantially higher were it not for the fact that hundreds of thousands have, at least temporarily, forsaken the job market by entering the universities.

The Urban League, under the direction of its able research director, Dr. Robert B. Hill, probed into the "hidden" and "forbidden" territories so long ignored by the Census Bureau and Department of Labor. This Black organization found that while the official figure on unemployment among the nation's eligible work force stood at 11.1% for Blacks, the "actual" computation showed 23.8%. The report "was based on a survey of 44 cities, comparing statistics with a special survey by the United States Bureau of the Census between August, 1970, and March, 1971."[36] Thus, while government statistics compute Black unemployment at twice the White rate, the Urban League found Blacks were out of jobs at twice the percentage presented by the Government! In 1971, according to the Department of Labor, unemployment in Los Angeles' Watts stood at 16%; in 1965, the year of the Watts uprising, the figure was 13%.[37] Today, in the Black ghettoes of Chicago, it is estimated that upwards of 40% of the Blacks are without jobs;[38] in Buffalo, New York, one estimate puts Black unemployment at 50%;[39] in Newark, N.J., it is estimated to be approximately 30%;[40] and about 40% for Detroit's inner-city Black population.[41] While these estimates may exaggerate somewhat the actual state of unemployment among Blacks, nonetheless Black unemployment cannot be less than 20% and is probably closer to 25–30%. The unemployment among Black teenagers is simply astronomical even by the official count of 38%; the figure would be still higher, as already noted, if the 1973 Black college enrollment of 684,000 had not expanded by 41% since 1967,[42] and if it were not for the fact that a disproportionate number of Black youths volunteer for military induction "if only because the military offers jobs for unemployed black youths."[43] The Black percentage within all military branches expanded from 11% in 1970 to 16% in 1974; 27% of all current recruits into the Army are Black, while only 11% of the nation's population between the ages of 17 and 44 are Black.[44]

Unemployment is surely a sufficient plight for any people to endure in a society such as ours where the reward system remains intrinsically attributable to employment; jobs mean the income for purchasing the necessary material goods for a sustaining living standard. Yet, not only are greater numbers of Blacks unemployed, but more are increasingly being rejected from any possibility for procuring work; unemployment among Blacks is a permanent, not a momentary, condition. The socio-economic difficulties now besetting Blacks are not only racial but economic as well; the crisis is caused not so much by the transition from slavery to equality as by a change from an economics of exploitation to an economics of uselessness.[45] With the onset of automation the Black is moving out of his historical state of oppression into economic obsolescence; increasingly, he is not so much economically exploited as he is irrelevant. The tremendous historical change for the Black person in America, under present circumstances, is taking place in these terms: he is not needed. He is not so much oppressed as unwanted; not so much unwanted as unnecessary; not so much abused as ignored. As automation proceeds, it will be easier and easier to disregard White dependence upon Black labor to sustain economic production of goods and to provide services for people. That this is increasingly becoming the fate of Black people is revealed even by the Manpower Report of the President as prepared by the U.S. Department of Labor in March, 1972.[46] The nonwhite civilian labor force participation* for males 16 years and over stood at 80.1 in 1960, 74.7 in 1970, and 73.73 in 1972; the figures for Whites were 82.6 in 1960, 79.7 in 1970, and 79.6 in 1972.[47] Thus, during the '60s and into the '70s, males of both races were less likely to participate in the labor force—yet the reduction was substantially greater for Blacks than for Whites, a drop of 6.4 percentage points for Blacks and 3.0 percentage points for Whites—a 2-to-1 ratio. Herbert Bienstock, Head of the Department of Labor's regional Bureau of Statistics in New York City, told a New York *Times* reporter in August, 1974, that the participation rate for nonwhites in the City—where more Blacks reside than in any other state of the union—dropped sharply from 61.1% in 1969 to 54.6% in 1973.[48] "This is a frightening trend," Bienstock exclaimed. "If this 6 per cent change had shown up on the unemployment rate instead of the participation rate, somebody somewhere would have gotten excited about it."[49] The point is, of course, that by not entering the work force Blacks are simply treated as invisible persons by our society; in dropping out of employment altogether, they become totally irrelevant. The extent of this Black invisibility is vividly demonstrated in a matter as relatively simple as taking a population count; for the 1970 census, the Bureau of Census estimates that it overlooked 1.9% of the total White population (3.45 million), yet, at the same time, it failed to count 7.7% of the total Black population (1.88 million)—a Black/White ratio of 4-to-1![50]

Blacks also are being compelled out of the labor force as industrialization in the form of mechanization continues to expand in southern agriculture. The *last* stronghold for Black employment in the South's agriculture economy is the tobacco field where, in the mid-sixties,

*"*Participation*" refers only to people actually employed and/or unemployed individuals who are actively seeking employment; it is a computation designed to show how many people are not holding or seeking jobs.*

1,000,000 out of the 1,500,000 Black farm workers concentrated. In 1971, however, the mechanical tobacco machine harvested the crop for at least four North Carolina farmers, and it is expected that the "four-legged, four-wheeled contraption of conveyor belts and hydraulic motors that moves down a row of tobacco plants and strips leaves from stalks almost as gently as a human hand would" will soon displace 50,000 farm people just in North Carolina. "The blacks will [most] probably be totally out of North Carolina agriculture by the end of this decade, and certainly by the end of the next decade," stated Dr. Selz C. Mayo, head of sociology and anthropology at North Carolina State College.[51] What is true for North Carolina will not be denied for the entire tobacco production throughout the South.

The uprooting of Black farmers is matched by unemployment within the cities as automation persists at a rapid pace. The automated automobile plant recently constructed by General Motors in Lordstown, Ohio, for the production of Vegas turns out 40% more automobiles without any increase in employment over the conventional assembly-line mode of production.[52] An automated bakery produces bread without the touch of a human hand on any ingredient until the bread emerges from the oven; "one plant run by one man could supply the needs of all Southern California."[53] In 1965, just prior to the introduction of automatic equipment, the steel industry employed 584,000 workers to turn out 131 million tons of steel; six years later, following the initial phase of automation, the work force dropped to 520,000—a loss of 64,000—in producing the same 131 million tons.[54] Daniel Mason, writing in the November, 1971 issue of *Political Affairs*, contends that "2 million jobs are eliminated every year as the result of automation and cybernation."[55] With labor costs rising approximately 6% per year, American businesses increasingly resort to automated robots inasmuch as "Replacing one [human] operator on two shifts results in a [profit] return of 56%";[56] although a most recent development, nonetheless, already 14% of America's 500 largest manufacturers use industrial robots simply because robotic equipment "can perform work of uniform superior quality in greater volume than can be done by a human operator, and it can pay for itself handsomely in a remarkably short period of time."[57]

BABIES BORN TO DIE

Health is another area of deterioration for Black people. The infant mortality rates reveal that "the ratio of the nonwhite to the white was higher in 1968 than in 1940."[58] Further, "the infant death rate for white children *dropped* from 18.8 per 1000 in 1969 to 18.0 [in 1970] . . ., while the death rate for non-white children *increased* from 32.3 to 32.5."[59] Blacks are more likely to die during infancy upon approaching the 1970s than 30 years earlier! Demographers commonly consider that the infant mortality rate reflects a country's living conditions and, therefore, according to this interpretation, the living standard for Black people *must* be taking a downward thrust. Death due to cancer was no greater by race in 1950, but in 1969 the Black rate was 25% higher than for Whites.[60] Dr. M. Harvey Brenner of Johns Hopkins University reported to the American Public Health Association that "Deaths in Black adults under 55 years of age from heart disease is 10 to 20 percent higher than in whites during periods of higher unemployment."[61] These setbacks in health appear as residential areas turn from White to Black. A 55 block area in the Bronx of New York City had, when it was White, 25 doctors so that there was a physician for every 700 people; in 1974, the same blocks were Black and only four doctors were residents, a ratio of one for every 10,000.[62] In 1971, there were only 5,800 to 6,000 Black doctors throughout the nation, just 2% of all physicians.[63]

This composite summary of the Black living standard displaying decisive handicaps and an overall worsening condition takes place in what is otherwise a prospering American economy. *Newsweek* proclaimed, in its November 4, 1972 issue, that "For months, the U.S. economy has been sinking deeper into a recession, but corporate profits, paradoxically [sic], have gone higher and higher. Last week, as third-quarter reports poured in, it was all but certain that earnings during the period had established another record [high]" for American corporations.[64] The corporations get wealthier while the poor people, particularly Blacks, plunge into utter destitution. That is, corporate capitalism is not in a paradoxical moment; it is in its full glory any time profits reach new levels.

WHITE ON BLACK: REPRESSION AND RETALIATION

The Republican administration which assumed control during the late 1960s, as so cogently analyzed by Arthur I. Blaustein and Geoffrey Faux in *The Star Spangled Hustle*,[65] not only ignored but retaliated against Blacks in formulating its socioeconomic policies toward minorities. Governmentally speaking, more Blacks have indeed been elected to political office; yet not only is the percentage insignificant, amounting to a mere one-half of one percent in 1973,[66] but also the actual power of government remains, and increasingly becomes, repressive. Key events capture the essence of Government retaliation against an ever-increasingly impoverished Black people:

- Although the Supreme Court set aside the death penalty applied arbitrarily and capriciously, revamped state laws have, nonetheless, resulted in a current death-row population of 140, 60% of whom are Black. "They are," in the editorial words of the *Nation*, "predominantly the type whom judges and juries tend to regard as social outcasts and irredeemable burdens on society."[67] The police rate of homicide against Blacks remains nine times as great as against Whites.[68]

The 11 documents the NBC news reporter, Carl Stern, secured through court proceedings in December, 1973 reveal the extensive plans drawn, and thereafter implemented, by the FBI during the 'sixties in a concerted effort to bring about the "disruption, exposure and neutralization" of "new left and Black nationalist groups."[69] This material also conveys the tactical plans for close cooperation among the Oakland and San Francisco police departments with the FBI in order to exterminate the Black Panther Party. "From May 2, 1967, to September 28, 1968—the date of Huey Newton's trial—there were 55 cases against members of the Black Panther Party—from September 28, 1968, to December 8, 1969, we find that there were 373 cases against the Panthers."[70] One explicit objective in the memorandi called upon the FBI to "prevent the rise of a black messiah who could unify and electrify the militant Black nationalist movement."[71] This directive is so forceful that Black leaders have demanded, and with reasonable cause, that the FBI itself be investigated as a potential collaborator in the deaths of Martin Luther King, Malcolm X, and Fred Hampton.[72] Needless to say, the call has gone unheeded.

That racial lines are being drawn more tightly is shown in the interpretation offered by Samuel Lubell, a well-known public opinion analyst, of the 1972 presidential election:

> First, the voting returns reveal that the President's [i.e., former President Richard Nixon] strongest gains over 1968 erupted in areas of the most intense racial polarization—through the whole South and in such big city Democratic strongholds as Cleveland, Chicago, New York and Philadelphia.
>
> This suggests that any Democratic effort to reassert a new drive for government-sponsored Black advances could invite defeat. . . .
>
> Southerners when interviewed now feel: "The Republicans have become the white man's party."[73]

Thus, if the Republican Party is now a "white" organization and the Democrats cannot court the Black vote without incurring defeat, where does this leave Blacks—but out and, in the event of open defiance, faced with the prospects, like the Black Panther Party, of destruction. "The cities, [Richard] Scammon [a former Census Bureau chief] speculates, could then come increasingly to resemble urban models of the old Indian reservations, kept alive by the state, but ruled by a kind of internal jungle law. The surrounding middle-class suburbs would be heavily guarded . . ., the chief function of the guards being to protect the middle-class majority in the suburbs from marauding bands from the cities."[74]

What took place in the Attica Correctional Facility, Attica, New York, is the most telling event of what is taking place.[75] The Attica uprising by inmates on September 13, 1971, merely duplicates the domestic lesson America intends to impose. What commentators somehow overlook in regard to what happened on that fateful day is that there emerged another instance of a race war upon American soil, another step among many toward the final solution. 73% of the inmates in the rebellious D. Yard were nonwhite; no Black person, but rather a White governor and presently the Vice-President of the United States, Nelson Rockefeller, ordered the military assault; and there were no Blacks among the 600 state troopers who chanted "white power, white power" when surging into the yard.[76] The insurrection, therefore, represents not an uprising within a penal institution but a racist massacre. In the words of I. F. Stone, ". . . the State troopers went in with murder in their hearts, like a lynch mob in the South 'to get them niggers.' "[77] The intensity of hatred toward Blacks is so strong that White troopers willingly paid the price for killing not only scores of *unarmed* and *trapped* Blacks, but ten of their very own! "Every hostage who died on Sept. 13, 1971, was killed by state police guns. . . . We now know thanks to the McKay Commission hearing that between fourteen and seventeen corrections officers, without permission, fired into the yard of D. Block with with their own hunting guns, and that they killed two inmates. We now know that the state police were firing dumdum bullets, . . . outlawed under international law and the Geneva Convention [among nations at war]. We now know that 450 rounds of ammunition were fired into the yard in that 'efficient' action, hitting one out of every ten inmates. We now know the inmates had no guns and fired no bullets. We now know . . . that the first warning to the inmates to surrender came after four minutes and twenty seconds of heavy shooting [by the troopers]."[78] And we now know that when an inmate sought treatment from the prison's physician, Dr. Williams, to obtain relief from severe chest pains days after the uprising, he was refused medication and the doctor told him, "You should have died in the yard, nigger."[79] As with American genocide in Vietnam, it was necessary, within the confines of Attica, to kill *anyone* in the administration of the ultimate solution.

The similarity between White hostility upon Blacks at Attica and atrocity in Vietnam did not go unnoticed before New York State's official McKay Commission investigation; Dr. John Cudmore, a surgeon and major in the National Guard on duty during the assault, testified that "he saw inmates shoved and beaten by guards as they were herded into a yard and forced to crawl. He reported . . . [inmates] were 'struck with blows to the elbows and genitalis.' "[80] Dr. Cudmore concluded, "That day tore from those guards the shreds of their humanity. *For the first time* I understood what had happened at Mylai."[81] But how many more Mylais and how many more Atticas must this country endure before *all of us* will awaken "for the first time" and understand that the same genocidal fate is besetting Black people in America and before our very eyes? For the White massacre of yesterday's Red people looms over Black people today. The McKay Report points out that "With the exception of Indian massacres in the late 19th century, the State Police assault which ended the four-day prison uprising was the bloodiest one-day encounter between Americans since the Civil War."[82] Indeed, "Governor [Nelson Rockefeller] and his Corrections Commissioner, Russell G. Oswald, were much more concerned to crush 'revolution' than to preserve the lives of the hostages or inmates. Once Governor Rockefeller and his subordinates decided that the rebellion was no longer tolerable, the [McKay] Commission concludes, 'the lives of the hostages were expendable.' "[83]

• Increasingly, the Government endeavors to transform the economically disposable and restless Black into a listless and irrelevant Black by resorting to the equivalent of the "Indian handout" —and thereby confirming further the Indian analogy for interpreting Black-White relations. In 1969, 17% of Black families received some form of public assistance, yet just two years later, in 1971, one-quarter of all Black families were accepting such aid.[84]

WHITE ON BLACK: EXTERMINATION

In light of the above survey and analysis, I believe it is reasonable to perceive increased destitution, oppression, and racial isolation of Blacks upon the ghetto-reservation. This can only mean that today's Black is destined to experience the Indian fate. In late 1974, the City Council in Hartford, Connecticut, initiated a debate concerning the erection of a fence around the city's ghetto to confine the Black and Puerto Rican people in order to prepare for a discontent that might, in the near future, assume the form of open rebellion; in the face of insurrection by the nonwhites, White people, businesses, and homes could be preserved from harm by keeping the threatening racial minorities bottled up within the ghetto.[85]

George Wald, Professor of Biology at Harvard and winner of the Nobel Prize in Physiology of Medicine for 1967, stated in his address at the 20th World Conference Against Atomic and Hydrogen Bombs in Tokyo on August 2, 1974:

The work that used to be done by human and animal muscle is increasingly done by machines. . . . With the increasing mechanization, increasing numbers of persons have become not only unemployed but superfluous. There is no use for them in the free-market economy. They are wanted neither as workers nor customers. They are not wanted at all. Their existence is a burden, an embarrassment. . . .

In his report to the World Bank in September, 1970, [Wald continues] its president, Robert McNamara, former Ford [Motor Company] executive and Secretary of Defense, spoke of such persons as "marginal men." He estimated that in 1970 there were 500 million of them—twice the population of the United States—that by 1980 there would be one billion, and by 1990, two billion. That would be half the world population.[86]

And Professor Samuel Yette of Howard University contends:

Black Americans have outlived their usefulness . . . Once an economic asset, they are now considered an economic drag. . . .

Thanks to old Black backs and newfangled machines, the sweat chores of the nation are done. Now some 25 million Blacks face a society that is brutally pragmatic, technologically accomplished, deeply racist, increasingly overcrowded, and surly.[87]

Finally, H. Rap Brown asserts in his, *Die Nigger Die,* "There is no more work. Machines do the jobs . . .";[88] he charges that "This country [of the U.S. of America] is waging a genocidal war against people of color . . ."[89]

CONCLUSION

It is becoming more widely acknowledged that America is a nation of White people marking time for a Black people. While assuring majestic prospects for acceptance, the nation deliberately removes the basic opportunities for Black achievement. The process, while by no means taking place overnight, is, nevertheless, well underway toward the same final resolve Whites imposed upon the Indian: Blacks will be forced to live in isolation upon the ghetto-reservation where, as the evidence concerning the Black condition documented here in this essay clearly conveys, they will become increasingly impoverished and, in the event of open rebellion within their midst, exterminated by armed Whites. The new economics of automation blends in harmony with America's everpresent racism and forewarns of the destitution and potential destruction of a Black people.[90]

ENDNOTES

1. For a survey of the view, see my *Who Needs the Negro?* (Garden City, New York, 1971), Ch. V.
2. Lewis M. Killian, "Optimism and Pessimism in Sociological Analysis," *The American Sociologist,* Vol. 6, November, 1971, p. 284.
3. For further substantiation see my "Equality: America's Racist Ideology," in *Radical Sociology,* David J. Colfax and Jack L. Roach, eds. (New York: Basic Books, 1971), pp. 246–262.
4. Fred M. Hechinger, "Education" column, New York *Times,* October 17, 1971.
5. United Press International newswire, Buffalo *Evening News,* March 18, 1971.
6. Ellen Kay Trimberger, "Open Admissions: A New Form of Tracking?" *The Insurgent Sociologist,* Vol. IV, Fall, 1973, pp. 29–43.
7. Associated Press newswire, "Educators Criticize Group's Proposal to Double College Tuition Rates," Buffalo *Evening News,* October 1, 1973, p. 7.
8. National Commission on the Financing of Post-Secondary Education as cited by Robert Nielsen, "Tuition and Enrollment in Higher Education," *American Teacher,* Vol. 59, September, 1974, p. 30.
9. An extensive bibliography and an outstanding critique of the genetic inferiority of Blacks *vis-a-vis* White intelligence is to be found in *Racism, Intelligence, and the Working Class* (Boston, Massachusetts: Progressive Labor Party, 1974).
10. Norval D. Glenn, "Recent Changes in the Social and Economic Conditions of Black Americans," in *Social Stratification: A Reader,* Joseph Lopreato and Lionel S. Lewis, eds. (New York: Harper & Row, 1974), pp. 453.
11. Cited by Charles S. Benson, "Why the Schools Flunk Out," *The Nation,* Vol. 205, April 10, 1967, p. 436.
12. New York *Times,* May 4, 1974, p. 24.
13. Roy Reed and Paul Delaney, "Year of Desegregation a Trying One in South," New York *Times,* April 18, 1971, p. 1.
14. William E. Farrell, "School Integration Fight Hardens in Shift North," New York *Times,* May 13, 1974, p. 24.
15. *Ibid.*
16. Martin Waldron, "White Pupils' Rolls Drop as Families Flee the Cities," New York *Times,* November 26, 1972, p. 74.
17. Seth S. King, "Integration Lag Noted in Chicago," New York *Times,* December 13, 1970.
18. "Tight Money Is Said to Keep Whites in Chicago's Schools," New York *Times,* December 1, 1974, p. 28.
19. United Press International newswire, Buffalo *Evening News,* September 3, 1972, p. 3.
20. Evan Jenkins, "School Conflict in South Is Intensifying As Academics Challenge Public System," New York *Times,* August 9, 1973, p. 1+.

21. "Black America Now," *Newsweek*, February 19, 1973, p. 33.
22. United Press International newswire, "One-Race Schools Called Fact of Life in Some Cities," New York *Times*, December 6, 1973, p. 24.
23. New York *Times*, October 3, 1971.
24. Glenn, *op. cit.*, pp. 447–448.
25. New York *Times*, July 23, 1973, p. 1.
26. *Ibid.*
27. Robert B. Hill, "Benign Neglect Revisited: The Illusion of Black Progress," National Urban League (Washington, D.C., July 24, 1973), Table 3.
28. Jack Rosenthal, "Poor in Nation Rise by 5%, Reversing 10-Year Trend," New York *Times*, May 8, 1973, p. 1.
29. *Ibid.*
30. Bill Kovach, "Million People in U.S. Escaped From the Ranks of Poor in 1972," New York *Times*, July 5, 1973, p. 35.
31. *Time*, October 31, 1969, p. 84.
32. Associated Press newswire, Buffalo *Evening News*, September 24, 1969.
33. "Intelligence Report," *Parade*, September 30, 1973, p. 9.
34. *Ibid.*
35. See Harry Brill, "Unemployment: Official & Real," *The Nation*, Vol. 212, January 23, 1971, p. 100, and John C. Leggett, Claudette Cervinka, and Lila Ward, "Let's Count the Unemployed," pp. 42–61 in this book.
36. Rudy Johnson, "U.S. is Criticized on Black Jobless," New York *Times*, September 2, 1972.
37. Curtis J. Sitomer, "It's Grim in Watts, But There's Pride, Maybe Progress," Buffalo *Evening News*, February 23, 1972, p. 34.
38. Reported on the NBC Nightly News during October, 1974.
39. Buffalo *Courier-Express*, November 8, 1974.
40. Ben Bedell, "Behind the Rebellion in Newark," *Guardian*, September 18, 1974, p. 3.
41. "Murder on the Rise in Detroit," *Guardian*, July 10, 1974, p. 5.
42. U.S. Census Bureau annual report for 1973 as carried by the Associated Press newswire, Buffalo *Evening News*, July 24, 1974, p. 13.
43. John W. Finney, "Very Soon Now the Army Will be R.A., All The Way," New York *Times*, November 3, 1974, p. E 3.
44. *Ibid.*
45. For a fuller analysis of this point see Sidney M. Willhelm and Elwin H. Powell, "Who Needs the Negro?", *Trans-Action*, Vol. 1, September-October, 1964, pp. 3–6; and my *Who Needs the Negro?, op. cit.*, especially Chapters VI and VII.
46. U.S. Department of Labor, *Manpower Report to the President*, March 1972 (Washington, D.C.: U.S. Government Printing Office), Table E-4.
47. *Ibid.*
48. As reported by Soma Colden, "Recession Is Not a Threat, It's a Fact

in New York City," New York *Times*, September 1, 1974, p. 5.

49. *Ibid.*

50. Bill Kovach, "Census Says It Overlooked 5,300,000," New York *Times*, April 26, 1973, pp. 1+.

51. William K. Stevens, "Tobacco Farming Enters Machine Age," New York *Times*, October 4, 1971, pp. 1+.

52. James Wargo, "Car Sales Soar, but Increase in Related Jobs Is Myth," Monitor News Service, Buffalo *Evening News*, September 20, 1972.

53. *Change*, Vol. I, October, 1965, p. 1.

54. Jerry M. Flint, "Big Industries Not Likely to Cut Down Jobless," New York *Times*, January 30, 1972, pp. 1+.

55. Daniel Mason, "The Problem of Unemployment," *Political Affairs*, Vol. 50, November, 1971, p. 35.

56. *Report on the Robot Revolution* (Englewood Cliffs, N.J.: Prentice-Hall, 1972), p. 8.

57. *Ibid.*, p. 3.

58. Glenn, *op. cit.*, p. 455.

59. United Press International newswire, Buffalo *Evening News*, March 24, 1971; emphasis supplied.

60. United Press International newswire, "22,000 to Conquer Cancer Report Notes," Buffalo *Evening News*, November 11, 1974, p. 6. For a fuller discussion on the health situation for Blacks see H. Roy Kaplan, "The Fee-For-Service System," in *Humanistic Perspectives in Medical Ethics*, Maurice B. Visscher, ed. (Buffalo: Promethus Books, 1972), pp. 148–149.

61. *Guardian*, December 25, 1974, p. 5.

62. Testimony presented by Dr. Harold B. Wise in *Costs and Delivery of Health Services to Older Americans*, Hearings before the Special Committee on Aging of the United States Senate, Part II, October, 1967 (Washington, D.C.: U.S. Government Printing Office, 1968), p. 416.

63. C. Gerald Fraser, "Negroes to Offer Own Health Plan," New York *Times*, August 15, 1971.

64. "Profits: The Best Ever," *Newsweek*, November 4, 1974, p. 80.

65. Arthur I. Blaustein and Geoffrey Faux, *The Star-Spangled Hustle: The Story of a Nixon Promise* (Garden City, New York: Doubleday Anchor, 1973).

66. "Black Americans Now," *Newsweek*, *op. cit.*, p. 34.

67. "The Death Penalty's Comeback," *The Nation*, Vol. 219, November 9, 1974, p. 453.

68. Paul Takagi, "A Garrison State in 'Democratic' Society," *Crime and Social Justice*, Vol. 1, Spring-Summer, 1974, p. 29.

69. Benjamin Bedell, "FBI Data Reveals Anti-Black Repression," *Guardian*, April 24, 1974, p. 5; for a more complete coverage see Baxter Smith, "FBI Memos Detail Government Plot to Crush Black Movement," *The Militant*, March 22, 1974. For the charge that key Black leaders have indeed been assassinated by a conspiracy,

see Louis E. Lomax, *To Kill A Black Man* (Los Angeles: Holloway Publishing Co., 1968).

70. Jean Genet, "Here and Now for Bobby Seal," *Ramparts*, Vol. 8, June, 1970, p. 39.

71. Bedell, *op. cit.*, p. 5.

72. *Ibid.*

73. Samuel Lubell, "Nixon Landslide Indicates Strong Public Support on Blacks, Defense, Peace with Honor," Buffalo *Evening News*, November 15, 1972, p. 14.

74. Quoted by Stewart Alsop, " 'The Cities Are Finished,' " *Newsweek*, April 5, 1971, p. 100.

75. For accounts on the Attica uprising see: New York State Special Commission on Attica [i.e., the "McKay Report"], *Attica* (New York: Praeger, 1972); Russell G. Oswald, *Attica—My Story* (Garden City, New York: Doubleday Anchor, 1972); and Herman Badillo and Milton Haynes, *A Bill of No Rights: Attica and the American Prison System* (New York: Outerbridge & Lazard, 1972).

76. Jack Newfield, "An Anniversary for Attica," New York *Times*, September 12, 1972, p. 43.

77. *I. F. Stone's Bi-Weekly*, October 4, 1971, p. 2.

78. Newfield, *op. cit.*, p. 43.

79. *Ibid.*

80. Quoted by Michael T. Kaulman, "Doctor Testifies on Attica Abuses," New York *Times*, April 28, 1972, pp. 1+; emphasis supplied.

81. *Ibid.*

82. New York State Special Commission on Attica, *op. cit.*, p. *xi*.

83. Bryce Nelson, book review, *New York Times Book Review*, December 17, 1972, p. 1.

84. Delaney, *op cit.*. p. 17.

85. *Guardian*, November 6, 1974, p. 2.

86. George Wald, " 'It Is Too Late for Declarations, for Popular Appeals,' " New York *Times*, August 17, 1974, p. 23.

87. Samuel Yette, *The Choice: The Issue of Black Survival in America* (New York: G. P. Putnam's Sons, 1971), p. 18.

88. H. Rap Brown, *Die Nigger Die* (New York: Dial Press, 1969), p. 139.

89. *Ibid.*, p. 138.

90. For a more extensive documentation that sustains this conclusion see my *Who Needs the Negro?*, *op. cit.*, especially Chapter VIII.

11

Peter Collier

The Red Man's Burden

We need fewer and fewer "experts" on Indians. What we need is a cultural leave-us-alone agreement, in spirit and in fact.

Vine Deloria, Jr.

Each generation of Americans rediscovers for itself what is fashionably called the "plight" of the Indian. The American Indian today has a life expectancy of approximately 44 years, more than 25 years below the national average. He has the highest infant-mortality rate in the country (among the more than 50,000 Alaskan natives, one of every four babies dies before reaching his first birthday). He suffers from epidemics of diseases which were supposed to have disappeared from America long ago.

A recent Department of Public Health report states that among California Indians, "water from contaminated sources is used in 38 to 42 percent of the homes, and water must be hauled under unsanitary conditions by 40 to 50 percent of all Indian families." Conditions are similar in other states. A high proportion of reservation housing throughout the country is officially classified as "substandard," an antiseptic term which fails to conjure up a tiny, two-room log cabin holding a family of thirteen at Fort Hall; a crumbling Navajo hogan surrounded by broken plumbing fixtures hauled in to serve as woodbins; or a gutted automobile body in which a Pine Ridge Sioux family huddles against the South Dakota winter.

On most reservations, a 50 percent unemployment rate is not considered high. Income per family among Indian people is just over $1,500 per year—the lowest of any group in the country. But this, like the other figures, is deceptive. It does not suggest, for instance, the quality of the daily life of families on the Navajo reservation who live on $600 per year (exchanging sheep's wool and hand-woven rugs with white traders for beans and flour), who never have real money and who are perpetually sinking a little further into credit debt.

To most Americans, the conditions under which the Indian is forced to live are a perennial revelation. On one level, the symptoms are always being tinkered with half-heartedly and the causes ignored; on another level, the whole thrust of the government's Indian policy appears calculated to perpetuate the Indians' "plight." This is why La Nada Means and the other Indians have joined what Janet McCloud, a leader of the Washington fishing protests, calls "the last, continuing Indian War." The enemies are legion, and they press in from every side: the studiously ignorant politicians, the continuously negligent Department of the Interior, and the white business interests who are allowed to prey upon the reservations' manpower and resources. But as the Indian has struggled to free himself from the suffocating embrace of white history, no enemy has held the death grip more tightly than has his supposed guardian, in effect his "keeper": the Bureau of Indian Affairs.

The bureau came into being in 1834 as a division of the War Department. Fifteen years later it was shifted to the Department of the Interior, the transition symbolizing the fact that the Indian was beginning to be seen not as a member of a sovereign, independent nation, but as a "ward," his land and life requiring constant management. This is the view that has informed the BIA for over a century. With its 16,000 employees and its outposts all over the country, the bureau has become what Cherokee anthropologist Robert Thomas calls "the most complete colonial system in the world."

It is also a classic bureaucratic miasma. A recent book on Indian Affairs, *Our Brother's Keeper*, notes that on the large Pine Ridge reservation, "$8,040 a year is spent per family to help the Oglala Sioux Indians out of poverty. Yet median income among these Indians is $1,910 per family. At last count there was nearly one bureaucrat for each and every family on the reservation."

The paternalism of the BIA, endless and debilitating, is calculated to keep the Indian in a state of perpetual juvenilization, without rights, dependent upon the meager and capricious beneficence of power. The bureau's power over its "wards," whom it defines and treats as children, seems limitless. The BIA takes care of the Indian's money, doling it out to him when it considers his requests worthy; it determines the use of the Indian's land; it is in charge of the development of his natural resources; it relocates him from the reservation to the big-city ghetto; it educates his children. It relinquishes its hold over him only reluctantly, even deciding whether or not his will is valid after he dies.

This bureaucratic paternalism hems the Indian in with an incomprehensible maze of procedures and regulations, never allowing him to know quite where he stands or what he can demand and how. Over 5,000 laws, statutes, and court decisions apply to the Indians alone. As one Indian student says, "Our people have to go to law school just to live a daily life."

The BIA is the Indian's point of contact with the white world, the concrete expression of this society's attitude towards him. The BIA manifests both stupidity and malice; but it is purely neither. It is guided by something more elusive, a whole world view regarding the Indian and what is good for him. Thus the BIA's overseership of human devastation begins by teaching bright-eyed youngsters the first formative lessons in what it is to be an Indian.

> It is unnecessary to mention the power which schools would have over the rising generation of Indians. Next to teaching them to work, the most important thing is to teach them the English language. Into their own language there is woven so much mythology and sorcery that a new one is needed in order to aid them in advancing beyond their baneful superstitions.
> —John Wesley Powell

The Darwinian educational system which La Nada Means endured is not a thing of the past. Last spring, for instance, the BIA's own Educational Division studied Chilocco and came to the following conclusions: "There is evidence of criminal malpractice, not to mention physical and mental perversion, by certain staff members." The report went on to outline the disastrous conditions at the school, noting among other things that "youngsters reported they were handcuffed for as long as eighteen hours in the dormitory . . . or chained to a basement pillar or from a suspended pipe. One team member . . . verified a youngster's hurt arms, the deformed hands of another boy, and an obviously broken rib of another. . . ."

The BIA responded to this report by suppressing it and transferring the investigators who submitted it. The principal of Chilocco was fired, but more as punishment for letting such things be discovered than for the conditions themselves. The same story is repeated at other BIA boarding schools. At the Intermountain Indian School in Utah, Indian children suspected of drinking have their heads ducked into filthy toilets by school disciplinarians. At Sherman Institute in Riverside, California, students of high-school age are fed on a budget of 76 cents a day.

But there is a far more damaging and subtle kind of violence at work in the school as well. It is, in the jargon of educational psychology, the initiation of a "failure-orientation," and it derives from the fact that the children and their culture are held in such obviously low regard. Twenty-five percent of all BIA teachers admit that they would rather be teaching whites; up to 70 percent leave the BIA schools after one year. If a teacher has any knowledge at all of his student's needs and backgrounds, he gets it from a two-week, noncompulsory course offered at the beginning of the year. One teacher, a former Peace Corps volunteer who returned to teach at the Navajo reservation, told the Senate Subcommittee on Indian Education that the principal of her BIA school habitually made statements such as "All Navajos are brain-damaged," and "Navajo culture belongs in a museum."

The results of the Indian's education, whether it be supervised by the BIA or by the public-school system, indicates how greatly the system fails him. Twenty percent of all Indian men have less than five years of schooling. According to a recent report to the Carnegie Foundation, there is a 60 percent dropout rate among Indian children as a whole, and those who do manage to stay in school fall further behind the longer they attend. A study of the Stewart Institute in Carson City, Nevada, for instance, shows that Indian sixth graders score 5.2 on the California Achievement Test. Six years later, at graduation, their achievement level is 8.4.

In a strange sense, the Indian student's education does prepare him for what lies ahead. What it teaches him is that he is powerless and inferior, and that he was destined to be so when he was born an Indian. Having spent his youth being managed and manhandled, the Indian is accustomed to the notion that his business must be taken care of for him. He is thus ideally equipped to stand by and watch the BIA collect mortgages on his future.

> We should test our thinking against the thinking of the wisest Indians and their friends, [but] this does not mean that we are going to let, as someone put it, Indian people themselves decide what the policy should be.
>
> —Stuart Udall

The Indians of California have more than their share of troubles—in part because they never received an adequate land base by government treaty. They are scattered up and down the state on reservations which are rarely larger than 10,000 acres and on rancherias as small as one acre. It takes a special determination to find these Indians, for most of them live in backwoods shacks, hidden from view as well as from water and electricity.

They have to struggle for every bit of federal service they get; disservice, however, comes easy. In 1969 the only irrigation money the BIA spent in all of southern California, where water is an especially precious commodity to the Indians, was not for an Indian at all, but for a white farmer who had bought an Indian's land on the Pala reservation. The BIA spent $2,500—of money appropriated by Congress for the Indians—to run a 900-foot pipeline to this white man's land. The Indians at Pala have been asking for irrigation lines for years, but less than one-half of their lands have them.

At the Resighini rancheria, a 228-acre reservation in northern California, the Simpson Timber Company had been paying the Indians 25 cents per 1,000 feet for the lumber it transported across their land. The total paid to the Indians in 1964 was $4,725, and the right of way was increasing in value every year. Then the BIA, acting without warning, sold the right of way outright to Simpson Timber Company for $2,500, or something less than one-half its yearly value.

The tiny Agua Caliente band of Indians sits on top of some of the most valuable land in the country: over 600 acres in the heart of Palm Springs. In the late fifties, the BIA, reacting to pressure from developers, obligingly transferred its jurisdiction over the Agua Caliente to a judge of the State Superior Court in the Palm Springs area who appointed "conservators" and "guardians" to make sure that the Indians would not be swindled as development took place. Ten years later, in 1967, a *Riverside Press Enterprise* reporter wrote a devastating series of articles showing the incredible fees collected for "protecting" the Agua Calientes. One conservator collected a fee of $9,000 from his Indian's $9,170 bank account; an Indian minor wound up with $3,000 out of a $23,000 income, his guardian taking the rest. The "abdication of responsibility" with which the BIA was charged is surely a mild description of what happened to the Agua Calientes, who are supposedly the "richest Indians in the world" living on what is regarded as "an ermine-lined reservation."

The Indian Claims Commission was set up in the 1940's to compensate tribes for the lands stolen during the period of white conquest. In the California claims award of 1964, the Indians were given 47 cents an acre, based on the land's fair market value in 1851. The total sum, $29 million, less "offsets" for the BIA's services over the years, still has not been distributed. When it is, the per capita payout will come to about $600, and the poorest Indians in the state will have to go off welfare to spend it. The BIA opposed an amendment to the Claims Award which would have exempted this money in determining welfare eligibility. The BIA testified that such an amendment constituted preferential treatment, and that it had been struggling for years to get *equal* treatment for the Indian. The amendment failed, and California's Indians will have to pay for a few months bread and rent with the money they are getting in return for the land that was taken from them.

Cases such as these exist in every state where Indian people live. If the Indian is the Vanishing American, it is the BIA's magic which makes him so. California Indians are fortunate only in one respect: they have an OEO-funded legal-rights organization, the California Indian Legal Services, which attempts to minimize the depredations. Most Indians have no one to protect them from the agency which is supposed to be their advocate.

Once we were happy in our own country and we were seldom hungry, for then the two-leggeds and the four-leggeds lived together like relatives, and there was plenty for them and for us. But the Wasichus [white men] came, and they have made little islands for us . . . and always these islands are becoming smaller, for around them surges the gnawing flood of Wasichu; and it is dirty with lies and greed. . . .

—Black Elk, An Oglala Holy Man

At the entrance to the Fort Hall reservation, where La Nada Means grew up, there is a plaque which commemorates the appearance in 1834 of the first white traders and indicates that the Hudson Bay Company later acquired the Fort and made it into an important stopover on the Oregon Trail. But other aspects of the history of Fort Hall are left unmentioned. It is not noted, for instance, that by the time a formal treaty was signed with the Bannock and northern Shoshone in 1868, the whites who settled this part of southern Idaho were paying between $25 and $100 for a good Indian scalp.

Today, the approximately 2,800 Shoshone-Bannocks live on the 520,000-acre reservation, all that remains of the 1.8 million acres of their land which the treaty originally set aside for their ancestors to keep. The largest single reduction came in 1900, when the government took over 416,000 acres, paying the Indians a little more than $1 an acre for the land. As late as the beginning of World War II, the government took over another 3,000 acres to make an airfield. It paid the Indians $10 an acre; after the war, it deeded the land to the city of Pocatello for $1 an acre, for use as a municipal airport. Each acre is now worth $500.

But the big problem on the Fort Hall reservation today is not the loss of large sections of land; rather it is the slow and steady attrition of Indian holdings and their absolute powerlessness to do anything about it. In 1887, the Dawes Allotment Act was passed as a major piece of "progressive" Indian legislation, providing for the breakup of community-held reservation land so that each individual Indian would receive his plot of irrigable farming land and some grazing land. The federal government would still hold the land in trust, so it could be sold only with BIA approval, the assumption being that an individual holding would give the Indian incentive to be a farmer and thus ease him into American agricultural patterns. Fort Hall shows that the law had quite different effects.

Today, some of these original allotments are owned by anywhere from two to forty heirs. Because of the complexity of kinship relationships, some Indian people own fractional interests in several of these "heirship lands" but have no ground that is all their own. These lands are one of the symbols of the ambiguity and inertia that rule at Fort Hall. As Edward Boyer, a former chairman of the tribal council, says,

Some of the people, they might want to exchange interests in the land or buy some of the other heirs out so they can have a piece of ground to hold a house on and do some farming. Also, a lot of us would like the tribe to buy these lands up and then assign them to the young people who don't have any place of their own. But the BIA has this policy of leasing out these lands to the white farmers. A lot of the time the owners don't even know about it.

The BIA at Fort Hall doesn't like the idea of any Indian lands laying idle. And the land is rich, some of the best potato-growing land there is. Its value and its yield are increasing every year. Driving through the reservation, you can't avoid being struck by the green symmetry of the long cultivated rows and by the efficiency of the army of men and machinery working them. The only trouble is that the men are white, and the profits from Fort Hall's rich land all flow out of the Indian community. The BIA is like any technocracy: it is more interested in "efficient" use than in proper use. The most "efficient" way for Fort Hall's lands to be used is by white industrialist-farmers with capital. Thus the pattern has been established: white lessees using Indian land, irrigating with Indian water, and then harvesting with bracero workers.

All leases must be approved by the BIA superintendent's office; they may be and are given without the consent of the Indians who own the land. The BIA has also allowed white lessees to seek "consents" from the Indians, which in effect provide for blank leases, the specific terms to be filled in later on. The BIA authorizes extremely long leases of the land. This leads to what a recent field study of Fort Hall, conducted by the Senate Subcommittee on Indian Education, calls "small fortunes" for white developers:

> One non-Indian in 1964 leased a large tract of Indian land for 13 years at $.30–$.50/acre/year. While the lease did stipulate that once the lessee installed sprinkler irrigation the annual rent would rise to $1.50–$2.00/acre, Indians in 1968 could have demanded $20–$30 for such land. Meanwhile, the independent University Agriculture Extension Service estimates that such potato operations bring the non-Indian lessee an annual *net* profit of $200 per acre.

In addition, these leases are usually given by the BIA on a noncompetitive, nonbidding basis to assure "the good will of the surrounding community." Fort Hall has rich and loamy land, but Indian people now work less than 17 percent of it themselves and the figure is declining.

The power of white farmer-developers and businessmen within the local Bureau of Indian Affairs office is a sore point with most people at

Fort Hall. They have rich lands, but theirs is one of the poorest reservations. They are told that much revenue comes both to the tribe and to individuals as a result of the BIA farm- and mine-leasing program, yet they know that if all the revenues were divided up the yield would be about $300 per capita a year. But for some of them, men like Joseph "Frank" Thorpe, Jr., the question of farming and mining leases is academic. Thorpe was a successful cattleman until BIA policies cut down the herds; now he is in the business of letting other people's cattle graze on his land.

Livestock are something of a fixation with Thorpe. He comes from a people who were proud horsemen, and he owns an Apaloosa mare and a couple of other horses. As he drives over the reservation, he often stops to look at others' cattle. In the basement of his home are several scrapbooks filled with documents tracing the destruction of the cattle business at Fort Hall. There is a yellowing clipping from the *Salt Lake City Tribune* of November 4, 1950, which says: "Fort Hall Indians have been more successful in cattle raising than any other activity. Theirs is the oldest Indian Cattleman's Association in the country. Association members raise more than 10,000 head of purebred herefords, and plan gradually to increase the herd. . . ." That was how it was twenty years ago. Thorpe, just back from war-time duty with the Marines, worked his herd and provided jobs for many of his kinsmen; the future was promising. Yet by 1958, there were only 3,000 head of Indian-owned cattle left, and today there are only ten families still involved in full-time cattle operation.

"Around the early 1950's," Thorpe says, "the BIA decided that the Indians who'd been using tribal grazing lands without paying a grazing fee were going to be charged. The BIA also made us cattle people set up a sinking fund to pay grazing fees in advance. The bills just got higher and higher, and pretty soon we found we had to start selling off our seed stock to pay them."

Less than 30 percent of all Fort Hall Indians are permanently employed today. Men like Frank Thorpe once had a going business that harked back to the old times and also provided jobs on the reservation. The BIA had decided that the best use for Fort Hall land was farming; it removed the Indians' cattle from trust status, which meant they could be sold, and began the accelerated program of leasing Indian lands to whites that is still in effect today.

Thorpe spends a good deal of time driving his dust-covered station wagon along the reservation's unpaved roads. A former tribal chairman, he spends much time checking up on the BIA and trying to function as a sort of ombudsman. He drives slowly down the dirt highways where magpies pick at the remains of rabbits slaughtered by cars. He points out where white farmers have begun to crop-dust their leased fields from airplanes. "The game, rabbits and pheasants and all, is disappearing," he says. "Our Indian people here rely on them for food, but the animals are dying out because of the sprays. And sometimes our kids get real sick. These sprays, they drift over and get in the swimming holes. The kids get real bad coughs and sometimes rashes all over their bodies."

Near the BIA agency office on the reservation sits a squat, weathered concrete building. "That's the old blouse factory," he says. "The BIA cooked up this deal where some outfit from Salt Lake City came in here to start a garment plant. The tribe put up the money for the factory, about $30,000, and in return the Salt Lake people were going to hire Indians and train them to sew. It lasted for about a year, and now we've still got the building. The last few years, they've used it to store the government surplus food that a lot of Indians get."

The old blouse factory is one symbol of the despair that has seized Fort Hall. Thorpe points out another one nearby. It is known as a "holding center," and it is a place for Fort Hall Indians who are suspected of being suicidal. The reservation has one of the highest suicide rates in the nation. Last year there were 35 attempts, mostly among the 18–25 age group. Many of them occurred in the nearby Blackfoot City Jail.

Blackfoot town authorities, embarrassed by the number of Indian suicides which have occurred in their jail, now use the holding facility at Fort Hall. It is headed by John Bopp, a former Navy man who is the public-health officer on the reservation. "I guess kids here just feel that their future is cut off," he says. "A lot of them are dropouts and rejects from schools. They look around and see their elders pretty downtrodden. They get angry, but the only thing they can do is take it out on themselves. From reading some of their suicide notes, I'd say that they see it as an honorable way out of a bad situation."

"The young people," says Thorpe, "they're our only hope. They've got to clean things up here. But a lot of our young guys, they've just given up." The human resources at Fort Hall, like the land, seem to be slipping away. The best interpretation that could be placed on the BIA's role in it all is to use the words of a teacher at nearby Idaho State College who says that they are "guardians of the poorhouse."

There are other reservations that seem to be in better shape. One is the mammoth Navajo reservation, whose 25,000 square miles reach into portions of Arizona, New Mexico, Utah, and Colorado. On the one hand, it too is a place of despair: many of the 120,000 Navajos live in shocking poverty, doing a little subsistence farming and sheep-raising, suffering severe discrimination when they go outside the reservation for a job, and being preyed upon by the white traders and the exotic diseases which infest the reservation. But it is also a place of hope: Navajo land is rich in resources—coal, oil, uranium, and other minerals—and the tribe gets about $30 million a year from rents and royalties. While this would come to less than $1,000 a year if distributed to each family, the Navajos have tried, and to some extent succeeded, in using it as seed money to begin a small but growing series of tribal industries—a sawmill, a handcrafts center, a tourist motel—which provide valuable jobs and income organized around the tribal community.

Private enterprise has also come onto the reservation, epitomized by the large Fairchild Industries plant. There has been much discussion of giving tax incentives to get industry to locate on reservations all over the country, but in general little has come of it. Of an estimated 10,000 jobs opened up by industries on Indian lands, more than half of them have been filled by whites. On the Navajo reservation, however, the tribe has seen to it that practically all the employees hired are Indian, and it seems like a good beginning. Everything there, in fact, appears to be on the upswing: the Navajos seem to be the one tribe that is beginning to solve its problems. This, however, is an oversimplification.

As far as private enterprise is concerned, the plants are mainly defense-oriented: they use federal money for job training and then work on a cost-plus basis. In effect, the government is underwriting private profit, when the same money could have gone into setting up community businesses. The Navajos do get about 1,000 jobs, but they are generally low-paying and are given to women, thus destroying the ecology of the Indian family.

Roughly the same thing applies to the rapid development of their natural resources. The way in which these resources are exploited—be it strip-mining or otherwise—depends on the desires of the businesses exploiting them, not on what the Navajos want or need. One result is that the Navajos have no way of planning the development of resources for their own future needs as a community. Navajos get royalties, but private concerns off the reservation get the profits (as well as the depletion allowances, though it is Navajo resources which are being depleted). Indian people have often brought up the possibility of joint economic development of their reservation with the help of private firms. This is always rejected by the BIA, which has an age-old bias against "socialistic" tribal enterprise as well as a very contemporary regard for big business.

The Navajos are seemingly doing well, but their environment is in the hands of others who are interested only in revenue, and not in the Indians' future. The Navajos are thankful, however, for short-term gains, which most tribes don't have; and they have no choice but to leave tomorrow up to the BIA. As anthropologist David Aberle has pointed out,

> Let us suppose that we cut a cross-section through the reservation territory . . . and make a rapid-motion picture of the flow of population, money, and resources. . . . We would see oil, helium, coal, uranium, and vanadium draining off into the surrounding

economy; we would see rents and royalties flowing into the tribal treasury, but, of course, major profits accruing to the corporations exploiting the reservation. We would see the slow development of roads, water for stock and drinking, government facilities, and so forth, and a flow of welfare funds coming in, to go out again via the trader. The net flow of many physical resources would be outward; the flow of profits would be outward; and the only major increases to be seen would be population, with a minor increment in physical facilities and consumer goods. This is the picture of a colony.

The BIA is an easy organization to whip. Its abuses are flagrant, and the Indians it is charged with protecting are in great jeopardy. But if places like the Navajo reservation resemble a colony, the BIA is no more than a corps of colonial officers whose role is not to make policy but rather to carry it out. It is impossible not to feel that the bureau itself has, over the years, taken on the most outstanding feature of the Indians it administers: their utter lack of power. It could make life on the reservation less complicated and cruel and establish some provisions for the Indians' cultural future, but it could never solve the larger issues that lie behind federal Indian policy. The BIA is only a unit within the Department of Interior, and not a very important one at that—certainly nothing like the powerful Bureaus of Land Management and Reclamation. It is the Department of Interior itself which is involved in the big power moves in Indian affairs. As trustees both for the Indians' private trust lands and for public trust lands, it is involved in an irremediable conflict of interest which it solves by taking from the red man's vanishing domains.

Ernesto Galarza

12

Mexican-Americans and
The American Culture

My working definition of culture runs like this: A culture is characterized by the uses it makes of its material environment; the accepted
or tolerated relations between the individuals that compose it; the
symbols, conventional signs, and utilities of everyday behavior; and
the values by which the society measures its moral performance.

By this rule of thumb I see only one culture in the United States: it
is the culture of the American people—all of them.

Thus, I do not think we can legitimately presume that there is a subculture of Mexican-Americans which explains their depressed conditions of life, or that there is a subculture of blacks which explains their
economic deprivation these past three hundred years.

What the concept of subculture implies, but does not say in so many
words, is that alien cultures of a lower grade somehow intruded themselves into the American superculture. If the black family today, for
instance, is too often damaged by the absentee father, the working
mother, and the delinquent youth, it is said to be a characteristic of their
subculture. The concept shines most brightly when we talk about the
discomforts of American society—dilapidated housing, crime, and unemployment. It is upon the minorities that these discomforts fall most
heavily. It is they, to be sure, who populate the ghettos, but it is our
entire society, the American society, that spawns slums and breeds
poverty.

I am not attempting to lay blame. I am trying to discover connections and relationships. What I see is that, among black and Mexican-
American minorities, what show up vividly as local color and dra-

From the September-October 1971 issue of The Center Magazine, *a publication of the Center for the Study of Democratic Institutions, Santa Barbara,
California. Reprinted by permission.*

matic contrast are, in truth, cracks and tears in the seamless fabric of American society.

It is not the subcultures that are in trouble. It is the American culture itself.

And what have been some of the major strikes against Mexican-Americans and blacks?

One is the pattern of land ownership, control, and use that has developed in America during the past half-century. Out of this pattern came the tractoring-out of the Southern sharecropper, the withering of the family farm, and the massive importation of foreign agricultural laborers.

The resulting flight from the soil took millions to the cities, which were already suffering from urban cramps. We have begun to call these cities "ports of entry." The term has happy connotations: it suggests the migrant minority is on its way to better things—that it has *made* connections, not *broken* them.

But, in fact, the minority man finds the port congested with people like himself. They, like him, are becoming obsolete as a result of mechanization, automation, and cybernation—American cultural products that are radically altering job requirements, opportunities, and tenure. He finds that those sections of the big city where he has found transient refuge are also becoming obsolete. Here, another American culture concept, acted out with bulldozers, awaits him—urban redevelopment. As soon as a section shows speculative promise, it attracts speculative capital and entire neighborhoods go under. The Mexican-American poor move with their anxieties to another place.

These and other massive social decisions are not for the Mexican-American poor to make, or even take part in. These choices, and the complicated devices by which they are applied, are not even understood by the poor. To understand them, they would need an educational system that would deal factually and critically with them. But the Mexican-American, on the average, barely gets through eight or nine years of school, so that even if the high schools and colleges were undertaking the task, which by and large they are not, they would not be reaching the minority man.

Mexican-Americans in California have made progress since the nineteen-forties. They are subject to less ethnic discrimination. They have also begun to climb the lower rungs of the economic ladder. Ninety per cent of the people I knew as a boy were farm workers; now, far more than ten per cent of us work as professors, journalists, bureaucrats, and so on. This change is only recent, but the process is increasing in scope and pace. With new jobs has come an ability to articulate. Today perhaps we even have too many spokesmen. In any event, the time is past when the Mexican-American was not heard from. Now he says what he wants.

So far, we have been testing the mechanics of American democracy. Those of us who have climbed two or three rungs up the ladder have had opportunities to learn how Anglo-Americans do things—how they run political parties; how they caucus; how they lobby; how they manipulate all of those niceties of political contrivance, some clean and some unclean; how they use them, sometimes for personal benefit and sometimes for the good of the commonwealth.

At the same time, the Mexican-American community has lost ground—important ground. Our leadership has been dispersed. Political appointments have sent men of distinction to Sacramento, Washington, and abroad. Distance does something to these men: their values and ideas change; politically and ideologically, not just residentially, they are separated from the community. Individuals are entitled to personal satisfaction in life, but, for the community, political dispersal has meant and means political decapitation.

Strains have also occurred within the community. Mechanization and automation, in industry, agriculture, and trade services, have thrown many thousands of Mexican-Americans out of work. In farming, machines now pick tomatoes, grapes, oranges, and so on. Where the packing houses and canneries used to employ eighty-five thousand people at the peak of production, they now employ around forty-five thousand. Large groups of Mexican-American families have had a steady income cut away, and have been forced to disperse and be mobile. These nuclei of community have broken down as a result.

Marginal workers have not been helped by the trade-union movement. Indeed, the trade-union leadership helped destroy the farm labor union we organized in the nineteen-forties. We had posed the twin issues of power and exploitation in agriculture, but the union leaders shrank from their responsibility to help farm workers, leaving thousands to a cruel fate. However, they taught the Mexican-American community a lesson: the trade unions cannot be a taproot of our salvation. They are interested only in workers who are continuously employed, even though vast numbers of people are now unemployed and probably always will be. Lose your job, or stop paying union dues, and you are no longer "sir" or "brother."

The disintegration of the Mexican-American community is apparent in the numerous "shoestring" and "doughnut" communities in which thousands of Mexican-Americans live. The "shoestrings" grow along the banks of irrigation ditches, where water is available and land is cheap; here, displaced migrants have their trailers and shacks, and the profile of their settlements is a shoestring; the classical example is South Dos Palos. The "doughnut" type is found in the city, in places like *La Rana* (The Frog) in Torrance. There, as in many other places,

Mexican-American families settled as farm workers, but now they are surrounded by progress, and they can only wait to be pushed out by urban redevelopment. This community, one might say, is a hole where poor people live surrounded by people with dough.

Does the Mexican-American community merely want to catch up with the Anglo-American culture? The question is important, and we had better be careful before we say yes. My experience—in farm labor, in academic work, in politics—has taught me a lot of things about the Anglo-American culture that I do not like. Its economic system, for instance, produces certain values and behavior that I don't want to catch up with. Mexican-Americans have an opportunity to discriminate between the different values, behavior, and institutions in the pervading culture, and we had better choose wisely.

All my life I have heard that the trouble with the Mexican-American is that he is too apathetic. As a boy in Mexico I lived among people who, viewed from the outside, were extremely apathetic. Nobody was interested in knowing who was going to be the next president of Mexico, or who the military commander of our zone was. Nobody cared about the location of the nearest college or high school. They were interested in tomorrow's ration of corn.

When we came to California, Anglo-Americans preached to us about our apathy and scolded us. And I thought: Are we really so? Of course we are not. What is mistaken for apathy is simply a system of self-defense inherited by people with a long history of being kicked around. And if they don't inherit it, they learn quickly. They learn that they are surrounded by hostile men and forces that will do them in at every turn. They naturally become indifferent and unresponsive. But it is not apathy: it is self-protection. *"La mula no nació arisca"*—the mule is not born stubborn, he is made stubborn.

In the village where I was born, men carried a money belt tied around their waists, and in it they kept all the money they possessed. They worked with the belt on, and they slept with it; they trusted nobody. As they progressed a little further, they put their money in a sock, which was purchased specially for the purpose, since nobody wore socks. Their circle of confidence had increased, but still they hid the sock under the corn crib in their cottage and left their women to protect it. Still a little further along came the piggy bank, which they usually placed on a shelf. Their circle of confidence had expanded further: all the family was trusted, friends too, even strangers who would drop by. Finally there came the sign of maturity: the bank account. Now, not only men were trusted but also a system, run by men who were not seen or even known.

These four stages of social evolution illustrate the so-called apathy of Mexican-Americans. How can anybody accuse that villager who kept his money in a belt tied around his body of being apathetic? Considering the circumstances, he was a pretty smart fellow.

It is often assumed that Mexican-Americans need to be "emancipated"; after all, a lot of us used to live in a different culture in Mexico, and survived a feudal economy and society. The mayor of San Francisco remarked once that his city was going to build such a wonderful cultural center that it would make Los Angeles look "like a little Mexican village." Well, what is so wrong with that village? I have some good memories of Janco, my birthplace. There were no electric lights there, but in the evening, as the sun went down, people would sit in front of their cottages and talk by the twilight. And when it was dark the kids were sent to bed, and later the young men and women. Then the men would talk, not about small things but important ones. Some nights we heard a rumble of voices, lasting far into the morning. When I would awaken I would go to the yard and count the number of slits made by machetes in the hard-baked earth, and I would know how many men had gathered. It was these men who sparked the revolution in my village. And it was villages like these that started one of the most portentous events in the history of the Americas: the Mexican Revolution. In my yard.

13

Michael Reich

Economic Theories of Racism

In the early 1960s it seemed to many that the elimination of racism in the United States was proceeding without requiring a radical restructuring of the entire society. There was a growing civil rights movement, and hundreds of thousands of blacks were moving to northern cities where discrimination was supposedly less severe than in the South. Government reports pointed to the rapid improvement in the quantity of black schooling as blacks moved out of the South: in 1966 the gap between the median years of schooling of black males aged 25–29 and white males in the same age group had shrunk to one-quarter the size of the gap that had existed in 1960.[1]

But by 1970 the optimism of earlier decades had vanished. Despite new civil rights laws, elaborate White House conferences, special ghetto manpower programs, the War on Poverty, and stepped-up tokenist hiring, racism and the economic exploitation of blacks has not lessened. During the past twenty-five years there has been virtually no permanent improvement in the relative economic position of blacks in America. Median black incomes have been fluctuating at a level between 47 percent and 62 percent of median white incomes, the ratio rising during economic expansions and falling to previous low levels during recessions.[2] Segregation in schools and neighborhoods has been steadily increasing in almost all cities, and the atmosphere of distrust between blacks and whites has been intensifying. Racism, instead of disappearing, seems to be on the increase.

Racism has been as persistent in the United States in the twentieth century as it was in previous centuries. The industrialization of the economy led to the transformation of the black worker's economic role from one of agricultural sharecropper and household servant to one of urban industrial operative and service worker, but it did not result in substantial relative improvement for blacks. Quantitative comparisons using U.S. Census data of occupational distributions by race show that the occupational status of black males relative to white males is virtually the same today as it was in 1910, the earliest year for which racial data is available.[3]

Besides systematically subjugating blacks so that their median income is 55 percent that of whites, racism is of profound importance for the distribution of income among white landowners, capitalists, and workers. For example, racism clearly benefits owners of housing in the ghetto, where blacks have no choice but to pay higher rents than for comparable housing elsewhere in the city. But more important, racism is a key mechanism for the stabilization of capitalism and the legitimization of inequality. We shall return to the question of who benefits from racism later, but first let us review some of the economic means used to subjugate blacks.

Beginning in the first grade, blacks go to schools of inferior quality and obtain little of the basic training and skills needed in the labor market. Finding school of little relevance, more in need of immediate income, and less able to finance their way through school, the average black student still drops out at a lower grade. In 1965 only 7.4 percent of black males aged 25–34 were college graduates, compared to 17.9 percent of whites in the same age bracket.

But exploitation really begins in earnest when the black youth enters the labor market. A black worker with the same number of years of schooling and the same scores on achievement tests as a white worker receives much less income. The black worker cannot get as good a job because the better-paying jobs are located too far from the ghetto, or because he was turned down by racist personnel agencies and employers, or because a union denied admittance, or perhaps because of an arrest record. Going to school after a certain point does not seem to increase a black person's job possibilities very much. The more educated a black person is, the greater is the disparity between his income and that of a white man with the same schooling. The result: in 1966 black college graduates earned less than white high school dropouts. And the higher the average wage or salary of an occupation, the lower the percentage of workers in that occupation who are black.

The rate of unemployment among blacks is twice as high as among whites. Layoffs and recessions hit blacks with twice the impact they hit whites, since blacks are the "last hired, first fired." The ratio of average black to white incomes follows the business cycle closely, buffering white workers from some of the impact of the recession.

Blacks pay higher rents for inferior housing, higher prices in ghetto stores, higher insurance premiums, higher interest rates in banks and lending companies, travel longer distances at greater expense to their jobs, suffer from inferior garbage collection and less access to public recreational facilities, and are assessed at higher property tax rates when they own housing. Beyond this, blacks are further harassed by police, the courts, and the prisons.

When conventional economists attempt to analyze racism they usually begin by trying to separate various forms of racial discrimination. For example, they define "pure wage discrimination" as the racial differential in wages paid to equivalent workers, that is, those with similar years and quality of schooling, skill training, previous employment experience and seniority, age, health, job attitudes, and a host of other factors. They presume that they can analyze the sources of "pure wage discrimination" without simultaneously analyzing the extent to which discrimination also affects the factors they hold constant.

But such a technique distorts reality. The various forms of discrimination are not separable in real life. Employers' hiring and promotion practices, resource allocation in city schools, the structure of transportation systems, residential segregation and housing quality, availability of decent health care, behavior of policemen and judges, foremen's prejudices, images of blacks presented in the media and the schools, price gouging in ghetto stores—these and the other forms of social and economic discrimination interact strongly with each other in determining the occupational status and annual income, and the welfare, of black people. The processes are not simply additive, but are mutually reinforcing. Often, a decrease in one narrow form of discrimination is accompanied by an increase in another form. Since all aspects of racism interact, an analysis of racism should incorporate all its aspects in a unified manner.

No single quantitative index could adequately measure racism in all its social, cultural, psychological and economic dimensions. But, while racism is far more than a narrow economic phenomenon, it does have very definite economic consequences: blacks have far lower incomes than whites. The ratio of median black to median white incomes thus provides a rough but useful quantitative index of the economic consequences of racism for blacks. We shall use this index statistically to analyze the causes of racism's persistence in the United States. While this approach overemphasizes the economic aspects of racism, it is nevertheless an improvement over the narrower approach taken by conventional economists.

How is the historical persistence of racism in the United States to be explained? Historically, the American Empire was founded on the racist extermination of American Indians, was financed in large part by profits from slavery, and was extended by a string of interventions, beginning with the Mexican War of the 1840s, which have been at least partly justified by white supremacist ideology.

Today by transferring white resentment toward blacks and away from capitalism, racism continues to serve the needs of the capitalist system. Although individual employers might gain by refusing to discriminate, hiring more blacks, and thus raising the black wage rate, it is not true that the capitalist class as a whole would profit if racism were eliminated and labor were more efficiently allocated without regard to skin color.

We will show below that the divisiveness of racism weakens workers' strength when bargaining with employers; the economic consequences of racism are not only lower incomes for blacks, but also higher incomes for the capitalist class coupled with lower incomes for white workers. Although capitalists may not have conspired consciously to create racism, and although capitalists may not be its principal perpetuators, nevertheless racism does support the continued well-being of the American capitalist system.

The statistical relationship between the extent of racism and the degree of inequality among whites provides a simple, yet clear test of the approach. This section describes that test and its results.

First, we shall need a measure of racism. The index to be used, for reasons already mentioned, is the ratio of black median family income to white median family income (abbreviated as B/W). A low numerical value for this ratio indicates a high degree of racism. We have calculated values of this racism index, using data from the 1960 Census, for each of the largest forty-eight Standard Metropolitan Statistical Areas (SMSAs). It turns out that there is a great deal of variation from SMSA to SMSA in the B/W index of racism, even within the North; southern SMSAs generally demonstrated a greater degree of racism. The statistical techniques used exploit this variation.

We shall also need measures of inequality among whites. Two convenient measures are (1) the percentage share of all white income which is received by the top 1 percent of white families, and (2) the Gini coefficient of white incomes, a measure that captures inequality within as well as between social classes.[4]

Both of these inequality measures vary considerably among the SMSAs; there is also a substantial amount of variation in these within the subsample of northern SMSAs. Therefore, it is interesting to examine whether the pattern of variation of the inequality and racism variables can be explained by causal hypotheses. This is our first source of empirical evidence.

A systematic relationship across SMSAs between racism and white inequality does exist and is highly significant: the correlation coefficient is =.47 (the negative sign indicates that where racism is greater, income inequality *among whites* is also greater).[5] This result is consistent with our model.

This evidence, however, should not be accepted too quickly. The correlations reported may not reflect actual causality, since other independent forces may be simultaneously influencing both variables in the same way. As is the case with many other statistical analyses, the model must be expanded to control for such other factors. We know from previous inter-SMSA income-distribution studies that the most important additional factors that should be introduced into our model are: (1) the industrial and occupational structure of the SMSAs, (2) the region in which the SMSAs are located, (3) the average income of the SMSAs, and (4) the proportion of the SMSA population that is black. These factors were introduced into the model by the technique of multiple regression analysis. We estimated separate equations using the Gini index and the top one percent share as measures of white inequality.

All the equations showed strikingly uniform statistical results: racism was a significantly un-equalizing force on the white income distribution, even when other factors were held constant. A 1 percent increase in the ratio of black-to-white median incomes (that is, a 1 percent decrease in racism) was associated with a .2 percent decrease in white inequality, as measured by the Gini coefficient. The corresponding effect on the top 1 percent share of white income was two and a half times as large, indicating that most of the inequality among whites generated by racism was associated with increased income for the richest 1 percent of white families. Further statistical investigation reveals that increases in racism had an insignificant effect on the share received by the poorest whites, and resulted in a decrease in the income share of the whites in the middling income brackets.[6] This is true even when the southern SMSAs are excluded.

Within our model, we can specify a number of mechanisms that further explain the statistical finding that racism increases inequality among whites. We shall consider two mechanisms here: (1) total wages of white labor are reduced by racial antagonisms, in part because union growth and labor militancy are inhibited; and (2) the supply of public services, especially in. education, available to low- and middle-income whites is reduced as a result of racial antagonisms.

Wages of white labor are lessened by racism because the fear of a cheaper and underemployed black labor supply in the area is invoked by employers when labor presents its wage demands. Racial antagonisms on the shop floor deflect attention from labor grievances related to working conditions, permitting employers to cut costs. Racial divisions among labor prevent the development of united worker organizations both within the work place and in the labor movement as a whole. As a result, union militancy will be less, the greater the extent of racism. A historical example of this process is the use of racial and ethnic divisions to destroy the solidarity of the 1919 steel strikers. By contrast, during the 1890s, black-white class solidarity greatly aided mineworkers in building militant unions among workers in Alabama, West Virginia, and other coal-field areas.[7]

The above argument and examples contradict the common belief that an exclusionary racial policy strengthens, rather than weakens the bargaining power of unions. Racial exclusion increases bargaining power only when entry into an occupation or industry can be effectively limited. Industrial-type unions are much less able to restrict entry than craft unions or organizations such as the American Medical Association. This is not to deny that much of organized labor is egregiously racist or that *some* skilled craft unionists may benefit from racism.[8] But it is important to distinguish actual discrimination practice from the objective economic self-interest of union members.

The second mechanism concerns the allocation of expenditures for public services. The most important of these services is education. Racial antagonisms dilute both the desire and the ability of poor white parents to improve educational opportunities for their children. Antagonisms between blacks and poor whites drive wedges between the two groups and reduce their ability to join in a united political movement pressing for improved and more equal education. Moreover, many poor whites recognize that, however inferior their own schools, black schools are even worse. This provides some degree of satisfaction and identification with the status quo, reducing the desire of poor whites to press politically for better schools in their neighborhoods. Ghettos tend to be located near poor white neighborhoods more often than near rich white neighborhoods; racism thus reduces the potential tax base of school districts containing poor whites. Also, pressures by teachers' groups to improve all poor schools is reduced by racial antagonisms between predominantly white teaching staffs and black children and parents.[9]

The statistical validity of the above mechanisms can be tested in a causal model. The effect of racism on unionism is tested by estimating an equation in which the percentage of the SMSA labor force which is unionized is the dependent variable, with racism and the structural variables (such as the SMSA industrial structure) as the independent variables. The schooling mechanism is tested by estimating a similar equation in which the dependent variable is inequality in years of schooling completed among white males aged 25–29 years old.[10]

Once again, the results of this statistical test appear to confirm the hypothesis of the radical model. The racism variable is statistically significant in both education equations and its sign predicts that a greater degree of racism results in greater amount of schooling inequality among whites. The effect of racism on unionization rates is less clear: although the coefficient of racism is positive and significant (implying a higher degree of unionization where there is less racism) for all the SMSAs, together, the estimate for non-southern SMSAs yields a coefficient of racism not significantly different from zero. The racism variable in the "all SMSAs" equation may therefore be picking up *regional* differences in unionization.

All in all, the empirical evidence suggests that racism is in the economic interests of capitalists and other rich whites, and against the economic interests of poor whites and white workers. Nevertheless, a full assessment of the importance of racism for capitalism would probably conclude that the primary significance of racism is not strictly economic. The simple economics of racism does not explain why many workers seem to be so vehemently racist when racism is not in their economic self-interest. In extra-economic ways, racism helps to legitimize inequality, alienation, and powerlessness—legitimization necessary for the stability of the capitalist system as a whole. For example, many whites believe that welfare payments to blacks are a far more important factor in their taxes than is military spending. Through racism, poor whites come to believe that their poverty is caused by blacks who are willing to take away their jobs, and at lower wages, thus concealing the fact that a substantial amount of income inequality is inevitable in a capitalist society. Racism thus transfers the locus of whites' resentment toward blacks and away from capitalism.

ENDNOTES

1. U.S. Bureau of Labor Statistics, *The Social and Economic Status of Negroes in the United States*, 1969, no. 375, p. 50.
2. The data refer to male incomes, and are published annually by the U.S. Census Bureau in its P-60 Series, *Income of Families and Persons*. Using data for the years 1948 to 1964, Rasmussen found that, after controlling for the effects of the business cycle, the average increase in the racial ratio of median incomes was only .3 percent per year, or 5 percent over the 16 years. See David Rasmussen, "A Note on the Relative Income of Nonwhite Men, 1948–64," *Quarterly Journal of Economics*, 84, no. 1 (1970): 168–172. Thurow, using a slightly different technique, estimated that no relative increase in black incomes would occur after unemployment was reduced to 3 percent. See L. Thurow, *Poverty and Discrimination*, (Washington, D.C.: Brookings Institution, 1969), pp. 58–61. Batchelder found stability in the ratio over time despite migration from the South to the North; within regions in the North, the ratio declined. Alan Batchelder, "Decline in the Relative Income of Negro Men," *Quarterly Journal of Economics*, 78 (November 1964): 525–548.
3. Since income data by race are not available before 1940, a relative index must be based on racial occupational data. Hiestand has computed such an index: he finds at most a 5 percent increase in

blacks' status between 1910 and 1960; most of this improvement occurred during the labor shortages of the 1940s. See D. Hiestand *Economic Growth and Employment Opportunities for Minorities.* (New York: Columbia University Press, 1964), p. 53.

4. The Gini coefficient varies between zero and 1, with zero indicating perfect equality, and 1 indicating perfect inequality. For a more complete exposition, see H. Miller, *Income Distribution in the United States* (Washington, D.C.: Government Printing Office, 1966). Data for the computation of G_w and S_1 for 48 SMSAs were taken from the 1960 Census. A full description of the computational techniques used is available in my dissertation.

5. The correlation coefficient reported in the text is between G_w and B/W. The equivalent correlation between S_1 and B/W is $R = -.55$. A similar calculation by S. Bowles, across states instead of SMSAs, resulted in an $R = -.58$.

6. A more rigorous presentation of these variables and the statistical results is available in my dissertation.

7. See Brody, *Steelworkers in America*; Gutman, "Negro and the United Mineworkers"; and Spero and Harris, *Black Worker*.

8. See, for example, H. Hill, "The Racial Practices of Organized Labor; the Contemporary Record," in *The Negro and the American Labor Movement*.

9. In a similar fashion, racial antagonisms reduce the political pressure on governmental agencies to provide other public services which would have a pro-poor distributional impact. The two principal items in this category are public health services and welfare payments in the Aid to Families with Dependent Children program.

10. These dependent variables do not perfectly represent the phenomena described, but serve as reasonable proxy variables for these purposes.

Ageism

It is not pleasant to grow old in American society. Ours is a youth dominated culture in which the old represent a despised commodity. Unlike the situation in traditional cultures where old age represents accumulated wisdom that generates respect and admiration, old age in our technological culture represents a way of life that no longer applies. Old people and their orientations to life have become irrelevant, as technology has ushered in a swirl of changes that demand corresponding change on the part of all.

Old people have been left behind in this process of change, and as their way of life has become irrelevant, so they have become irrelevant. Accordingly, they are assigned an insignificant role in our culture. They are not allowed to work, and they thereby become cut off from a major source of personal and social identity. They ultimately become an embarrassment to the young who do not have a satisfactory "cultural script" to follow in their dealings with old people.

In Article 14, Henslin analyzes the youth emphasis in our culture and its effects on our ideas of the old, our throw-away orientation to commodities and people, the effects of mandatory retirement in a function oriented society and its benefits for capitalism, the myth of Medicare, and the question of how much security is provided by Social Security. As he analyzes these aspects of aging in our culture, he also examines how old people are "deculturated" or disengaged from the dominant orientations of this culture as they begin the torturous process of "social death." Finally, he examines the "spoiled identity" of old people and the situation that has led to them becoming another minority group in American society.

Article 15 proposes specific solutions to the problems of ageism in American society. In this article, a "Manifesto for the Aged" is proposed in the form of OPERA (Old People's Equal Rights Amendment). Henslin focuses on the quality of life that a guaranteed annual income could provide old people in our society. His proposals also involve free access to housing, food, education, and medical care, and he proposes specific jobs in which old people could make valuable contributions to both society and to their own well-being. Note that at the essence of these specific suggestions is the active involvement of the old in deciding their own future, in forging their own fate.

James M. Henslin

14

Growing Old in the Land of the Young

In each culture some personal characteristics or attributes are selected out for high evaluation, admiration, and esteem, while other characteristics are selected for low evaluation, denigration, and reproach. People are evaluated according to how they match valued attributes. People who have characteristics that are devalued are themselves also devalued. They become objects of prejudice and discrimination. Such persons become characterized by negative stereotypes and find themselves on the receiving end of negative treatment. They are thought to possess less social worth than others and are systematically excluded from social activities.

Such prejudice and discrimination directed against people on the basis of their race is known as racism and has been studied by social scientists for generations. When prejudice and discrimination are directed against people on the basis of their sex, it is called sexism; awareness of sexism in our society has been growing steadily as women have militantly reacted against their devalued status. Old age is another physical characteristic on the basis of which prejudice and discrimination are directed against people in our society. In recent years, ageism has also increasingly been called to our attention. The cultural context that feeds ageism in our society and its consequences for those against whom it is directed are the subjects of this article.

THE ILLUSORY FOUNTAIN OF YOUTH

Stereotypes of persons with devalued characteristics abound in our society. They lump people together into a social category that obliterates

I wish to express my appreciation to Linda K. Henslin for her help in formulating some of the initial ideas that preceded this article, which was written for this volume.

individual differences and depicts people in unflattering terms. Our common stereotypes of women, Jews, blacks, Puerto Ricans, Indians, and Chicanos clothe their victims in negative imagery. This stereotypical victimization is not limited to women and minority groups. It is also directed against the aged in our society.

The youth cult has come to characterize American culture. As with other valued commodities, such as white and male, we associate a number of highly desirable traits with people who are younger. Youth is viewed as a period of happiness, characterized by beauty and health, intelligence, sexual vigor, useful goals and activities, and even life itself. In contrast, we associate a number of highly undesirable traits with old age, viewing it as a period of unhappiness characterized by ugliness and sickness, mental dullness, sexual debilitation, uselessness, and death. Consequently, practically no one in our society wants to become old, for we learn that old age is a time of misery, and old people are pitiable; they are liabilities as workers, they are cantankerous, behind the times, rigid in their ways, and arrogant in their manner (Rosenfelt 1965:39).

Our mass media encourage such stereotypical perceptions. Advertising on our mass media almost invariably associates good things solely with youth. It is the young who are shown happily puffing on cigarettes, enjoying leisure moments, demonstrating sexual capacities, and, in general, enjoying a good time in life as they lustily consume a cornucopia of technological products. We are told that "we only go around once in life"—and it is obviously the youth who are doing the going around. The same mass media inform us that we should quickly remove any and all telltale signs of approaching old age, and even of middle age. We are told to disguise the gray in our hair, to use wrinkle creams, and even to get our faces lifted and our hair transplanted. If the noses of old people looked significantly different from the noses of the young, we would probably be taught to undergo nose transplants!

Life expectancy in our country has surged during this century. In 1900, the life expectancy of Americans was 47; today it is 70. In 1900, one of eleven Americans was 65 or over; today it is one in eight. The average man who lives to be 65 can expect to live to be 78, while the average woman who lives to be 65 can expect to live to be 80. The 25 million or so Americans who are 65 or over equal the combined population of 21 of our states (Anderson 1972:210).

With our technological achievements, we have extended the life span of Americans by about one-half, but we do not know what to do with those added years in our technological society. Our general attitude is that the old are washed up and over the hill. The common attitude is that they cannot contribute anything worthwhile to our society, but have, instead, become leeches living off the productive energies of the young. Our attitudes have become so negative that when the highly prestigious "think tank" of Stanford University, Rand Corporation, studied the capability of the United States to survive in the event of nuclear war, these "scholars" concluded that we would be "better off without old and feeble citizens," and suggested that no provisions be made to care for the surviving elderly! (*Time*, June 2, 1975:44). We have come to the point in society that we basically have no place for old people, nuclear war or not.

THE NO DEPOSIT, NO RETURN SOCIETY

"No deposit, no return." "Throw away only." "Do not refill." Our typical practice is to use and to discard. We approach most commodities in this way, from plastic containers to appliances and clothing. Junkyards are filled with our discarded automobiles, and our discard rate has become so great that we do not know how to dispose of all that we throw away.

This throw away syndrome is not limited to material commodities. We also discard old people. They have performed their service, and they are no longer needed. Their skills have become obsolete in our rapidly changing technological society, so out they go—many to the human trash heaps and junkyards we euphemistically call nursing homes.

Doing the Dirty Work: Nursing Home Blues

Each society develops its own ways of handling its disvalued people. In some, the machinery of the State becomes focused on eliminating them as undesirables. Such was the case with Nazi Germany and the Jews. The dirty work of administering the "final solution" had to be done by someone, and the Nazis were able to recruit sufficient numbers of "good people" to take care of their dirty work (Hughes 1962).

It is not often that such an extreme solution as the Nazis' is decided upon, but it does happen, as with the former American genocide policy for the Indians. More common and less extreme is the development of institutions that segregate and isolate the disvalued. Almshouses of the past were such places to remove the disvalued from sight. They were collecting pots for the orphaned, the lame, the sick, the blind, the deaf, the aged, and often the insane (Shore 1966; Gold and Kaufman 1970). The back wards of our mental hospitals and VA hospitals serve this same function, as do our prisons and many of our jails.

Because they have become a disvalued commodity, we in American society also do not know what to do with the aged. Those who are able to care for themselves and those who have the financial resources to hire someone to care for them do not present real problems. The presence of such people is bothersome because they represent what we are told we should *not* be, but they are usually docile and quietly remain in the background. It is those who are old and sick who present the real problem. What should we do with them?

The American solution is called the nursing home. We used to call them Old Folks' Homes, but negative imagery was so greatly associated with this term that many old people refused to go to them, knowing that Old Folks' Homes were places to die. So we gave them a new name. This new term was meant to convey the idea of humane care for the elderly, but a change in name does not mean a change in actuality (Orlans 1948).

And what are they? They are the places in which we lock up our old and sick. We put them out of sight and out of mind. Just as we do with our prisoners, we do with the unfortunate old—but we call their prisons nursing homes instead of jails. In our nursing homes, we deposit those on the journey of no return—those who have not broken the law, but who carry a stigma so great that others feel they might catch it if they get too close to those who have it.

Not all nursing homes are bad, of course. We could not tolerate that in our enlightened society. But over 50 percent have one or more major violations of the supposed standards that have been set for them. Being substandard means more than having a burned out light bulb or dirty hallways. According to the Senate Committee on Aging, American nursing homes are characterized by widespread abuse, including negligence that leads to the death and injury of patients. They are not only unsanitary but they also provide poor food, lack proper medical care, and inflict reprisals against those who complain about their treatment. The pattern of victimization includes a lack of activities, inadequate fire protection, inadequate staffing, false advertising, and profiteering (*Nursing Home Care: Senate Hearings*).

The listing of specific instances from across the United States (including those that lead to slow, torturous deaths) are appalling, and I encourage you to read the Senate document cited above. The Senate Committee found that nursing homes typically have inadequate staffs because they hire untrained personnel and consequently experience a high turnover of employees and high rates of absenteeism. Another researcher found that it is not uncommon for the staff to abuse patients, especially those the staff finds "difficult." For such patients, it is considered legitimate by some staff members to retaliate by kicking, hitting, pulling hair, slapping, pinching, violently shaking, throwing water or food on them, or terrorizing them by word or gesture. And patients who complain are looked at as troublemakers or as being crazy (Stannard 1973).

Certainly not all nursing homes are like this. But the Senate Committee found such a pattern of abuse of nursing home patients that they concluded that it was not a matter of individual homes and staff but, rather, was connected to what nursing homes in the United States mean today. Old people are probably aware of this situation more than are younger people, and for them nursing homes have often become synonomous with death and protracted suffering before death. Being placed in a nursing home is often a bitter confirmation of the fears of a lifetime.

To be a patient in a nursing home typically means to lose control over one's life, to become dependent on hostile and uncaring personnel, to live in crowded conditions, to be separated from family and friends, to suffer from loneliness and lack of privacy, to lose one's identity, to become desexualized and infantile. Consequently, institutionalized old people undergo an impaired level of overall adjustment; their capacity for independent thought and action lessens, their self-esteem lowers, and they become depressed. Such reactions to nursing home placement are so common that they have been given their own name— the institutional syndrome (*Nursing Home Care: Senate Hearings:* 217).

It does not seem too far-fetched to draw an analogy between prisoners and nursing home patients. The family of a new member of a nursing home is often required to sign a medical "permission to treat" form that in some cases will be in effect for many years. Often medications that were formerly self-administered are removed. Alcoholic beverages, cigarettes, and certain foods may be prohibited. There are few options about such basic activities as rising and bedtimes, mealtimes and menus (*Nursing Home Care: Senate Hearings:* 218). If the patient doesn't like it, too bad. For he is a prisoner. He has entered a total institution that eliminates or makes irrelevant his outside statuses by means of rituals that strip away outside identities and replace them with the salient identity of patient—an old, sick, dependent, worthless person on his way to death. (Cf., Goffman 1961.)

Fortunately, only about 5 percent of our elderly are forced to live in nursing homes, but that represents about one million people. We have developed an American way of handling the most troublesome of the aged, a socially acceptable means of abandoning the old and sick. In this process, the owners of nursing homes are running them in our best capitalistic tradition—for the purpose of making profit (Mendelson, 1974). As they pursue their profit, our nursing home entrepreneurs cut costs to the bone and fill their rosters with unskilled attendants who are paid rock-bottom wages. With these profit-seeking entrepreneurs leeching off Medicaid and sometimes feeding patients on less than what is spent for prisoners in our jails, nursing homes can yield an annual return of up to 40 percent on their investment (*Time*, June 2, 1975:47).

THOSE GOLDEN YEARS

The worker becomes 62, and he is encouraged to quit his job. He turns 65, and he is forced into retirement. Although 65 is an arbitrary age, decided on in 1937 when our Social Security legislation came into effect, it has become a magical number in our society. As one old worker said:

> You know, one day you are sought after by all of your colleagues, your associates and citizens for advice, counsel, and assistance and for your participation and involvement. The next day nobody wants you at all. You are the same person that you were the day before. What's different? You are one day older. You've had your birthday. You are 65. (*Retirement and the Individual, Senate Hearings:* 72)

The old know they are being discarded. In spite of ideological trappings about "those golden years," most old people know there's hardly a nugget of gold to be found. Retirement, more often than not, represents being thrown out of work—somewhat like a compulsory divorce from a spouse. Retirement does not have to be this way, of course, but with our cultural dictates concerning the values of youth and productivity, retirement is often seen as entering the dependent role we have all been taught to studiously avoid.

The central problem is that when we "put people to pasture" we are forcing them from positions which were major rootings of their self concept. In our industrialized society we build a large portion of our identities around our occupational role. What we do for a living represents a good part of what we become, of who we are, and what we consider ourselves to be. We tend to incorporate our occupational role into our self-concept.

The occupational role also becomes a major *social* identifier. When we first meet someone, one of the first things we want to know about that person is what he does for a living. When we learn this, we assume that we know a great deal about that person. We tie that person into what we know about that occupation, associating it with various attitudes and orientations to life. Consequently, our occupation is one of the major means by which we identify ourselves to one another.

By removing them from their jobs and positions, we successfully remove old people from that around which a major portion of their self and social identities has been constructed. With what do they fill this void? Many are able to construct alternate identities, but retirement frequently leads to a state of normlessness or anomie. If someone asks "What do you do?" and the person replies, "I'm retired," one doesn't know exactly how to respond, as "being retired" reveals little about who the person is. We can inquire about what the person *used* to do, but that primarily tells us something about how he or she *used to be.*

We have provided no satisfactory alternate identity for the aged in our society. We give them neither "honorific" positions nor worthwhile activities in which they can take pride. In spite of all the hoopla in our society about the joys of retirement, it is essentially a functionless position in a function oriented society, a society in which positive approval and consequent self and social identities are given for *doing* something. To be retired in our society, however, is taken to mean *not* doing something and, ultimately, to be useless. Thus, to put this matter in the strongest terms, to currently be retired in our society is to *not* be.

We are all familiar with the problems of jobs, with the requirements and demands they make. Most workers appear to complain regularly about their jobs, and some quite bitterly. The feeling is not uncommon about how good it would be to be free from work. In spite of this, retirement has become so negative in our society that most workers prefer to continue working at their jobs than to retire. Eighty to eighty-nine percent state that they would prefer to continue to work, even if they received enough money to live comfortably without working (Carter 1970).

Although work is the major integrating activity around which the self is lodged, we increasingly are *requiring* retirement. The extent to which retirement at the age of 65 has become common in our country is illustrated by Figure 1. Note that where about one-half of workers 65 and over were in the labor force in 1947, now only approximately one-fourth remain working.

Forced retirement further contributes to our stereotypes of the aged, as they self-evidently are "over the hill." After all, being *forced* to retire at 65 must be based on the inability to adequately perform. The retired become inactive and nonproductive in our highly production oriented society. The old come to be viewed as persons who must be supported by others. This ignominious position into which we force people sometimes leads to resentment on the part of younger workers who feel that they must work to sustain the useless. Who, after all, appreciates that which has been discarded?

BENEFITS TO CAPITALISM

As with other forms of discrimination in our society, capitalism is a major beneficiary. As racism and sexism have traditionally maintained a pool of unskilled and low paid workers available for our economic directors, so ageism serves this same sector of our social structure. Putting a mandatory retirement age into effect has the consequence of force-

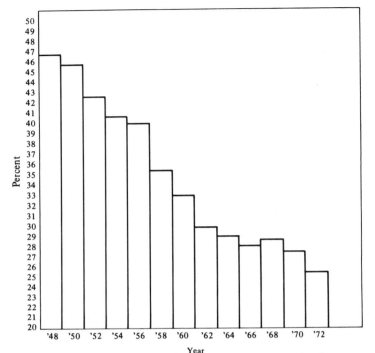

Year

[1] For the age cohort represented by these persons, only a low proportion of women ever worked in the labor force. Their labor force participation rates at age 65 and over for 1948 to 1972 have consistently hovered between eight and ten per cent.

Source: Future Directions in Social Security; Hearings Before the Special Committee on Aging, United States Senate, January 15, 1973, p. 334.

FIGURE 1   Labor Force Participation Rates for Males[1] 65 Years of Age and Older

fully removing our higher paid workers from the labor force. Those who have been with a corporation for many years are generally paid more than beginning workers. Forcing workers out of their jobs at the age of 65 or earlier means that they can be replaced at a much lower salary by those who are just entering the job market.

Inflation also combines with mandatory retirement to benefit the corporate elite at the expense of the workers. While employed by a corporation, workers never see a good part of their salary. Money is withheld from their paychecks in the form of pension plans and retirement funds. When workers put money into such plans and funds, it has a much higher purchasing power than when it is returned to them during retirement. Inflation means that they pay "hard" dollars into retirement plans but, in turn, are paid "soft" dollars from them. During the years that this money has been withheld, it is used by banks and other financial institutions controlled by the wealthy to make more money for the wealthy, with a proportion of the earnings returned to the retirement fund in the form of interest.

Inflation also continues to work against workers when they are retired. When older workers are forced out of their jobs, they are usually left with a fixed retirement income. While this income may have been adequate when they first retired, it often becomes inadequate as their purchasing power is dramatically eaten away by inflation.

We are a mobile people, and it is the old who are left behind. The average American moves to a different residence once every five years. One consequence of our mobility is that it makes it extremely difficult to maintain a closely knit family. The younger people move to a house designed for the nuclear family, a home with just enough bedrooms for the parents and their children. With the generally ample space in our homes, it is probable that there is sufficient room for the older generation—but the older generation is not wanted in the homes of the younger. Our cultural view is that old people are intruders, persons who have no business living with the younger generation. Our scheme of cultural values encourages married couples to live by themselves, and they become embarrassed if they are unable to afford a home or apartment of their own. Even young singles are encouraged to strike out on their own, and they usually feel deprived if they are unable to do so. This "split in the generations" is also a boon to capitalism, as it multiplies the need for new housing, home furnishings, and the like.

THE MYTH OF MEDICARE

Among the problems that old people in our society face are those of illness and inadequate medical care. The aged obviously suffer from more health problems than do younger persons. They are more likely to suffer from such chronic conditions as arthritis, cardiovascular diseases, and cancer. Almost everyone over 60 has at least one chronic health problem. But since the passage of Medicare, many people assume that the old are now receiving medical care free or almost free, and are well provided for medically. The truth is far from this assumption.

Medicare does not provide for care at home, and if a person is hospitalized he or she must be in the hospital for at least three days before Medicare goes into effect (Cottrell 1974). Nor does Medicare cover preventive medicine, the cost of out-of-hospital drugs, dental work, eyeglasses, or hearing aids (*Senate Hearings*). With these conditions, it almost sounds as though Medicare was designed to discriminate against the elderly, for it is they who most often need dental work, eyeglasses, and hearing aids. And without covering preventive medical care, someone with a Machiavellian orientation might conclude that Medicare is designed to get rid of old people since it doesn't put out money to prevent them from becoming sick.

To gain some idea of the inadequacy of Medicare, we can note that the average old person now pays *more* for his own medical treatment than he did when Medicare began. This anomalous situation is illustrated by Figure 2 which shows the deterioration of Medicare benefits

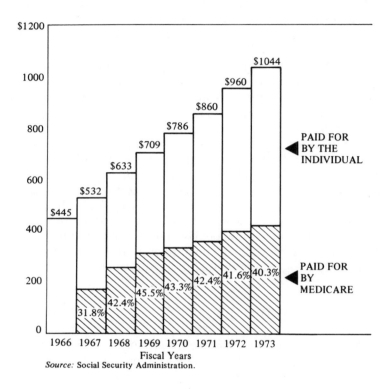

Source: Social Security Administration.

FIGURE 2   Medical Care Bill per Aged Person and Proportion Covered by Medicare, 1966–1973

in the last few years. For example, in 1969 the average annual medical bill for those covered by Medicare was $709. Of this amount, Medicare paid 45.5 percent, or $322, while the patient paid 54.5 percent, or $387. By 1973, medical bills for the elderly soared to an annual average of $1,044. The percentage Medicare paid, however, *dropped* to 40.3 percent, or $431. During a period in which inflation was eating away at their skimpy incomes, this left the old saddled with average annual medical expenses of $613. By 1973, Medicare patients found themselves paying 38 percent *more* for their medical care than they had before Medicare came into being! Three years later Medicare patients found they also had to cover the first $104 of hospitalization expenses (NBC-TV September 30, 1975).

THE SEMBLANCE OF SOCIAL SECURITY

In 1937, the Social Security Act was adopted in the United States. This legislation was a giant step forward in providing Americans with security in their old age. Rather than allowing former workers or their widows and children to starve, those who had contributed to Social Security were guaranteed a minimum compensation upon retirement. With its current minimum payment of $85 a month, however, in some cases Social Security benefits allow the aged and poor to barely stay alive. Most benefits are considerably greater than this minimum, however, as illustrated by Figure 3, which shows the average cash benefits paid by Social Security.

But does Social Security provide security?

As everyone has experienced, most to their sorrow, galloping inflation has been the order of the day in our country. While most of us have experienced losses due to inflation, it has hit hardest those who are on fixed incomes. This has left the aged in a bind. Social Security benefits have increased, however, leaving most people with the idea that the aged are being taken care of adequately. Social Security benefit increases, however, have *not* kept pace with the increases in the cost of living. From 1970 to 1975, the purchasing power of the dollar declined at least 27¢ per dollar. During this same period, Social Security payments increased eighteen percent. The millions who rely solely on Social Security suffered a minimum loss of nine percent during this period (Associated Press, March 24, 1975). For those already living on the border of subsistence, to undergo a loss of nine percent of the little they have means that they face a crisis of immense proportions.

Poverty in old age is by no means restricted to the lifelong poor, the profligate, or the shortsighted. Our public assistance programs include aged recipients of middle class biographies, many of whom simply outlived their economic resources. It is an unfortunate economic fact of social life in the United States that the longer one lives past retirement, the greater one's chances for impoverishment (Sheppard 1965:67). And if one becomes impoverished, but still has a little property, such as a small home, many states will put such a person on welfare—but only after taking a lien on the property that gives the state the right to dispose of it (Cottrell 1974).

Old people in our society also face credit discrimination. Many national credit card companies, department stores, gasoline companies, banks, and other financial institutions use an arbitrary age cut-off on credit privileges. Simply because they are old, numerous people are

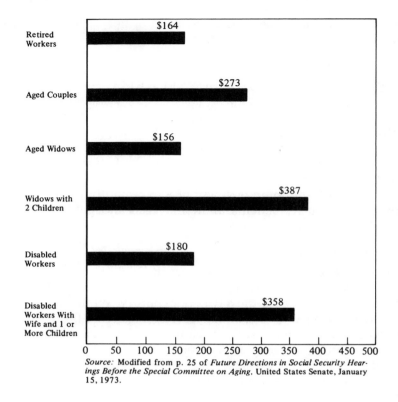

Source: Modified from p. 25 of *Future Directions in Social Security Hearings Before the Special Committee on Aging.* United States Senate, January 15, 1973.

FIGURE 3   Average Cash Benefits of Social Security, January 1973

denied credit. Credit can be denied even though one has $30,000 a year income and a good credit record. Being over 65 is considered a justifiable reason to deny someone credit. Yet we have moved into a credit card society, and increasingly stores no longer take personal checks. Being denied credit cards, many of our old people are forced to the literally dangerous act of carrying cash for their purchases (Associated Press, April 24, 1975).

To grow old in our society means to be confronted with deep-rooted problems of adjustment. The old are usually separated from their children, they suffer from diseases and illnesses for which they often cannot afford a physician, they have fear of the future, a dread of helplessness, a fear of abandonment, reduced income, often the loss of spouse and friends through death, and the feeling that one's problems are of little interest to others. And as life expectancy has increased, so has the number of years the typical worker can expect to spend outside the labor force.

The unstructured anomic status into which we force old people frequently leads to tension, depression, and a feeling of hopelessness. Because of the many problems faced by the old, retirement is not uncommonly viewed as the beginning step in the inevitable slide into oblivion, a sort of protracted purgatory before death ends the sufferings of this life. Regardless of chronological age, the retired in our society tend to have a lower morale than the employed. Such lowered morale among the retired also holds true regardless of income level (Thompson 1973: 342–343).

SOCIAL DEATH BEFORE PHYSICAL DEATH: THE PROCESS OF DECULTURATION

Financial difficulties are only part of the problems Americans experience when they become old. The major difficulty is social death. Old Americans are gradually groomed for total cultural withdrawal. In many ways, this process is the reverse of the enculturative process of childhood. As it is during childhood that the individual comes to learn the customary ways of society in order to be able to function within it, so in the United States it is during old age that the individual is made to unlearn these ways so he or she can eventually cease to function culturally (Anderson 1972).

In a traditional society, old people represent the same culture as the young; the accumulated experience of the aged is taken as wisdom gained through living, an experience which is respected because it can be passed on to the young. In our technologically changing society, in contrast, old people represent a "lost generation," as they are carriers of outmoded and bypassed culture. They are displaced persons, being replaced by the young who bear the new culture. Their accumulated experience represents another age, a period whose other ways of doing things are irrelevant to the present. Accordingly, in our culture old people become irrelevant. As their experiences are insignificant for the present, so they themselves become insignificant.

The destination of old people is clear to all, including the aged. With their irrelevance and insignificance for modern life, they enter a period of "temporary tangential identity" that is soon "followed by dissolution and social death" (Anderson 1972:211). They are shunted into irrelevant and insignificant corners of American life, allowed to be only peripherally present until they can finally be relegated to a box and be carried out of this life for good.

In this process of deculturation, the old are removed from the traditional activities, goals, and even ideologies of our culture. The old learn that it is wrong for them to think in terms of being mobile, acquisitive, and innovative (Anderson 1972). Such characteristics now belong to the young, to those who have taken the reins of social life. The old are to withdraw from the mainstream, to sit back and let those who are capable run things. They are to move to a less active, less responsible, and more dependent role. They are to become as children. They are, moreover, to be resigned to fate, to be humble, and also to be self-centered.

During this process of deculturation, dominant stereotypes of the aged do their destructive work. Old people are also well acquainted with our stereotypes of old people, and these stereotypes color their own perception of themselves. The older worker, for example, has also internalized dominant attitudes toward and ideas about the aged, and this leads to a lower evaluation of his own capacities than a younger worker with comparable skills has of himself (*Retirement and the Individual; Senate Hearings:* 168). As they internalize the attitudes culturally appropriate to their assigned status, they learn to think of themselves as others think of them. They consequently come to think of themselves as more useless and as having less social worth than others (Anderson 1972). They have entered the limbo state of social death that precedes, and often hastens, their physical death.

OLD AGE AS A MASTER TRAIT OF A MINORITY GROUP

Social characteristics which override all others are called master traits. These are traits that predominate over other characteristics and roles. Other people react to persons who have them primarily in terms of the master trait. The master trait dominates, and people cannot quite seem to get it out of their minds. Examples include being an ex-con among "straights," or a black in white society, or a midget among tall people, or a physician among nonphysicians, or a congressman among the ordinary citizenry.

Old age is another such master trait, and a highly visible one. The master trait of old age is so negative that we can say that old people in our culture suffer from a "spoiled identity;" that is, old age in our culture is a discrediting attribute, a major stigma (Goffman 1963). As one old man put it, "Being old is like having bad breath—a built-in distancing mechanism" (Anderson 1972:213). Regardless of whatever else one may be, an old person is old. And in our youth dominated society Americans are constantly aware of age. One may be a woman, but one is an *old* woman. One may be a professor, but one is an *old* professor. One may be a bongo player, but one is an *old* bongo player. (And the young are surprised that the person can *still* teach, play the bongos —or even walk.)

Part of the stereotype surrounding this master trait in our society is that the old are desexualized. It simply becomes unthinkable for many that old people have a sex life. Sex belongs to the young, and the old have no business having anything to do with sex. There must be something wrong with them if they want to be sexually active. This part of the stereotype also affects old people's perceptions of themselves and their behavior. Tending to think of themselves along the lines of the stereotype, they tend to become sexless. The sex drive does decrease with age, but such internalized social expectations further decrease it. Old people are capable of enjoying sex into advanced old age, but the effect of dominant stereotypes is so great that people even respond to them biologically. (Cf., Christenson and Gagnon 1965; Masters and Johnson 1966.)

As we increasingly shunt people on the basis of this master trait or stigma, old people are becoming more and more similar to a minority group. They are typified by negative stereotypes; they are discriminated against in employment and credit; they are being segregated in housing; and a subculture of the aged is developing. Dissimilarities between the aged and the young are on the increase, with growing income and educational gaps, characteristics which typically separate our dominant group and the minorities. The aged are also being kept at a geographical distance. As the younger have moved to the metropolitan areas and then to the suburbs, the aged have not kept pace. Increasingly higher proportions of the aged live in nonmetropolitan areas and the central cities. As whites are leaving the central cities to blacks, so the younger are leaving them to the old. Similarly, the aged are characterized by the same inferior socio-economic indices that characterize minority groups in our country; from one-third to one-half of the aged are poorer, are employed less, work in lower-status occupations, and have less education and poorer health than similar proportions of the younger. And their relative status is continuing to decline (Palmore 1969; Palmore and Whittington 1971).

FOR THE FORTUNATE FEW:
REVERSE DISCRIMINATION

Being old is not bad for all old people, of course. Many old people live in homes they have paid for, enjoy modest pensions along with their Social Security, grow gardens, and enjoy a good life. Many are healthy until the day they die and do not have to go through the agonies of seeing their life savings gouged into nothingness by an avaricious medical profession. Many continue to enjoy intimate relationships with beloved children who live close to them. About a half million of our old people are so well off that they are even able to move to Florida and the Southwest where they segregate themselves into gerontopolises. They live in well designed apartments or cottages and enjoy dancing, crafts, swimming, and golf. In some, as in Arizona's Sun City, reverse discrimination is practiced, and no one under 50 is allowed to buy or lease property. In another, a three-week limit is put on visits by children (*Time*, June 2, 1975:45).

But these are the fortunate ones. At the other end of the spectrum are the aged of our inner cities who are forced to live in cheaply furnished rooms, and the million or so who find themselves prisoners of the nursing home business. While the average old person probably manages to adequately get by on his savings, pension, and social security—combined with a good deal of frugality—about a third of all old Americans live in poverty. About five million live on less than $2,000 a year.

CONCLUSION

For most Americans, growing old and retiring is not something to look forward to. It means entering a period of life marked by hardship and discrimination, by negative attitudes and stereotypes one must face daily, by uncertainty of the future, and by medical expenses which are approaching a never never land of affordability. It also means to be subjected to the rigors of deculturation and to live with the certainty that the only release from the physical and social pains and frustrations is death.

Our cultural form of old age is what people face after a lifetime of work in one of the wealthiest countries in the world, a country that can well afford much better for its old people. It is no exaggeration to say that this country could make the golden years truly golden. And it does not seem much of an exaggeration to say that, in general, the inhabitants of this country just plain don't give a damn—although each of the noncaring must one day find himself or herself in the same anomalous situation, unless death's mysterious hand intervenes first.

REFERENCES

Barbara Gallatin Anderson, "The Process of Deculturation—Its Dynamics Among United States Aged," *Anthropological Quarterly, 45,* October 1972, pp. 209–216.

Reginald Carter, "The Myth of Increasing Non-Work Vs. Work Activities," *Social Problems, 18,* Summer 1970, pp. 52–67.

Cornelia V. Christenson and John H. Gagnon, "Sexual Behavior in a Group of Older Women," *Journal of Gerontology, 20,* 1965, pp. 351–356.

Fred Cottrell, *Aging and the Aged*, Dubuque, Iowa: Wm. C. Brown Company Publishers, 1974.

Erving Goffman, *Asylums*, Chicago: Aldine Publishers, 1961.

Erving Goffman, *Stigma: Notes on the Management of Spoiled Identity*, Englewood Cliffs, N.J.: Prentice-Hall, 1963.

Jacob G. Gold and Saul M. Kaufman, "Development of Care of the Elderly: Tracing the History of Institutional Facilities," *The Gerontologist, 10*, Winter 1970, Part I.

Lawrence D. Haber, "Aging and Capacity Devaluation," *Journal of Health and Social Behavior, 11*, September 1970, pp. 167–182.

Everett C. Hughes, "Good People and Dirty Work," *Social Problems, 10*, Summer 1962.

William H. Masters and Virginia E. Johnson, *Human Sexual Response*, Boston: Little, Brown and Company, 1966.

Mary Adelaide Mendelson, *Tender Loving Greed*, New York: Alfred A. Knopf, Inc., 1974.

Harold Orlans, "An American Death Camp," in *Politics*, Summer 1948, pp. 162–167, 205.

Erdman Palmore, "Sociological Aspects of Aging," in *Behavior and Adaptation in Late Life*, Ewald W. Busse and Eric Pfeiffer, eds., Boston: Little, Brown, 1969, pp. 33–69.

Erdman Palmore and Frank Whittington, "Trends in the Relative Status of the Aged," *Social Forces, 50*, September 1971, pp. 84–91.

Rosalie H. Rosenfelt, "The Elderly Mystique," *Journal of Social Issues, 21*, October 1965, pp. 37–43.

Senate Hearings, *Nursing Home Care in the United States: Failure in Public Policy;* Supporting Paper No. 1; The Litany of Nursing Home Abuses and an Examination of the Roots of Controversy: Subcommittee on Long-Term Care of the Special Committee on Aging, United States Senate, December 1974.

Senate Hearings, *Retirement and the Individual*, Hearings Before the Subcommittee on Retirement and the Individual of the Special Committee on Aging, United States Senate, Part 1, June 7 and 8, 1967.

H. L. Sheppard, "The Poverty of Aging," in *Poverty as a Social Issue*, Ben B. Seligman, ed., New York: The Free Press, 1965.

S. Shore, "New Ideas in Institutional Care," *Professional Nursing Home*, June 1966.

Charles I. Stannard, "Old Folks and Dirty Work: The Social Conditions for Patient Abuse in a Nursing Home," *Social Problems, 20*, Winter 1973, pp. 329–342.

Gayle B. Thompson, "Work Versus Leisure Roles: An Investigation of Morale Among Employed and Retired Men," *Journal of Gerontology, 38,* 1973, pp. 339–344.

James M. Henslin

15

On OPERA and Human Dignity:
Proposals for Social Change

A major criticism directed at sociologists is that they are long on analyses of what is wrong with society and short on proposals for solving social problems. This is a legitimate criticism. In our professional training, we sociologists generally receive a heavy emphasis on how to analyze the "ills" of society, but receive little corresponding emphasis on how to program positive social change. Innovation is usually left for "others," whoever those others may be. To analytically criticize is certainly the safer course to follow, for whatever one proposes can never be perfect in this imperfect world—and there are always many who are eager to find fault with any constructive proposals, although they themselves fail to provide guidance for social change.

Yet our professional education should also equip us for actively developing models and proposals for social change. We are trained in systemic analysis; that is, we are sensitized to look for the effects of the social system on people. This sensitivity, in fact, is the basis for our analytical talents which we use in diagnosing what is wrong with society. That same training and those same talents can also be used for developing programs of social change, for any effective change must involve change in the social system, since it is arrangements of the social system that lead to our social problems in the first place.

This brief article is an attempt at applying sociological analysis to the solution of the social problem of ageism in our society. I shall not be advocating the abolishment of capitalism, although that would be the real place to begin. It is not that I consider capitalism to be a good economic system, for I am too well acquainted with its deleterious effects on people. It is, rather, that while such a proposal gets to the heart of the matter, it is simply too utopian; it is like saying, "My pro-

This article was written for this volume.

posal for solving the problem is to not have the problem." Nice, if you can get by with it. But we live in a society firmly entrenched in the capitalist framework. Accordingly, any practical proposals for constructive change must take this historical situation into account and be made within the framework of our current economic system. The proposals which follow, then, are suggestions for social change that, in my opinion, are viable; that is, they have the potential for leading to widesweeping change in the lives and social conditions of old people in our society and a chance for success if the right pressures are properly exerted.

This article, then, is dedicated to old people, who deserve much better than they are now getting, and to those persons, whether young or old or in between, who want to see society change in the direction of greater equality. You may disagree with any of the particulars that I am suggesting, but they are only proposals. They are not meant to be a final analysis of the way change must go. On the contrary, they are put forward with the hope that they will stimulate discussion and in the light of that discussion be modified.

The basic proposal is a manifesto for old people. This would be best in the form of an amendment to the Constitution of the United States. The Old People's Equal Rights Amendment, OPERA, would read somewhat as follows:

> *The basic rights of old people to independence, security, and freedom shall not be abridged by the Federal or State governments in either their laws or practices. It shall furthermore be the duty of the Government of the United States to take every reasonable step to eliminate discrimination against people on the basis of their having reached old age.*

Independence, security, and freedom are only hollow words unless they are backed up by positive action. To have freedom, security, and independence, opportunities must be opened up, opportunities that represent aspects of living that the old desire and from which they can choose.

That which leads to independence, security, and freedom in our society is money. A basic means of attaining these rights, then, would be a guaranteed annual income for all old people. This income must be sufficient to maintain "quality of life," and be automatically escalated to keep pace with inflation.

Certainly quality of life is a difficult term to define, but, at the minimum, it includes adequate housing and diet and access to education and medical care. "Adequate" is similarly a difficult term to define because it can be interpreted in so many different ways and because it changes as standards change. Rather than pegging these terms with particulars, such as so many calories per day or so many square feet of living space, it is better to let "quality of life" and "adequate" match the standards that prevail for the general society. If standards for the "average" person in our society become modified with changes in historical circumstance, so they would change for old people.

As citizens of one of the wealthiest lands in the world, old people should never have to worry about having sufficient food to eat, or a place to live, or the opportunity to continue their education, or whether or not they can afford to get a doctor to treat their illnesses. If this sounds like socialized education and socialized medicine, then let that term stand. It is also socialized food and socialized housing, for that matter. I would, in fact, suggest that all citizens of the United States have the basic rights to food, housing, education, and medicine, regardless of their age, but I am here applying these rights only to old people.

Guaranteed employment *and* guaranteed retirement should be *options* available to people at some set age, say 55, or 60, or 65. Guaranteed employment must be offered to those old people who want to and are able to continue working. There is nothing about the age of 65 that automatically removes a person's abilities, and we must get old age out of the Dark Ages. Far from being "over the hill," old people are still in the process of "becoming." They are simply at a different stage in life. By the same token, guaranteed retirement should be available to those who desire that option. Those who wish to work can do so, while those who wish not to work can do so. The guaranteed annual income would make this option viable. Guaranteed employment should also contain a guaranteed "slowing down;" that is, workers who desire to continue to work but who prefer to work less than they formerly did should be guaranteed some combination of shorter work days, shorter work weeks, and longer vacations.

Repealing mandatory retirement laws and instituting guaranteed employment will lead to a change in the common ideas people now have about the old. Those old people who wish to continue contributing to the welfare of others through their employment would be able to do so. They would be seen as productive people. Those who select the retirement option would be living in dignity and security and would also be representing a desirable goal in life that the younger can have hope of some day attaining. The old who decide to continue to work would be working at jobs that they find self-fulfilling or else they would select the retirement option. Younger workers would then be around *happier* older colleagues and work associates. As it now is, as workers get old, they become increasingly uneasy concerning the future, for they do not know what it will bring them. Under this program, there will be no such thing as outliving one's resources, and true social *security* will be provided all old people.

Certainly not having to work for a living is not in and of itself evil. Not having to work can be a tremendous blessing, as many wealthy people in our society have known all their lives. The basic problem is not retiring from work, but both the insecurity retiring now brings and the negative attitudes associated with not working. If the retired have retired by choice, however, and they have retired into security readily visible to others, such ideas will undergo profound change. Younger workers will have something to look forward to as they grow older, for they will not be forced into a style of life they do not want, but will be able to freely choose that which they do want. To have freedom of choice means to have the opportunity to choose from among options that are desirable. If someone who wants to live is given the choice of taking poison or being garrotted, that is not freedom of choice. He has only a choice of how to bring about what he does not want.

Where choice of working or not working takes place within a framework of financial security and guaranteed access to medical care, as well as the right to continue one's education if so desired, retirement can be beautiful. Retirement can mean a wonderfully self-fulfilling period in a person's life. Retirement can be a time for reflection; a time for enjoying the fruits of one's labors, the contributions one has made to society through a lifetime of work; a time to dream; a time to enjoy; a time to relax; a time to take up new interests and activities; a time to pursue ambitions once longed for but put aside due to the press of making a living and providing for one's family.

Old people can no longer be thought of as passive receptors of the actions of younger people. The loss to our society of their many years of experience and the worthwhile orientation to life that they could share with others is a luxury we can no longer afford. For example, child neglect is a major problem in this country. Millions of children across the nation are being neglected by their parents. It appears that this negligence is dooming many of these children to a lifetime of poverty and crime. But our old people provide a vast reservoir from which to draw to help remedy this situation. Many old people would find deep satisfaction in working closely with a child on a one-to-one basis in order to shape young lives in a positive direction. To salvage now makes more sense than to incarcerate later—and it would be cheaper in the long run. But the real cost of such a current waste is not in dollars and cents; it is in the loss of potential for human development and fulfillment.

A step in this direction has already been taken with Congress' approval of a limited Foster Grandparent Program. Such programs should be expanded across the country, but not simply with old people taking directions from the younger. Old people are not children; nor should they be treated as children. Abilities do not disappear with old age, and old people are quite capable of administering such a program, supervising the program, and carrying it out in all of its details. They are capable, moreover, of doing so with both efficiency and compassion.

Similarly, old people can be trained for work as counselors in our prisons, in our halfway houses, in our jails, and for work with the disabled and handicapped. Coupled with training in communications skills, their experience in living could be a real boon in such endeavors. Over a lifetime of experience, old people have gained much that is worthwhile that can be passed on to others. If old people are despised, however, no one will listen to their accumulated experience. But with such other changes as are being suggested, attitudes toward old people will be sharply modified, and the experience of the old can be put to productive use in these and many other areas.

The old also should be actively involved in shaping their own fate in life. They should be able to actively make decisions concerning matters that directly affect themselves, especially concerning the conditions under which they will live. For example, in housing, old people should have the choice of whether or not they will live alone. For those who have a preference for living alone, this should be honored. Still others will prefer to live in residential developments designed exclusively for old people. Such housing should be made available, also well within range of their guaranteed annual income.

In providing residential choice for old people, the issue goes beyond where they desire to live. If old people want to live in developments that cater to the special needs of people who reach advanced age, for example, why should they be forced to choose among buildings designed by the young for the old? Old people should be the ones who compose the planning committees, site selection committees, and the like. They should be able to choose their own architects and make certain that their input, based on their own perceptions of their own needs, is incorporated into the design of these residences. Who, after all, better knows the needs of the old than the old themselves? Rather than basing plans on "*If* we were old, this is what we *would* like," plans should be based on people saying, "We *are* old, and this *is* what we like."

Old people have their own unique health and social needs, and even in meeting these needs they can be actively involved. I would suggest that courses in social gerontology be established across the nation. They should not, however, be designed only by "experts" who may or may not be in touch with the needs of the old; rather, they should have input from old people built into them. In order to recruit highly qualified gerontological workers, the federal government should subsidize trainees, both paying them reasonable salaries while they are in training and guaranteeing them employment at good salaries after they have completed their programs in social gerontology. I would suggest that their training be approximately evenly divided between theoretical and other academic course work in our colleges and universities and practical, supervised experience with old people. It is at this point especially that input from old people would be valuable. They can provide feedback on the practical work experience of trainees to help make solid evaluations of whether or not the trainee is qualified for this type of work. Old people themselves should be hired to help place, supervise, train, and evaluate the progress of trainees.

If nursing homes must continue to exist, then they should be staffed with persons who have been rigorously trained in meeting the needs of gerontological patients—whether those needs are physical, emotional, social, or spiritual. To accomplish this, some nursing homes can remain under the control of individuals and private and public organizations, but should immediately be removed from profit making, with the federal government financing the buildings, facilities, and the salaries of staff. Others could be run by the federal government itself. The right of choosing a public or private nursing home should remain with the patient.

All nursing homes, whether government or private, should be inspected by qualified old people, those from the legal, medical, and paramedical professions, as well as old people from other backgrounds who are specifically recruited and trained for this task. These inspections should be *solely* on an irregular and surprise basis. If the visiting team finds conditions detrimental to the well-being of patients, they should have the right and power to investigate, subpoena, hold hearings, and fix responsibility. Any persons they adjudge to be responsible for such conditions should be immediately removed from their jobs. These persons should have the right to appeal to a higher Board, which also should be composed of old people. If the accused does not appeal, or if his or her appeal fails, that person should no longer be allowed to participate in nursing home care in any capacity whatsoever. In cases appearing to be criminal negligence, the committee should bring the matter to the attention of a higher committee that convenes solely for such purposes. If this higher committee, also composed of old people, agrees that it is a case of criminal negligence, they should be empowered to bring the matter to the attention of the criminal prosecutor. If the prosecutor drags his feet in pressing charges, this committee should be empowered both to bring the case to another jurisdiction and to press charges against the prosecutor for malfeasance of duty.

In providing opportunities for old people to actively participate in matters affecting their own welfare, they also should be encouraged to form their own pressure groups. These would be groups composed of old people, who, in order to make their needs known and to secure redress of wrongs, would march, strike, demonstrate, publicize, and make use of all tactics we have come to accept as legitimate. As with the Gray Panthers of Philadelphia, their goal should be to force change in the system, instead of trying to adjust old people to the system. Funds, perhaps on a matching basis between the government and private sources, should be made available for old people who want to organize groups for advocating and working toward social change. This funding would also be administered by old people.

Among the many areas of social life toward which organizations can direct their energies are "media watches," such as the ones the Gray Panthers are trying to develop. When prejudicing stereotypes of old people are presented in the mass media, they can protest and pressure the media to drop them. Just as we no longer (or seldom) tolerate on our mass media ethnic jokes, skits, and characters that degrade people on the basis of race or ethnicity, so we should no longer tolerate degrading stereotypes of the old. Such organizations can be extremely effective in sensitizing people to age propaganda.

Because primary groups are the most significant groups to which we are exposed in life, and, indeed, our continued well-being ordinarily depends on our maintaining good relationships with them, we should develop programs that encourage younger people to maintain their ties with the old. One effective step in this direction would be to provide subsidies for families that do maintain such ties with old people and that provide places for them to live in their homes. Living with a family, whether or not the old person is related to the family, should always be at the discretion of *both* the family and the old person. Such relationships are debilitating if they are forced on either, but when freely chosen, they can be self-actualizing for all.

There are some who think that the industrialization of a society is incompatible with maintaining respect for the aged and with several generations living in the same home. There is nothing inherent in industrialization that makes this incompatibility a necessity. Japan is a case in point (Erdman Palmore, "The Status and Integration of the Aged in Japanese Society," *Journal of Gerontology, 30,* March 1975, pp. 199–208). Although Japan is highly industrialized, with 98.5 percent of its population literate, 84 percent of its labor force in nonagricultural occupations, 68 percent of its population living in urban areas, and a per capita gross national product about the same as Great Britain, old people are highly integrated into the family, the work force, and the community. Where the three generation household is rare in our industrialized society, this is the *typical* Japanese family. Over three-fourths of Japanese who are 65 and over live with their children, while only 5 percent of Japanese aged live alone.

What kind of "quality of life" do old people in Japan have? They ordinarily are not living with their families out of economic necessity, but out of mutual desire. Living together provides them companionship and mutual aid. The old perform valuable roles in the home—from taking care of younger children, preparing meals, doing the gardening, and helping with the laundry for the women, to taking care of children and helping with family businesses for men.

The old in Japan gradually change their roles, step by step retiring from a full work load and full authority to a routine of light tasks, advisory functions, and skilled handicrafts. The old are provided welfare centers with educational, recreational, and consultational services. They are also given annual health examinations, while housekeeping help is provided to those living alone. Their 1963 National Law for the Welfare of Elders reads as follows:

> The elders shall be *loved* and *respected* as those who have for many years contributed toward the development of society, and a *wholesome* and *peaceful* life shall be *guaranteed* to them. In accordance with their desire and ability, the elders shall be given opportunities to engage in suitable work or to participate in social activities. (Emphasis added.) (As quoted in Palmore)

If old people in our society are going to be able to live in human dignity, we must reconceptualize old age. It cannot be a category of worthlessness, but it must signify worthfulness. Old age as an experience common to large proportions of our people has just now arrived on the historical scene, and we have not yet sufficiently adapted to this change. We need to think of old age as another stage in the life cycle, a stage which is different from those that preceded it, and one which, like the earlier stages, has its own interests, goals, and appropriate self-images. We must develop adaptive techniques that maximize self-potential and human dignity. We must strike out and develop new cultural models and images of what being old is and means, a model that the young can admire, respect, and look forward to becoming a part of—and a model that the old can apply to themselves with pride, for it provides directions for a healthy, vigorous, fruitful, and self-satisfying life.

To this end, I have proposed OPERA and the specific suggestions for change delineated in this article. Such changes would not only improve social conditions for the aged, but would also make the United States a more humane society for us all.

Population and Resources

The social problems of American society are not separate entities, but are highly interrelated. Consequently, any division of our social problems is arbitrary, as each social problem is part of another social problem. Ecology is one such example. Ecology involves many interrelated issues such as pollution, energy, resources, population growth, the destruction of our life support system, national policies in urbanization, transportation, conservation, decisions made by Detroit, Washington, the government of India, and so forth. Where and how to divide the interrelated aspects of just this one social problem is in itself problematic and arbitrary. In this instance, problems concerning population and resources are the focus of this section, while analyses of ecology and pollution have been placed in the next section. The section following ecology and pollution will then focus on the crisis of energy, another part of this complexly interrelated social problem. These issues could logically have been grouped together, as could the earlier sections on sexism, racism, and ageism that deal with discrimination against people on the basis of their membership in sociobiological categories.

In the first selection dealing with population and resources, Lyle says that we are in the midst of a population explosion such as the world has never before seen. Hunger haunts the world's population, and many areas of the world suffer from a lack of space. Will the result be that the world's population will continue to grow without planning, only to be ultimately decimated by famine, disease, or warfare? Or will rigorous action be taken in order to level off population growth and maintain some reasonable level? Current population increases around the world are anything but encouraging, and some experts are convinced that humanity is rapidly treading a precipitous path by which it will breed itself into oblivion.

Although the United States is far from being overpopulated, and has even approached Zero Population Growth in recent years, we are not isolated from problems due to population increases. The globe has become an interrelated socio-political unit, with events in one part having repercussions in others. With precipitous international relationships, the burgeoning population increases around the world carry direct consequences for our own welfare.

In the second selection, Lekachman indicates that there are both pessimists and optimists concerning the population-resource problem. The pessimists are people, like Lyle, who see population increasing unchecked, natural resources being exhausted, and the technological means utilized to cope with resource problems bringing disastrous side effects for humanity. The optimists are those who see viable solutions being proposed and adopted, with the future bringing either expanded resources to meet population growth or population growth being curtailed and brought in line with available resources.

Lekachman provides an historical background for understanding the concept of zero growth. From the background he provides on Mill and Malthus, we see that concerns with population growth, food production, and quality of life are not simply recent issues. Awareness of the problem has existed for a century and a half or so. Technological developments in food production and a declining birth rate in the industrialized nations have staved off the impasse—but many now feel that the day of reckoning is near. Zero growth can alter this impasse, Lekachman proposes—not only zero population growth, but also zero industrial growth. Lekachman sees such a stabilized world as being necessary for human survival, but he expresses pessimism concerning the cost that such a social order would necessitate in terms of quality of life.

What sort of life will we experience in the future? Will it be some utopian dream come true due to technological advances that are applied for the benefit of all? Such a future is certainly a possibility, given the technological expertise of this historical period. But such a future appears highly unlikely, given the current ordering of priorities devoted to the maintenance of the wealthy and powerful in their positions of power and wealth. Such a utopian future would necessitate the wholesale reordering of priorities, and the possibility of such a reordering appears dim indeed. We appear, rather, to be continuing on a course that leads to greater control of the masses by the minority in positions of dominance. Given our technological capacity for social control, especially that provided by our electronics revolution, the possibility of almost complete social control over the masses is dawning —presenting a picture of an Orwellian world from which few shall escape. If this be our future, population problems shall no longer confront us, as birth shall have become a privilege that is licensed by those in control. Stability in such a future will indeed be given society, but the cost will be the ushering in of *1984*.

The third and final article in this section deals with a developing technological breakthrough that poses a solution to the population problem. The subject of this concluding article is cloning, a topic of which few persons are aware, but one with which we should become familiar because of the serious consequences it holds for radically altering our lives. Cloning is asexual human reproduction. Rorvik indicates that with recent startling advances in biology, we may soon be able to reproduce, without sexual relations, any *particular* living individual whom we desire in *any quantities* that we wish. With cloning, each offspring is literally a *reproduction*, being the identical twin of the "father."

If cloning is perfected, the ramifications for social change are almost unthinkable. This one technological development, if matched with social control mechanisms, might bring the end of social life as we know it. Cloning holds forth the possibility of such pervasive control over population as even Aldous Huxley did not conceive in his *Brave New World*. Cloning could, for example, radically alter our family structure; by being coupled with mandatory sterilization, political leaders easily could fall heir to the complete responsibility for human reproduction. What implications this would have for humanity! As a possible example, the control over reproducing human life might pass to a nameless, faceless regulatory agency.

With the problems posed by burgeoning populations and limited resources, and with technological controls in the hands of the powerful, no one can say with certainty what the world of the future will be. But if we do not take steps at rational planning now, it may be too late to later take such steps. At some point, the problem will have mushroomed beyond human scope—if it has not already done so.

16

David Lyle

The Human Race Has, Maybe, Thirty-Five Years Left

In the seventh century, according to the records of the Church of Mayo, two kings of Erin summoned the principal clergy and laity to a council at Temora, in consequence of a general dearth, the land not being sufficient to support the increasing population. The chiefs . . . decreed that a fast should be observed both by clergy and laity so that they might with one accord solicit God to prayer to remove by some species of pestilence the burthensome multitudes of the inferior people. . . . St. Gerald and his associates suggested that it would be more conformable to the Divine Nature and not more difficult to multiply the fruits of the earth than to destroy its inhabitants. An amendment was accordingly moved "to supplicate the Almighty not to reduce the number of men till it answered the quantity of corn usually produced, but to increase the produce of the land so that it might satisfy the wants of the people." However, the nobles and clergy, headed by St. Fechin, bore down the opposition and called for a pestilence on the lower orders of the people. According to the records a pestilence was given, which included in its ravages the authors of the petition, the two kings who had summoned the convention, with St. Fechin, the King of Ulster and Munster and a third of the nobles concerned. . . .

A Treatise on Plague, by W. J. Simpson

In a year of poor harvest, the weight of the burthensome multitudes lies heavy upon the shoulders of the affluent. My grandfather had a book that his father gave him, presented upon his reaching young manhood; and whether it was given with a kind word or a black look, I can't say, but the title was *Where to Emigrate and Why*. My grandfather headed

West—this at a time when emigration remained plausible for young men found to be surplus upon the home ground.

Today the crowd is global. There is no place to go. There has never been such a crowd, and in no time at all now, it's going to be twice as big. As for man's efforts to cope, the performance of St. Fechin suggests a certain lack of promise. Perhaps the mildest we can hope for is the suggestion of a prominent anthropologist that birth-control agents be applied liberally to the public water supply.

The case is this: Fifteen thousand years ago the earth probably held fewer people than New York City does today. The population doubled slowly at that time—say every forty thousand years. Today there are more than three billion people in the world and the rate of increase is almost a thousand times greater. Doubling occurs in less than forty years.

On a graph the human population line now rises almost vertically, which will not continue—there must be leveling off or decline. Leveling seems rational. Decline can be a landslide, as the history of the Irish and the lemming imply. The critical period near a population peak is likely to be a time of anxiety, of extreme unease. Thus President Johnson told the troops in Korea last year: "Don't forget, there are only two hundred million of us in the world of three billion. They want what we've got and we aren't going to give it to them." (Quoted by John Gerassi, in *The New York Review of Books*.)

In the United States a huge majority sees population as infinitely less threatening than crime and communism. Population crisis in America tends to become a cliché—a joke in the newspapers about standing room only in the year 2600. After which the matter may be dismissed— possibly it's something the Chinese are up to.

A few—the ecologically-minded, some Senators and scientists and academicians—cry out that growth and change are tearing the world apart. But on television the audience cheers a father of ten; and in Washington the political leadership continues heavily occupied in the shadows, scuffling with crime and communism, hustling money for defense and space and the war, and plotting ways to insure more growth and change.

Population increase and technological change are immense forces driving the world ahead at an accelerating pace into a turbulent and highly uncertain future. The effect of these forces upon the United States is already profound; no Island of Affluence or Fortress America notions are likely for long to fend off the future, or to make a particle of difference in the logic of vertical increase.

To grasp the implications, look first at the world that remains poor, then at the changes wrought in man and animal by extreme crowding, and finally at the consequences in the U.S.

Begin with India.

I: THE CITY OF THE FUTURE

> *At Sealdah Station, Calcutta, misery radiates outward . . . dusty*
> *streets straggle away in every direction lined with tiny shacks built*
> *of metal scraps, pieces of old baskets, strips of wood, and gunny-*
> *sacks. In the dark interiors of the shacks, small fires glow through*
> *the smoke, and dark faces gaze out at children playing in the*
> *urinous-smelling, fly-infested streets. In a few years the children*
> *who survive . . . will grow taller and thinner and stand in the streets*
> *like ragged skeletons, barefoot, hollow-eyed, blinking their apathetic*
> *stares out of grey, dusty faces . . . Calcutta today . . . swollen by*
> *millions of refugees until the streets are spotted with their sleeping*
> *bodies . . . may very well represent the City of the Future.*
> Philip Appleman, in The Silent Explosion

In Calcutta, six hundred thousand people sleep, eat, live in the streets—lacking even the shacks Appleman saw at Sealdah Station. The American visitor sees these thousands lying upon the ground "like little bundles of rags"; sees "women huddling over little piles of manure, patting it into cakes for fuel; children competing with dogs for refuse" —and reacts with shock and revulsion. A student told Appleman, "I wanted to run away, to weep. I was disgusted, horrified, saddened. . . ."

Calcutta stands for three worldwide forces—burgeoning population; food shortage; a torrent of migration to the cities.

Today there are about five hundred million people in India. In thirty years or so there may well be one billion. Most Indians live in rural villages—but the villages are overflowing. The surrounding lands no longer produce enough food. The excess population drifts into the big coastal cities where there is hope for food; Calcutta has become an immense breadline where the starving from the countryside gather to feed on grain from American ships.

The vision of six hundred thousand people lying in the streets at night—a prostrate breadline waiting for Midwestern grain—must be burned into the mind if the fate of the third world (and of the United States) is to assume reality. Because as the population rises, the supply of grain is running out. This is true not only for India but for two-thirds of the human population. All over the third world the City of the Future is a place where the rural poor gather to await the grain handout from abroad, while it lasts.

From Calcutta, draw the implications for the third (so-called "underdeveloped") world—briefly, as follows:

- The 1960 population of the developed world was about 900,000,000; that of the third world ran over 2,000,000,000.

- The agricultural land resources of the two parts of the world are approximately equal.
- By the year 2000—in less than thirty-three years—the developed world must feed 1,300,000,000 on its half of the world's croplands. The third world will have to feed about 5,000,000,000 people on its half.
- The industrial states have moved on to high-yield agriculture, getting maximum production from the land. The third world must make the same transition but there very well may not be time to make it before mass famine sets in.

The bind is this: There is a desperate need to cut population growth and to raise food production within the next three decades. The most urgent period will be the ten or fifteen years immediately ahead. All right, then, say the hopeful—birth control; but Dora Du Bois, an anthropologist with much experience in India, reports that ". . . any effective reduction of population growth among heavily breeding rural populations is not foreseeable in less than possibly fifty years. I believe this is a question on which it is wise to have no illusions."

Nor is the prospect for rapid increase in food supply much brighter. On the contrary, according to Lester R. Brown, an economist with the U.S. Department of Agriculture: "The food problem emerging in the less-developed regions may be one of the most nearly insoluble problems facing man over the next few decades."

There are, nevertheless, a few optimists. Some talk of farming the sea, eating plankton; but this will not help anyone soon. Anyway, says William Vogt, who is experienced, "Few of the people who advocate this, I am sure, have tasted plankton. . . ."

Recently, an optimist of some renown appeared—Donald J. Bogue, a sociologist at the University of Chicago. He said the United Nations' projections of about six billion people by the year 2000 are exaggerated; Dr. Bogue predicted a rapid decline in growth after 1975. The immediate reaction of his colleagues was disappointing. Dr. Bogue said, "Most were angry. I found no one who agreed with me."

Perhaps the most disturbing thing about the present world-population situation, as Dr. Bogue himself suggested, is the almost uniformly pessimistic outlook of so many very capable people who have examined the matter closely. Lloyd V. Berkner, a leading American scientist, remarked that in the third world, "We are probably already beyond the point at which a sensible solution is possible." Eugene R. Black, when he was president of the World Bank, said, "We are coming to a situation in which the optimist will be the man who thinks that present living standards can be maintained."

Dr. B. R. Sen, Director-General of the United Nations Food and Agriculture Organization, has said, "The next thirty-five years . . . will be a most critical period in man's history. Either we take the fullest measures to raise productivity and to stabilize population growth, or we will face disaster of an unprecedented magnitude. We must be warned . . . of unlimited disaster."

In Pakistan, President Ayub said in 1964, "In ten years' time, human beings will eat human beings in Pakistan."

The third world, then, is in acute danger of entering into a descending spiral where each successive failure reinforces the last in a descent toward chaos. The process may have begun. There is a tendency in the U.S. to believe it will be possible to isolate ourselves from this, retreat into the land of affluence. For a while perhaps.

Consider this: As of 1954 the United States was using about fifty percent of the raw material resources consumed in the world each year. The rate of consumption has been rising and by 1980 the U.S. could be consuming more than eighty-three percent of the total.

Today the U.S. is a net importer of goods. Its reliance on foreign trade grows each year. The third world, in the meantime, sees industrialization as the road to salvation; its demand for raw material can be expected to accelerate. Today we can soothe the hungry by offering a certain amount of food and aid. Tomorrow we will be competing for raw material and there will be no spare food to offer.

The prospect is not bright. As Professor Harold A. Thomas, Jr. of Harvard's Center for Population Studies put it, ". . . unless we engage ourselves today in problems of development of the poor nations, the conditions under which we live during the next two generations may not be attractive. The fuel required to sustain our mammoth technological apparatus may constitute a gross drain on the resources of the earth. Other societies cannot be expected to regard this favorably. A vista of an enclave of privilege in an isolated West is not pleasant to contemplate. Wise and human political institutions do not thrive in beleaguered citadels."

II: THE MOUSE EXPLOSION

Mice were generated and "boiled over" the towns and fields in the midst of that region, and there was a confusion of great death in the land.

Vulgate 1, Kings, v. 6

The periodic, vast increase in numbers of field mice is a peculiar and ancient phenomenon, and men have long feared it. In the cult of Apollo this fear gave rise to religious ceremonies—the keepers of Apollo's temple kept tame mice in the sanctuary and a colony of them beneath the altar.

Aristotle was astounded by the capacity of mice to increase. "The rate of propagation of field mice in country places, and the destruction that they cause, are beyond all telling. In many places their number is so incalculable that but very little of the corn crop is left to the farmer; and so rapid is their mode of proceeding that sometimes a small farmer will one day observe that it is time for reaping, and on the following morning, when he takes his reapers afield, he finds his entire crop devoured. Their disappearance is unaccountable: in a few days not a mouse will be there to be seen. . . ."

The mouse horde has for centuries represented a serious problem in Europe. Charles Elton, the director of the Bureau of Animal Population at Oxford, has described one historic outbreak in France: ". . . an impressive picture of insurgent subterranean activity, of devastation breaking like a flood upon the crops. All man's vigilance and care are taxed by the multitude of small, swift, flitting forms that infest the ground and devour all living plants. Poison, plowing, fumigation, trenches, and prayers, all these can scarcely stop the destruction. . . . In [1822] Alsace was absolutely in the power of mice. 'It was a living and hideous scourging of the earth, which appeared perforated all over, like a sieve.' "

The animal responsible for this devastation is normally quite inconspicuous—a tiny creature, short-legged, short-tailed, broad of face—known commonly as the meadow mouse, or vole. The vole rarely travels more than twenty-five feet from its burrow. It lives less than a year. But during its short life it is absolutely voracious. Each day it consumes its own weight in food. First it takes care of the plants above ground; then it burrows down after roots and tubers. In an orchard, voles may girdle and kill trees.

The vole population follows a typical four-year cycle of rise and fall, proceeding from relative scarcity to a peak of abundance, then declining and beginning the cycle all over again. The remarkable thing about voles is their capacity under certain circumstances to increase to enormous numbers within a single breeding season. On occasion—in Europe this occurs perhaps once in a generation—there is an increase of truly catastrophic proportions, a "scourging of the earth," as in Alsace in 1822.

There have been a good many locally catastrophic mouse population explosions in the United States, the most severe in the far West. Perhaps the most devastating of all was centered in Oregon just a few years ago, and the damage to crops ran into millions of dollars. Wells were polluted because of the numbers of voles that fell into them. In the most heavily infested areas there were two or three thousand mice to the acre and their burrows crisscrossed the ground like a lace network. One man counted twenty-eight thousand burrow entrances in an area a little over two hundred feet square.

The end of a mouse outbreak is always abrupt. At the peak, food begins to run short and crowding leads to tension and fighting. It is as though a tremor of anxiety had begun to run through the whole population—tension, food shortage, the stress of crowding (with demonstrable physical effects), disease, fighting, cannibalism—all these appear and lead into the descending spiral, a rapid decline that ends in mass die-off. Toward the end, predatory birds gather in spectacular numbers to feed on the mouse horde. Only then does the earth begin to recover.

The vole cycle gives a broad picture of population dynamics, of catastrophic increase in numbers. In recent years, studies done by John B. Calhoun have shown in great detail just what happens to social behavior under such circumstances. Dr. Calhoun worked with rats in captivity, and he found that under extreme crowding startling behavioral changes occurred. Among male rats these changes ranged from "sexual deviation to cannibalism and from frenetic overactivity to a pathological withdrawal." Among female rats the number of miscarriages increased, nest-building ability deteriorated, and so did the ability to care for the young.

The female rats built no nests at all under extreme crowding, but bore their young on the floor of the pen where the young rats were easily scattered and few survived. Females lost the ability to transport the young. En route somewhere a female would set a young rat down and then, distracted, wander off and forget it. The scattered young were seldom nursed, finally were left to die.

Dr. Calhoun developed a term for the social deterioration occurring under extreme crowding; he called it the "behavioral sink."

III: CANDELARIA

India gets the publicity; but Latin America is the fastest-growing region of the world and one of the most unstable. The shock of population growth there can be incredible. By one estimate there are a million deaths a year from starvation and malnutrition. A Notre Dame sociologist, Professor Donald N. Barrett, describes a slum where "two or three children [are] dying per week because of the ravenous dogs." Today the populations of Latin America and North America are not far apart; by the end of this century Latin America could easily have as many people as China today—750,000,000, dwarfing the U.S.

The population of India doubles every thirty-one years; in Colombia it doubles in twenty-three years and there are rural areas doubling in sixteen. In a brief space, it is probably impossible really to convey what this means. A Colombian doctor who has been in the midst of it has said the implications are "almost beyond comprehension." To see, even to a small extent, what this means, look at the village of Candelaria and what Dr. Alfredo Aguirre found there—as he reported it to *The Population Council.*

Candelaria is semi-rural—a village where, quite literally, people are multiplying at such a rate in relation to resources that almost everything has broken down. Big families are crammed into tiny rooms in flimsy shacks; there isn't enough food; what food there is goes mainly to the father because he must work in the nearby cane fields or sugar mills. The children go hungry and, as Dr. Aguirre put it, "undernourishment means early death for many of the children, and if death fails to intervene . . . [there will be] delay in walking, retardation in speech development, difficulties in relating to other people . . . a diminished capacity to adapt."

The adolescent in this world "may exhibit antisocial tendencies [and] ultimately abandons school without having developed any skills. Finally he joins the mass of unemployed . . . tends to flout authority . . . cannot adapt to a social system that involves laws and mores of which he is unaware because nobody has ever taught him, and that apparently deny to him and his family the right of survival." This is the analytical language of social science; behind it is the reality of Colombia: a country on the edge of revolution, with guerrilla bands in the mountains, disaffection in the cities, extremes of poverty and affluence, and one of the highest homicide rates in the world.

The typical young girl in Candelaria has a child or two in her teens. She is unmarried, illiterate or semiliterate, has no way to support the children. She has, Dr. Aguirre says, two options:

"One is to seek a more or less stable marital relationship, not just out of sexual instinct but from economic necessity, although this means sacrificing her own freedom, since in this type of relationship it is the man who decides how long it shall last, who distributes the family income according to his own convenience (other women, alcoholic beverages, etc.), and who determines the number of children to be conceived.

"The other solution to the mother's problems is the death of the child ('masked infanticide') in which children between six months and four years of age are often allowed to die when attacked by any disease. . . . We have even seen mothers who objected to their children being treated and [who] were upset when curative measures were successful. No less rarely, such children are abandoned in the hospital. . . . A frequent indication of 'masked infanticide' is apparent when a mother or a couple of very limited means approaches the physician for a 'death certificate' for their child without any emotion or anguish. . . ."

Candelaria is the human equivalent of Calhoun's behavioral sink.

IV: REUNION AND TIKOPIA

Reunion is an island in the Indian Ocean: *"The accounts of the first visitors* [sixteenth century] *are a description of Eden."*

The French geographer Pierre Gourou has described what happened thereafter. First, European settlers set up coffee and sugar plantations on the island and ran them with slave labor. (Islands were favored; the slaves couldn't run off.) By 1848 there were 61,000 slaves and 45,000 free, and in that year the slaves were freed. The planters were unwilling to change their approach—that is, to pay and otherwise treat the blacks as free men. So the ex-slaves tended to move up onto the island's steep interior slopes, where they practiced subsistence farming on small plots. The big planters imported Indian labor to work the plantations. The smaller planters found they could no longer compete. They were forced to abandon their plantations; they moved up onto the slopes with the freed slaves.

Through World War II, the population grew with fair speed and regularity. The island changed—plants and animals native to it were exterminated. Cultivation of the steep slopes caused heavy erosion, threatening the future of the subsistence farmers. And in the course of a century, the quality of the lives of those small planters driven onto the slopes with the former slaves had changed remarkably. "Their ancestors, three to four generations before, had stone houses and fireplaces, and spun and wove wool; but these people live in plank or leaf houses, have no fireplaces, and shiver in their thin cotton clothes."

After World War II modern medicine and sanitation brought a quick drop in the death rate, and the population began shooting upward. There were 310,000 inhabitants in 1957; there may well be 620,000 by 1980. There is no place for the overflow; unemployment is swelling. The situation, as Gourou says, "is really alarming."

Tikopia is an island in the Pacific where the "primitive" people in residence learned to regulate their own numbers by, as Raymond Firth put it, "restraint on the part of the male." The Tikopian recognized that their environment was limited, that the island could support only so many people. They acted accordingly, with a remarkably clear vision of the consequences if they should fail. An islander told Firth, "Families by Tikopia custom are made corresponding to orchards in the woods. If children are produced in plenty, then they go and steal because their orchards are few. So families in our land are not made large in truth; they are made small. If the family groups are large, they go and steal, they eat from the orchards, and if this goes on they kill each other."

It may be that the Tikopia were rare among human societies in their acute awareness of cause and effect. But the point is that they did have ways of limiting their numbers, and used them, as have many other premodern peoples. And in this they were typical of animals generally.

All animals produce more young than necessary to maintain their numbers. So if a species is to stay within the limits of its food supply, some check on numbers is essential. Such checks are quite common—predators, disease, the maintenance of territory or of hierarchies or peck orders, etc. The ultimate check of famine operates on a large scale rather rarely, because the other checks have kept population within limits of the food supply.

But all this assumes an undisturbed environment and a complex one. In a disturbed environment peculiar things begin to happen. For example, where man disturbs the plant environment through cultivation, weeds proliferate as they would not ordinarily in the wild. Where man cultivates a single crop over wide acreage, destructive insect populations like the boll weevil multiply as they would not normally in a natural environment. Great mouse plagues occur where man sets up ideal conditions for them. This suggests something about the difference between Reunion and Tikopia.

In Tikopia, over many generations men have learned to live within the limitations of their world. Every man is in close touch with the essentials of life—with food, water, shelter, education of the young. Every man is aware of outer limits. To put it in computer jargon, there is a daily feedback which tells a man what his situation is, and there is an ancient pattern of tradition which tells him how then to carry on.

Reunion is a disturbed environment, and in this it is typical of most of the modern world. Reunion is peopled with uprooted Europeans, uprooted Africans, uprooted Indians, people for whom all the old patterns and traditions have been smashed by a galaxy of new forces. In the shock of change all the old ways of dealing with the world are forgotten. Or they don't work anymore. Or they are illegal. The uprooted man is at first baffled and disorganized because nothing works anymore. Then, increasingly, he is bitter. The old self-regulating feedback systems will not be restored in a day; if they are restored at all, it will take generations.

In the meantime almost everyone on earth is out of touch with the essentials, with the clear view of outer limits possessed by the Tikopian. Nowhere is the evidence of shattered patterns, of drift away from the awareness of essentials, more apparent today than in the United States.

V: THE AMERICAN ENVIRONMENT

The U.S. birthrate has been declining since 1957. Even if this decline continues, population will grow at an accelerating pace for some decades to come. There were 100,000,000 Americans about fifty years ago. There are 200,000,000, now; there will be 300,000,000 by 2000, assuming the continued *decline* in the birthrate; and there could well be 400,000,000 by 2015 or 2020. Note that each time the population increases by 100,000,000, it takes far less time than it took to add the previous 100,000,000. This is one aspect of acceleration, and today acceleration touches everything.

Today, according to one student of American society, "It takes only a year or two for the exaggerations to come true. Nothing will remain in the next ten years. Or there will be twice as much of it." (Warren G. Bennis, in *Technology Review.*)

To Americans, growth has always been a "good"—growth stocks, the Soaring Sixties, the Baby Boom, the Biggest Little City in the West, etc. India has a population crisis; the U.S. has "growth," the booster philosophy, "Dig We Must for a Growing New York." The dismal side of all this is becoming only too apparent today: in the birth of the city that never ends; in the difficulty of getting anywhere within that city, or of getting out of it, or of finding (once out of it) any place worth getting to that isn't already overrun with other escapees; in the air and water pollution; in the difficulty of finding a doctor; in the evolution of the Kafkaesque bureaucracy, corporate and governmental.

All this is rather well-known. Some aspects of the situation are less well-known. For example:

1. Water. A recent writer in *Science* said, "A permanent water shortage affecting our standard of living will occur before the year 2,000." This, of course, has all kinds of ramifications. Consider just one. In the Western states forty percent of all agriculture (and much allied enterprise) depends on irrigation. Much of this may have to be abandoned. Gerald W. Thomas, the Dean of Agriculture at Texas Technological College, writes that some of this agriculture "may have to be shifted back to the more humid zones in the next fifty years." This is likely to mean higher costs to consumers. And of course the more humid Eastern zones are precisely the ones now urbanizing most rapidly.

2. Urbanization. We are spreading out over the landscape at a phenomenal rate. Highways now cover with concrete an area the size of Massachusetts, Connecticut, Vermont, Rhode Island and Delaware. William Vogt has recorded the fact that the National Golf Foundation desires to cover an area the size of New Hampshire and Rhode Island with new golf courses. In downtown Los Angeles sixty-six percent of the land is taken up by parking lots or streets; in the whole Los Angeles area one-third of the land is paved. The trend is toward the creation of Los Angeles everywhere. We are developing urban complexes so vast that one can travel a hundred and more miles before reaching open country. The leapfrogging, haphazard pattern of development hastens the process of spread; in California, housing that need have covered only twenty-six square miles actually knocked out two hundred square miles of farmland.

3. Mobility. Automobiles are multiplying three times faster than people and five times faster than roads necessary to accommodate them. Freeways are obsolete before completion. If all our registered vehicles were laid end to end, the line would begin to approach in length the total mileage of city streets in the United States. Which suggests why Boston had a traffic jam a few years ago—no special cause—that froze the entire downtown area for five hours. Or why a single New Jersey jam lasted seven hours and tied up a million and a half vehicles. Senator Claiborne Pell of Rhode Island, who put all these facts in a book called *Megalopolis Unbound*, believes that the search for perfect mobility is leading to total immobility.

4. Farmlands. The spread of the cities takes at least a million and a half acres of open land every year, fifty percent more than a decade ago. The popular outcry has been minor; after all we have had huge crop surpluses. But now there is some concern. Maurice L. Peterson, Dean of Agriculture for the University of California, has said that "urbanization of prime farmland is one of the most serious problems facing us in agriculture. The population is increasing at a far more rapid rate than our ability to produce food, and farmers are being forced up into the hills, where it costs more to produce." California produces twenty-five percent of the nation's table food, forty-three percent of fresh vegetables, forty-two percent of nut and fruit crops. By conservative estimate, half of California's prime cropland will go to housing and industry in the next thirty-three years; pessimists believe it will be eighty percent.

The U.S. seems unlikely to have a food problem soon; it has enormous capabilities in food production. This capability has a price, however, as two of our ecologists, William Vogt and Raymond F. Dasmann, have made quite clear. American rivers run brown because they are full of earth washed from the fields bordering them. Twenty years ago, Dr. Vogt wrote: "American civilization, founded on nine inches of topsoil, has now lost one third of this soil; Part of the Sahara and much of the barren wasteland of the Middle East is, to a large extent, man-made desert. In the dust-bowl regions of the American Southwest, Dr. Dasmann has said, "What the Bedouin took centuries to achieve, we have almost equaled in decades."

5. The economics of change. The biggest public-works project in history, according to President Eisenhower, was the $41,000,000,000 public highway project undertaken during his Administration. (When the American people voted for it through their Congress, said Lewis Mumford, "the most charitable thing to assume . . . is that they hadn't the faintest notion of what they were doing.") But the requirements just ahead make the highway program look like a county supervisors' boondoggle. A Congressional committee recently put the cost of providing clean water at $100,000,000,000. The effort to do something about air pollution is likely to cost at least as much in the next thirty years. Sen-

ator Ribicoff says city rehabilitation will require $1,000,000,000,000. A housing expert sees the need for $100,000,000,000 (a popular figure) in Federal housing aid. The population of the country will double in fifty years. This means—if the living standard is to be maintained or improved—something close to a doubling of facilities, public and private. Will we, then, duplicate in fifty years, and pay for, what has taken much of the nation's history to produce? Or will we balk at the effort and the cost, and suffer a gradual decline in the quality of our lives? The evidence is powerful—in failed school bond issues, deteriorating environment, overburdened public facilities—that we are balking already. Eugene Black's description of the optimist as a man who believes living standards can be maintained takes on new life.

6. Pollution. Everybody knows something about air and water pollution today. But there are exotic effects which remain less well known:

a. Pesticides are essential to high-yield agriculture as now practiced in the U.S. Pesticides wash from field to river to sea, where they are concentrated by diatoms. I quote now from Lloyd V. Berkner, who is studying the phenomenon in detail. "Now the point is this: Our supply of atmospheric oxygen comes largely from these diatoms—they replenish all of the atmospheric oxygen every two thousand years as it is used up. But if our pesticides should be reducing the supply of diatoms or forcing evolution of less productive mutants, we might find ourselves running out of atmospheric oxygen."

b. Agricultural fertilizers are another essential of high-yield agriculture, as now practiced. They are used in ever-greater quantities each year. Nitrates from these fertilizers are getting into water supplies both in the U.S. and Europe. At a certain level of concentration, the water becomes toxic. At least one town, Garden Grove, California, has had to shut down some of the wells providing its public water supply because of nitrate contamination. Other towns scattered around the nation have begun to discover similar problems. In Minnesota, during one three-year period, fourteen infant deaths were attributed to nitrates in well water.

c. Dr. Barry Commoner reported recently (in his book, *Science and Survival*) that the burning of fuels has caused the carbon-dioxide content of the earth's atmosphere to rise fourteen percent in the past century. This has produced a general warming effect on the atmosphere. The President's Science Advisory Committee concludes that this warming may begin melting the Antarctic ice cap by the year 2000 (raising sea levels four feet a decade and, of course, finally inundating huge land areas and major cities, like New York).

d. There is a call for nuclear power today to replace coal or oil-fired electric generating units and thus reduce air pollution. Frank M. Stead, when he was with the California Department of Public Health, concluded that in his state after 1980 "electrical power sources must be progressively replaced with nuclear sources if clean air is to be maintained."

A Congressional subcommittee headed by Representative Emilio Q. Daddario of Connecticut concerns itself specifically with science and the effects of technological change. The subcommittee reported recently: "There has been little progress in devising a way to get rid of the toxic by-products [of the nuclear power plant]. The best we can do with radio-active waste is what we first thought of—bury it. But someday that system will no longer be feasible. Then what? . . . At this point there is no convincing evidence that anyone really knows." Yet nuclear power plants are being planned or built countrywide.

The United States, of course, lacks a monopoly on nuclear power. In a recent book, *Inherit the Earth*, the zoologist N. J. Berrill finds that radio-active wastes from atomic-energy plants already constitute a world-wide problem—"country after country is already dumping them into the sea, to contaminate or poison whatever life there be. Our total inheritance seems to be at stake if no restraint appears."

e. More on California. Mr. Stead, the environmental health expert, has said: "It is clearly evident . . . that between now and 1980 the gasoline-powered engine must be phased out [in California] and replaced with an electrical power package. . . . The only realistic way . . . is to demand it by law." The forces working against this—considering many of our largest corporations are based on the auto industry—are vast.

The fundamental question here is this: To what extent today are we threatened by the very technology—and the institutions—we find essential to support a rapidly expanding population? The technology will not be abandoned. It is put to new uses every day, and with almost no thought of ultimate effects.

VI: THE CULTURAL SHOCK FRONT

The point should be clear—change occurs today at a fantastic pace in the U.S. and the pace is accelerating. We have no real idea where it all leads, any more than we know what to do with the hot waste from nuclear power plants. We rocket along, straight into the unknown, treasuring a Panglossian notion that somehow it will all work out for the best. This is true in the technological sense; equally so in the social sense.

For some the strain of contemporary life is already too great. Medicine links the stress ailments—heart disease, mental aberration, ulcers (which appear commonly in overcrowded animals)—to the tempo of modern life. Psychiatry recognizes an "automation syndrome" in which older workers, replaced by a machine, may break down, suffer amnesia or commit suicide. One sociologist predicts increasing alcoholism in the automated factory—this in a nation which now has one of the world's most substantial alcoholism problems.

In a sense today you can feel a tremor of anxiety through the whole society—feel it in the city riots, in the war, in the accelerating crime rate, in widespread unrest, unease, disaffection, tendency to drop out, turn on, drink up. You hear it in the cry for more police to "deal with the situation in the cities." You hear it in the shrillness of the extremist—the point being not what is said but the anxiety exhibited and the high decibel count. All this is directly related to population growth, to crowding, movement and swift social and technological change.

Sir Julian Huxley said the "stress effect of overcrowding and frustration . . . is undoubtedly operating on the inhabitants of any city with over a million inhabitants in the world today, and has, to my mind, very serious implications." (This idea was belittled at length recently in a rather strange article by Irving Kristol. My money remains on Sir Julian.)

Keeping in mind the stress effect, the pace of growth and change, consider this: Population will grow by at least fifty percent in the U.S. during the next thirty-three years, barring catastrophe. During the same period U.S. urban population will come close to doubling. Thus in the most congested areas the effects of simple population growth will be doubled by the effects of movement and migration. Urban areas in the U.S. will grow at about the same rate as the population of India. India today we consider to be in a state of population crisis—but in the U.S. the boosters are still in charge. When the population hit 170,000,000 in 1957, Secretary of Commerce Sinclair Weeks said, "I am happy to welcome this vast throng of new customers for America's goods and services. They help insure a rising standard of living. . . ." Four years later the population hit 185,000,000 and Secretary Luther Hodges led a round of cheers at the Commerce Department.

The effects of social and technological change, of growth and movement—these are already great in the United States and they will be compounded in the next thirty years. Some central cities will become highly unstable places, and what we now see in terms of crime, rioting and disaffection is just a preview. Today in the U.S. nearly everyone belongs to the class of the uprooted. The factory worker's daughter moves into the middle class; the commuter migrates daily to the city; the executive living in Louisville develops little concern for the affairs of his town because next year the company will shift him to Des Moines; the rural family migrates to the city and disintegrates; the more affluent flee the city for the suburbs; Easterners go West. Everyone, everything is in motion—as never before, anywhere.

The newspapers are filled with stories of turmoil in the world; factories harbor a new technology that is in the process of antiquating the skills of millions of workers; schools prepare the young for a world, and for jobs, that no longer exist; the accumulation of knowledge is so swift that "a major problem in research is to find out what has been done by others so as to avoid rediscovering the same information." Our institutions were formed for—and mentally and emotionally our political and other leaders exist in—a world that has ceased to be.

> "I think," said the biophysicist John R. Platt, "we may be now in the time of most rapid change in the whole evolution of the human race, either past or to come. It is a kind of cultural 'shock front,' like the shock fronts that occur in aerodynamics when the leading edge of an airplane wing moves faster than the speed of sound and generates the sharp pressure wave that causes the . . . sonic boom."

Look at what's coming. The first industrial revolution replaced the pick-and-shovel man. Skilled scientists and administrators may survive the second (cybernetic) revolution, as Norbert Wiener said, but "taking the second revolution as accomplished, the average man of mediocre attainments or less has nothing to sell that is worth anyone's money to buy." In other words, the computer today functions at the high-school graduate level. High-school graduates are becoming industrially superfluous: so is the middle-management echelon.

Automation creates some jobs, of course—there is a demand today for more skilled and educated workers. So it's essential to upgrade education, make everyone skilled. Yet there is evidence that American schools have declined steadily in quality for years now. Considering the pace at which the school system has grown, this will hardly come as a stunning surprise. In a sample study made during an eighteen-month period twenty-five percent of the men who took the Selective Service test failed the mental part of it. There are more than fifty million people in the country who failed to make it through high school, and sometime ago the Labor Department estimated that thirty percent of students might be high-school drop-outs in the 1960's. Whatever the demand for skills may be or may become, we are turning out masses of young who will be unable to cope in a cybernated world.

It becomes essential, then, to "improve the schools." But the rigidity of the educational bureaucracy is legendary. It would be difficult to change the direction of this bureaucracy in any circumstances. It will inevitably be far harder at a time when the attention of that bureaucracy is focused primarily on problems of growth and change—as it must be for the next thirty years at least.

As recently as 1963, thirty-six percent of all vocational education funds went to what must be the single most rapidly declining major area of employment in the nation—agriculture. An investment, that is, in training for non-jobs. Much of the rest of the vocational-education money went into home economics. All of which says something profound about the relevance of our education efforts, about the intellects in charge, and the capacity for change.

Today the United States has the highest rate of unemployment as well as the highest rate of public dependency and population growth of any modern industrial state. From here on, according to Philip M. Hauser, former chief of the Bureau of the Census, population growth will "worsen the U.S. employment problem, greatly increase the magnitude of juvenile delinquency, exacerbate already dangerous race tensions, inundate the secondary schools and colleges . . . augment urban congestion and further subvert the traditional American Government system."

There are between thirty and forty million people living below the poverty level in the U.S. today. The rural Negro's movement to the city and the middle-class flight to the suburbs is reaching a crescendo. In Washington ninety percent of the schoolchildren are Negro, in Manhattan seventy-five percent are Negro or Puerto Rican—indicating the future city population. In the cities Negro unemployment averages about ten percent—there are areas where it runs much higher, up to twenty-five percent or more. Nor is this likely to be the peak. Commissioner of Labor Statistics Arthur M. Ross of the U.S. Department of Labor has said Negro unemployment could be running three or four times higher within eight years if present trends continue.

This could mean unemployment rates of thirty or forty percent and up for the city Negro. The industries that might hire them are moving to the suburbs. In Chicago in recent years seventy-seven percent of new plants have located outside the main metropolitan area; in Los Angeles eighty-five percent. The newspapers lately have been full of the exodus from New York—the black man reaches the promised land, and the white man packs it up and takes it to Westchester.

The prospect ahead for the thirty-odd million of poor is more poverty, or the dole, or some form of Federal work project, perhaps all three; and it seems highly likely that even all three will provide no real solution. The crowd, or the mob, seems likely to reappear as a force in politics. Watts was a prelude.

The cultural shock front is an area of extreme turbulence, of buffeting, of exotic and swift currents. The question is whether the society we've known in the U.S. will survive passage through it.

VII: TRANSFORMATION

Dr. Platt is one of a group of people who sees the present as a critical period of transition. A brief composite of the group's view might go like this:

For most of his two million years, man has operated in a fairly stable—slow to change—world. Stone Age. From generation to generation there was almost no social or technological change. There was no gap between generations; father was like son was like grandson; they shared the same world, the same outlook. And every man was in touch with the essentials.

All this began to change with the advent of agriculture about 10,000 years ago. Food surpluses appeared. A few people, then, had time to do something other than hunt and cultivate. The efforts of the few led to civilization and to the accumulation of new knowledge. Knowledge brought innovation, changes in the accumulated human pattern of two million years. The more knowledge accumulated, the more innovation there was, until the process of change accelerated into the dizzy pattern of the present.

Dr. Platt sees the period of accelerating change—civilization—as transitional, the step between the old stability of the Stone Age and some new stability that may last equally long. Either we reach this new stability or, you might say, the whole thing goes belly-up. Because the pace of change can't accelerate indefinitely.

The present is probably the critical period in the transition. Dr. B. R. Sen, you remember, saw the next thirty-five years as decisive in terms of food. A sharp decline in population growth must come soon, or the likelihood is reduction through famine, war and disease. Aside from the population imbalance, the other major obstacle of the transition period is the danger of nuclear war.

Dr. Platt sees a limit here, too, because the big powers are playing nuclear roulette, and in the mathematical sense if you continue to do this, "It finally, certainly, kills you . . . some have estimated that our 'half-life' under these circumstances—that is, the probable number of years before these repeated confrontations add up to a fifty-fifty chance of destroying the human race forever—may be only about ten or twenty years . . . this cannot continue. No one lives very long walking on loose rocks at the edge of a precipice."

Do we make our way into the new stability, or do we not? The class divides into optimists and pessimists. Assume we make it. There is again a division into optimists and pessimists, the question being, this time: Do we emerge into Churchill's sunlit uplands or into Orwell's 1984?

To find an answer you have to consider that:

World population is almost certain to double before any final stability is reached.

The growth of a crowd inevitably restricts freedom. In the packed subway, finally, you are unable to raise your arms.

The crowd must be more highly organized as it grows, to avoid chaos and to permit the technology which supports the crowd to function.

Cybernetics and game theory will inform the actions of government

—the process is underway in the United States. This will, very likely, have effects foreseen by Norbert Wiener and the Dominican friar, Père Dubarle. The process is exquisitely simple. In the game with the individual, as Father Dubarle put it, "The *machines à gouverner* will define the State as the best-informed player. . . ."

The players are likely to be cooperative. Because each will be a specialist. Technology demands it, and the specialist is by definition the Dependent Man. He cannot provide the essentials of life for himself. He is dependent upon others to provide, to create opinion, order, to *know what must be done.*

Dependent Man, properly fed and educated, is Acquiescent Man— he who lets others do it. Programmed for conformity. "Orthodoxy means . . . not needing to think. Orthodoxy is unconscious," said George Orwell.

Herein lies the chief danger of the U.S. becoming a beleaguered citadel in a world entering the descending spiral; the already great pressures for conformity would become overwhelming.

Sometimes the elements of the Orwellian world seem remarkably close. "The control of human behavior by artificial means will have become by the year 2000 a frightening possibility. Government—'big brother'—might use tranquilizers, or hallucinogens like L.S.D., to keep the population from becoming unruly or over-independent. More and more subtle forms of conditioning will lead people to react in predictable ways desired by government or by commercial interests without people quite knowing how they are hoodwinked . . ."—thus H. Bentley Glass, biologist and vice-president of the State University of New York at Stony Brook.

Recently Representative Daddario's subcommittee raised the question whether we may not reach a day when "a magnetic public personality, provided with sufficient funds to place his image electronically before the populace as often as the psychologically programmed computers dictate, will automatically be guaranteed election."

Robert Lekachman   **17**

Mill, Malthus,
and Growth Without End

I

Last December, at the meetings of the American Economic Association,
there was a major address by MIT's generally admired theorist of economic growth, Robert M. Solow. He chose for his title, "The Economics
of Resources or the Resources of Economics," and began with this
quotation:

> Contemplation of the world's disappearing supplies of miner-
> als, forests, and other exhaustible assets has led to demands for
> regulation of their exploitation. The feeling that these products
> are now too cheap for the good of future generations, that they
> are being selfishly exploited at too rapid a rate, and that in con-
> sequence of their excessive cheapness they are being produced
> and consumed wastefully has given rise to the conservation
> movement.

Solow's intent was playful, for as he immediately revealed, "The
author of those sentences is not Dennis Meadows and associates, not
Ralph Nader and associates, not the president of the Sierra Club; it is a
very eminent economic theorist . . . Harold Hotelling," who confided
these fears to fellow economists way back in 1931. From this instance
of doom averted and scarcity denied, Solow inferred the encouraging
conclusion that "The world has been exhausting its exhaustible resources since the first caveman chipped a flint, and I imagine the process will go on for a long, long time."
After this preliminary skirmish with the catastrophists, Solow

*Robert Lekachman, "Mill, Malthus, and Growth Without End," Dissent, Fall
1974, pp. 492–500. Reprinted by permission.*

treated his auditors to an elegant analysis of the manner in which market forces in the future as in the past can be expected to evoke new resources, improve the technology of their extraction, and impose salutary cost constraints upon individuals and enterprises purchasing resources in either raw or processed form. Solow's nearly unqualified message was one of confidence in the capacity of societies organized on market principles to grow indefinitely into the future at the 3–4 percent annual per capita rates, which describe the economic history of the West since the Industrial Revolution.

If this conventional economic wisdom contains the root of the matter, then the current flood of gloomy social prophecy—of which Robert Heilbroner's eloquent *An Inquiry into the Human Prospect* is this year's best example, as Dennis Meadows' *Limits of Growth* was last year's—symbolizes no more than a recurrent fashion. A long time ago Malthus predicted doom because of too many people. A century ago Jevons feared that exhaustion of its coal deposits would halt England's progress. But here we are richer than ever.

Sound economics explains why pessimists err and optimists are wise. Pay heed to the market. Energy prices will drop for predictable reasons: the OPEC cartel, like cartels before it, will disintegrate as the interests of its members come into sharper and sharper conflict (already Iran and Saudi Arabia have semipublicly quarreled over crude oil prices); new deposits of conventional energy will be located because higher prices encourage exploration; alternative energy sources will be exploited by entrepreneurs for the usual profit-maximizing reasons; new technologies will become economically important for the same reasons; and energy-thrifty activities, appliances, autos, and residential patterns will displace their energy-wasteful alternatives. Little in the way of government action is necessary, for given half a chance, competitive markets will perform their routine miracles of allocation of existing resources and evocation of new ones. So it has been for two centuries at least. So it shall be.

I mention only parenthetically the embarrassing limitations which monopoly imposes upon market efficiency, certainly in petroleum extraction and marketing, as well as in autos, steel, and a long list of manufacturing industries. I assume that true believers in the efficacy of competitive behavior will do their bit to revivify the antitrust statutes and fragment concentrated industries. That economists tend, one suspects for their own convenience, drastically to underestimate the impact of monopoly is a story for another occasion.

What concerns me here is the continuing confidence of mainstream American economists and their colleagues in Japan and Western Europe that growth can and will continue at its usual pace. The implications of that conviction are momentous. One relates to the analysis of contemporary inflation. Most Keynesians accept continuous but slight inflation as on balance socially beneficial. Persistent 2–3 percent annual increases in the consumer price index tilt the odds in favor of debtors, entrepreneurs, and innovators at the expense of less active elements in the community such as creditors and rentiers. It was Keynes himself who set the tone by looking forward wistfully to the "euthanasia of the rentier, and, consequently, the euthanasia of the cumulative oppressive power of the capitalist to exploit the scarcity-value of capital. Interest today rewards no genuine sacrifice, any more than does the rent of land."

Dynamic capitalist societies flourish when businesses take shrewd gambles in the hope of great gain. When they calculate the odds correctly, inflation affords them the opportunity to sell their inventories at prices higher than those at which the merchandise was acquired. Inflation makes it easier to borrow and enlarges prospective capital gain as well as profit.

Businessmen are not the only winners. Since moderate inflation stimulates economic activity and reduces unemployment, well-organized unions can successfully bargain for wage gains in excess of the inflation rate. It follows that so long as output per worker grows faster than the cost of living, typical white- and blue-collar operatives can reasonably anticipate long-run improvements in their real income, which average the 3–4 percent secular improvement in per capita productivity. In 33 years a steady 3 percent annual increase in real wages ensures that real wages double those in force at the beginning of the period, even if an individual never becomes a foreman or supervisor.

As this account runs, the coincidence of steady growth and persistent inflation since the end of World War II is the necessary and benign consequence of the power of organized business and union groups to extract somewhat larger profits and wages than, at current prices, a given economy is capable of generating. Conventionally, the American Federal Reserve and the central banks of other nations validate the claims by printing enough new money and generating sufficient credit to pay into corporate treasuries and workers' hands the amounts targeted by corporate managers or embodied in union contracts.

Inflation is realistically unavoidable because depression has become a socially unacceptable technique for the treatment of rising prices. In the United States the Employment Act of 1946, emasculated though it was by congressional conservatives, nevertheless signaled political recognition of new public responsibility for the maintenance of high levels of employment and production, come what might. Although in the last generation American employment performance leaves much to be desired, particularly by comparison with Western Europe and Japan, the contrast between pre- and post-World War II experience is striking. In the worst month of the worst post-World War II recession, unemployment was less than 8 percent. By somber contrast, on the eve of World War II, after an early seven years of the New Deal, unemployment persisted at 12–14 percent levels.

These days wages, once flexible in both directions, are now flexible only upward. There have been times, most recently in 1969 and 1970, when wages actually advanced more rapidly during spells of mild contraction than in time of rapid expansion. Profits also tend to resist erosion, whatever the economic weather. During the 1973–74 recession profits increased more rapidly than they did in 1971 and 1972, and both were years of general business expansion.

Thus far I have written of slow inflation. What about the double-digit pace at which prices are now marching upward? Optimistic Keynesians argue that a combination of bad luck, poor national leadership, international politics, and coincidence explain the present price explosion. Bad luck has abounded. The Peruvian anchovies, now back in their usual haunts, swam mysteriously away, caused shortages of cattle feed, compelled substitution of soybeans, drove up soybean prices, and elevated American meat prices. In 1972 simultaneous Russian, Chinese, and Indian crop failures generated explosive demand for American food. Dollar devaluation, in addition, for a time turned American food into a world bargain. As luck would have it, business boomed simultaneously in Western Europe, the United States, and Japan, a coincidence of business cycle peaks which accentuated demand pressure upon all manner of finished goods and raw materials.

Administration blunders compounded misfortune. The list is familiar. Agriculture Secretary Earl Butz retained acreage limitations long after worldwide crop shortages dictated reversal of American policy. White House pursuit of détente as well as sheer incompetence allowed Russian trade negotiators quietly to purchase far more wheat at far lower prices than the Nixon administration realized or perhaps wished to realize until the damage had been done. Neglect of international commercial relationships necessitated three dollar devaluations, which predictably enlarged foreign demand for American products and contributed to domestic inflationary pressure. At exactly the wrong moment, the Administration in January 1973 dismantled its relatively effective (though inequitable) Phase II wage-price controls and moved into an ambiguous Phase III which was generally interpreted by the business community as a license to elevate prices and profits as high as the market would bear.

The near quadrupling of petroleum prices by the OPEC cartel reinforced these inflationary tendencies. And as the most cheerful will concede, in the short run no relief is in sight. For some time to come the multinational oil companies will continue to enjoy record windfall profits. Real transfers of wealth will continue to be made not only between oil consuming and oil producing nations but between average American motorists and Exxon, Mobil, and Texaco stockholders, a generally more affluent collection of men and women.

According to the optimists, however, these are transitional events. For the reasons earlier noted, energy prices will subside. Plentiful American and Russian harvests, for instance, are far more likely to revive apprehensions about the reappearance of crop surpluses than to demonstrate Malthusian theorems about faster growth in mouths to be fed than in food to feed them. And the new Ford administration may have learned enough from its predecessor's experience to avoid repetition of the most egregious blunders.

The watchword then is, Keep Cool. Economic growth, less alarming inflation, and renewed improvement in living standards will soon resume, *if* we don't panic and, following the lead of Dr. Arthur F. Burns, take such drastic anti-inflationary action as to cause a genuine deep recession.

II

Are the economists, our contemporary Dr. Panglosses, right? Is the specter of scarcity as distant as ever? I don't think that they are. If the world is Malthusian, we are likely to be better guided by Malthus and Mill than by Robert Solow.

Malthus would be at home in the 1970s. With the help of Robert Heilbroner[1] and Emile Benoit,[2] the situation can be readily summarized. With now approximately 4 billion, world population is increasing about 80 million annually, 13 million in India alone. At present rates of increase the globe's population by the end of the present century will be between 6 and 7 billion. The bulk of this growth is occurring not in the richer industrialized nations but in the poverty-stricken continents of Asia, South America, and Africa. As Heilbroner puts it,

> Southeast Asia . . . is growing at a rate that will double its numbers in less than 30 years; the African continent as a whole every 27 years; Latin America every 24 years. Thus, whereas we can expect that the industrialized areas of the world will have to support roughly 1.4 to 1.7 billion people a century hence, the underdeveloped world, which today totals around 2.5 billion, will have to support something like 40 billion by that date if it continues to double its numbers approximately every quarter-century.[3]

The Malthusian "solution," which Heilbroner judges to be probable, features famine, disease,[4] and other calamities. Or, as Malthus phrased the prospect, in a passage that led Thomas Carlyle to call political economy the dismal science,

Famine seems to be the last, the most dreadful resource of nature. The power of population is so superior to the power of the earth to produce subsistence for man, that premature death must in some shape or other visit the human race. The vices of mankind are active and able ministers of depopulation. They are the precursors in the great army of destruction; and they often finish the dreadful work themselves. But should they fail in this war of extermination, sickly seasons, epidemics, pestilence and plague, advance in terrific array, and sweep off their thousands and ten thousands. Should success be still incomplete; gigantic, inevitable famine stalks in the rear, and with one mighty blow, levels the population with the food of the world.

Effective limitation of population is essential to human survival. The routine marvels of science and technology by themselves do not suffice. For with all the ingenuity and imagination that science may muster, raw materials of some kind are essential, but as Benoit observes

The presently estimated usable reserves of most of the world's irreplaceable raw materials will be exhausted in 50 to 100 years if the present growth of demand continues.[5] Even if new discoveries succeed in quintupling usable reserves and social discipline novel to the American experience allows us to reclaim and recycle 75 per cent of the irreplaceable resources now discarded, the additions would accommodate our rising rates of consumption for only a pitifully brief additional period—one that would be measured in decades rather than centuries.

Moreover, hope for a technological "fix" is much less well-founded than economists and other optimists seem to believe. Generally speaking, alternatives to petroleum all entail either threats to safety (as in nuclear power plants), enormous pollution problems (as in strip-mining and oil shale extraction), vast water requirements, threats to marine life and protein supplies from the ocean, enormous capital expenditures, or some combination of these costs and hazards. If, by some succession of miracles, the scientific community invents solutions to each of these difficulties, there is still no reason to count on the technology improving at requisite speed. Benoit reminds his readers that

It is now a quarter of a century since the basic technology of nuclear power has been understood, yet nuclear plants still account for only a small fraction of world energy production, the breeder reactor is still in the development stage, and serious unresolved safety and pollution problems impede rapid expansion of the program.

The prospects for adequate food are even more discouraging. Despite a "green revolution" in wheat and rice cultivation, aggregate food supplies in recent years have increased only at about the same pace as population, leaving no margin for improvement in standards of nutrition and no cushion against localized famines, like the one in progress caused by a five-year sub-Saharan drought or the catastrophe looming in that new nuclear power, India. As a prototypical technological fix, the green revolution relied heavily on petrochemical fertilizers, chemical insecticides, forest clearing to extend cultivated land, and tilling of new land in regions of marginal rainfall. Unfortunately, just as though Emerson's law of compensation were malignly at work, artificial fertilizers tend to diminish the natural fertility of the earth. Insecticides frequently enter into food chains and imperil human health and life, encourage the breeding of poison-resistant strains of crop pests, and occasionally destroy the natural enemies of plant vandals. Attempts to clear forest and cultivate marginal land appear to increase soil erosion and lower water tables. Fishing, which has enjoyed its own technological revolution, is threatened by pollution as well as depletion of fish stock caused by the greed of the fishermen.

Even if we don't all starve, men and women may perish from the adverse effects of the pollution of their water, atmosphere, and immediate environment. Benoit cites a Japanese expert to the effect that in his country "where illnesses attributed to pollution number in the hundreds of thousands . . . half the population will be dead in twenty years if economic growth continues at present rates."

In sum, Robert Solow's optimism is close to fatuous at a time of demographic, raw material, food, and environmental threats to which the deified market, worshiped by every respectable economist, seems the most trivial of responses. The world that Malthus predicted and feared is our world. As Benoit aptly comments, "The fact that someone once cried 'wolf' does not prove that a wolf may not finally arrive. . . . Every extinct species and civilization was a success story for a while— often for a long while!"

III

What next? Should the middle-aged rejoice because they are likely to disappear before the steaks, lobsters, and vintage wines vanish from the tables of all but Greek billionaires? Should the living, to revise Herman Kahn, envy those who sooner then they themselves will be dead? Is it necessary, as the only viable alternative to such despair, to resign ourselves, as Robert Heilbroner appears to do, to the necessity of authoritarian governments, which alone, so his argument runs, can control resource use and regulate human reproduction in the interests of the survival of the species? In such a context it is sobering to note the almost casual comment of a Russian scientific humanist like Andrei D. Sakharov that "The scientific and democratic regulation of the world economy and all social life, *including the dynamics of population* [emphasis added], is not, I am profoundly convinced, a utopia but a very real necessity." But Sakharov, whose values approximate those of the editors and readers of DISSENT, does not pause to explain just how one "democratically" regulates human reproduction.

At worst, zero or negative rates of growth imply a Hobbesian universe, a specter that animated the British economist Rudolf Klein's June essay in the *New York Times Magazine*. Once growth stops,

> Immediately the competition for resources becomes a zero-sum game. One man's prize is another man's loss. If the blacks want to improve their share of desirable goods, it can only be at the expense of the whites. If the over-65's are to be given higher pensions, or improved medical services, it can only be at the expense of the working population or of the young.
>
> [Klein fears that] It would seem only too likely that the haves would man the barricades to defend their share of resources, against the have-nots. The politics of compromise would be replaced by the politics of revolution, because the have-nots would be forced to challenge the whole basis of society, and its distribution of wealth and power.

Such contests of each against all are likely to end in the extermination of some of the antagonists, the exhaustion of the remainder, and the emergence of the sort of authoritarian monarchs or governments that Hobbes postulated in his version of the social contract and Heilbroner describes as the likeliest of future political developments.

In the absence of that universal solvent, genuine and continuous economic growth, it is hard to deny the plausibility of the dreadful futures variously envisaged by Heilbroner, Klein, and other pessimists. The wars among nations over resources, the clashes within nations over income and wealth redistribution, and the games of nuclear blackmail that Heilbroner foresees, may indeed be the only responses to scarcity that "human nature," national egotism, and group hostility are capable of engendering once the realization becomes general that the economic pie cannot be indefinitely enlarged, that, in Malthus's words, there really are "unhappy persons who, in the great lottery of life, have drawn a blank." If so, magazines like DISSENT and essays like this one will be among the minor casualties in the regimented societies just over the horizon. It is unlikely in the extreme that the controllers of the printed word in this world to come would allot even recycled paper to their professional critics. Possibly no one ought to weep for a species so prone to aggression, cruelty, deception, and misuse of its own intellectual and esthetic powers. Why trouble about the fate of societies that prefer to evade rather than pursue the ethical goals of compassion, justice, and brotherhood, which spiritual leaders and secular prophets have vainly promoted over the millennia?

Still, hope, like despair, is a human tendency. Even terminal cancer victims dream of spontaneous remissions and new therapies. In this spirit, I shall briefly speculate about a somewhat different and less depressing response to the ending of the Era of Growth and the inauguration of the Era of Redistribution. There are plastic as well as stable elements in human behavior, just as there are instances of institutional improvement as well as rather more cases of institutional deterioration.

For reasons that will become speedily evident, I shall term what follows a Millian alternative. The first edition of John Stuart Mill's *Principles of Political Economy* was published in that year of failed revolution, 1848, the last during Mill's own lifetime in 1871. During the intervening generation, Mill's detestation of the moral and esthetic impact of English and American capitalism steadily deepened, partly as his *Autobiography* disclosed, because of the influence of his wife, Harriet Taylor. The chapters on socialism took an increasingly kindly view of the ethical desirability if not the economic practicality of the versions of Utopian socialism promulgated by Fourier and Owen. Powerful chapters entitled "Of the Stationary State" and "On the Probable Futurity of the Labouring Classes" grappled ever more devotedly with the definition of a state of society superior to Victorian capitalism.

Mill's intellectual strategy embraced the stationary, zero-growth state as a huge opportunity for personal development, not at all as a menace to humankind. In one place Mill phrased this vision of a better future in this way:

It must always have been seen, more or less distinctly, by political economists, that the increase of wealth is not boundless: that at the end of what they term the progressive state lies the stationary state, that all progress in wealth is but postponement of this, and that each step in advance is an approach to it. We have not been led to recognise that this ultimate goal is at all times near enough to be fully in view; that we are always on the verge of it, and that if we have not reached it long ago, it is because the goal itself flies before us. The richest and most prosperous countries would very soon attain the stationary state, if no further improvements were made in the productive arts, and if there were a suspension of the overflow of capital from those countries into the uncultivated or ill-cultivated regions of the earth.

The diagnosis embodied in this forecast was premised upon increasing population and diminishing returns from the cultivation of less and less fertile land, as well as overcultivation of higher quality farms.[6] As a result, both the pace of real growth and the rate of return upon capital declined. For orthodox contemporaries of Mill, who defined prosperity after the fashion of James R. McCulloch not as a "large production and a good distribution of wealth but a rapid increase of it" stimulated by "high profits," such a condition was unmitigated disaster, much as it appears today to writers like Rudolf Klein.

Perceiving much that was wrong with Victorian capitalism as remediable in a stationary state, Mill reached a precisely opposite evaluation:

> I cannot . . . regard the stationary state of capital and wealth with the unaffected aversion so generally manifested towards it by political economists of the old school. I am inclined to believe that it would be, on the whole, a very considerable improvement on our present condition. I confess that I am not charmed with the ideal of life held out by those who think that the normal state of human beings is that of struggling to get on; that the trampling, crushing, elbowing, and treading on each other's heels, which form the existing type of social life, are the most desirable lot of human kind, or anything but the disagreeable symptoms of one of the phases of industrial progress . . . the best state for human nature is that in which, while no one is poor, no one desires to be richer, nor has any reason to fear being thrust back, by the efforts of others to push themselves forward.

English capitalism was bad enough; the American version was plain dreadful, an object lesson of what happens to a society that pursues wealth above all other goals:

> The northern and middle states of America are a specimen of this state of civilization in very favourable circumstances; having, apparently, got rid of all social injustices and inequalities that affect persons of Caucasian race and of the male sex, while the proportion of population to capital and land is such as to ensure abundance to every able-bodied member of the community who does not forfeit it by misconduct. They have the six points of Chartism, and they have no poverty; and all that these advantages do for them is that the life of the whole of one sex is devoted to dollar-hunting, and of the other to breeding dollar-hunters.

Mill's prescription for a better society emphasized what now are called quality-of-life issues. Here a central dilemma was how to reconcile his admiration of competition as guarantor of free choice and economic efficiency, and his dislike of societies organized on the model of rat races. Very much like Karl Marx in his own time and our own analysts of worker alienation, Mill worried about the deficiencies of factories as social institutions. It was not only, in Mill's bitter judgment, that "hitherto it is questionable if all the mechanical inventions yet made have lightened the day's toil of any human being"; it was also and far more important, the circumstance that at the center of the factory operative's daily routine was a cancer. The relationship between worker and employer was diseased by the mutual suspicions of both parties. Employers coldly insisted upon the last possible ounce of effort from their employees, treating them as particularly refractory machines. For their part, the employees retaliated by conscientious malingering. The contest demeaned both groups. Reading Mill, one finds it easy to grasp his premonition of such recent episodes as the Lordstown strike, which centered on just such an effort by the General Motors Assembly Division to extract extra labor and just such a sabotaging reprisal by the human targets of its policy.

What, then, should be done simultaneously to preserve competition's benefits and dissipate its dehumanizing side effects? It seemed to Mill that a transformation of industrial relations was essential so that the interests and emotions of workers and owners might coincide instead of conflict. Profit-sharing was a promising technique. Examining numerous 19th-century French and English experiments, Mill concluded that under profit-sharing laborers worked harder, enlarged their incomes, and even raised the profits of capital. Moreover, because workers took into their own hands factory discipline and punished malingerers, the quality of workmanship tended steadily to rise.

Yet, even though profit-sharing improved normal industrial relations, Mill judged the form transitional. His ideal solution was syndicalist. Workers ought by peaceful purchase to acquire factories, run them in their own interest, and compete with other enterprises similarly managed. Although Mill's account of the internal governance of worker-owned factories was less than precise, his expectations of benefit were high: "The relation of masters and workpeople will be gradually superseded by partnership, in one of two forms; in some cases, associations of the labourers with the capitalists; in others, and perhaps finally in all, associations of labourers among themselves."

For Mill as for such spiritual descendants as William Morris, R. H. Tawney, and J. K. Galbraith, the relevant measure of social achievement was moral rather than material. Syndicalist solutions preserved the formal value of competition; but as Mill aged and witnessed ever more of market capitalism's corrupting effect on individual character, he became increasingly eager to soften the rigors of competition between persons, increasingly partisan to diminished inequality of income and wealth, more feminist than ever in his insistence upon the emancipation of women as a precondition to general progress, more inclined in 1871 than even in 1848 to judge English society harshly, and more confident than ever that only freedom of expression and parliamentary government promoted truth and enlightenment.

IV

Obviously there is no occasion for rejoicing that Mill more than a century ago sketched an agenda for industrial societies that today is not only incompletely resolved but in significant respects barely started upon. Today as in Victorian England population limitation is absolutely essential to human survival at least in any manner that one might prefer to survive. It is fair to say that contemporary scientific advances have actually accentuated Malthusian dangers. Notoriously uneven in its impact, science and technology have been better at draining marshes, controlling malaria, reducing infant mortality, eliminating epidemic disease, and purifying water supplies than in sweetening the routine of daily life, raising the level of public education, comprehending the roots of crime and mental disorder, moderating the hostile and aggressive impulses of individuals, groups, and nations, and generally promoting the altruistic, cooperative side of "human nature."

Population limitation is not an end, but a precondition of a society friendly to the best of human aspirations and potentialities. For us as for Mill such a society requires a decrease in the gap between rich and poor, managers and workers, educated and less educated, black and white, male and female. The human condition is now more desperate than in 1871, in good part because of the warlike uses of science. Inequality between rich and poor nations is now embittered by the demonstration efforts upon the poor of the life-styles of the affluent. Nuclear blackmail is a real possibility, for a community as poor as India can explode nuclear devices. The relatively puny military weaponry of the 19th century made genocide at worst a localized affair.

As I read our contemporary catastrophists, I find it hard not to nod my head in agreement. On the record, poor nations have preferred war to painful efforts at solution of their internal problems. Rich nations have erratically, at best, recognized a community of interest with less fortunate neighbors. Rich men have reluctantly surrendered their tithes to improve the condition of men and women of their own nationality and citizenship, let alone those lesser beings whose color, religion, ethnic origin, or geographical location enforce even smaller claims to succor.

Hunger, nuclear war, and authoritarian social control may lie just over the horizon. I have far less than complete confidence that we shall take the enlightened route sign-posted by Mill. We may and very possibly will fail to limit population, transform the character of work, transfer resources within rich societies and between rich societies and poor ones, and learn to prefer cooperation to competition. No divine principle insures human survival. In the absence of changes such as these, the human prospect would be truly dismal.

ENDNOTES

1. *An Inquiry into the Human Prospect* (New York: Norton, 1974).
2. "What Future Spaceship Earth?" *Social Policy*, November–December 1973, pp. 17–21.
3. In his *First Essay on Population* (1798), Malthus formulated the problem like this:

   > Taking the population of the world at any number, a thousand millions, for instance, the human species would increase in the ratio of 1, 2, 4, 8, 16, 32, 64, 128, 256, 512, &c. and subsistence as −1, 2, 3, 4, 5, 6, 7, 8, 9, 10, &c. In two centuries and a quarter, the population would be to the means of subsistence as 512 to 10; in three centuries as 4096 to 13, and in two thousand years the difference would be almost incalculable. . . .

   Although food output has increased rather faster than Malthus anticipated, Latin-American and African population growth rates are frighteningly close to his speculations.
4. In June 1973 an Indian smallpox epidemic has killed tens of thousands in the province of Bihar. A precursor of things to come?
5. American energy consumption has been steadily growing at 4.8 annual rates. Nor is the situation less ominous in other advanced communities.
6. In the trade jargon, cultivation at both the extensive and the intensive margin infallibly yields smaller and smaller additional outputs per additional unit of labor and capital.

18

David M. Rorvik

Cloning: Asexual Human Reproduction?

The place: A glass-domed conference room at the U.S. Manned Space Center, Houston.

A dozen leaders of the American space effort, the chairman of select Congressional committees and a representative of the President sit facing a lectern at the end of the long, oval table. Everyone is silent, expectant.

Dr. Eric Lehmann, NASA's Director of Space Colonization, enters the room, goes to the lectern and reads this statement: "Gentlemen, it is my pleasure to announce that our panel of distinguished geneticists, working with our experts in the field of bioastronautics, have selected from a field of 50 finalists the man whose 100 clonal offspring will—twenty-five years from today—begin the arduous task of colonizing the moon. The man, a twenty-five-year-old rookie in our training program, has been declared perfect in every respect to serve as the model moon man. This prototype, hereafter known as Mr. X, will be cloned immediately."

Cloning? What is this, you ask, a put-on—or the latest in science fiction? Actually, it's neither; cloning is strange enough, all right, and, in fact, is probably the most bizarre development to come along in the field of biology to date. But it is also one of the most significant, a scientific breakthrough with mind-stretching implications for the future. Cloning will make it possible for society to reproduce prize bulls, race horses, Olympic-caliber athletes, war heroes, great philosophers, leading scientists, even rock musicians like Ringo Starr by the tens, hundreds or even thousands. And each will be a precise duplicate, a carbon copy of the original.

If one Einstein could lay down the whole foundation of modern-day physics, what might a dozen—or 1,000—Einsteins, either working together or individually, accomplish? Think of the talents of a Mozart or a Beethoven amplified fifty or 100 times. (A million Ringo Starrs?) Imagine the power and discipline of an army whose members are all copies of a Congressional Medal of Honor winner, all united by the same attitudes and objectives and able to communicate with one another with a minimum of words. Apply the same imagination to astronauts, space colonizers, underwater explorers and surgical teams.

Cloning may even have a welcome surprise in store for the "common man," making it possible for him to achieve a sort of immortality; as soon as he dies, his family or friends can simply make a whole new copy of him. Less welcome to some may be the fact that cloning will almost surely take sex out of reproduction for all time. Cloning, in fact, is destined to revolutionize nearly every one of man's traditional notions about how he comes into the world and how Nature changes him over the centuries; it promises to take evolution out of Nature's hands and put it in man's, making him, for the first time, the master of his own fate, the architect of his own biological future.

As the Nobel Prize winning geneticist Joshua Lederberg puts it, cloning places man "on the brink of a major evolutionary perturbation." And though cloning has so far only been achieved in lower life forms, Dr. Lederberg adds that "there is nothing to suggest any particular difficulty about accomplishing this in mammals or man, though it will rightly be admired as a technical tour de force when it is first accomplished." Like Kimball Atwood, a professor of microbiology at the University of Illinois, he believes this could occur at almost any moment. With a crash program , Dr. Atwood claims, "it could be done now." But even in the normal course of things he expects it to take place "within a few years."

Cloning (a word which comes from a Greek root meaning "cutting") is generally defined as "asexual propagation," which simply means reproduction-without-sex or, put another way, reproduction-without fertilization.

Cloning makes it possible for a woman to bear a child without the hitherto necessary union of egg and sperm. More incredibly, it will also make possible the birth of a child whose only parent is a male. In either event, the clonal offspring will have only one parent and will become the *identical* twin of the parent.

To get a better grasp on this, let's go back to Houston for a minute, where Mr. X was about to give "birth" to centuplets, and listen to the rest of Dr. Lehmann's speech: "Several thousand body cells will be removed at once," he explains, "from a tiny patch on Mr. X's forearm. Each cell will be examined for minute chromosomal damage, and the

100 soundest cells will be retained for implantation into 100 host cells. Nine months from now 100 little Mr. X-es will arrive—identical in every detail to their sole parent. For the next twenty-five years a NASA team, headed by Mr. X himself, will train our 100-strong clone for the mission to come. Then, one fine day in the year 2000, Mr. X, then fifty years old, will lead the nation in bidding farewell to his 100 identical sons, if we may call them that, bound for a new life on the moon."

'SWITCHED ON' CELL

To understand this fantastic state-of-affairs, it is necessary to review a little basic biology. Remember, first of all, that there are two general kinds of cells: body cells, each of which has a nucleus containing forty-six chromosomes, and sex cells (sperm in the male, ova or eggs in the female), each of which has only half as many chromosomes as the body cells. (That's why you have to get two of them together to make a new individual; half of the chromosomes come from the mother, half from the father.)

The human egg cell is very tiny (one-hundredth of an inch in diameter) but is actually not much different from a chicken egg. The yoke, or nucleus is even the same color as the chicken's yoke. The clear material around the nucleus is called cytoplasm and can be compared to the "white" of the chicken egg. The cytoplasm contributes nothing to the genetic makeup of an individual, since the genes are inside the chromosomes and not the cytoplasm. The job of the cytoplasm is simply to protect and nourish the nucleus and its payload.

In recent years, however, a very important additional function has been revealed: the cytoplasm seems to act as a control center that tells the nucleus to "switch on," that is, when to start dividing, thus creating new cells and ultimately a new human being. As long as the egg nucleus just sits there with only twenty-three chromosomes the cytoplasm does nothing. But as soon as the sperm (much tinier than the egg) swims through the cytoplasm and penetrates the nucleus, the cytoplasm is chemically "programmed" to send a message to the nucleus which says, in effect: "You are now a fertilized egg cell, complete with forty-six chromosomes, and as such you must start dividing at once." Which is precisely what happens. The "switched on" cell takes off, dividing billions of times to make a whole new individual.

All of those billions of body cells, in any given individual, have a common ancestry: a single, fertilized egg cell; they all contain an identical set of chromosomes. Yet, *unlike* the fertilized egg cell, the body cells have limited and very specialized creative capabilities. Some make only teeth, others form nothing but liver and still others go into making up nothing but hair. And so on. Each body cell has the full number of chromosomes necessary to start an entire new individual, but most of the mechanisms inside them seem to be "switched off." The components in the forty-six chromosomes of a skin cell, for example, are all turned off except for those that go into making skin. So, in a sense, most of the cell is "wasted."

For years scientists have been fascinated with the idea of taking a body cell and switching it on so that it would start dividing, thus creating a replica of the individual from which it came. No sexual union would be necessary in this sort of reproduction, they reasoned, since all forty-six chromosomes would already be present in the single cell. Incredible as the whole theory seemed, nobody could think of any valid objections to it; but neither could anybody think of a way to bring this stunning feat off, even in the lowliest forms of life.

Nobody, that is, until Professor F. C. Steward of Cornell University scored the long-awaited breakthrough a few years ago. His experiments were with nothing more exalted than carrots, but the results electrified the scientific world. Dr. Steward scraped an unfertilized cell from the body of a carrot and placed it in a specifically prepared nutrient bath, which contained, among other things, coconut milk. In this solution the cell began dividing as if it thought it had been pollinated. As Dr. Steward puts it, "It was as if the coconut milk had acted like a clutch, putting the cell's idling engine of growth into gear." From a single body cells the Cornell team finally got a mature carrot, complete with roots, flowers and seeds. "We were hardly prepared," Dr. Steward said, "for such dramatic results." Since then many other carrots, tobacco and asparagus plants have been cloned in this fashion.

Now Dr. J. B. Gurdon of Oxford University has devised an ingenious method of duplicating this feat in the animal kingdom. Building on the pioneering work of Drs. R. Briggs and T. J. King, two American scientists, Dr. Gurdon uses the following technique to achieve asexual reproduction in the African clawed frog: First he takes an unfertilized egg cell from a frog and destroys its nucleus with ultraviolet radiation. Then he takes a body cell from another frog (often scraping it from such remote spots as an intestinal wall) and removes its nucleus with the help of a powerful microscope and tiny surgical tools. Next he implants the body cell nucleus into the egg cell, the original nucleus of which had only half as many chromosomes.

In this way the control center in the egg-cell cytoplasm is "tricked" into thinking that fertilization has taken place—because it suddenly notices that there is a full set of chromosomes in its nucleus. So it is that a body-cell nucleus, which previously was nothing more than a speck of intestine, is "turned on" to divide and produce a spanking new tadpole. And, of course, the most striking part of this is that the tadpole grows up to be an identical twin of the body cell donor. To demonstrate, even to the layman, that the new frog is the "offspring" of the body-cell donor and not the egg-cell donor, Dr. Gurdon uses frogs of clearly distinctive types as the two donors in each case. Invariably, the new frog is the exact image of the body cell donor, and microscopic studies show that it owes none of its inheritance whatever to the egg-cell donor. The egg cell cytoplasm is merely the nutrient material it feeds on in its formative stage.

Dr. Gurdon's work seems to define the state-of-the-art at the present time. Research into cloning is going on at the universities all over the world but most of this is simply an effort to catch up with the likes of Steward and Gurdon. Some scientists who, quite understandably, don't want to be named, however, "suggest" that some of their colleagues may—very quietly—be attempting to clone mammals right away.

Dr. Kurt Hirschhorn, chief of the Division of Medical Genetics at the Mount Sinai School of Medicine in New York, is one of the many scientists who think that cloning will be applied to man—"perhaps much sooner than people think." Without question, though, human cloning is going to be more difficult than the cloning of carrots or toads, partly because human cells are so small and partly because human eggs must be carried in the womb, not deposited under a rock or dropped into coconut milk in a test tube.

Still, a technique has already been developed to remove egg cells from such mammals as cows, sheep and horses and put them into other animals. This process, which could be very important to human cloning, is being used at the present time by shrewd livestock breeders to improve their herds. They take a prize cow, for example, and wash hundreds of egg cells out of her oviducts with special hormone preparations. These are then implanted into the uteruses of other, poorer quality, cows which, after being artificially inseminated as well, carry the fetuses to term, finally giving birth to calves that really belong to the prize cow. In this way an exceptional cow can be made to produce hundreds of offspring—instead of the normal seven or eight—in her lifetime. Soon it is expected that this technique will be applied to humans, primarily to permit the barren woman to carry and give birth to a child for the first time. It will also permit the wealthy woman who does not want to undergo the rigors of pregnancy to have her fertilized egg cell removed a few days after conception and implanted in another woman, whom she will pay to have the baby for her.

The importance of artificial inovulation to cloning humans is this: it offers a way around the nutrient-bath problem. To illustrate how the two techniques will work together, take the case again of Mr. X, the NASA rookie who was about to be cloned at the beginning of this article. He has been declared the perfect specimen to serve as a prototype for the 100 moon men the U.S. wants to send aloft in twenty-five years. So doctors take 100 cells from his arm (such a small quantity that he

doesn't even feel the scratch) and remove their nuclei. In the meantime they have secured 100 egg cells, the nuclei of which have been
destroyed with tiny beams of radiation from a laser. (The 100 egg cells
can be washed out of the same woman or out of 100 different women;
it makes no difference, so long as they are all good healthy cells.)
Then, using microsurgery, (See "Microsurgery," May 1969, p. 7.) the
doctors inject the body cell nuclei from Mr. X's arm into the 100 egg-cell
"packages" (and packages is all they are, since their contents have been
vaporized). Next, using the techniques of artificial inovulation, the
100 newly constructed cells are implanted into the wombs of 100
women. (These do not have to be the same women who donated the
egg cells in the first place; again, all that is necessary is that they be
healthy and capable of carrying an embryo to term.)

Women, of course, could contribute the body cells as well as men.
In this case all the clonal offspring would be females. And the same
woman who donates the egg cell and carries the baby to birth could
also contribute the body-cell nucleus. Almost any combination is possible, but, in every case, the new individual will always be identical to
the body-cell donor.

The biggest challenge for those who would achieve human cloning
is simply getting the tiny body-cell nucleus into the egg-cell cytoplasm.
"But once you get the chromosomes from the body cell in there," says
Dr. Hirschhorn, "there's no reason whatever why it won't grow just
like an ordinary fertilized egg cell."

A number of geneticists have noted that cloning offers a better
means of improving the human species than do such schemes as "germinal choice." Germinal choice involves the mating of physically and
mentally superior men and women in an effort to achieve a sort of super
race. It has received serious support from such eminent scientists as
the late Dr. H. J. Muller, a winner of the Nobel Prize in medicine. But
critics say that it "smacks of the human stud farm" and does not necessarily guarantee consistent improvement. There are millions of elements in the human genes and these can combine in millions of different and quite unpredictable ways. Geniuses, for example, quite often
give birth to children of only average intelligence. In cloning, on the
other hand, there are no unknown factors; you can see what you are
going to get in advance.

So, instead of the sperm and egg banks that Dr. Muller proposed,
Dr. Lederberg predicts that the future will see the development of
widespread body-cell banks. The late Dr. Jean Rostand, one of the "Im-
mortals" of the French Academy, suggested that even the average
man ought to set aside a few body cells (which can be preserved indefinitely in cell-culture solutions) to serve as the ultimate sort of life
insurance. In the event of untimely death these cells could be taken
out of storage and grown into an entire new copy of the deceased indi-

vidual. This process could be continued indefinitely, thus conferring a sort of quasi-immortality on the person in question.

Some scientists fear that the egotists among us will not wait for death before having copies of themselves made. Lord Rothschild, a noted physiologist, recently warned a gathering of scientists that self-centered fanatics, in the Hitler mold, might set up shop at home—making dozens of replicas of themselves before society could intervene. To try to forestall such disasters, he has proposed the eventual establishment of a Commission for Genetical Control to license clonists. But even more unsettling than the idea of a dozen Hitlers or a score of Stalins is one that originated with Dr. Lederberg. For the same reasons that tribalism and racism have flourished for the past several centuries, he says, "clonism and clonishness will prevail" in the future.

The internationally known biologist J. B. S. Haldane, who died recently, was one of the first to seriously suggest the cloning of people. He proposed that geniuses, and others who had made extraordinary contributions to society, be cloned. They could use their "retirement" to teach their clonal offspring all they knew. Exceptions would be made, of course, for individuals valued for their physical abilities—dancers, athletes, soldiers, astronauts and so on. These, Dr. Haldane said, should be cloned young so that they would have all the vigor necessary to train their replicas. And, practical to the end, he said some considerable effort should be given to seeking out and cloning individuals with "special effects," such as lack of the pain sense, night vision, resistance to radiation, inability to hear or be affected by high-pitched sounds (the sort which might be used in weapons in the future), dwarfism (which might come in handy in the high gravitational fields of some of the other planets we will eventually be visiting) and so on.

So even if you don't think you are one of the great thinkers of the 20th Century, take heart; cloning may yet have something for you. As one geneticist puts it, "Who is to say what the future will hold, particularly as we move out into space with its unknown environments. In the year 2000, for example, circumstances might be such that big feet will be in great demand and fat, stubby legs among the most highly valued attributes of the day." And then all size twelves to the fore.

Ecology and Pollution

We can stop pollution, if we but put our minds and energies to the task. Let's put antipollution devices on our automobiles, and stop littering, and clean up our streams, and pay more attention to the effects of what we do, and hire young people to watchdog industry— and we'll be all right. So say some.

But pollution is much more than a matter of exhaust fumes from automobiles. And ecology is much more than a matter of dead fish. Such things are but the surface manifestations of phenomena much more fundamental. It is to the roots that we must go if we are to understand ecology and pollution. Without understanding fundamental causes of the problem, we are doomed to deal only with symptoms and ailments, while the causes go unchecked.

It is on these root causes that Weisberg focuses in his opening article on the politics of ecology. He first indicates the extent of our pollution-ecology problem. He bluntly states that our natural environment is being destroyed, not merely polluted here and there. He then traces this destructive process of our natural environment to the basic orientation of industrialized technological society.

Political and economic power have become concentrated in the hands of a few, and these few are directing the wholesale rape and destruction of the physical world as they relentlessly pursue profit. This is resulting in the life-support capacity of our planet being destroyed—not simply upset or thrown into temporary disorder, but being destroyed. The very existence of humanity is what is at stake, not simply cleaner or dirtier air or water, or the threat to specific flora and fauna. Rather, for over 200 years, those directing our social institutions have guided the systematic slaughter of both human and other forms of life. The ecological catastrophe is part and parcel of this rapacious approach to the world, where the human world and the world of nature are being exploited for the sake of short term profit. As long as our political and economic framework remains the same, so remains the fundamental cause of the crisis on which our existence hangs in the balance. To reverse the course of ecological destruction requires not merely a "let's stop polluting this particular thing" approach, but it requires a fundamental change in our approach to life. Our current socio-economic system, however, is carrying on "business as usual."

Pessimistic, one might say in response to this first selection. Indeed, such a response would be putting the matter rather mildly, for it is entirely possible that through our basic exploitative economic system we have been set on a doomsday course. Although the public may have had no hand in selecting this course, they are riding the same spaceship as those who did—and there is no exit. Perhaps the course can be changed. Only time will tell for certain. But in the meantime, we are not taking even the measures necessary to determine if the course is reversible.

Rather than attempting to reverse our course of destruction, the American capitalistic system has made big business out of this crisis. Pollution control has simply become another major industry— American style. Pollution profit is pursued, although this time it is under the ideological camouflage of "cleaning up the environment." Ecology has become a good issue for increasing magazine circulation, for those campaigning for political office, and for big business. Shell puts out ads saying how good they are to the environment. Everything seems to get better because they are drilling for oil. So does Standard. And Exxon. And Mobil. And Texaco. And the rest. If we listen to such sources, as well as to our politicians, we would believe that the ecological crisis is being solved. Rather than finding solutions, however, pollution and ecology are simply being tamed into innocuous non-political issues. But innocuous they are not; and nonpolitical they are not.

In the second selection, Gellen analyzes the collusion taking place between the pollution control business and the industrial polluters. Many of the industrialists who are doing the polluting are now getting into the act of cleaning up pollution. They are not doing so out of any good intentions or out of concern for people or for the environment, Gellen says, but because there is now a healthy profit in the anti-pollution industry. Industries that have been polluting the environment will now be paid by the government, and ultimately by the taxpayer, to clean up the very pollutants with which they have fouled our environment. This is a most interesting situation—making profits by creating waste, and then making further profits by cleaning up that same waste. This is what one might well call "cleaning up" all the way around. It is also worth noting that the pollution control industries pollute the environment while they are manufacturing their anti-pollution products.

Can you possibly reverse this situation and imagine the poor polluting the streams used by the rich, and then not only getting away with it and avoiding arrest, but also being paid by the rich through the government to clean up their own pollution? The question reduces to power differential. Who has the power, and how is this power being manipulated for greater benefits to those who have it?

Is our present course reversible? I certainly hope so, but I am far from convinced that it is. The concluding article by Inglis deals with a particular type of pollution; one about which most of us are probably aware, one which threatens our existence—and one which continues as though it did not directly concern our fate. Nuclear pollution is the subject of this concluding essay.

Nuclear pollution brings to mind the threat of nuclear holocaust—a nuclear war that might destroy us all, including through radiation those generations that would otherwise have been born. But that is only one form of nuclear pollution—the unlikely one. Certainly nuclear warfare might come, and that might well mark the end of humanity. But there are other forms of nuclear pollution going on around us right now, at this very moment, that also hold the possibility of similar destruction of human existence. Radiation pollution. Nuclear wastes being produced in the form of plutonium, tritium, and uranium products. Waste that we don't know what to do with. Waste that stays radioactive for generations and generations. Waste that threatens the existence of humanity but is still being produced as though it were but another form of garbage. Waste that must be put in "perpetual care storage." Waste that is poured into steel and concrete underground tanks. Waste now in the amount of around 1,000,000 gallons—when just three gallons evenly distributed around the earth's population would bring every person's body to the danger point in radiation. Yet with all of these conditions, the production blindly goes on. Profit is involved—and the economic system dictates immediate profit, without consequence to the generations yet unborn.

19

Barry Weisberg

The Politics of Ecology

The critical importance of ecology as a developing source of political opposition in America stems from the realization that politics in our age has acquired an absolute character. While political decision making and control is steadily concentrated in the hands of a very few—the arena of control is steadily expanding. Fewer and fewer people control more and more—so that the very conditions which support life on this planet: the land we walk upon, the air we breathe, and the water we drink, are now the subjects of political management on a scale beyond normal comprehension. The politics of ecology must start from the premise that present-day reality is increasingly the product of a structure of economic and political power that consolidates and sustains itself through the systematic destruction of man and his physical world. The exploitation of man by man and nature by man are merely two sides of the same coin.

It is then folly to think that the destruction of our global life support systems under advanced industrial capitalism or communism is merely a by-product of progress, a case of bad management, the result of insufficient esthetic sensibilities on the part of business and engineers, or simply a matter of who owns the means of production. In an historical sense, we have reached the point where we can totally violate the processes and structures of the natural world; hence our relationship to nature is no longer determined by the forces of nature but by the rule of political management. The deterioration of the natural environment all around us is therefore clearly a product of the nature of production and consumption, of cultural values and social relationships that today hold sway over industrial technological society —American or Soviet.

In short, our present technical manipulation of the life-support ca-

Barry Weisberg, "The Politics of Ecology," Liberation, *January 1970, pp. 20–25. Reprinted by permission.*

pacity of the planet now threatens the totality of physical conditions which nurture life itself. The oxygen content in the atmosphere, the metabolism of our own bodies, food chains and the relationship between populations and the resources needed to support them, conditions upon which the existence of all plant and animal life today depends, are the products of evolutionary processes extending over billions of years. Our industrial civilization is now destroying them in a matter of decades. We are talking about processes which may well have worked their irrevocable consequences within a decade or two— after which there will be nothing within the human potential to restore their life-giving capacity.

The culture itself is aware of the explosive potential of the imbalances between society and nature. Government and industry through the media have begun to manage these issues on a daily basis. Scientists speak out, reports are called for and committees created. In fact the pattern of action and language emerging around pollution parallels exactly the failures of civil rights and poverty—"a war on pollution," the calling for a "pollution pentagon." Even new bureaucratic offices to replace the Department of Interior are suggested. What such proposals miss is that it is not the control of the land, air and water that is at stake but the control of man.

The obvious question resulting from this brief survey is whether or not these are matters of bad management, disfunction or the like, as mentioned earlier. The origins of our present destruction of the life-support capacity of this planet are rooted in the very fabric of our civilization, reaching their most insane dimensions in the present corporate America. The Greek rationalism of Aristotle, the Roman engineering mentality, the biblical anthropomorphic injunctions to "have dominion over the land and subdue every creeping thing," the post-Enlightenment notions of growth and progress, the present technical corporate economic systems motivated by competition—all dominate the Western mentality of man against nature. Where nature works toward harmony, cooperation and interdependence, advanced industrial society works toward growth, competition and independence. The advanced nation state works in direct opposition to those basic life giving instincts which have nourished our billion year evolution. To repeat, the domination of man by man and man over nature are two sides of the same coin. The precondition of our survival requires the most basic transformation of the cultural, social, political and economic mentalities and structures which dominate the developed nations and hang as a carrot over the never-to-be-developed nations.

In view of the sudden flurry of government-initiated programs (including the spate of officially endorsed campus "teach-ins"), it is especially chilling to contemplate the performance of government, industry and their conservationist junior partners. Here's a rundown:

GOVERNMENT

The proportion of the National Budget spent on all natural resource programs has declined steadily since 1959.

1965	2.3%
1966	2.2%
1967	2.0%
1968	1.9%
1969	1.9% est.
1970	1.8% est.

In other words, for fiscal 1969, we spent only 3.6 billion on all natural resource programs, of some 202 billion dollars, spending more (4 billion) to reach outer space than to make the earth habitable. The gap between authorization and appropriation on programs such as air and water pollution has widened every year. This is merely to demonstrate the inability of the Congress to achieve its own stated objectives —not that those objectives would have successfully dealt with any major issue. In fact, there is every reason to believe that more spending would have produced merely more pollution. Add to this a government which at the same time subsidizes the supersonic transport, maintains the depletion allowance for continued off-shore drilling, undermines efforts at consumer protection—and one begins to understand the meaning of federal efforts. While there are more committees, more reports, more research and more attention, less and less is actually done. The frightening conclusion, however, is not that government should do more, for the more it does the worse our ecological systems get.

INDUSTRY

What are we to make of the flurry of industrial ads depicting everything from Standard Oil to Dow Chemical to the American Rifle Association as conservation-minded people? Of the recent Business of Pollution Control Technology of the investment of industry in conservation organization? The answer I think is to be found, for instance, in the words of Robert O. Anderson, chairman of the board of Atlantic Richfield. In a recent address before a State Department–sponsored conference on Man and His Environment, Anderson argued that the costs of pollution control should be passed on to the consumer and that oil should remain the base of energy supply. In short, industry has made of the environmental crisis a commodity. Recent financial reports indicate that the business of pollution control will in fact make a profit out of pollution while at the same time generating more pollution: more growth will be the remedy applied to the perils of growth. In short, that advertising will continue to cost more for business than research, that the consumers will be passed on any costs of "pollution control," and that federal agencies, new or old, will continue to operate as captives of the industry they are to regulate.

CONSERVATION

More than any single element of the present collage of conservation activity, the conservation organizations themselves, to varying degrees, lead the public to believe that the Emperor has no clothes when in fact they serve as clothes for the Emperor. Such organizations act in the most fragmentary ways, attacking isolated problems and not complex patterns of social and political behavior. They save a nature area and fail to address the entire land use patterns of that region. They save a seashore from development when that seashore is threatened with the biological destruction of its wildlife. As such, their victories are at best stop gaps, always provisional. They foster the existence of centralized forms of authority through the support they lend to present elective procedures—"get the good guys in office." They have virtually no critical understanding of the governments of oil, agri-business, public utilities or chemicals. The conservationists frequently violence-bait the Left or shun it as revolutionary. "The country is tired of SDS and ready to see someone like us come to the forefront," a young conservationist recently noted. Increasingly motivated and supported by various governmental machinations, these people work in total isolation to the civil rights and peace movements, with no relationship to the varied forces of opposition and liberation in the society today—the revolutionary young, women's liberation, labor, and oppressed minorities. They seek private solutions to what more correctly are public issues—picking up litter rather than attacking the production of junk, refusing to use autos rather than struggling against oil and the auto manufacturers, to be merely suggestive.

But most important, the "new breed of young conservationists" fail to see that the crisis of the environment truly is but a reflective of the crisis of this culture itself, of the values, institutions, and procedures which has for some 200 years systematically guided the slaughter of human and all other forms of life at home and abroad. These tendencies were demonstrated too well by a recent selection of "youth" hand-picked by the Department of State to participate in the US Commission for UNESCO Conference on Man and His Environment in San Francisco last month. Virtually all "programs" suggested by these participants lent credence to the status quo by advocating "better" candidates, new ecology colleges, yet additional "research," and more jobs for conservation-minded college kids.

The barrage of petitions and letters to the President was greeted by the conference "adults" with adulation, for the kids turned out to be "reasonable men" just as their parents. The popular press billed their performance as revolutionary—defined as "non-violent," get-your-man-in-office, and increased student participation. But the role of our benign media goes much further.

By and large, the media has purposely obscured the political and social content of the environmental crisis by confining problems as well as solutions solely to the realm of science and technology. The result is that blind faith in the omnipotence of expertise and technocracy wholly dominates current thinking on ecological issues. Technological innovation and more reasonable methods of resource allocation cannot possibly reverse the present logic of the environment unless the overriding political, social and economic framework which has actually generated that trend is radically rebuilt. Such a transformation cannot reside solely in the realm of culture and values—as most often proposed by the youthful elites of conservation. The critical task today is to raise the issue of pollution/destruction, imperialistic styles of consumption, and of over-population to a political status in order to reveal an arena of political opposition in America which the Left has hitherto ignored. That is not to say that the Left can simply absorb the ecological crisis into its own kind of "business as usual" behavior. For the patterns of life in which most of us partake are not much different than those of the ruling class. This is not to say that true solutions reside in private action, but that public transformation without an entirely different style of life is futile. Thus the development of an ecological politics on a practical level may provide the only framework in which the alienated and oppressed can achieve true liberation.

That potential for liberation doesn't lie in the Save the Bay Campaigns, the protection of a redwood grove or planned parenthood. It does not reside alone in the culturally symbolic acts of many ecology action groups around the country. The true origin of what has yet to become an authentic movement is in the People's Park episode, in militant actions against corporate despoilers (including sabotage) and in the private as well as public attempts to create ecologically sound lives.

While the traditional conservationists have made no imaginative attempt to understand what our cities would look like without autos, with decentralized agriculture or power, with neighborhood control and rationed resources, save for few scant efforts, the Left, with few exceptions, has been equally derelict. "Radical" economists still contem-

plate growth-motivated economies grounded in false notions of affluence and unlimited resources.

The New Left has at this point made little serious effort to understand or relate to the politics of ecology. While the battles in the streets
appear more pressing and more direct, it ought to be understood that
unless something very basic and very revolutionary is done about the
continued destruction of our life support systems, there may well be no
wind to weather in the near future.

Dismissing over-population as simply a matter of genocide, efforts
to take back the land as bourgeois or the necessity for clean air and
water as a luxury completely fails to grasp what can only properly be
understood as a matter of life or death.

The task of ecological radicals is to continually raise those issues
which sort those which would seek to patch up the status quo from
those who struggle for basic transformation. The polarization of the
rulers and the ruled is the authentic growth of any true movement for
liberation. When conservationists argue that everyone is in the same
boat (or on the same raft), that everyone must work together, temper-
ing their action to suit the imperatives of coalition, they are in fact
arguing for the further consolidation of power and profit in the hands
of those responsible for the present dilemma.

There is no easy way to summarize exactly how the Movement must
respond to the growing politics of ecology. Publishing special magazine
editions and flimsy attacks on "sewermen" will not do. Few models exist
to lend direction to organizing efforts. Already throughout the country
people have been organized around industrial accidents and health
hazards, consumer boycotts, women's liberation and the nuclear family, the extinction of animal species or the struggle against a new
highway. This is just the beginning. This winter and spring we can
expect a series of radical ecological actions: the bombing of more corporate headquarters, sabotage to the industrial machinery that pollutes
and obstruction at airports and other transportation corridors.

It is safe to suggest that organizing around environment issues that
fails immediately to lead to the political causes and implications of that
peril is misguided. For too long eco news and reports have begun and
ended with nature—without understanding that nature itself is today
the product of manipulation by man. We should have learned from the
People's Park that the road ahead will be perilous and paved with a life
and death struggle. If the State of California would defend a parking
lot with the life of one person and the shooting of another 150, imagine
the cost of taking back a forest, preventing an off-shore drilling rig
from being placed, blocking the construction of a nuclear power plant or
tampering with the power/communication/food/transport systems
which make America grow. But the sooner this happens the better. The
sooner the spirit of the People's Park infuses every ecological action, the

brighter will be our chances to insure the conditions for our survival and, beyond that, a decent society.

Educating "the people about the impending ecological disaster" without pointing to possible forms of action available is at this point a disservice to the Movement. As people engage in direct struggle against the Con Edisons, the Standard Oils, the pollution control agencies, and the United Fruit companies of the world, more and more new insights for strategy will develop. What has been happening to poor whites and blacks for several hundred years, what America has done to the Vietnamese, America is now doing to its own population, en masse. The organizing implications of this single fact may be profound. In a world of total biological slavery, liberation is the very condition of Life itself. To fail does not mean growing up absurd, but not growing up at all.

Martin Gellen

20

The Making of a Pollution-
Industrial Complex

In January of this year Coca-Cola Company announced its purchase
of Aqua-Chem, a leading manufacturer of water treatment equipment
and desalination systems. "The acquisition will permit Coca-Cola to
enter the mainstream of environmental control systems," declared a
spokesman for the company. Perhaps the people at Coke have seen the
handwriting on the wall and realize that their livelihood depends on
having clean water to make brown. But whatever the precise reasoning, the marriage of Coke and Aqua-Chem is just one among a rash of
similar developments on Wall Street where pollution control has
emerged as one of the hottest growth industries of the '70's. As Forbes
Magazine put it in a recent cover story, there's "cash in all that trash."

Since the beginning of December 1969, despite a market engaged
in a remarkably stubborn downward spiral, stock issues of companies
with substantial interests in pollution control have made price advances of often better than fifty percent. For instance, Research-Cottrell,
Inc., the largest of the corporations devoted entirely to environmental
systems, has quadrupled its sales in five years. For the pollution control
industry as a whole, the average annual growth rate for the next five
years is expected to climb to better than twenty percent, which is almost three times that of most manufacturing groups.

Lester Krellenstein, an engineer and pollution control promoter for
the brokerage firm of H. Hentz and Company, believes that President
Nixon's appointment of a Council of Environmental Quality triggered
the heavy buying. According to Krellenstein, "A great deal of money is
going to be made in this business." Present estimates of the potential
market start at $25 billion.

But of all the developments in the fledgling industry, by far the most instructive is the corporate integration of polluters and controllers. About two dozen pollution control companies are subsidiaries or divisions of the largest corporations and polluters in the United States. Represented among this latter group are Dow Chemical Co., Monsanto Chemical, W. R. Grace, DuPont, Merck, Nalco, Union Carbide, General Electric, Westinghouse, Combustion Engineering, Honeywell, Beckman Instruments, Alcoa, Universal Oil Products, North American Rockwell, and many others. Although these supercorporations currently make less in sales from pollution control than do smaller firms like Research-Cottrell and Wheelabrator, their superior access to capital, resources, markets, management skills and political power will invariably be translated into a superior competitive position as the ecology movement flowers and the control industry grows.

II

The pollution control industry is really an extension of both the technological capabilities and the marketing patterns of the capital goods sector of the economy. Most of the companies involved in pollution control are not only polluters themselves but are the same firms which supply the chemicals, machines, plant fuels and parts for even bigger polluters, such as General Motors, U.S. Steel, Boeing, Standard Oil, Philco-Ford, American Can Co. and Consolidated Edison. For many of these firms, pollution control is merely one aspect of a program of "environmental diversification," which is generally accompanied by heavy investment and aggressive acquisition programs.

Koppers, for instance, is an engineering and construction firm that designs municipal sewage plants as well as air and water purification systems. Among its many specialists in pollution abatement is the production of gas removal devices for electric utilities, steel plants, coke plants, and foundries. At the same time, however, Koppers is one of the world's leading builders of steelmaking equipment and is responsible for designing over 25 percent of all basic steelmaking facilities in the U.S., as well as half of the present domestic coke plants in operation. Thus it gets the business coming and going. Since 80 percent of the coke plants in the nation will require modernization in the '70's, and the steel industry expects to increase its overall capacity by 50 percent, Koppers can expect good profits designing the pollution control systems needed to curb the pollution caused by all the new coke ovens, steel furnaces and foundries which it will construct.

It is the chemical industry, however, that best illustrates the consequences of the incest between the pollution control business and the industrial polluters. First, the chemical industry is in the enviable position of reaping sizable profits by attempting to clean up rivers and lakes (at public expense) which they have profitably polluted in the first place. To facilitate this, practically every major chemical company in the U.S. has established a pollution abatement division or is in the process of doing so. Dow Chemical, for example, produces a wide variety of products and services for water pollution abatement, including measuring instruments, specialty treatment chemicals, and a special biological filter medium called SURF-PAC. The company designs, engineers, builds and services waste water treatment plants and is currently supervising municipal sewage plants in Cleveland and working on waste disposal problems for lumber companies in Pensacola, Florida, and West Nyack, New York. All of these projects are funded by the Federal Water Pollution Control Administration (FWPCA).

Thus, the chemical industry—which ranks second in production of polluted waste water and generates close to 50 percent of the biological oxygen demand in industrial water before treatment—has, at the same time, established a dominant position in the water pollution control business.

A second consequence of placing the "control" of pollution in the hands of big business is that the official abatement levels will inevitably be set low enough to protect industry's power to pollute and therefore its ability to keep costs down and revenues high. According to a recent study by the FWPCA, if the chemical industry were to reduce its pollution of water to zero, the costs involved would amount to almost $2.7 billion per year. This would cut profits almost by half.

Fortunately for the chemical industry, the present abatement target is only 75 percent reduction in water pollution through "secondary treatment" methods which will clean up the solids but leave the phosphates, nitrogen compounds and a host of other poisonous substances which secondary treatment can't possibly catch.

Of course, it is precisely the profit incentive as the criterion of what shall and shall not be produced that makes it impossible to stop the proliferation and profusion of poisons in even the most obvious places. Thus, the chemical industry has polluted the housewife's food package not only through the unintended absorption of pesticide residues, but also through innumerable colorings, additives (like the cyclamates) and preservatives designed to increase food purchases and consumption, in order to buoy up sagging sales curves. The package itself, which is a sales boosting device par excellence, can be both the most polluting and dangerous feature of all. As a pièce de résistance the chemical industry produces the non-biodegradable plastic container, which comes in all sizes, shapes and colors, and, if made from polyvinyl plastic, like Dow's Saran-Wrap, can be deadly in the most literal sense of the word. When Saran-Wrap is accumulated as trash and burned, it produces phosgene gas—a poison gas used in World War I and currently stockpiled by the Department of Defense. Exposure for only a short duration to fifty parts of phosgene per million parts of air will cause death. The chemical industry currently makes approximately five billion pounds of polyvinyl plastic per year and output is expected to rise by seven per cent this year alone.

Another consequence of business control of cleaning up the environment is cost to the public. Most municipal water treatment plants in large urban areas are currently constructed to handle an excess capacity frequently 100 percent greater than the volume of waste actually produced by their resident populations. Much of this surplus capacity is used by big business (especially the chemical industry) to dispose of its wastes. Although industries are charged for this use, it is the consumers and taxpayers, through federal grants and state bonds, who bear the cost of construction and maintenance of the treatment facilities. Thus the public pays the polluters to construct the treatment facilities necessitated by the polluters in the first place.

Thus pollution control, developed as a complementary industry, is a way to insure that the favorable balance between cost, sales and profits can be maintained and business can continue as usual—indeed, better than usual, for pollution control means new investment outlets, new income and new profits; the more waste, the better. Pollution control as conceived by the pollution control industry is merely an extension of the same pattern of profit-seeking exploitation and market economics which is at the root of the environmental crisis itself.

III

The most salient fact about the crisis that now threatens to overwhelm us is that it is first and foremost a product of the so-called free-enterprise system. "American business," as Fortune admits, "since it organizes and channels a high proportion of the total action of this society, has been and still is deeply implicated in depredations against the environment." It is not technology per se, but the way technology is employed (its organization and channeling) that creates the problems. Take, for example, the automobile. What logic determined man's use, as his central mode of transportation, of a device which threw concrete highways across the plains, cut up the forests, poisoned the atmosphere, congested the cities and created the sprawling conurbations that have smothered the land? Was it safe? Computed as fatalities per mile, the death rate for cars is twenty-five times that for trains and ten times that for planes. Was it efficient? A traffic study made in 1907 shows that horse-drawn vehicles in New York moved at an average speed of 11.5 miles per hour. Today, automobiles crawl at the average daytime rate of six miles per hour.

At the beginning of the '60's it was estimated that in a single day, motor vehicles burned about seven million gallons of gasoline and in the process produced enough carbon monoxide to pollute the air to a depth of 400 feet over an area of 681 square miles. One-third of the entire land area of Los Angeles (two-thirds of the downtown section) had been absorbed by cars and trucks and the facilities to service them. The area was so congested that plans were laid to spend another $7.5 billion over the next decade on highway construction. The highway program would cost $10,000 per family, while during the same period only $3090 per family would be spent in Los Angeles County for schools, hospitals, parks, water supply, recreation and all other facilities. And Los Angeles is no worse in this respect than other city or urban areas. New York is now spending $100 million per mile to construct a cross-town highway. But in the peak hours, 87.6 percent of the people entering the central business district come by public transport (71 percent by subway).

Is there any rationality in all this? There is. But it is a private rationality. The essence of the private property system is that social technology and production are privately or corporately organized and channeled through the market. Thus, in launching his new product, Henry Ford had only private costs to reckon (i.e., the costs to him in labor, materials, etc.). The individual consumer who bought the car had only to reckon his personal preferences versus the purchase price. The question of who would pay the costs of roads, of restructuring cities and organizing the flow of traffic, was taken care of by Ford, the rubber industry, the glass industry, the concrete industry and related interests getting together and twisting the arm of the government. They saw to it that the public would pay for solving the problems created by the new machine.

The costs of pollution are borne by our lungs and in individual cleaning bills; the costs of lack of safety are paid in individual hospital bills and individual deaths. Suppose Ford had been forced from the outset to reckon the social costs (at least the ones that could be quantified) and to put that in the price of his autos. At that price, people would have bought trains as their mass transportation, or more reasonably, they would have been forced to structure their cities and communities in a way which would have enabled them to walk to virtually all of the places necessary.

The problems created by the market system are thus like original sin: their implications keep spreading and diversifying. Now, when the demand for cars shows signs of being saturated, the market strategists get to work and—by changing models, manipulating consumers and planning the obsolescence of their product—generate the need for more and more cars, ad infinitum. The waste in resources is staggering (it has been estimated that style changes in autos alone cost $4 billion annually) and the increase in pollution incalculable.

The pollution control industry itself reflects this irrationality in production for profit. It, too, is a growth industry. It, too, depends for its existence on society's capacity to make waste. The production of steel, copper, aluminum, asbestos and beryllium components for air pollution systems and sewage plants will probably create more air pollution and kill more rivers. The waste involved in the production of all the specialty chemicals and biological agents needed for water treatment alone is staggering. Moreover, the waste in resources required to operate $100 billion worth of control systems will certainly not reduce the despoliation of the environment.

Instead of reorganizing the productive system for social ends, thereby eliminating the problem of waste production and distribution at its source, pollution control under business auspices amounts to no more than rationalizing and improving waste production by making it less ugly, less harmful, less objectionable, and more pleasant for everybody. The object of this kind of pollution control is to make pollution "functional" in society, to institutionalize it, to change it into a necessary and regular part of the everyday world. There is no more effective way to do that than to make it possible for a whole industry to make money out of it. To the military-industrial complex, we can now add an eco-pollution-industrial complex, with a vested interest in continuing economic growth and environmental malaise.

The philosophical justifications for this "solution" are already well developed. As President Nixon's science adviser, Dr. Lee A. DuBridge, puts it, "Let's face it—waste products are a fact of life we have to recognize. . . . Clearly, the U.S. will be producing more waste in the future—not less." The purpose of pollution control, DuBridge explains, is simply to "determine reasonable levels of pollution consistent with good health." Such a logic simultaneously justifies the political economy of waste, effectively de-politicizes the issues of the environment, and defines the problem of pollution in terms of technological solutions and bureaucratic directives. As such it is the normal logic of a society whose business, as Coolidge once said, is business.

Following every failure of the business system in a major social area, the government has stepped in to create a new social-industrial complex, passing the costs of rehabilitation and correction on to the tax-paying public, and reserving the benefits for the corporations. Like the defense suppliers and the educational-manpower conglomerates, the pollution control industry now enjoys the good fortune of being legislated into success. Lavish profits will come from ready-made markets bolstered by special laws controlling pollution levels of factories, special tax write-offs for the industrial buyers of abatement equipment, and plenty of R&D money for the pollution controllers themselves. As government outlays on abatement grow, so will the profits accruing to the pollution control industry. With Uncle Sam posing as Mr. Clean, the crisis of the environment can't help being profitable.

At the National Executives Conference on Water Pollution Abatement, convened last fall by the Department of Interior in order to "bring the environmental programs of business and government into close alignment," John Gillis, president of Monsanto Chemical Co., led the business executives in calling for immediate federal financial aid in the form of quick tax write-offs and investment credits. The Tax Reform Bill passed by Congress early this winter answered the call. While abolishing the seven percent investment credit, Congress instituted a special five-year amortization allowance for pollution control equipment, which will actually allow a lot of corporations somewhat larger tax deductions than did the investment credit. In addition, some twenty-two states also offer such subsidies for installation of pollution control equipment. California, for example, provides for a special five-year write-off, while Connecticut gives anti-polluters a five percent tax credit.

With the prospects of rising R&D expenditures by the federal government, everyone is getting into the act. Anaconda and Alcoa have recently established environmental divisions. Esso Research has started a five-year planning study to determine the National Air Pollution Control Administration (NAPCA) needs in the area of nitrogen oxide emission control. The presence of aerospace corporations and other major defense contractors like Dow, G.E. and Westinghouse on the federal pollution control payroll is of course more than mere coincidence. Currently, the aerospace industry receives about twenty-five percent of all the research contracts awarded by NAPCA. Aerojet-General, Avco Industries, Bendix Corporation and Litton Industries are some of the more prominent newcomers to the field. For Litton, Bendix and Aerojet-General, pollution control is a spin-off from their government-sponsored programs for development of biological weapons. Aerojet-General has also received over a million dollars in contracts from the Federal Water Pollution Control Administration for control of toxic agents in water supplies.

After riot control, pollution control is another area in which North American Rockwell, builder of Apollo and one of the country's biggest defense contractors, expects to make "important social contributions as well as profits," according to Robert T. Chambers, chairman of Envirotech, which is NAR's new pollution abatement subsidiary. Envirotech will market some of the measuring devices which NAR has developed through work for FWPCA, NAPCA, the Defense Department's chemical and biological warfare programs, and the space program. Just to keep it all in the family, President Nixon is reportedly planning to place the coordination of pollution control R&D programs under the aegis of the National Aeronautics and Space Administration instead of setting up a special agency for this purpose.

Nixon is also arranging to whip up a little business for investment bankers. As a part of Nixon's $10 billion program for municipal sewage plant construction, state and local governments will finance their $6 billion share of the deal through tax-exempt bonds. The President will also establish an Environmental Funding Authority to buy up any of the bonds which the locals can't sell. The EFA will probably handle a good number of them, since the municipal and state government bond markets are currently glutted. Its own funds would come from the sale of bonds at the even higher non-municipal rates. The Treasury Department (headed by banker David Kennedy) would make up the difference between the interest the EFA would receive on local bonds and what it would have to pay out on its own. In other words, the taxpayers would once again pay the bill.

Thus, pollution control programs illustrate the ways in which government promotes the welfare of business at the expense of the taxpaying public. The non-taxpaying poor will also suffer. It's all a matter of priorities. More federal spending for pollution control will mean less for the war on poverty. "Ultimately," pontificates the Wall Street Journal, "preservation of the environment may have to take absolute priority over social stability and welfare."

The crisis of the environment must be viewed in terms of a paradox central to modern society. The mobilization of the productive energies of society and the physical forces of nature for the purpose of accumulating profits or enhancing private power and privilege now conflicts directly with the universal dependence of men upon nature for the means of their common survival. A society whose principal ends and incentives are monetary and expansionist inevitably produces material and cultural impoverishment—in part precisely because of the abundance of profitable goods. To make an industry out of cleaning up the mess that industry itself makes is a logical extension of corporate capitalism. What is needed, however, is not an extension of what is already bad, but its transformation into something better.

David R. Inglis

21

Nuclear Pollution
and
the Arms Race

Both the arms race between the nuclear giants and the rapid growth of industry are making appalling inroads on our environment. The manufacture and testing of nuclear weapons add to the world's burden of radioactive contamination, while industrial activity, stimulated by the arms race and civilian demand, belches noxious contaminants into the atmosphere and water courses.

Yet in our ardor for preserving the environment we must not forget that there is a far more compelling reason for putting a lid on the arms race, namely, reducing the risk of nuclear war.

The direct way to modify the arms race is by negotiation and wise example. It is our country that has principally fired the nuclear arms race by insisting on being way ahead in most categories. Our overkill is such that we could afford to set an example of moderation and watch for reciprocal restraint on the other side. The U.S. negotiation stance at the Vienna arms reduction talks should be one of initiative to attain substantial mutual limitations and reductions, rather than one of stalling until we get ABMs and MIRVs before talking seriously.

The recent sudden shift of liberal concern from the ABM to the environment seems to be leaving a vacuum where pressure is urgently needed to stop the arms race by diplomacy and restraint.

The way President Nixon has hopped on the environment bandwagon with enthusiastic words, if little substance, suggests he may have sensed its importance in weakening the opposition that was nearly successful last time, as he seeks to step up the ABM program. With the perpetual expansion of the military establishment, nuclear weapons production is likely to grow, increasing radioactive pollution at home and around the world, strengthening the military-industrial complex, and moving mankind closer to the full horror of nuclear war.

Concern for the environment, and even legislation protecting it, can mildly shackle some of the details of weapons production, but only a change of foreign policy can stop it. The basic shortcoming of the President's budget message was that it called for no really substantial transfer of funds from Vietnam and the arms race to the anti-pollution effort, and gave no indication of an intention to taper off the arms race and make this transfer possible in the future.

The production of nuclear materials—plutonium, tritium, and separated uranium—involves the production of enormous amounts of radioactive materials that must be disposed of as waste, and in the production of power which ends up by heating rivers and lakes enough to affect aquatic life. Furthermore, the uranium separation consumes a lot of power generated by burning coal. It is the disposal of radioactive wastes that is the most serious problem nuclear power presents to the environment. Nuclear materials are produced to fuel both the arms race and the electric utilities industry. The needs of both threaten the environment in a cumulative way.

The most dramatic effect of the arms race on the environment came from the testing of nuclear weapons in the atmosphere in the era before the partial test ban of 1963. Radioactive fission products in unprecedented quantities were carried high in the atmosphere by the mushroom clouds of the big H-bomb explosions, and gradually settled over much of the earth. Yet people went about their daily lives without noticing any tangible or identifiable effects on the environment. We normally live with a weak exposure of radiation from cosmic rays and from ordinary rocks. In terms of this natural background, the increase of overall radiation was not large and some authorities scoffed at misgivings. The normal background causes some cancer and genetic change, and a slight increase could not be easily isolated and recognized.

Yet this oft-quoted comparison with natural background is unfair because the fission process, that which takes place in bomb explosions and in electric power generating reactors, does not merely increase the background radiation. It produces kinds of radioactive substances that are different and which settle in and attack the human body in specific ways, unlike the natural background radiation. Rocks and cosmic rays provide a natural background of gamma rays (deeply penetrating X-rays) and less penetrating beta-rays (electrons) that pass through the whole body indiscriminately, causing weak ionization on the way; cosmic rays passing through the atmosphere also make a special radioactive substance, carbon-14, that becomes rather generally distributed through body tissues. But the fission process creates new types of radioactive atoms that do not exist in nature, and that are dissipated through the air (and water and food supplies) until they settle in the body. Depending on their chemical nature, some of them locate preferentially in certain sensitive parts to do their radioactive damage in a concentrated fashion. Thus, while the overall radiation dosage may be raised only a few per cent by bomb test fallout, the biological damage is disproportionately serious.

During the course of nuclear bomb testing, the danger of one particular element of fallout, strontium 90, was initially denied by Federal Government spokesmen. Its threat was first established by university scientists in independent research. Strontium 90 has a long-lived radioactivity. It is chemically similar to calcium and settles in bone. It concentrates particularly rapidly in the fast-growing bone of fetuses and young children. It gets there by settling on grass eaten by cows and is concentrated in milk. Starting in St. Louis, and then more widely, records have been kept of strontium 90 in the teeth normally lost by children, as well as in fetal skeletons. As a radioactive part of the bone, within which blood is made, strontium 90 can cause leukemia and other forms of cancer. It also attacks the genes, and can cause birth defects and infant death. Yet these maladies arise also from other causes and one cannot pinpoint which cases are caused by the arms race. Invisible though the fallout was, we are well rid of the insidious atmospheric testing which might have been much heavier by now if we had had no test ban.

We should be eager to preserve and extend the test ban. Instead, after all our early worries about the Russians, it is we who are callously breaking it. Of more than two hundred U.S. underground tests, seventeen have vented seriously and the radioactivity from two has been officially reported as observed in Canada. Further pressure to abandon the test ban is apt to come with the growth of the ABM system.

Yet even without nuclear war and without nuclear testing, the arms race still has its effect on the environment through the preparation of nuclear materials. The mine and uranium mill tailings—the waste products—are themselves a serious local danger. They expose ores that were once locked underground to leaching by rain and consequent radioactive pollution of our rivers. But this is still only an accelerated recirculation of nature's radioactivity, mainly that of radium with its slow and therefore relatively weak decay.

More serious are the new man-made radioactive elements, byproducts of the reactors that make plutonium and tritium for bombs. Some of these have lifetimes that are short enough to make the immediate radiation intense and yet long enough that they create a hazard for tens or hundreds of years, such as strontium 90 and cesium 137, which have half-value decay times of about thirty years. This means that after a hundred years, they would still be about one-tenth as radioactive as now and still a grave hazard in view of the huge amounts being put in perpetual-care storage.

Some of the nuclear reactors are operated for the Federal Government exclusively for the production of bomb materials. Such plants are at Hanford, Washington (the site of the original wartime plant), Paducah, Kentucky, and Savannah River, South Carolina.

Still other nuclear reactors are owned and operated by the electric utilities industry under Government subsidy for the dual purpose of producing plutonium (much of it for bombs) and electric power.

The subsidies provided by the Atomic Energy Commission at the taxpayers' expense take several forms. One is risk insurance. The Federal Government pays for most of what limited insurance coverage there is, and beyond that lets the public take the risk of the possible consequences of a serious reactor-runaway accident.

As another form of subsidy, the Government runs the huge, expensive, energy-consuming, thermal-diffusion plants. These supply the enriched uranium used as fuel in the industrial reactors at a favorable price to industry. A third form of subsidy is the guaranteed price at which the Government will buy all the plutonium industry produces. It is hoped that plutonium as well as enriched uranium will be used to fuel future reactors, but we do not yet know how.

The only current use for plutonium is for bombs. Both because this subsidy was necessary to make the rather marginal hoped-for profits sufficiently attractive to get the industrial program started and because the plutonium is used for bombs, the nuclear electric power program may be considered a handmaiden of the armaments program and its contribution to environmental pollution may be blamed partly on the arms race.

Most of the radioactivity produced by a reactor stays inside the metal fuel elements in the reactor core. After a period of a year or two the reactor is shut down while the fuel is removed and replaced. The partially spent fuel is sent to a reprocessing plant where the radioactive wastes are extracted in acid solution that is kept so hot by the radioactive decay that it boils if it is not continually cooled. This extremely lethal brew must be prevented from entering the environment, but the containment is not perfect despite all the care taken.

At present, such high-level wastes in this country are stored in about 200 large underground steel-and-concrete tanks, holding as much as a million gallons each. Most of these wastes came from weapons production not associated with electric power production. The radioactive intensity of the liquid (measured in a unit known as a "curie") may run as high as a thousand curies per gallon or more. This is so lethal that if only three gallons were distributed equally among the entire world's population, this would suffice to reach in everyone on earth what is considered the danger point in radiation for the human body.

Yet we already have in those buried tanks a hundred million gallons of the stuff, and apparently plan to go on producing it at an ever-increasing rate. These storage tanks require most elaborate perpetual care. They not only need power to cool them, but new high-quality tanks must be installed about every twenty years, on through the centuries, to replace old tanks damaged by radiation. Already failure of one tank has spilled 60,000 gallons of that lethal brew to find its uncertain way through the soil.

During the routine operation of reactors and fuel-processing plants there are also both planned and inadvertent releases of low-level wastes that contaminate air and water. The hot fuel elements in a reactor are sealed in a thin metal bonding intended to prevent the cooling fluid from coming into direct contact with the uranium and absorbing the radioactive fission products. However, in the power-generating plants, technology is pushed to its limit of high temperature and the metal seal frequently fails. It would be too expensive to interrupt operation for each failure, so leaks are tolerated in something like one per cent of the fuel elements before shutdown. This is one route by which strontium and other radioactive fission products get into rivers.

Krypton 85 is a radioactive gas which, like neon and argon, does not easily react with other atoms to form solids, and remains a gas that escapes into the atmosphere. Some of it goes up the stack at the reactor, because of leaks, and the rest of it escapes at the fuel-processing plant. When breathed in air, a little of it dissolves in body fats. Radioactive tritium, the stuff of the H-bomb, is also produced in reactors and finds its way both into the atmosphere and into water supplies. It enters into bodily processes as part of water molecules.

The annual amount of the release of hazardous elements from any nuclear plant is limited by standards set up by the Atomic Energy Commission. Since it is impossible to pinpoint all radioactive damage at low levels, the standards necessarily depend on somewhat arbitrary judgments. At high levels, it is known how much radiation will probably kill a man, and how much will probably give him serious radiation sickness. Permissible doses for workers in atomic plants are set well below that level, about one per cent of the lethal standard per year. But for the general populace, the permissible is set about ten times lower, partly because of the possible seriousness of genetic damage.

Thus, the "maximum permissible dose" for the public is far below the level of identifiably radioactive damage to the individual and may seem to be a conservative standard. The guideline figure for the permitted level of radiation exposure for the general public as a result of reactor operation is set at such a level that if the whole population of the United States were to receive this additional exposure continuously, data now available on cancer incidence show that it would result in more than ten thousand deaths annually. While this number is small compared with the population, it is a large number of people to kill with a deliberate change in the environment. The radiation specialists who arrived at this conclusion, J. W. Gofman and A. R. Tamplin of Berkeley and Livermore, California, advocate that the permitted limit be reduced tenfold. Such a reduction, if enforced, would drastically modify the operation of commercial reactors.

The release from the stack of a single atomic plant is limited, so that it may not exceed the permitted level for people in the neighborhood, on a yearly average. If it does exceed the permitted level for a short time in an accidental release, as sometimes happens, the power level must be reduced the rest of the year to compensate. But a combination of a temperature inversion to keep the gases close to the ground, wind direction, and an accidental release can give some people a dose far above the "maximum permissible." As nuclear power plants become more numerous, the release from many plants may compound the exposure to radiation for persons in a wider area.

The commercial fuel processing plant at West Valley, New York, is responsible for keeping its low-level waste within permissible limits after discharge into a creek. It remained for University of Rochester scientists, acting on their own initiative as environment buffs, to discover that the radioactivity of the creek was far above the maximum permissible limit. Such considerations have led to clamor for an effective independent agency to set and enforce the safety standards, since AEC is now both promoter of nuclear power and its own policeman.

Radiation does its damage to individual cells within the body, and there is good reason to believe that genes and the rapidly multiplying cells in unborn and young children are more sensitive to such damage than are the cells in adults. Study of survivors of Hiroshima showed little genetic damage, but there the bomb burst high in the air and its debris was carried away in the mushroom cloud. More recent studies on mice have shown that strontium 90, which is spread from bomb debris and reactors, has a special affinity for causing genetic damage leading to fetal and infant mortality, in addition to its tendency to settle in bone and cause cancer and leukemia more in the young than in adults. It thus appears that radiation-induced fetal and infant mortality may pose a more serious problem than cancer in adults.

As the arms race goes on piling overkill on overkill, an all-out nuclear war could cause fallout extremely more intense than that caused by testing in the late 1950s and early 1960s. If testing caused fetal and infant deaths at the rate of something like one per 100 births, as Dr. E. J. Sternglass of the University of Pittsburgh claims, then a nuclear war causing 100 times as much fallout could presumably kill approximately all children born, and thus end the human race. From the way heavier doses affect adults, it could be surmised that considerably less than 100 times the test-era fallout might eliminate the next generation.

Even though we take the view that the Sternglass thesis has not been proved, the very possibility that all-out nuclear war could end the human race is a more cogent reason than any other that such large-scale nuclear war should be avoided, and that the arms race should be terminated.

The marvelous natural resources that eons of geologic history have provided for us are limited indeed. We have used as much fossil fuel in the last quarter century as in all previous history, and we are beginning to feel the pinch. Rather than planning still more rapid consumption, madly doubling power consumption every ten years, we should be acting as careful stewards of the planet's resources for the maximum long-term benefit of mankind. Every gallon of valuable fuel, every pound of copper and uranium that goes into the arms race is robbed from the present and future quality of human life. If we could stop this arms-race robbery from human needs and if we could evolve an economic system dependent on stability rather than continual growth, then we could both spread the bounty of our environment more equitably over the centuries and get rid of the awful pollution with which our Twentieth Century gluttony is poisoning us.

Energy

Just as the social problem of ecology and pollution is related to the problem of population and resources, so it is interrelated with the problem of energy resources. This is also an area of social life which we are just now coming to realize as a problem for humanity. In spite of our traditional natural resources being limited, they are being utilized in a highly wasteful fashion. The articles in this section are designed to acquaint the reader with some of the basic statistics on energy resources and utilization, and to indicate the structural arrangements that underlie this problem. Both the opening and concluding articles point to potential solutions to the energy crisis.

The first selection is by a coal miner. Miller formerly worked in the coal mines, and he now is President of the United Mine Workers of America. With his work experience and his current union leadership, he is in a strategic position to evaluate what is occurring in the coal industry. Look at some of the statistics he provides: 590,000,000 tons of coal are being mined each year in the United States, with 300,000,000 tons being mined by just fifteen companies. The significance of this industrial concentration is that these companies form an essential part of an energy cartel that vitally affects the lives of each of us. This domestic energy cartel has concentrated its extensive holdings in coal, oil, natural gas, and uranium, with the power being directed by the oil industry. Eight oil companies control 51 percent of the crude oil production in the United States, 58 percent of all refining, 59 percent of our refined gasoline, and 55 percent of gasoline marketing. With such power, this cartel is able to dominate not only prices but also national energy policy. They vitally influence, and often direct, the decision making on energetics, which has a vital effect on both us and the generations to come.

Although we have run into serious problems with oil and natural gas reserves, it has not been in the best interest of the oil companies to expand coal production. The oil companies have found it more to their advantage to concentrate on the production and marketing of oil products. Since they sit in the director's seat of the coal companies, they have been able to have their own way. Consequently, even though we have over a trillion tons of coal reserves, with 390 billion tons being readily recoverable, the emphasis of our energy policy has been placed on oil, oil products, and the development and use of machinery dependent on these products. Even though we have a 600 year supply of coal in reserve, these companies have found it to their advantage to concentrate on oil.

In spite of the threat of import restrictions and embargo posed by OPEC, the foreign oil cartel, the direction of our national energy policy remains unchanged. It is difficult not to conclude that OPEC does not pose a threat to our domestic energy barons, but rather, represents another opportunity for profit making. Indeed, the activities of the foreign oil cartel directly profit our domestic cartel. When OPEC raises its prices, our domestic cartel directly benefits by a rapid increase in the value of their own oil holdings and an upsurge in profits. By minimizing the development of alternative sources of energy and by controlling competing sources of energy, our domestic monopolizers keep our nation dependent on oil. Any increase in the cost of oil to the consumer is money in the oil companies' pockets. It's a nice game, if you can play it; and they are playing it very well indeed, for when Mr. Nelson Rockefeller was appointed Vice-President of the United States, they had gained a spectacular victory—their direct representative became the holder of the second highest office in the land and the Presider over the United States Senate. The Rockefellers control much of the exploration, refining, and marketing of the oil industry and have done so for a generation or more. If one directs a powerful monopoly, it is most beneficial in terms of profits to have a representative political liaison in the White House, certainly much more effective than simply having him head only one of the states.

The statistics provided by our second selection shed some light on the profits of the oil industry. This full page advertisement by the Oil, Chemical, and Atomic Workers International Union ran in newspapers across the country. It reveals that oil profits soared *360* percent from 1961 to 1974, increasing 146 percent between 1972 and 1974. The 1974 profits of the American oil industry were $17,000,000,000. The oil "shortage" worked so much in their favor that the oil industry was able to give *$22 an hour raises* to their executives. That's not bad at all.

With such profits, the oil industry has been able to buy into coal, natural gas, oil shale leases, geothermal energy leases, chemicals, plastics, fertilizers, building products, and even department stores, real estate, and the entertainment industry. On top of consolidating power in energy resources and cashing in on the "oil shortage," they have been directly purchasing political power by buying off corrupt politicians in both this country and abroad. For example, among their other bribes, Gulf Oil Company paid $4,000,000 to the Democratic Republican

Party of South Korea and $460,000 to political rulers in Bolivia (*Time*, May 26, 1975: 72). The criminal activities of the oil industry have become widespread, with profit as the goal and dire consequences for the public. For example, while the Arab oil embargo was on, our domestic oil companies falsified their import documents to show that they paid per barrel of imported oil four to five times what they actually paid. During those few months, they gouged customers from one to three *billion* dollars (Associated Press, March 31, 1975). Who else has the power to steal on such a grand scale—much less to get away with it? Yet, while they engage in such corrupt practices for which anyone else without their powerful political connections would be sent to jail with the key being thrown away, the oil companies have received only a slap on the wrist.

Our supposedly progressive income tax also strangely works to the advantage of oil companies. For example, in 1973 Occidental Petroleum Corporation paid 1.8 percent of their income in taxes, Texaco Incorporated paid 2.3 percent, Gulf Oil Corporation paid 3.1 percent, Standard Oil of Ohio paid 3.5 percent, Mobil Oil paid 5 percent, Union Oil Company of California paid 9.6 percent, and Continental Oil paid 9.9 percent (United Press International, December 9, 1974). (Continental and Union will probably hire Occidental's tax accountants!) Now those are tax rates most of us would like to pay, even if our income is $10,000 or less. With their billions in income, how can they get away with it? The oil companies represent an immense concentration of power and wealth in the United States. This power and wealth are so firmly established that they can successfully manipulate, and bribe, and corrupt. Remember playing the board game called Monopoly? Well, that is what the oil companies have been playing—except they are playing it for real. They are the owners of the properties that we land on, and they can successfully demand what they want—regardless of the consequence for others.

The concluding article of this section is written by Seaborg, a Nobel Prize winner and a former Chairman of the United States Atomic Energy Commission. As one would anticipate, with such credentials Seaborg takes a very conservative approach to energetics. Although he overlooks the role of the energy monopoly and minimizes radioactive pollution and other deleterious effects of our energy policies, he does delineate several alternative sources of energy which we could develop. His points about our waste of energy, the need for developing solar, geothermal, and thermonuclear fusion as sources of energy, and the possibility of recycling organic wastes are especially noteworthy.

22

Arnold Miller

The Energy Crisis
As A Coal Miner Sees It

I was born in the mountains of West Virginia, and my views are the views of a coal miner. Coal mining is hard, dirty work, and when you have time to think on the job, you mainly think about your survival. I have spent most of my life just trying to survive, and what free time I had left over I spent on trying to reform the union I belonged to. That is hard work.

When I was still working underground, long before I knew any people who called themselves environmentalists, I ran across what the founder of the Sierra Club, John Muir, said: "When we try to pick out anything by itself, we find it hitched to everything else in the universe." I think that is about as true as any idea I ever heard. You can't talk about coal without talking about energy. You can't talk about energy without talking about oil. You can't talk about oil without talking about politics. You can't talk about politics without talking about corruption. You can't talk about corruption without talking about companies that are so big that they can give half a million dollars to a politician without its even showing up on their books. You can't talk about companies like that without talking about energy, because they supply it. And you can't talk about energy without talking about coal. So I will talk about all of these things, and if I wander around, you can blame it on the Sierra Club. That is what the coal industry does.

I still run into people who think that the coal industry died when railroads converted from steam locomotives to diesel. They are very surprised when I point out to them that their electrical appliances burn coal. They don't see it because it is delivered by wire. The steel that goes

Excerpted from Arnold Miller, "The Energy Crisis as a Coal Miner Sees It," The Center Magazine, *a publication of the Center for the Study of Democratic Institutions, Santa Barbara, California.*

into their cars could not have been produced without coal. That is true even if they are driving a Japanese car, because it is exported American coal that the Japanese steel industry uses—and then sends back to us, at a comfortable profit. I am sure, though, that you all know enough about our economy to realize that coal is the basis of it. If we stopped digging coal in September, the country would shut down in October, after the stockpiles ran out. It is that simple.

We are producing, at this point, about 590 million tons of coal a year from twenty-four states. West Virginia and Kentucky are the leading producers. They account for about forty per cent of last year's total between them. In the east, the other principal coal-producing states are Pennsylvania, Ohio, Illinois, Indiana, Maryland, Virginia, Tennessee, and Alabama. Moving westward, there is production in Oklahoma, Arkansas, Iowa, Kansas, and Missouri. The big reserves are in the Rocky Mountains and the Northern Plains.

All this coal is being mined by an estimated 150,000 men, which makes coal one of the most productive industries in the country. About 125,000 of those men belong to the United Mine Workers (our total membership, including retired miners, is about two hundred thousand). You can get some sense of how the coal industry has changed through mechanization by realizing that thirty years ago we were producing roughly the same amount of coal every year, but then it required a work force of about six hundred thousand to do it. Today the coal industry is about ninety-eight per cent mechanized.

More than half of the coal we produce goes to electric utilities. We deliver about ninety million tons to the steel industry. We export about fifty-seven million tons. We deliver the rest to a wide variety of other industries, particularly those producing chemicals, which rely heavily on coal and coal by-products.

Mainly because of mechanization and the high productivity that results from it, the price of coal traditionally has stayed low. That is the price to the consumer. The hidden cost of coal is the one we pay—the people who mine it. It is a high price. We get killed. Since the Bureau of Mines started keeping records of such things back in 1910, about eighty thousand of us have been killed. No other industry comes close to that. And we get black lung, from exposure to fine coal dust in the mine air. That problem has been with us through the history of the industry, but the companies and the company doctors have denied it even existed. They were still denying it in 1969 when the Public Health Service finally got around to releasing a study it had been sitting on for sixteen years that showed that one hundred thousand or more miners and retired miners were afflicted. And "afflicted" isn't a strong enough word. Dying of cancer is no worse. This old disease has become worse with mechanization because the high-speed mining machines stir the coal dust up much more intensely than in the old pick-and-shovel days. We have had our technological progress in coal, just as in other industries, but we are still being smothered to death.

There are other hidden costs in coal. Underground mining produces acid wastes and gob piles. Strip mining destroys mountains and poisons watersheds. It also poisons people's lives. There is probably nothing worse than knowing those big shovels are coming to take your land and the house you grew up in. If you are poor, you don't have too many ways to fight back, and it is tempting to take whatever they offer you. That brings me back to John Muir's idea about everything's being hitched together to everything else. You are poor in the first place because of the coal industry—if you live in an Appalachian coal camp. They make you poor and then they come and take advantage of it. That is a hidden cost. Anybody who has had to fight the coal industry knows what it is like to pay it.

We have learned from bitter experience that when you fight the coal industry, there are terrible odds against you. The concentration in the industry is extreme. Of course, the industry says this is ridiculous. The industry spokesmen are always pointing out that there are five thousand mines and 1,200 mining companies. And then they ask how any industry with that many companies in it could possibly be concentrated. They get away with this question because so few people know anything about the industry. But the simple fact is that fifteen companies produced 301,208,359 tons last year, which was fifty-one per cent of the total. The top fifty companies combined produced 400,000,000 tons—two-thirds of the total. I am not an economist, but you don't have to be to know that any industry which has half of its production controlled by fifteen companies is concentrated.

You realize very quickly that the coal industry is not what it seems to be at first glance. You have oil companies controlling two of the top three. Kennecott Copper controls the biggest of them all—a company which produced nearly seventy-two million tons last year and plans to double that by 1980. This one company, which gets about eighty per cent of its coal from strip mining, produces about twelve per cent of the industry total. In fact, Peabody alone outproduces the combined effort of the seven companies at the bottom of the top-fifteen list.

In the coal industry a very small number of very large companies not only sets the pace for the rest but also has the power to swamp them financially. What other industry has this same pattern? Everybody knows: oil. But not everybody knows that the oil industry effectively controls the coal industry. It shares that control to some degree with other industries—with Kennecott, with the steel people, and with utilities. I don't deny that they have their differences of opinion from time to time, and maybe even a little competition. But not very much competition, and less of it every day.

We are all slowly learning that the oil industry is more than that now. It has wide-ranging interests: coal, natural gas, uranium. It is an energy industry, though that is too polite a name. The Federal Trade Commission recently observed that "the industry operates much like a cartel" and filed suit to try to break it up. Exxon, Texaco, Gulf, Shell, Standard Oil of California, Atlantic-Richfield, Standard Oil of Indiana, and Mobil between them control fifty-one per cent of crude oil production, sixty-four per cent of crude oil reserves, fifty-eight per cent of all refining, fifty-nine per cent of refined gasoline, and fifty-five per cent of gasoline marketing. "A nation that runs on oil can't afford to run short," they say in their advertising. In the long run, it may be much more true that a nation that runs on energy can't afford to fall into the hands of a cartel. We already have some firsthand experience with shortages. But today's are nothing compared to tomorrow's. I think shortages are directly connected with concentration.

What is true of all the giants is that ordinary citizens can't get at them. They are not accountable to us.

They should be, because there are some important questions they should be forced to answer—and not just with the usual symphony of public relations they pump out whenever they are being criticized. First of all, they should be forced to explain how they are going to deal with the future energy needs of this country. Lately we have had truckloads of studies indicating one thing: by 1985, the United States will be running out of domestic oil and domestic gas, and relying even more heavily than we already are on supplies imported from the Middle East. Most of the studies also give some passing mention to coal. Some of them point out that we will need to produce about 1.5 billion tons of it a year in order to keep our lights burning. That is more than double the six hundred million tons per year we produce now. In effect, it means building a whole new industry on top of the one we already have.

That might be possible if the coal industry were expanding production steadily, about ten per cent each year. But total production last year was less than in 1947. The National Coal Association forecast for 1973 shows little or no increase over 1972. At this point even that forecast seems to be off the mark; production is now running five to ten per cent behind last year, and it is likely to stay that way for some time. At this rate, there is no way that the coal industry will be producing 1.5 billion tons a year by 1985—or for that matter, at any time after that.

The bigger companies, with effective control of their market, have no incentive to expand except when they are absolutely certain in advance of selling every ton of coal at acceptable prices. Their goal is to remove every last bit of risk from the business (except in the area of safety, where they are still willing to take all kinds of risks).

This was true even before they started being devoured by the oil industry; it is twice as true now. The oil industry knows that you don't refine more gasoline than you think the country will need, because if you do, the price will go down. In the days of competition you had less chance of manipulating the total production. These days, when competition in the oil industry is a joke, you can manipulate whatever you feel like manipulating, starting with the White House and the Interior Department and going on from there. The biggest oil-coal combines are sitting on vast reserves of readily recoverable coal. But that coal will come out of the ground only when the men who own it can be sure of the price they will get for it.

That is a simple objective, but it immediately becomes complicated. Coal, oil, and gas are largely interchangeable as far as electric utilities are concerned. They all produce Btu's. Many generating plants have been designed to take any or all three. If coal were still one hundred per cent competitive, there would be an incentive to mine more of it, sell it to the utilities at the lowest possible prices, and undercut oil and gas, which are increasingly difficult to find and bring to market, especially if you have to go overseas to do it. But coal is not one hundred per cent competitive. It has problems of environmental damage and it is hard to transport efficiently. More importantly, however, it is being kept in the back room by the oil industry. When the other commodities are gone from the shelves, the industry will bring out coal. And it will sell for what the industry wants it to sell for.

For coal miners, this isn't just a little spare-time exercise in industry-baiting. The idea of an unrestrained oil-coal-gas-uranium cartel is terrifying to us. We already know what it is to work for people who think of themselves as above the law. The coal industry has always been that way. If you don't believe it, look at what is left of the company towns they built—and then sold to us when they no longer needed them. Look at the schools in eastern Kentucky. Look at the roads all over Appalachia. Look at the men who were battered and broken in the mines, and then forgotten. Look at the stripped hills and the rivers running red with acid. Look at all that, and look at the coal companies' tax returns, and then tell me the coal industry isn't above the law.

Let us look at a few aspects of the current energy situation. We are already using twenty-four trillion cubic feet of natural gas per year, and finding less than half that much in our reserves. Demand has increased about seven per cent per year since World War II. There is no leveling off in sight. The Federal Power Commission says we have a sixty-five-year supply of natural gas, but that figure is based on a demand increase of 1.4 per cent a year, which is ridiculously out of date. With luck, assuming there are more undiscovered reserves than we think, we might make it to 1995.

We are not quite as badly off in oil reserves, but the forecast is no more encouraging. We were using 14.7 million barrels a day in 1970. We were producing 11.6 million barrels a day from domestic wells. That gave us a deficit of 3.1 million barrels a day. We made it up with imports. Looking ahead, even the most conservative estimates for 1985 show domestic demand running at 30.2 million barrels a day, more than twice the consumption of 1970. With luck, domestic wells will be producing fifteen million barrels.

That is a deficit of 15.2 million barrels a day to be accounted for. It has to come from the Middle East, for the most part. In the back of my mind right now is the question: What are we going to be doing with all those B-52 bombers now that they are not bombing Cambodia any more? I don't think it is wrong to start worrying about what the Pentagon is up to—or will be up to. When we have too much dependence on foreign supply, as we now do, the temptation to go in there on some flimsy pretense and clean out all those shieks will be strong. If the B-52's are too clumsy, we will do it with subversion and the C.I.A.

We don't have to do that, of course. We could be pouring money into research that would speed the day when we can convert coal to pipeline gas and synthetic gasoline. Very few people have come to grips with one vitally important fact. That fact is that we could run this country on coal, if we wanted to. Not tomorrow, no. But, with a sufficient commitment, we could be doing it before 1985.

Some time in the future, we will be running this country with fast-breeder nuclear reactors, though I won't live to see it. When my children are my age the first of these reactors will be making an impact. Beyond that, we will get the sun's energy harnessed. My children won't live to see that—at least not on a nationwide commercial scale. Meanwhile, we ought to be concentrating on figuring out how to use our conventional fuels. We have just about run out of gas. We are low on oil. What about coal?

We sit squarely on top of the largest readily available supply of coal on earth—about 1.3 trillion tons in all, with about 390 billion tons considered to be readily recoverable. That is a six-hundred years supply, at current consumption levels. Even when you double or triple our consumption, the supply will outlast any conceivable period of demand.

Coal overpowers gas and oil in terms of available reserves. The U.S. Geological Survey figures that coal accounts for 87.1 per cent of everything we have left. Oil is 3.5 per cent. Gas is 4.6 per cent. Sheer common sense should tell us to put all our efforts into developing coal.

Unfortunately, common sense has almost nothing to do with the way we consume energy in America. Not only do we consume more of it than we should—it is a widely quoted statistic that we add up to six per cent of the world's people and burn up about forty per cent of the world's energy—but we consume more of it all the time. Population increased fourteen per cent from 1961 to 1973; per-capita consumption of energy went up forty per cent. And while we are busily consuming more every day, we are burning up the wrong things. Oil and natural gas account for 77.9 per cent of our current total energy consumption—almost a direct inversion of the figure for available reserves. Coal accounts for 17.5 per cent. Hydroelectric and nuclear sources provide the remaining 4.6 per cent. It is not just because I am a coal miner that I consider this a ridiculous situation. It is also because I am a citizen. My interests as a citizen are not being served by this kind of arrangement.

There are various reasons why coal is low on the list of fuels currently supplying our energy requirements. The biggest reason has to do with simple expediency. Aside from the fact that coal is difficult to transport and requires large storage facilities, it also comes out of the ground mixed with various impurities. The most serious is sulphur. The burning of coal produces other impurities—fly ash, particulates—but electrostatic precipitators and redesigned boilers have largely brought those under control, and that is a very serious problem, since a high percentage of the coal we mine in the East is high-sulphur.

A few months ago I was in a meeting with some coal barons who were wringing their hands about the sulphur problem and how it was affecting their sales. I couldn't argue that it was having that effect, but I could still ask them a question: "Gentlemen, when did you first discover there was sulphur in coal?" I knew the answer as well as they did. The discovery goes back hundreds of years. The next question was: "Gentlemen, how much money has each of your companies spent researching ways to handle the sulphur problem?" They changed the subject.

I can understand that they would, because research is not something the coal industry has been comfortable with. Some coal companies will tell you that they have a research department, and in the annual report you will find a picture of a man in a white coat squinting at a piece of coal; but when you go to their headquarters and ask to see the research department, either they have nothing at all or their "research" consists of a technician working out of a converted broom closet fixed up with a Bunsen burner and two or three beakers. All he does by way of research is to analyze random samples coming out of the company's mines.

Industry and government are much closer together and much less distinguishable than they have a right to be. And I believe that when we talk about developing an intelligent energy policy in this country—a policy designed to serve us all, not just a corporate few—we'd better know that the odds are bad, and the size of the job is almost overwhelming.

As far as coal is concerned, I define the job this way: we must greatly expand total production, on a crash basis, and aim at a goal of domestic energy self-sufficiency as quickly as possible.

We owe it to ourselves and our children to develop a National Energy Policy. To do that, we will have to make some very tough decisions that nobody is going to be entirely happy about. What I mean by that is that there must be some form of authority empowered to say no to the most powerful corporations in the United States. At the moment there is no such authority anywhere.

I know that sounds pessimistic. I am not a pessimist but I would prefer to try to be realistic now than to be taken by surprise later.

23 Oil Workers of America

They Can't Rob Us Blind
If We Open Our Eyes

We, the refinery workers of America, are about to take an unprecedented step in the relationship between worker and employer.
   We're going to open up one of the most secretive industries in America to public scrutiny.
   We're going to tell you why oil prices are so high.
   How the oil industry causes the inflation that robs our paychecks.
   And . . . what we can do about it.

We're the Oil, Chemical and Atomic Workers, the people who make the petroleum products that keep America running.

We hope to influence the industry we've served long and well to make some basic changes in the way it treats its workers and the public.

We all know the effects of inflation. We feel them every time we buy food or clothing. Every time we buy gasoline or pay our utility bills. We don't need any lessons in economic theory; we can see what's happening every time we struggle over our family budget, then read about huge profit increases for corporations.

WHAT CAUSES INFLATION?

Increased oil prices were responsible, directly or indirectly, for almost half of last year's increase in the cost of living, according to a congressional study. So what causes high oil prices?

They're partly due to increased prices for foreign crude. But not entirely.

Reprinted by permission of the Oil, Chemical, and Atomic Workers International Union.

Oil industry profits are up 146% since 1972, 360% since 1961. We may be paying more for foreign crude, but we're also paying a lot more for industry profits. The oil companies would like to believe they need all the money they're making—$17 *billion* in 1974 alone—to find more oil.

But we know different.

Being inside the industry, we have a pretty good idea of how it works. And how, as workers and consumers, we're being robbed blind. We took a good hard look at where the money we pay for oil goes. And we found some interesting things.

We knew the extra money wasn't going to pay our salaries.

Since 1961, the refinery labor cost of refined products has risen one one-hundredth of a cent per gallon—to slightly more than seven-tenths of one cent per gallon—while the price of a barrel of refined products has increased from $3.85 to $10.10. Proportionately, the refinery labor cost per barrel has been cut in half, from 7.1% of the total cost in 1961 to 3.3% today.

Obviously, the money's going somewhere else. We found that oil executives got average salary raises of more than 21% last year.

They got an average *increase* of more than *$22 per hour.*

Their *raise* was almost four times *our total wages.*

THE MONOPOLY GAME

We also found that oil companies are using tremendous amounts of money to buy up other companies. Some of them are energy companies, giving them a horizontal monopoly in energy to go along with their vertical monopoly in oil. Oil companies control most of America's natural gas, 50% of its nuclear fuels, seven of the fifteen largest coal companies, most of the oil shale leases and most of the geothermal energy leases.

They're also investing heavily in chemicals and other petroleum derivatives. Between 1961 and 1967, the industry spent as much on chemical plants as on oil refineries. They're using their current profits to invest in plastics, fertilizers, building products and other downstream applications of oil. They're even investing in companies that have nothing to do with oil.

Other companies are putting their money into real estate, entertainment, commodities and other areas that will never give the public one drop of oil. And, finally, a segment of the oil industry spent huge sums on illegal campaign contributions in 1972, to influence government supervision of their activities.

If the oil companies have all that money to spend on executive raises, outside investments and political contributions, they must be making too much money.

The money we pay for oil shouldn't go for *anything* except finding, refining and delivering oil.

The industry *can* and *should* lower its prices.

A FAIR PRICE FOR LABOR

At the same time, it can afford to pay its workers a decent wage. While the industry has prospered, we've suffered. In 1966, our average wage was $3.45 an hour. Today, we get $3.27 an hour in 1966 dollars. For some of the most dangerous, unhealthy work in America.

Our productivity has increased by 71% in the past fifteen years. But all the benefits of our increased productivity are going to the industry. They should be going to lower prices and fairer wages.

As we said, the total cost of refinery labor is around *seven-tenths of one cent* for each gallon of refined products we turn out. That means it would take a 143% wage increase to raise the cost of a gallon just one cent.

But even a large wage increase could be absorbed now from current high profits and soon be offset by the constantly increasing productivity of oil workers.

Thus, we do not believe any price increase would be justified—and we don't want any price increase.

A QUESTION OF RESPONSIBILITY

We hope we've helped you understand who's responsible for inflation, who's benefiting from it, who's suffering.

But there's one final point we'd like to make.

Corporations would like you to believe that workers cause inflation, just as they wanted you to believe that consumers caused the energy crisis. We've shown that that's not so.

Our real wages haven't gone up; they've gone down.

We're not profiting at your expense; the industry is.

Our real returns for each barrel of oil we process have decreased 28% since 1961; the industry's real returns for each barrel of oil we process have increased 135% since 1961. The oil industry has reaped windfall profits while pursuing policies that can only be called irresponsible and contrary to the national interest. Besides their contribution to inflation, they've shifted much of their production and refining capacity overseas.

Despite their huge profits, the seven largest oil companies have been paying federal taxes at a rate of about five cents on the dollar—about the same rate that a worker, with a family of four to support, would pay if he earned $125 a week. If the oil companies paid their fair share in taxes, it would help balance the federal budget and would help ease inflation.

WHAT TO DO?

We can't let the oil industry get away with blaming workers and consumers for our nation's ills. When we recognize what's really behind our inflation and energy problems, we can begin to do something about them. But if we allow corporations to continue playing off one segment of the public against another, we'll never get to the real root of the problem.

They may keep trying to rob us. But if we open our eyes, they can't rob us blind.

24
Glenn Seaborg

Finding a New Approach to Energetics—Fast!

The traumatic impact of our energy crisis has provided us with a not-too-early recognition of the realities of the boundaries of our energy supply. Thus warned, we can get down to the business of planning for the future. Fortunately, we can foresee solutions to our energy problem provided that we can garner a national sense of determination which will guide us toward the conception and implementation of a coherent and realistic national energy policy. I believe we can and will.

The foundation for such an energy policy must be based on approximately equal doses of energy conservation and the development of additional sources through a judicious application of science and technology. Both of these prescriptions can be successfully applied provided that we have the courage to make some difficult choices.

We can—we must—develop an energy-conservation ethic in the United States. The energy that we waste in heating, in cooling and lighting poorly designed and badly insulated buildings, and in inefficient transportation systems contributes nothing to our standard of living. The large automobile, which has become the hallmark of the American way of life, is unnecessarily costly in the consumption of fuel, material, and space. We suffer as much from excess energy consumption as from energy shortage. More than 50 percent of the energy consumed in the United States is discarded as waste heat. Technical knowhow and the laws of thermodynamics permit substantial reduction in this wastage through the development of more efficient engines, industrial products and processes, transportation systems, air conditioners, furnaces, household appliances, and the construction of better-designed and -insulated buildings. Some such waste heat can be used for heating

Reprinted by permission from Saturday Review/World, *December 14, 1974, pp. 44–47.*

homes and buildings, as the Soviet Union has successfully done. And each of us certainly can draw less from our energy bank and still get along very well.

On the energy-supply side, our most serious problem is on the short-time scale, until about 1985—a result of inadequate national planning. We have a plethora of possible technical solutions, which in general require 10 or more years of research and development. Had an adequate research-and-development program been in effect during the last 25 years, we would not be faced with our present dilemma. Now we must play a catch-up game—a difficult, but by no means hopeless, situation.

Let me make a somewhat more quantitative assessment of our energy problem and then turn to a discussion of the technical solutions. If we were to continue for another decade (until 1985) our recent rate of growth of energy consumption, about 4.5 percent per year, an increase of about 60 percent would result. Close to 50 percent of our energy today derives from oil, and we now import about one-third of our supply of this fossil fuel. As for the rest of our energy: About 30 percent is provided from gas (which we are importing in increasing proportion), less than 20 percent from coal, the small remainder from hydroelectric (whose practical potential essentially is exhausted) and nuclear power. To compound the problem, we are consuming oil and gas faster than we are finding new supplies, and in a few decades we will have depleted the supply of these resources. More than 90 percent of our fossil-fuel reserves, sufficient for meeting our needs for hundreds of years, reside in coal, which we are consuming at the lowest rate.

Oil recovery can be increased by exploration for new origins, including off-shore sources, by using improved drilling techniques, and by additional recovery from already-exploited sources (so-called secondary recovery). Oil from Alaska, transported via the famous trans-Alaskan pipeline, capable of increasing our supply by some 10 percent, will make little impact before 1985.

Coal is capable of making the largest contribution. As fuel for power-generating plants and industrial processes, it can be substituted for oil or gas, thus freeing them for their specialized uses as sources of chemicals, fertilizer, and fuel for transportation and reducing the import of these fossil fuels. Coal can be the source of gas through the gasification process and, together with oil shale, the source of oil through liquefication; short of an extraordinary, unlikely, national effort, we can expect only limited contributions from these processes before 1985. The potential supplies greatly exceed those of ordinary gas and oil recoverable directly from the ground or sea. Such conversion processes, with an aggressive research and development program, can be economically competitive at the recent high prices for imported oil and gas but will require very large investments—on the order of tens of billions of dollars—and it will require the solution of serious problems of man-power, water supply, and land lease before production is achieved at appreciable levels.

As the result of a unique program of research and development during the last 25 years, an exception to the neglect that has contributed so much to our present plight, nuclear (fission) power is reaching the stage where it can make an appreciable contribution. In the United States the total nuclear-power capacity that is in operation, under construction, or committed for construction is about 200 million kilowatts, indicating that some 25 percent of all our electrical energy could come from the nuclear source by 1985. All of the industrialized countries are turning toward this source of energy, at faster or slower rates than the United States, depending on their domestic resources of fossil fuels.

All three of these categories of energy sources have problems, varying in degree, with respect to public health and safety, and they have an adverse impact on the environment, the preservation of which belatedly has now become our highest priority.

Oil recovery has the risks of leakage in offshore drilling, spills during transportation, air pollution from the burning of sulfur-containing sources. Natural gas and low-sulfur oil have clean burning properties and are almost ideal energy sources. However, they are severely limited in availability.

The use of coal suffers from serious problems in its removal from underground, the need for land reclamation after strip-mining, extensive new transportation requirements, and the need for removing air pollutants before, during, or after its burning. Air pollution from the burning of coal contributes widely to respiratory and heart ailments. A large number of coal miners suffer from black-lung disease and work-induced injuries. Conversion to gas and oil on an appreciable scale requires the mining of tremendous quantities of coal or oil shale, seriously aggravating our strip-mining and water-supply problems. These difficulties can be overcome by improvements in mining technology, location of electric generating plants at mine mouths, dispersal of air pollutants by high stacks, research and development to produce clean burning techniques, and development of underground (*in situ*) methods for conversion to gas and oil.

Although nuclear power does not contribute any noxious fumes or particulates to our air, it has offsetting disadvantages—a radioactive waste-disposal problem, the possible danger of widespread dissemination of radioactive fission products and poisonous plutonium, the problems of thermal pollution (in common with fossil fuels) and routine emission of low levels of radioactive effluents, and the possibility that fissionable material may be diverted for use in the production of weapons. These problems can be mitigated by the judicious design and placement of waste repositories, careful design and operation of the reactors, concentration of reactors, fuel fabrication and reprocessing plants in "energy parks," the use of cooling towers, and improved coordinated nuclear safeguarding procedures.

Of the other potential contributors on the early time scale—solar, geothermal, wind—the most help probably will come from some specialized uses of solar energy, although the others will give some aid. More than half of the United States has a sufficient supply of sunshine to allow the widespread use of solar energy in the heating and cooling of homes and other buildings. This technology can be developed rapidly; its implementation depends chiefly on the inception of a national energy policy that encourages or demands the necessary construction, renovation, and design changes.

Now let us consider the longer-range picture, beyond 1985. During the early post-1985 period, our hopes will ride on the expanding exploitation of coal, oil shale, and nuclear power, with increasing help from the other new sources. Beyond the year 2000, as our fossil fuels diminish, we will turn more and more to nuclear (including the new fusion power) and solar energy. Eventually we will consume all of our fossil fuels and will have to depend entirely on nuclear and solar energy.

Realistic projections suggest that 50 percent of our electric power might be generated through nuclear (fission) energy by the year 2000. This power will come chiefly from our present type of reactors—that is, conventional ones; but our national program contemplates the introduction of the breeder reactor before then, perhaps in time to make a contribution in the 1990s. The need for breeders is predicated upon the much greater efficiency that they have in the utilization of the nuclear fuel uranium, which is available in limited supply at the present purchase price. However, in order to find a place in our energy repertoire, the breeder will have to generate electricity at a cost competitive with that from non-breeder reactors, some of which can use both uranium and thorium as fuel with relatively high efficiency. Because the cost of uranium accounts for less than 10 percent of the total cost of electricity from any of the conventional reactors, the supply of uranium can be considerably increased by mining lower-grade uranium ores at higher cost without increasing the price of nuclear electricity to an unacceptable level. All advanced industrialized countries are working on the development of the breeder reactor with the objective of including it among their future energy sources. Some nuclear reactors have the long-range possibility of furnishing heat energy at temperatures sufficiently high to split water for producing hydrogen gas, a very versatile potential fuel; clean-burning hydrogen, from whatever source, can be used as fuel for industrial and central-station power plants, in automobiles, and for fuel cells (to provide individual sources of electricity), and it can be stored and transported with negligible loss.

The production of electricity and other forms of energy through controlled thermonuclear fusion—the source of energy of our sun—in the period beyond the year 2000 will make it possible for us to use the unlimited supply of heavy hydrogen of the world's oceans as nuclear fuel. They will provide an energy source that can meet the world's needs for millions of years. Technical feasibility has not yet been demonstrated, but there are indications that it will be achieved within the next 5 or 10 years. We will then have the scientific basis for the building of prototype and demonstration reactors preparatory to the construction of practical, large, economical fusion reactors. Research on nuclear fusion is proceeding in most industrialized countries. The effort in the Soviet Union is particularly noteworthy; fortunately, we have excellent technical cooperation with the Soviet Union in this field.

Solar energy represents our ultimate source—continuously renewable, inexhaustible, available as long as our sun shines. The economical production of electricity on a large scale by solar energy offers many technical difficulties because of its low intensity, and predictions indicate that it will not be achieved before the year 2000. Imaginative proposals are under investigation, including "solar farms" for collecting and converting solar energy over areas of many square miles and the placing of solar-energy collectors and converters, more than one mile in diameter, into synchronous orbit 22,300 miles above the earth. Perhaps the best method for wide-scale utilization of solar energy will result from basic scientific discoveries yet to be made, such as the synthesis of chemicals capable of converting sunlight directly into electricity or into such fuels as hydrogen gas.

Geothermal energy is another natural source for conversion to electrical power. Available in specific areas on a world-wide basis, this has encouraging long-range potential. There are three main types—steam, hot water, and hot rock—which are found at varying depths below the earth's surface. Assessment of the ultimate total potential of geothermal energy, in terms of quantity, duration, and time scale, depends on a great deal of developmental work. The long-range future of wind energy is difficult to assess. The other natural sources, providing energy from the tides or temperature variations at different ocean depths, apparently have only limited practical potential according to our present understanding.

Recognition of our energy problem should prepare us for an inevitable, related series of future problems. Largely on the longer time scale, beyond 1985, these relate to the impending shortages of metals essential to our economy—copper, aluminum, chromium, nickel, tin, manganese, and so on. As our domestic supplies dwindle and the competition for purchase on the international market increases, we will have to make the transition to a "recycle society." At that stage of our development, virtually all materials will be reused indefinitely, and virgin resources will be used primarily as "make-up" materials. Akin to recycling is the potential conversion of organic wastes (garbage, manure, and so on), by hydrogenation, pyrolysis, or bioconversion, to synthetic fuels (oil and gas); and cellulosic wastes (wood and paper products), by microbial-produced enzymes, to edible protein and carbohydrate sources. A society set up to reuse most of its resources systematically and habitually will affect enormous energy savings. This eventually must be the industrial philosophy of a stabilized society.

Institutional Subservience: Religion, Science, Education, and Mass Communications

A major theme running through our previous sections has been the dominance of the elites in the industrial and political sectors of American society and their contributory maintenance to our social problems. In this section, we focus on the subservience of our other social institutions to this concentration of economic and political power, specifically examining religion, science, education, and mass communications. In the following section, we shall deal with the role of the military and its joint decision making in partnership with our top industrial and political leaders.

According to its own teachings and ideals, the Church should be in the vanguard of protest against those conditions that give rise to social problems which lead to such extensive suffering among the masses of the United States. The Church traditionally has been silent regarding social problems, however, at least regarding social problems that are intricately connected with the powerful of society. The Church most certainly speaks out against vices affecting individuals (such as alcoholism, prostitution, adultery, lying, disobedience, and stealing), but it doesn't say much about most of the problems which we have detailed in previous selections. When it does deal with social problems, the focus is almost invariably individualistic. That is, the emphasis is on individuals doing better or being different. When the subject is racism, for example, the message is that individuals should be fairer, not discriminate, have love in their hearts, and so forth. The Church conveniently overlooks how racism and our other social problems are built into our social structure. Consequently, it seldom focuses on the evils of our current social arrangements.

The theme of Henslin's article is that this stance is not surprising; indeed, it is normal for the Church to side with the Establishment because the Church is also subservient to the dominant social institutions of our society. Will the Church perhaps change in the future and positively contribute effective social change in American society? With its numbers, it has such potential; but because the Church is firmly entrenched in the Establishment and has a vested interest in maintaining this entrenchment, it is highly likely that it will not be a force for social change and that it will not provide solutions for our social problems.

In the second selection, Willhelm presents an overview of scientific mythology. He illustrates how science, through its myths, provides rationales which support corporate capitalism. The dominant myths in American society justify whatever needs to be done in order to expand our economy, and both the natural and social sciences have helped to supply these myths. Individualsm, Social Darwinism, rationality, bureaucracy, professionalism, truth, objectivity, value neutrality, imperialism, expansion, knowledge, technology, Scientism, and Statism—all become interrelating, interlocking concepts providing justification for the dominant economic orientation of the United States. Science does not arise, nor does it exist, in a social vacuum, and the social context within which science arises and within which it functions affects what science is and what it does.

Another of our major social institutions is education. In each society, knowledge and skills must be transmitted across generational lines. Our society has developed a vast formal educational system to accomplish this process of cross-generational transmission. Most of us realize that our extensive system of mass education helps to stabilize society, but few of us realize just how it does so. In the third selection, Henslin, Henslin, and Keiser analyze the subservience of the American educational institution to our economic system and its role in preserving the status quo. They analyze the biases in our standardized tests that serve to discriminate against the lower social classes and minority groups, the orientation of the educational system around middle class values, and the current tracking of students into different types of programs. They illustrate how students from middle class backgrounds are selected for success in our educational system, while students from lower class backgrounds are selected for failure. They then relate this selection process to the maintenance of the social class system and its service for the economic order. They also analyze techniques by which those doomed for failure are "cooled out."

In the following selection Henslin examines changes that are taking place in higher education—changes that are turning the university into a factory. He analyzes how these changes are forcing a reconceptualization of what students and faculty are and how these changes are destroying the American university. He then draws the connection between these changes and the power elite of our society, showing how the power elite is becoming even more firmly entrenched in their positions of power through these changes in higher education.

With power so solidly concentrated in the hands of a few, is there possibility for social change? This possibility is indeed slight, given the current concentration of power and its readiness to be wielded against those who do not peacefully acquiesce to the decisions of our leaders. It is true that the press can work for social change, as it did in its concerted attempt to remove Mr. Nixon from office, but the mass communications system of the United States is also largely under the control of those in power. For an easy demonstration of their control, try flipping the channels during any evening news presentation on television. Note how the same national news is presented on each channel in an almost identical manner. It does not take long to conclude that the major television stations primarily pass along a predigested format. There is almost no disagreement among the channels, and what little difference there is comes through as mild, innocuous, and irrelevant. We have no news alternative with our current mass media; we are given the views that the power elite decides are good for us in a format designed to augment the status quo of power.

It is in response to these canned presentations that Cirino makes his proposal for an alternative range of viewpoints to be broadcast and telecast, with the consumers being able to choose the viewpoint they prefer. His proposal is sound and should provide for the exchange of a wide range of viewpoints and orientations. However, since we do not live in a "marketplace of ideas" when it comes to the presentation of political viewpoints on our mass media, it is highly unlikely that the Power Establishment will pay any heed to such a proposal. In fact, it could well be dangerous to their position—for alternative viewpoints may threaten their power. Ideas still are powerful, but with the weaponry of the Power Elite (as with Kent State) combined with our current censorship of dissenting opinion in our mass communications, the powerful are firmly entrenched in their elite positions of dominance.

25

James M. Henslin

From Prophets to Profits: The
Church and the Establishment

Many churches have become slumlords. In 1966 Friendship Baptist Church had to shut down rooming houses it operated on West 130th Street between 17th and Lenox Avenue, since the buildings were "no longer fit for human habitation" according to church officials.— Look Magazine, May 1970, p. 26.

Behold . . . The voice of one crying in the wilderness.

Mark 1:2,3

The theme of this essay is that it is *normal* for the Church[1] *not* to effectively protest or to actively seek solutions on behalf of those being victimized by the social order. I am not referring to the innocuous pap the Church routinely hands out in muted and safe tones on quiet Sunday mornings to yawning and bored parishioners. This it does with the regularity of ritual—and is regularly ineffectual. I am, rather, referring to the Church, with its millions of members and its potential power, not protesting the Established Order on behalf of the downtrodden of society, not taking a stand for those persons who are being systematically brutalized by a discriminatory social system.

Why, for example, is the Church largely silent when it exists in the midst of a white supremacist society which selected its most physically fit and able youth (primarily from the ranks of its lower income groups —those groups which didn't have the privileged protection of deferments—its blacks, Indians, and Appalachian whites) and sent them thousands of miles in a genocidal onslaught against a yellow peasant population? Where was the voice of the Church when our corporate

This article was written for this volume. Excerpt from Look Magazine, May *1970, reprinted by permission of the publisher, Cowles Communications.*

warlords spouted their democratic ideology as the basis for napalming women and children, with never a word about the profits being raked off the war industries based on the production of wholesale death and destruction? Why didn't the Church protest when the military dehumanized our youth by teaching them to slaughter *groups* of yellow peasants as regular policy and ordered them by direct command to cold-bloodedly shoot *individual* peasants whose only "guilt" was that of being *suspected* of having collaborated with the Viet Cong? Where was the voice of the Church when those youth, who learned their lesson so well, applied it to a village such as My Lai? Why was the Church mostly silent when a dehumanized American public initially reacted with a "That's war" philosophy or a "We-don't-know-enough-about-it-to-make-a-judgment" attitude? Where is the Church when it is surrounded by a populace so brainwashed that it cannot see that the My Lai massacre was the logical extension of an inhuman, demoralizing policy being systematically and cruelly followed by the United States Government for the sake of profit and power?

Even when the social malaise came to the point where the poverty-stricken and our students began to riot and government troops, tanks, and helicopters were brought into play in order to hold down the masses, it was only a small part of the Church which responded in protest. When our corrupting and corrupted leaders dehumanize large numbers of our citizens by placing profits before human values, and when, through inadequate diets, the minds of our poor are blunted, their bodies debilitated, while at the same time others stuff themselves to the point that concern with too much fat on the figure becomes a major preoccupation, the Church is strangely silent.

One wonders where the Church is when more money is annually spent in the United States on alcohol (16.4 *billion* dollars) than the combined amount spent on public aid by federal, state, and local governments (13.2 billion dollars). Or when more than *eight* times as much is spent on tobacco (10.2 billion dollars) than on funding the Job Corps (1.2 billion dollars). Or when more money is spent annually on cat and dog food (1 billion 160 million dollars) than the total amount spent by all our federal, state, and local governments on meals for public school children (896 million dollars).[2]

The reason the Church seldom joins social protest is because the Church itself typically sides with the Established Order of society. It does not view discriminatory and victimizing social arrangements as evil so much as it does the disturbances arising from these social arrangements. For example, the Church does not protest the conditions which lead to riots as much as it does rioting. It gives out insipid statements about deploring conditions which lead men to riot but then comes down firmly and with no hesitation solidly against those who riot, pointing to the evils of destroying that which is so sacred in American society—property. In this way the Church defends the propertied, those in control (and, not incidentally, its own larger contributors), and comes down hard with its predictable lines about "respect" for "law and order."

Can we really expect anything different from the Church? If we take the lessons of history seriously instead of paying attention to ecclesiastical ideology, we would find that it is normal for the Church *not* to speak out, *not* to take the side of the impoverished, the weak, and the defenseless, or when it does speak out, to do so in such a muted and weak way that it affects no one. Historically, it is only rarely that the privileged classes of a society have effectively worked to change the conditions of the less fortunate of their society: This is because those very conditions serve to maintain the privileged in their exalted positions. Those who protest run the risk of bringing into play forces which lead to their own destruction. If members of the privileged classes were to protest, they would run the risk of losing their positions of privilege. And, as we shall discuss shortly, the Church is part of the privileged sector of American society.

It is true that from time to time some leaders and other members of the Church attempt to effectively protest the victimizing of members of society, but these are primarily its Young Turks. The Church ordinarily responds to these protesters in its midst by either rejecting them or by uncomfortably putting up with them in the hope that they will soon "mature" and abandon such attitudes and activities and allow the Church to rest in the security of "the way things used to be." At other times, the Church is reluctantly pulled into social protest, as when secular groups take a strong moral stance in favor of America's poor, or work on behalf of American minority groups. At such times, the Church *sometimes* belatedly realizes on whose side it should be and queasily joins the opposition to such social abuse.

But primarily only after secular groups have taken up the defense of the oppressed does today's Church even begin to think beyond its own position of privilege and reluctantly realize that there might be a connection between the plight of the towntrodden of its own society and the founder of Christianity. It is most difficult for a wealthy Church to draw the implications of, or for that matter to even remember, that its founder was a member of a disenfranchised and enslaved group of poverty-stricken people, that he was himself a vagrant who ate, slept, and wept among the poor, and who chose his close followers from among them, and not from the rich, and that he died a painful ignominious death between two disreputable thieves. It is only with extreme reluctance that today's Church recognizes the connection between its founder and the current social, political, and economic situation in which it finds itself imbedded—and, at that, only rarely.

It appears that the Church begins to listen and to speak only after the downtrodden have ceased to accept quietly and passively their lot in life. Even when the victimized loudly protest, however, the Church is likely to say, paternalistically, as it has countless times in the past in similar situations, "Moderation, children, moderation. It is all part of God's will that you suffer now, for in the Kingdom to Come you shall be rewarded . . . ," and then the Church looks on in desperation as the Older Order is threatened along with its own privileged position—its property and wealth, tax exemptions, automatic draft exemptions, clergy perquisites, the fawning respect of the masses, and the aloof deference of society's "respectables."

When the Church does speak out, it is primarily *pro forma*, the making of ritualistic, ineffectual statements which hardly arouse an angry populace to oppose their oppressive regime. For example, the Church usually exercises its "prophetic voice" by merely formulating safe committee resolutions at its annual conventions, convincing itself and others that it is doing the right thing, that it is on the side of the oppressed and not the side of the oppressor. By speaking about conditions which *appear* to be evil, by disclaiming any desire for the continuance of such conditions, and by expressing its heartfelt dismay that they do continue, the Church sweetly and inexpensively salves its conscience and continues to go about its daily routines.

By its resolutions, which it indefatigably draws up, the Church commits itself neither to action nor to change. It has "spoken," and its "voice" has been quietly filed away in dusty tomes. If anyone wants to see what the Church's "official position" is, he can be directed to a resolution which triumphantly points to a "firm" position. The unfortunate consequence of this approach is that by it the Church effects no change: the oppressors continue to oppress, the oppressed continue to chafe and rebel, or become despondent and de-energized while the Church, like Pontius Pilate, washes its hands of the whole matter, perplexedly wondering and academically debating as to where "truth" really lies.

By its silence, inaction, acquiescence, and irrelevancies, *the Church contributes to the problems which it condemns in its endless resolutions*. By either defining social problems as lying outside its power or outside its "theological domain," the Church defines itself as powerless to effect change in the conditions which bring about these problems. The Church conveniently sees problematic factors in society as being caused by persons and institutions external to itself. For example, the Church refuses to acknowledge that the factors making it possible for its critics to call the Sunday morning church service "the most segregated hour in the United States" did *not* come about without the Church's cooperation. The Church has acquiesced to the social conditions affecting it, many created by its own members, and by acceptance and inaction has helped perpetuate the very social problems it condemns in its resolutions.

If through nothing else than by means of her embarrassing history of silence during the past three or four hundred years, the Church itself has played an active role in bringing about and perpetuating social problems. One could ask:

Where were you, Church,
 when the Indians were systematically slaughtered?
Where were you, Church,
 when the Blacks were brought in chains from Africa?
Where were you, Church,
 when the Jews were gassed by the Schutz-Staffeln?
That may all be in the past,
 as you say,
 but where are you today—
  As we exploit the "undeveloped" world and support
   oppressive regimes?
  As we isolate Blacks into reservations called the
   "inner city"?
  As males continue to suppress females?
  As our prisoners begin to reject the violence directed
   against them and organize for collective redress of
   their grievances—only to be put down by more
   violence?
  As our courts continue to give unequal justice based
   on income?
  As medical care, nutritional diets, and decent
   housing are still not rights, but privileges?
  As our resources are raped, along with our people,
   for the sake of profit?
In the Middle Ages you gave up counting
 the number of angels that can stand on the head of a pin . . .
But is it money I hear you counting today?

"But," say the defenders of the Church, "There always have been those within the Church who have spoken out against such evils." And by such statements the Church's conscience is again salved because it is true that some within the Church have spoken out. In fact, within the Church there have been individuals who have done much more than speak, persons who have stood up and died for the principles that the Church professes. In addition to thousands of laity, many clergy, nuns, and seminarians, for example, participated in the Civil Rights Movement. Many of them are today participating in the Black Liberation Movement—and some of them have been brutally murdered for their convictions.

But to the Church's shame we must also note that the leadership of the Church has shunted off many of its social activists into quiet parishes and educational institutions, where they can be occupied with less threatening concerns. It is the Church's typical reaction to deal bureaucratically with its Young Turks, to move them to places where they will "get along" and "be happier" (read: less troublesome and less upsetting to the more complacent members and to the Church's wealthier contributors).

"Our job is to heal souls and not to meddle in politics," say the saintly defenders of the ecclesiastical status quo. By means of such ideology the Church further salves its conscience, turns away from pressing issues of the day, avoids seriously questioning what is occurring in society, concurs with the status quo, and busies itself with mundane, routine, and ritualistic day-to-day tasks.

The Church and the Establishment, the Establishment and the Church—all neatly entertwined. Why? One reason is that the Establishment represents the virtues or values which the Church has adopted. The Church, for example, stands for respectability. The Church represents "rightness" and "morality," and when around people who are more expressive in their emotions and who are not as "uptight" as the middle class, the Church becomes uncomfortable. The Church appears to have forgotten that its founder was one of the "unrespectables" in the eyes of the Establishment of his society. The founder of what has become respectable Christianity was himself a challenger of the status quo, calling the scribes, Pharisees, and priests such choice names as white-washed gravestones. He eventually was condemned by both the religious and legal systems of his day and put to death by means of the cultural equivalent of our electric chair. And the Church of his day rejoiced to see that such a rabble-rousing antagonist of established virtue got what he deserved.

In a related manner, both the Church and the Establishment stand for *cleanliness*. "Cleanliness is next to godliness" is thought by many American Christians to be an exact quotation from the Bible itself. Is this just an accident? Or has cleanliness come to be such a high representation of virtue, being so greatly reinforced by the Church, that the two are forever paired in the minds of our people? In this context, I can't help but wonder about Christ's dirty, sweaty, stinking feet as he walked those dusty roads of Galilee. Since there weren't many showers around in those days, and Gillette hadn't yet come out with Right Guard, one wonders how Christ would match up to today's standards of physical cleanliness?

Individualism is another "virtue" loved by the Establishment, and, needless to say, by the Church. The teaching of individualism is that each of us should stand on his own two feet and fight for survival in a "dog-eat-dog" world. In this neo-Darwinian approach to life which the Church has adopted, it is taught that the fittest survive in a social world where *success* is held to be the highest value. Accordingly, the Church praises the successful man, for in this circular reasoning, success, by definition, becomes a virtue. This emphasis on individualism makes *upward social mobility* a related value on which the Establishment and the Church again agree. Never mind that actually there is little social mobility in the United States—it is sufficient that the issue of social mobility remain an unexamined part of both ecclesiastical and secular ideology, since the idea of social mobility helps to keep the masses from despairing. For those who fail to attain upward mobility, the Church provides comforting words about "God's will," "doing one's best where one is," and "rewards in the after-life," a sort of theological equivalent of the secular "better-luck-next-time" pat on the back.

Closely related is the virtue of *hard work*, which the Church also wholeheartedly supports. The Church and the Establishment form a harmonious chorus in support of St. Paul when he says, "If a man shall not work, neither shall he eat." At one point in its history, the Church was overt in such an approach to life, and hand-in-hand with the Establishment, the Church struggled against legislation for the well-being of the masses; it opposed legislation for shorter work days, industrial legislation to protect women and children, and sided against labor in the bitter and bloody struggle to gain the right to form labor unions which could effectively bargain for its membership. Such an approach to human dignity was thought to undermine ambition. Even today, welfare payments to the poor, especially to blacks, are suspect by both the Church and the Establishment. But today the Church has "advanced" to the point, as has the Establishment, that it primarily attacks welfare payments covertly, and it would rather see people eat through welfare payments than starve without them (with the exception of "able-bodied men," of course).

Both the Establishment and the Church also stand for *education.* Education has become one of the supreme values in American life. Though not taught in the Scriptures, people who have the opportunity to receive a higher education and don't take it frequently are thought to be committing an immoral act.

The point should be clear—the Church and the Establishment are mostly in agreement on the virtues or values which people should be taught. By teaching such values, the Church helps the Establishment to maintain the status quo. (And by teaching related values, such as diligence, honesty, and respect, the Church also helps to produce docile workers, buttresses our capitalistic system, and lends foundational support to the value of private property.)[3] Reciprocally, the Establishment supports the status quo of organized religion through favoritisms such as tax and draft exemptions, and by incorporating many of the Church teachings into law, into what are called "moral crimes," e.g., laws against adultery, homosexuality, gambling, and prostitution.

The second reason that the Church sides with the Establishment is that the Church has "arrived" in American society. Although the

Church is not sitting at the top of the heap, it has a secure position above the masses. If the Church were to speak out against those in power, it would be speaking directly against those on whom its present position of privilege largely depends. It would run the risk of losing one of the virtues for which it now stands, respectability, and of becoming associated with "sin."

Apart from a few small things such as clergy perquisites, some might question whether the Church has really "arrived" in a worldly sense. I am convinced that the answer is, "Indeed it has! And how!" For example, the construction of new religious buildings in the United States for 1966 alone ran well over a *billion* dollars.[4] Annual contributions to religious bodies in 1969 topped the three-and-a-half-billion-dollar mark.[5] The Roman Catholic denomination alone holds art works valued at over a billion dollars, plus more than *five billion* dollars of negotiable securities—and all this in addition to its world-wide real estate empire of buildings and lands.[6] In 1972 the Archdiocese of New York had a net worth of $643,000,000. Of this amount, a hefty $51,-000,000 was in cash.[7] Even Boys Town has an endowment fund of *at least* 209 million dollars. The Boys Town investment portfolio alone yields 8.1 million dollars a year. In 1970 Boys Town raked in 17.7 million dollars from just its mailings.[8] There is little doubt that the Church is wealthy.[9]

When an individual or organization is wealthy, it is usual to take steps to protect that wealth and the privileged position it brings. The Church is no exception. Being an integral part of the secular order, the Church, as we have just discussed, sacralizes the normative order, reinforcing the values of those in power. It is also usual that if an existing order is overthrown by revolution, then institutions which represent the old values are also overthrown. In cases where the Church has been overthrown by revolution, this is not, as has been frequently thought, because of some inherent antipathy between revolutionaries and what Christ himself represented. Rather, it has occurred because of antipathy between the values which the revolutionaries held and what they saw that the Church represented. Only vague strands connect the values of the Church and the founder of the Church, since Christ, as he demonstrated by his actions and his teachings, was not aligned with those in power.

It is not by accident that the Church suffered at the hands of the revolutionaries of France in 1789, Mexico in 1859 and again in 1917, Russia in 1907, China in 1949, and Cuba in 1959. In each country the Church had become part and parcel of the Establishment. The Church represented an institution which stood for wealth and privilege of the few and poverty and privation for the many. The Church became an institution which could build magnificent edifices for its own greater glory while the masses lived in squalor. It became transformed into an institution which could take money from hungry peasants, while in Rome it amassed unheard of fortunes in gold and jewels. Whatever it did in these countries was, of course, done "to the glory of God."

It is true that it was a priest of the Church who issued the *Grito de Dolores,* the signal for revolution in Mexico. But what was Father Hidalgo's fate with his own Church—excommunication before his execution. It is also true, in the case of Mexico, that it was another priest of the Church, José María Morelos, who led the revolution and developed a democratic constitution for Mexico in 1813. This constitution decreed racial equality, the division of large landed estates into small holdings for the peasants, the abolition of special privileges for clergymen, a general redistribution of wealth, a sales tax, and the confiscation of the vast accumulated Church funds to be used for the general welfare of Mexicans. And what was the fate of Morelos? He also was excommunicated by the Church and executed by the Establishment.[10]

There is probably nothing that the Church cannot rationalize as being to the "glory of God." The Church has systematically done this from the slaughter of the Innocents during the Spanish Inquisition of 1481 to the enslavement of Africans. In fact, a "respectable" theological source says of John Newton (1725–1821): "The six following years, during which he commanded a slave ship, matured his Christian faith."[11] That is quite a way to have one's faith mature! With such experiences under his belt, this slave trader was able to write such sensitive words as:

> How sweet the Name of Jesus sounds
> In a believer's ear!
> It soothes his sorrows, heals his wounds,
> And drives away his fear.

> It makes the wounded spirit whole
> And calms the troubled breast;
> 'Tis manna to the hungry soul
> And to the weary, rest.

> Jesus, my Shepherd, Guardian, Friend,
> My Prophet, Priest, and King,
> My Lord, my Life, my Way, my End,
> Accept the praise I bring.

> Till then I would Thy love proclaim
> With every fleeting breath;
> And may the music of Thy name
> Refresh my soul in death![12]

The poetic hymnic worship of this slave trader has been so appreciated by contemporary Christians that eight of his hymns are contained in *The Lutheran Hymnal.*[13]

The Church became such an integral part of the established way of doing things in society that the American Church was not only even able to accept slavery, but in many cases from its own holy writings it justified the enslavement of blacks. The Church was able to look upon blacks as being "Sons of Ham," fit only for cutting wood and carrying water. Segments of the Church became so adjusted to this aspect of Americana that some "respectable and religious" whites thought it quite proper to invest in slaves in order to pay the salary of their pastor. For example:

> In 1767 some members of Presbyterian churches in Prince Edward County, Virginia, subscribed a sum of money and purchased two slave girls. These and their descendants were annually hired out and "the hires appropriated to the payment of the salaries of the (common) pastor," till 1835, when they numbered about seventy. Then the owners, believing that it would be better for the slaves, ordered their sale and the investment of the money obtained.[14]

Not only was the Church such a part of the Establishment that it was able to make peace between slavery and its own teachings, but when the country split on the slavery question, the Northern churches for the most part decided that slavery was an evil which should be stamped out, while the churches in the South decided that slavery was not really that evil and even in some cases that slavery was what God intended. "After all, they couldn't have been Christianized if they hadn't become slaves," so went, amazingly enough, the argument. It wasn't by accident that a denomination sometimes split geographically, as with the Northern and Southern Methodists.

With the Church's interconnection with the Establishment, it is small wonder that the present-day Church can justify its policy of sending chaplains to our armed forces. These chaplains are paid by the federal government, and they teach our soldiers "to kill with morality." "For God and country!" they say to our soldiers. These chaplains have the divine task of consoling soldiers when their conscience begins to bother them. ("You only did your duty, and, although it was hard, God wants you to do your duty," or, "There is a larger plan in all this than the deaths of the individuals you have seen.") This is nothing new for the Church. In the same way and for the same reasons, the German Church in the Second World War sent chaplains to their troops. Because of this vital interconnection between the Church and the Establishment, the Pope even blessed troops, tanks, men, and weapons when Mussolini's fittest went out to defend and forcibly extend Fascism. The Pope even gave his blessings before Mussolini's army left Italy to plunder and ravage the primitive Ethiopians, who were forced to defend themselves with spears. The Pope, moreover, even said that Mussolini was "sent by Providence."[15] And German soldiers once had an emblem on their uniforms which said, "Gott Mit Uns."

It would be strange for today's Church to foster noncooperation with nationalistic imperialism, since it has such a high stake in the perpetuation of the status quo. Silence, acquiescence, acceptance, tolerance, and active involvement in imperialistic ventures by the Church is what is usual—once we understand some of the connections between the Church and the Establishment. Those in the Church who protest the Establishment are the ones who are out of line, for it is those who protest who are the ones who are threatening not only the present domestic political order but also the present ecclesiastical order. Such persons are a threat to both the Establishment and the Church—just as Christ was a threat to both the Church and Establishment of his day—and he was put to death for his disruptions of the accepted and respected religious and secular orders.

It is no wonder, then, that the Church today accepts the present established order of this country because *the Church is itself an integral part of that order*. The virtues of "democracy" and "Christianity" (and I use quotes advisedly in *both* instances) are all tied together into a single package. To challenge one is to challenge the other. It is not too unusual, for example, based on my experiences, to have both clergy and laity believe that God himself had something to do with establishing our form of government, to believe that participatory capitalism is the economic order desired by God.

"Go to Church this Sunday," billboards outside small, rural towns frequently exhort travelers—compliments of the local Junior Chamber of Commerce. Go to church, any church. It doesn't matter to the JCCs which "mainstream" church you choose because they all align themselves in their own peculiar way with the Established Order. Churches are good for business because they tend to maintain the status quo, to perpetuate the way things are, and thus to keep in power those who already have power. They also help maintain the status quo by stifling dissent: "God is for peace. He doesn't want revolution. So run along and be a good boy or girl, and he'll take care of things in his own way and in his own time." Which isn't now.

Over and over in the Church the emphasis is on individualism. You, as an individual, the Church says, are to do what you can where you are to help alleviate suffering, to feed the poor, to help the sick, etc., etc., *ad nauseam*. And as someone follows these exhortations to help those less fortunate than himself, what a marvelous sense of warmth and goodness fills his very being. "Everything is O.K. between God and yourself. You've done his will. He is smiling cherubically down from his lofty place in the heavens. Oh, wouldn't this be a dandy world if we all just acted as good Christians!"

Well, it probably would. But, as has been so astutely noted by some anonymous observer of the religious and social scene, "No one can say Christianity is a failure. It's never been tried." The noble virtues of Christianity will probably continue to remain hidden between the dusty covers of household Bibles as the Church and its membership continue to perpetuate the evils and miseries of our present political order. Only time will tell, of course. But except for a fantastic beginning and a marvelous couple of hundred years, as the early Christians stood *against* the Established Political Order, and with isolated exceptions from time to time in local history, almost 2,000 years of characteristic behavior provides a fairly solid basis for predicting the future. It appears that only a revolution *within* the Church could change this interconnection. At any rate, there is little to hope for from a Church which is corruptly intertwined with our current Political-Military-Industrial Order to such an extent that in 1971 it invested 203 million dollars in war industries. The twenty-nine war-related companies in which the Church invested produced over ten *billion* dollars in war supplies in 1971, ranging from firearms to missiles.[16]

Change in this interconnection between the Church and the Establishment probably can only come about by revolution—either revolution in the secular social order, which also will overthrow the Church, or revolution from *within* the Church. 450 years ago Martin Luther attempted a revolution within the Church, but his revolution was centered on purifying some of the doctrines of the Church. Perhaps now is the time for a revolution which will bring the Church back to poverty. For it is only in poverty that the Church can ever hope to again find its founder. Not because poverty is a virtue, but because the Establishment does not identify with poverty.

ENDNOTES

1. The term "Church," as used in this paper, refers to Christianity in general and the American-brand of Christianity in particular.
2. The figures in this paragraph are for 1969 and are computed from the *Statistical Abstract of the United States*, 1971, Tables 431 and 521. The amounts for cat and dog food are from "Pet Food: Pedigreed Profits," *The Magazine of Wall Street and Business Analyst, 127*, December 5, 1970, p. 14.
3. For a classic source in this area, see Liston Pope, *Millhands and Preachers*, second edition, 1965 (New Haven, Conn.: Yale University Press, 1942). For some differences in socialization effects between Roman Catholics and Protestants, see Gerhard Lenski, *The Religious Factor*, Anchor Book edition, 1963 (New York: Doubleday and Company, 1961).

4.   *Yearbook of American Churches*, Lauris B. Whitman, ed. (New York: Council Press, 1969), p. 193.
5.   *Yearbook of American Churches*, Constant H. Jacquet, Jr., ed. (New York: Council Press, 1970), p. 200.
6.   Nino Lo Bello, *The Vatican Empire* (New York: Trident Press, 1968), pp. 13, 135.
7.   *St. Louis Post-Dispatch*, April 5, 1972, p. 16-A.
8.   *Newsweek*, April 10, 1972, p. 55.
9.   It is interesting to note that some people who have become aware of the privileged position of the Church in our society are beginning to utilize it to their advantage. Note, for example, the current upsurge in diploma mills offering Bachelor of Divinity degrees for ten dollars, no questions asked, and which supposedly entitle the bearers to both tax and draft exemptions. (For $50 one can even become a bishop!)
10.   For an excellent account of the violent history of Mexico, see Hudson Strode, *Timeless Mexico* (New York: Harcourt Brace Jovanovich, Inc., 1944). See in particular pp. 105 and 106. My thanks to Larry T. Reynolds for drawing this source to my attention. This source (pp. 256, 257) states that the Constitution of 1917 removed the right of Churches to own real property and banned foreign priests from Mexico.
11.   *The Handbook to the Lutheran Hymnal*, W. G. Pollack, ed. (St. Louis, Mo.: Concordia Publishing House, 1942), p. 555.
12.   Stanzas 1, 2, 5, and 7 of hymn 364 of *The Lutheran Hymnal* (St. Louis, Mo.: Concordia Publishing House, 1945). It should be noted that this hymn was written some time after Newton's slave-trading.
13.   For those who are interested, these hymns are numbers 11, 46, 51, 113, 364, 456, and 469.
14.   Frederic Bancroft, *Slave-trading in the Old South* (Baltimore, Md.: J. H. Furst Company, 1931), p. 87. We might parenthetically note that knowledge of such history should lead to greater insight and understanding of animosity towards the Church on the part of many blacks in the Black Liberation movement, and why a demand for reparations from the Church has been made.
15.   Lo Bello, *op cit.*, p. 63.
16.   *St. Louis Post-Dispatch*, January 9, 1972, p. 16-A. It should be noted that these figures include the three major religions in the United States—Protestant, Roman Catholic, *and* Jewish.

For a most insightful statement of the thesis of this paper, and one which is much more appealing in its form, see the song by Bob Dylan, "With God on Our Side."

Sidney M. Willhelm

26

Scientific Mythology:
A Speculative Overview

Human kind cannot bear very much reality.
T. S. Eliot

Dissension within professional associations reflects precisely what "scientific" inquiry itself must not acknowledge, namely, the ethics of human relations. An allegiance to value-neutrality has supposedly made it possible for academics sharing a common disciplinary interest to come together in such a manner as to minimize conflict among themselves[1] and dissociate overtly from ideological judgments. Allegedly, the purge of ethical concerns allows for a dispassionate discovery of scientific laws and insulates society from subversive scholarship; the public welfare is served by allowing the pursuit of objective research and teaching.

For all its purification, the denunciation of values does not eradicate the issue of morality. Instead, it deludes the scientific practitioners, on the one hand, and, on the other, intensifies dedication to special interests within American society. Basically, the professional scholar has so internalized values enhancing the legitimacy of State Rule over all Americans that he boldly declares his moral commitment as an "objective" view of what is "true." The anguish among those voicing support for "professional" integrity is enormous, for they must enunciate their beliefs in the very process of proclaiming "value neutrality." Thus, if there is a crisis within professional associations, it is found

This article was written for this volume. The author expresses appreciation for the assistance given by Lionel S. Lewis and Dusky Lee Smith in writing this article. Printed by permission.

precisely in the one element which was to be expunged by scientific inquiry: social ethics.

MYTH-MAKING

Many are called but few are chosen.
Biblical quotation

Social myths prescribe social conduct in accord with a compelling force; they are the beliefs we profess to sanctify the righteousness of our deeds. We subordinate ourselves to one another according to the transcendental qualities of our myth. It is within the myth that man cultivates the essence, and expresses the universals, of his social experiences; myths provide us with our "First Law," our "First Principles" from which we derive other conclusions for ordering our lives. They are not, however, the genuine values motivating human behavior but are, instead, rationalizations justifying whatever we undertake; they reflect and validate our enduring values. Furthermore, the social myth is temporal, subject to modification or removal "when new centers of power, not yet legitimated, not able to cloak themselves in established symbols of authority, arise . . ."[2] As such, myths are society's ornaments to enshrine the select with the absolutes of their command and the subordinates of their obedience to rulers. Moreover, rulers and the ruled seek to hold one another accountable by direct appeal to the authority of myths.

What is constant within all myths is the ascendancy of the superlative with an imprint so forceful as to be beyond reproach: "We hold these truths to be self-evident." What is so readily conspicuous has no urge for inquiry but rather trust, i.e., faith. But while righteousness owes no explanation, there is the obvious need for a spokesman, an individual or group, with a special designation to speak out and inform others of the invincible Final Authority. Consequently, a very special rationale elaborates the way for mortal man being able to know and bestow immortal Authority for an entire people. Since, in the words of Thomas Browne, "God hath not made a creature that can comprehend him," the anointment of a priesthood is a task undertaken by mortals.

Man does not stand alone and in coming together some system of order gets formulated and given a sense of finality with an absolutely binding force. Social rulers are admittedly temporal, but their authority is attuned to the superlatives of myths. The right to rule over others must be legitimated by a source clearly external and beyond the command of those who rule, since "a right abstracted from the power necessary to protect it, is a nonentity."[3] The responsibility to germinate and exhort the social myths of literate societies is delegated to intellectuals;

intellectuals set about making moral judgments, in terms of a written body of ethics, whereby the reign of rulers within a society exonerates the control exerted over the lives of men. Insofar as intellectuals expound teachings sustaining their rulers, they are apologists; whenever they extend teachings challenging those in power, they are critics.[4] A stable society will have intellectuals who receive sufficient rewards to uphold its prevailing myths.[5]

AMERICAN MYTHS

> *God alters no law of Nature.*
> John Preston, Puritan theologian

Since its establishment, American society has been based on an economic system requiring constant expansion for its prosperity,[6] and its dominant myths, therefore, expound justifications to assure whatever needs to be done for expanding the economy would be a compelling edict of transcendental entities. Our myths have been shaped by American intellectuals who, for the most part, obediently reformulate our creeds to harmonize with shifting economic circumstances.

The nation's initial myth came from white, Christian settlers of the New World who set themselves apart as God's chosen People and designated the native Indian as "heathen" and hence inferior. Expropriation of lands from Indians merely fulfilled the economics of settlement; needless to say, the economics of settlement came to be the Word of God. God destined His people to populate the earth; the settlers could seize land not under till since it was the Will of Heaven that all things be improved. The "heathen" Indians were transformed by definition into savages, and their resistance to whites truthful to God's commands meant extermination/or isolation upon reservations.

When economic expansion in the American Colonies reached the point of pertinent competition with England, the voice of Providence resounded with a conviction of justified independence. Colonists perceived themselves as economically oppressed, although they simultaneously conceived founding an American empire extending from coast to coast and, eventually, from continent to continent.[7] At this moment of economic transition, the Word of God inspired independent-minded colonists to speak of the "natural rights" of mankind. First used in America by New England clergymen, the doctrine quickly entered into public discourse by the 1760's. The *Commentaries* (1765–69) of Sir William Blackstone provided considerable argumentation for Divine creation of natural laws and rights for a budding nation to severe governance exerted by Britain:

> This law of nature being coeval with mankind, and dictated by God himself, is of course superior in obligation to any other. It is binding over all the globe, in all countries and at all times; no human laws are of any validity, if contrary to this; and such of them as are valid derive all their forces and all their authority, mediately or immediately, from this original.

By 1775 Alexander Hamilton proclaimed that

> Good and wise men, in all ages . . . have supposed that the Deity, from the relations we stand in to Himself, and to each other, has constituted an eternal and immutable law, which is indispensably obligatory upon all mankind, prior to any human institution whatever. . . .

> Upon this law depend the natural rights of mankind: The Supreme Being gave existence to man, together with the means of preserving and beautifying that existence.

Any government, it was concluded, which impeded or threatened the natural rights of man gave just cause for revolution.

Increasingly, ideological justifications moved into the realm of Nature. As man learned more about physical and biological processes, the more man had to reckon with his place in an ordered universe; the ways of Nature, hopefully, would enhance the ways of coping with the social order. Newton had uncovered Nature's secrets of motion; Carolus Linnaeus, in the 1730's, sealed man *into* the animal kingdom by his catalog of organisms; and about a century later, Charles Darwin announced the very origin of species through descent in accord with the principle of natural selection based upon adaptation to survive in the struggle for existence. The transfiguration of man was initially accomplished through the salvation of one's soul, but with greater attention being given to worldly wonders, the inner, spiritual dimensions faded. Consequently, Nature was willed by God, but the rights of man were established upon the Natural premise. The hierarchical formulation—God, Nature, man—minimized direct confrontations between what would otherwise have been two highly competitive systems of Absolutes.

By the nineteenth century, dramatic changes emerged for channeling wealth which would have profound bearing upon the course of human events. Up until modern times, wealth, for the most part, had to be extracted from tilling the soil. The rise of technology to replace human energy in the production of goods for profits allowed for new wealth. Through inventions, men began to transform Nature into goods for consumption; economic production expanded by *applying*, rather than abiding by, the Laws of Nature. Nature, then, became redefined into a composite of objects subject to transformation by technological know-how drawing upon scientific understandings. Mankind would no longer conceive its destiny in the immutables of Nature since technology could be implemented to command Nature. And religion, relegated to a greater distance from worldly affairs by the intrusion of Nature, became even less relevant; as man seized control over Nature, God could not remain in an exalted position.

In short, man placed himself into his own hands in the most direct sense possible. Henceforth, immutable truths would be established within the very social life man lives. And, in one sense, this is a calamity of the first order: the burden of man's own responsibility came to rest with social actions and could not be traced to transcendental entities preceding human existence.

As we shall explore in the next section of this paper, we have yet to succeed in easing this burden, for no satisfactory myth has risen to replace that of God and Nature. Indeed, we should remind ourselves what has already been stated to emphasize the difficulty: "A right abstracted from the power necessary to protect it, is a nonentity." Otherwise, just Everyman could proclaim Any Right when, however, social relations involve the authority to exert a right—a claim—upon one another; a right by one announces an obligation from another which, therefore, introduces a rationale of social responsibility. It is precisely this linkage which is cemented by the founding of a compelling myth.

Where have Americans turned in search of a new myth sanctifying the economic interests of the 20th century?

THE SOCIAL MYTH

> *No one is exempt from talking nonsense;*
> *the misfortune is to do it solemnly.*
>
> Montaigne

In his *Notes on Virginia*, Jefferson set forth the view that "those who labor *in the earth* are the chosen people of God, if ever he had a chosen people, whose breasts he has made his peculiar deposit for substantial and genuine virtue." With the rise of industry, labor moved from the landed gentry to industrialists bent upon extracting fortunes not from "labor in the earth" but labor per se. Henceforth, as Nature succumbed to human manipulation there could be no Godly creed affirming the economics of mankind. "The whole modern system," Richard Henry Dana prophetically observed in 1853, "seems to me to be gounded on a false view of man . . . as acknowledging no God, nor the need of any. . . . There is a spirit of self-confidence in it, which, left to its natural tendencies, will inevitably bring a deeper and wider woe upon man than earth has ever yet known."[8] That "deeper and wider woe," I suggest, is the American Empire forged upon the anvil of capitalism into a militaristic state on the brink of exterminating the human race through massive technological destruction.

The doctrine of laissez-faire demonstrates the ideological transitions justifying economic interests. From the inspiration of diligence sanctioned by God, the ideologues moved into the natural rights of laissez-faire. Early in the 19th century the economist Daniel Raymond broke from mercantilism and formulated a theory of laissez-faire predicated upon the privileges of manufacturing corporations. By 1836, this new economics had captivated Henry Carey whose essay, *The Harmony of Nature*, presented a "natural law" imperative: "Arguing a rather sophisticated version of Smith's laissez-faire, he stressed three interrelated principles: happiness and the general welfare were most effectively produced by giving *men of property* the freedom of action that was theirs by *natural law,* and in particular by recognizing that even greater (and faster) rewards would be gained by encouraging and accepting the industrial corporation and other large business enterprise."[9] It was felt that the efforts to invoke Nature would encourage not only property interests but would also instill semblances of stability—lawful behavior for all persons with assurances of an orderly system reflecting the order established by the physical sciences. When, however, capitalism yielded neither a public welfare of happiness nor stability but fostered instead one economic crisis after another, social harmony based upon "natural law" floundered. The crass aggrandizement by business promoted pleasure of a few at the expense of the many.

The crisis of laissez-faire acquired a new dress following the biological formulations of Charles Darwin just beyond mid-19th century. In a society ravaged by an unstable economy of capitalization, there came forth a brief flurry of writers vigorously advocating intense individual competition: the most talented persons evolve out of economic competition, while those failing to secure sufficient resources manifest an inherent inability to survive. Consequently, an economic elite represents an inevitable process of evolution testifying to its qualities to prevail; individuals in poverty are the least talented and can only expect a life of hardship. The former, therefore, have every right to claim their wealth, and the latter are to be obedient to their fate. Any measure by government to introduce public welfare and ameliorate the lot of the poor only interferes with natural evolutionary processes, allowing persons least able to survive to prevail at the expense of those who demonstrate the faculties to win. Economic competition was thus viewed as the natural process by which a society removes its social dregs for replacement by superior persons.

Social Darwinists moved intellectual thought through the transition from natural to social causation. Although applying a biological analogy to social processes, their basic efforts were explicit in the devotion to found a science of *social* laws matching the conclusiveness of *physical* laws. The laws they intended to discover would then become social mandates—maxims to be learned and obeyed. For society abided by irrefutable principles equivalent to the compliance of matter to physical laws; social evolution was one such determinism within human society. Doctrines contrary to social laws, such as socialism and communism, were exercises in futility for placing priority upon a collective welfare in preference to the individualism of laissez-faire.

It is only appropriate, then, to expect the growth of a science devoted to the discovery of social laws, namely, sociology. "The chaos of the [18]70's and the development of American sociology," Dusky Lee Smith suggests, "are not unrelated phenomena; rather, sociology developed within the reform movements created to salvage the capitalist system."[10] The founding fathers of American sociology declared their faith in capitalism, denounced socialism and communism (i.e., Karl Marx), and insisted that the fantastic economic dislocations between 1870–1900 could be eliminated by convincing capitalists of an obligation toward those inferior in station who had limited opportunities. Economic anomalies under capitalism were transformed into social problems subject to scientific analysis for amelioration. In short, sociology, a science of society, would discover the social processes necessary for securing the reign of corporate capitalism much as physical science serviced capitalism by discovering laws applicable to factory production.

A dominant view, at the moment, is that the bureaucratic administration is rationality par excellence, and that persons merely hold offices carrying out duties mandated by the very positions they possess. Contemporary orthodox teachings of large-scale social organization endeavor to subordinate all persons to the supremacy of rationality attributed to the intrinsic quality of the bureaucracy which, after all, is the foremost form of corporate capitalist production. A new Social Myth has been founded upon a new kind of authority arguing for a rationality established within the collective rather than among men.[11] Over the past century rational *man* has been subdued, indeed, destroyed; in his stead has come the rational *system* of corporate capitalism in the disguise of bureaucratic systems analysis propagated by social scientists. Social science itself has come into greater prominence by the need for capitalists to have an enunciation of new myths to legitimate the corporate structure as the proper source for authority following the disintegration of Faith and Nature. It is no wonder, then, to find so many scholars denouncing challenges external to bureaucratic organizations as irrational. For if bureaucracies act rationally, assaults must be attacks upon rationality by irrational persons. Nowhere is this more apparent than in the case of academics denouncing the college student critical of administrative rule; administrators and professors, however, present themselves as persons seeking resolutions based upon reason simply because rationality is part and parcel of being an office-holder within a well-defined bureaucracy. The bureaucratic structure is now the repository for a supreme attribute: the faculty to reason.

Throughout the transition from one myth to another, the persistent opposition to socialist doctrines continued; advocates of collectivism, especially variations of Marxist thought, would not be easily tolerated and would be subject to harsh suppression. From the "red scares" under Attorney General Palmer during the administration of Woodrow Wilson through Progressivism of the New Deal during the Depression era of the 1930's; from the fictional creation of a "Cold War" during post-World-War-II America through the "thaw" of the '60's, sufficient ways to contain the spread of communistic interpretations are apparent.[12] The hysteria of a Bolshevik bogeyman foreclosed all opportunity for an effective leftist "third party" force—from Populism at the turn of the century through Henry Wallace's Progressive Party. Intellectuals of socialist inclinations were frozen out while social thinkers justifying property interests bent upon imperialistic ventures over foreign territories—from the historian Brooks Adams ("I take it our destiny is to reorganize the Asiatic end of the vast chaotic mass we call Russia.") to the post-World-War-II social scientist promoting "modernization" for "underdeveloped" nations—were amply rewarded.

The task for intellectuals, therefore, has been made patently clear by men of property: to compose a Social Myth legitimating the populace's acquiescence to the corporate takeover of wealth necessarily requiring expansion of the American Empire throughout the world. Notions of a cosmic reality for sanctioning the shift from laissez-faire to corporate capitalism—all bound to the preservation of private property and staunchly opposed to socialism—have gone from religious to strictly social conceptualization. The affairs of men were once viewed as reflecting the dogma of religion, then the laws of nature, and, today, unalterable principles of society enunciated by social scientists. Intellectuals refusing to weave their judgments into the framework of capitalist economics endure a relentless wrath: conform or face expulsion from respectability conferred by the scions of knowledge.

THE SCIENTIFIC ENTERPRISE

Scientific research is a method whereby
private curiosity is satisfied at public expense.
L. A. Artsimovitch, Soviet physicist

Just as Christian intellectuals convinced themselves of the righteousness of God while furnishing justification for laissez-faire capitalism, social scientists cloak themselves in transcendental myths to absolve any need for atonement for servicing corporate capitalism. Just as the teachings of God were revelations to prophetic individuals, somehow especially "called" and thus privileged to be anointed, the professional social scientist rises to the fore to "discover" scientific truths through methodological confirmation; as the holder of "scientific" qualifications, he declares himself the expert for comprehending the patterns of our lives. Unlike their predecessors, however, social scientists declare principles of "value neutrality" to argue that they are examining, not judging, the social lives of men.

A scientific creed, buttressed by the professional organization, has come to replace religious dogma. Professionalism has become the by-word and the mark of excellence for the truly matured social scientist; it is intended to enshrine not only "the truth" but also the bearer of that "truth"—namely, the scholar of scientific investigations. The scholar's ascendancy in the profession's hierarchy of membership and office-holding validates his claim for prominence and anoints his particular writings with an official imprimatur; the prestige conferred by professionalization of scholarship warrants respect from other bureaucracies such as the university, government, foundations, publishing houses, and business corporations.

The professional cult is now fully implanted in the college education of an upcoming generation of social science recruits, and scientific college education thus supplants the "laying on of hands" ordaining yesterday's religious intellectual. The prime word for handling prospective recruits is "training"; an apprenticeship is expected of those seeking to follow in the footsteps of the professional mentor. The professional teacher believes his discipline possesses, and he, in turn, commands a body of knowledge to be passed on; education consists of disciplining students into on-going "scientific truths" and the "scientific method" for elaborating mostly what is already known. "Standards" become the means by which professional control is exerted throughout the educational process, especially over graduates. Students, therefore, *ascend* to knowledge in orderly procession by adhering to professional expectations enunciated by the professional teacher; conformity, or at least the appearance of such, is mandatory. Once professional certification is administered, the graduating student is expected to become a producer, filling gaps of knowledge in meticulous fashion so as to demonstrate his technical competence.

Still, it has never been demonstrated that "objectivity" assures greater accuracy for the social scientist; instead, as a canon of science, it is intended to convey the purity of innocence required for academic piety. Increased professionalization decreases the exploration of motivation, for what is studied is the "objective" world and not the inner, subjective desires of persons. Consequently, it is not intentions but rather results which interest professionally-minded social scientists.

That such a commitment ignores or distorts what is to be explained is very much beside the point since myths are to sanctify, not analyze, the beliefs directing the course of human experiences. Thomas S. Szasz is explicit on the meaning of casting aside morality: "The omission from psychiatric theories of moral issues and normative standards, as explicitly stated goals and rules of conduct, has divorced psychiatry from precisely that reality which it has tried to describe and explain."[13] The historian, Charles Beard, made the same observation about political science: "We are therefore confronted by an inherent antagonism between our generally accepted political doctrines, and the actual facts of political life. . . . Shall we in the field of political science cling to a delusion that we have to deal only with an abstract man divorced from all economic interests and group sentiments?"[14] The escape from values pardoned by scientific impartiality can only mean, according to the anthropologist, A. L. Kroeber, that

> . . . we are refusing to deal with what has most meaning in particular cultures as well as in human culture seen as a whole. . . .
>
> What we have left on elimination of values is an arid roster of cultural events which we are constantly tempted to animate by reintroducing the values we have banned, or else by backhandedly introducing values from our own culture. . . .[15]

In political science, morality has no place when formulating international theories and national policies among nations; only national interests hold forth according to the professionalized political analyst. Consequently, at a moment in history when four-fifths of the world's foreign investment is made by Americans for assuring corporate profits, most professional experts on international relations only hint at an American Empire predicated upon the outpouring of capital unmatched by any nation any time in history. Instead, we are fed the pablum that "a country like the United States probably cannot maintain self-confidence if just about the greatest thing it ever attempted, namely to create the basis for decency and prosperity and democratic government in the underdeveloped world, had to be acknowledged as a failure or as an attempt that we wouldn't try again."[16] It is as though the nation must not suffer a deflated ego rather than admit to the economic expansion anticipated even when America was still part of the British Empire. It is *Realpolitik*—supposedly free from sentimentality —passing for analysis which led Professor David N. Rowe, Director of Graduate Studies in International Relations at Yale University, to encourage the U.S. government's purchase of surplus Canadian and Australian wheat being sold to China so as to induce mass starvation in order to destroy another *government* (not a people!):

> Mind you, [were his reassuring words] I am not talking about this as a weapon against the Chinese people. It will be. But that

is only incidental. The weapon will be a weapon against the Government because the internal stability of that country cannot be sustained by an unfriendly Government in the face of general starvation.[17]

It is clear from this testimony that people don't count and that the political scientist creates a Social Entity at the heart of his analysis in keeping with the need for a Social Myth: the Nation-State. Suffering people are "incidental" to *any* transcendental entity—God, Nature, and now, the Social. It was "unfortunate" that a native population had to be exterminated because white Christians, in "settling" the New World, believed in a religious freedom requiring obedience to the Will of God; it was a "natural" fate for the poor to be left "unfit" according to the Law of Nature since advocates of Social Darwinism insisted freedom meant the liberty of human society to evolve according to Nature's mandates; and it is "incidental" to exterminate millions to implant the American reign in Asia inasmuch as the Social Myth of Statism vouchsafes any nation the freedom to do whatever America's national interests dictate. Thus do we hear Dean G. Acheson, Secretary of State under President Truman, justifying America's post-World-War-II empire-building.

> We are willing to help people *who believe the way we do,* to continue to live the way *they want* to live.[18]

MILITARIZATION OF THE SOCIAL MYTH

> *Mass murder . . . has become our most important product.*
> *The Pentagon dwarfs the biggest of American big business.*
> I. F. Stone (1971)

We have the assurance of the ideologue, Daniel Bell, that "the economic philosophy of American liberalism . . . [is] rooted in the idea of growth,"[19] and that, according to William Appleman Williams, such expansion means the active creation of new markets outside national boundaries —all of which equals imperialism. Such expansion, furthermore, has been massive: direct investment amounted to $11 billion in 1950 and exceeded $70 billion during 1969; when one adds to the latter figure the foreign capital controlled by American enterprise, the astronomical sum of $100 billion is reached. The claim is made that just as private wealth is now concentrated in the top 100 corporations, it will not be long before 300 corporations monopolize international industrial output—and ⅔ of the 300 will be American enterprises.

Presenting such figures as these, Professor Robert L. Heilbroner searches for an explanation to account for the arrival of what he calls "the multinational corporation."[20] He finds his answer in one of the most recent popular brands of Social Myths—technology. "Thus," he argues, "behind the rise of the interlocking, interpenetrating webs of overseas production there lies a certain logic of technology and organization."[21] To be sure, Heilbroner acknowledges "the gradual 'saturation' of national markets . . . provided the *initial* stimulus for a shift from mere export-orientation to true international production" and "corporations typically send home more profits than the capital that they originally introduce into the 'host' country."[22] Yet, such observations are but mere asides while the "logic of technology" remains the central thrust. Although Heilbroner admits of "the nation-state with its vicious force and shameful irrationality, and the corporation with its bureaucratic hierarchies and its reliance on greed and carefully inculcated dissatisfaction," he nonetheless concludes by saying, "I suspect that the interaction of the international corporation and the nation-state is less comprehensible as a conflict between 'capitalism' . . . and 'socialism' . . . than as part of the ignorant and often desperate processes by which we seek to contain *the demon of technology* and to organize the collective endeavors of men at a time when the level of human understanding is still pitiably low, even in the most 'advanced' countries."[23] This analysis leads, then, to an omnipotent determinant—the logic of technology— which, though unmotivated, besets the destiny of mankind. And this *deus ex machina* exonerates what Heilbroner never mentions, even should one accept his presentation, namely, the fact that it is the American military which has made people expendable by exporting technology over the entire globe; if the "logic of technology" prevails and it is the military which is the foremost source of technological expansion throughout the world, then how can one avoid the implications of this?

With the maturity of industrialization and military expansion during, particularly, the Second World War, it became apparent to the heads of corporations, and, especially, government officials, that knowledge and technology were indispensable ingredients. No longer would inventions be accomplished by men tinkering in makeshift quarters, nor would knowledge come from scientists doodling in makeshift laboratories. The growth of massive technology through massive discoveries by scientists meant massive financing, an economic burden which corporations would not accept and which, therefore, became the responsibility of government. No other event so vividly demonstrates the shift from private business to government for financing research as the support given scientists for constructing atomic weapons. Since then, billions of research dollars have flowed from the public treasury. Accordingly, the loyalty of scientists had to be squarely faced and determined: if the economics for funding research became concentrated in the Department of Defense, could scientists afford an allegiance to any organization other than the military branches of government?[24] Furthermore, if knowledge is so vital to technological development and thereby an important input to power, can corporate capitalism continue as the dominant economic momentum when the military monopolizes the knowledge and technology which provide the basis for economic growth?

These economic considerations surrounding knowledge and technology establish a fundamental transition within American society— a shift from the corporate enterprise to the military. This basic alteration necessitated a fundamental examination of the ethical system by which intellectuals assured economic validation of corporations. Such questioning was initially raised by nuclear scientists themselves. "The nuclear scientists," Ralph E. Lapp explains, "realized more than anyone else that the bombs dropped at Hiroshima and Nagasaki were not the end of the matter. *Control of nuclear research and of the use of nuclear power was at stake.* . . . The *single* topic which served both to focus the sicentists' efforts and to excite them to the need for group action was *the issue of civilian versus military control of atomic energy.*"[25]

In short, the business ethic diminishes in response to the rise of government in dominating scientific undertakings. As government acquired control over the economics of knowledge, scientists faced the imperative to demonstrate a *government* loyalty which, in turn, initiated a new situation calling for reformulating the Social Myth which was, as explained above, devoted to capitalism. Such realignments invited severe strain, for it is no simple matter to move from the myths of capitalism to a myth supporting military rule over inquiry. The fear of Nazi Germany during World War II furnished a ready rationale to place oneself in service to the State and produce military weapons capable of destroying all humans. But the defeat of the Axis powers broke ranks among scientists—as most vividly shown by the issue surrounding the decision to develop the hydrogen bomb.

The moral strain among nuclear scientists was the first instance of acute dissatisfaction which forced both scientists and intellectuals to experience direct regulation by the state. The transition is not an easy one; it initiated all kinds of imputations of disloyalty as resistance developed in the professional community of scholars. Loyalty tests similar to military clearance moved onto university campuses where intellectuals concentrated; the Cold War was played up to generate the pressure for allegiance to the government which, like capitalists, was unwilling to finance knowledge without control over personnel; and the McCarthy era capped the loyalty-testing momentum. Intimidation became commonplace, but intellectuals willing to justify the righteousness of the Cold War flourished along with scientists willing to become technicians in the militarization of knowledge and technology.

Now that appropriations emanate from the Department of Defense, the accumulation of knowledge and creation of technology by members of professional organizations and universities cannot be reconciled with traditional concepts of social order previously accredited to the corporate system. The election of Glenn T. Seaborg, Chairman of the Atomic Energy Commission, to the presidency of the American Association for the Advancement of Science (AAAS) conveys the militarization trend set forth in this analysis. His speech, which he intended to give before the assembled participants of the AAAS's December 1970 convention but was prevented from doing so by members of the Scientists and Engineers for Social and Political Action, blamed success for the deep malcontent within his organization:

> I think [he wrote] we must realize that science is suffering today from a kind of dislocation and disunity brought on by its own success. That is, it has fostered changes in our society faster and with far more impact than our social and political institutions can absorb and manage them.[26]

To blame "dislocation and disunity" upon scientific success diverts attention from professional subservience to the Pentagon. It was an "outsider" who made the more pertinent charge before the AAAS convention. Stewart L. Udall, former Secretary of the Interior and presently an environmental consultant, accused the American scientific community of seeking a "special status for itself" with a sense of responsibility confined to its professional ethic in keeping with its clientele, the Pentagon. He argued that the nation's foremost scientists maneuver "all too often as a virtual puppet of the *Government*" rather than serving "as an independent, critical voice." "While courageous individuals," Udall continued, "in the scientific community were raising the alarm about the lethal threat of chemical and biological warfare, what was the [National] Academy [of Sciences] doing? It was working under contract to the Defense Department to select bright young scientists to work in the Defense Department's chemical and biological weapons centers."[27]

We are moving, ever so rapidly, into an era of *direct state rule*,[28] and that part of the Federal government which commands technology will command society. For it is by exercising control over technology that greater knowledge is acquired which enables a group to rank supreme. It is the military which has the greatest *interest* in sponsoring research to advance weapons of destruction.[29] And it will be through technological devices that greater social control over the American people will be accomplished. Therefore, the military now ascends into prominence and stands in need of the legitimacy propounded by the Social Myth professed by American scholars. The founding of such a myth means, then, the outbreak of dissension to make the transition from corporate capitalism to State militarism. It is this struggle which bursts forth before so many professional academic organizations and upon the university campus—the foremost places where intellectual myth-making goes on; indeed, it is this struggle—civilian vs. military rule—which is now the struggle we all confront.

The military-industrial complex we hear so much about as the demon besetting America is itself a transitory stage in moving towards our rapidly-approaching Military State. The alliance grew out of mutual weaknesses following World War II; the return to civilian rule would all but liquidate the Pentagon, and the absence of military expenditures would deplete corporate capitalism of prosperity following saturation of consumer demand pent up by wartime scarcity. The pact would be momentary, however, and beneficial to the more dominant member, namely, the military.

The Vietnam war provided an empirical confirmation that economic policies of the nation are to be arranged according to military specifications. It is not merely that the Federal budget sacrifices civilian and business welfare to the Pentagon, but that traditional business concerns get suppressed; inflation, profits, wages, dividends—all such standardized indices of economic prosperity—are subverted so that military rule suffices. Surely corporations, even in terms of selfish interests at the expense of the public treasury, perceived the damaging economics of this conflict, for the war did not preserve the capitalistic imperial system but rather constituted a drain upon the foreign exchange servicing a Pax Americana by and for the military. Capitalists must balance military expenditures abroad at a cost to their own international profits thereby creating the deficits now undermining the American dollar in the international marketplace. In brief, the military has taken on a life of its own, charting an autonomous path for itself with economic needs which must be extracted from the corporation as well as the public generally. The bookkeeping system of corporate capitalism simply fails to dictate foreign policy but is instead being groomed to the economics of consumption for the massive budgetary demands exerted by the Pentagon. It should be apparent that the economic instability growing out of inflation and foreign exchange leading to a loss of confidence in the American dollar is to be traced to military priority over business judgment; capitalists yield to profit losses as a consequence of their diminishing control over the economy.

Moving into a form of direct State Rule—an autocracy of the State, by the State, and for the State—we increasingly hear the rhetoric to enshrine the State with ultimate authority: "Ask not what your country can do for you—," instructed the late President John F. Kennedy, "Ask what you can do for your country." He was preparing the guideline for new-frontiersmen myth-makers such as the historian Arthur

Schlesinger who would eventually explain America's Vietnamese policies of 1954 as "part of our general program of international goodwill,"[30] defend the bombing of North Vietnam and military escalation in Vietnam as decisions based upon a "perfectly rational argument,"[31] and designate his own concoctions of the U.S.-sponsored Bay of Pigs invasion of Cuba as nothing more than lying in defense of national interests.

Words of warning concerning the drift toward Statism, however, have been with us for some time. Tocqueville cautioned, "war does not always give democratic societies over to military government, but it must invariably and immeasurably increase the powers of civil government; it must almost automatically concentrate the direction of all men and the control of all things in the hands of the government. If that does not lead to despotism by sudden violence, it leads men gently in that direction by their habits." When, at the turn of the century, the nation embarked upon active imperialistic expansion and seized control over territories detached from the continent, it was the outspoken leader of the Populists, Tom Watson, who damned the Spanish-American War and exclaimed that "Republics cannot go into the conquering business and remain republics. Militarism leads to military domination, military despotism."[32] At this same historical moment, it was the liberal Republican, Carl Schurz, who "understood that the dilemma of empire was in a real sense *the* dilemma of laissez-faire. Without [expanding] the markets [for American capitalists] . . . depressions and class conflict would follow; but getting the markets would lead to moral degradation, big government, and militarism at home."[33] President Herbert Hoover declared his fear that "if the government itself came to extend its power under the leadership of purely political leaders as narrowly interest-conscious in their [own] way, and for their [own] careers, as their opposite numbers in the capital group, the result would be bureaucratic tyranny."[34]

The most conspicuous "bureaucratic" tyrant is, of course, none other than the Pentagon.

CONCLUSION

We are in the throes of another intense period of military exertion in need of the legitimacy provided by myths. The professional association, having sponsored the forum for what C. Wright Mills called the "celebration" of American society, now becomes a center for controversy; being the custodian of a myth which had once provided justification for corporate capitalization, it is now the arena in which contestants vie with one another for the creation of a new Social Myth. When a myth is no longer operative and must therefore be discarded, the issue must be taken directly to the Temple providing sanctuary for status-quo-oriented myths. We can therefore expect to undergo another period of repression over, as well as from within, the repositories of ideology— American universities and professional associations. We are going through another testing period when ideologies will either enunciate justifications reflecting militarized economics and thereby win research grants, or stand in defiance with advocacies of doctrines inimical to the military. Intellectuals who are successful in formulating thoughts complying with the dominant economic interests of their day stand on the threshold of victory; the challengers incur defeat, loss of jobs, and subordination. There is no reason to doubt the outcome of our present contests within professional associations. And we will find, before long, many who have strayed from the fold finding intractable "truths" compatible with the militarization of the economy in order to enter the spheres of acceptability.

In one of his last essays, Theodore W. Adorno wrote that "sanctioned delusions allow a dispensation from comparison with reality . . ." for "of the world as it exists, one cannot be enough afraid." American intellectuals fear any configurations of reality which jeopardize the rewards they receive through myth-making. Their activities, furthermore, require substantial financing. Today, it is the Federal government—the military branches more specifically—which provides the billions in research funds. Consequently, Dr. Karl W. Deutsch, the Harvard University political scientist, boasts, "We are moving into an age of reform in the United States. . . . One of the great reform tasks is making available to policymakers the cognitive resources of the social sciences in the next thirty years."[35] Can intellectuals bite the feeding hand? Can we expect business supremacy in our Social Myths now that economic dependency for intellectuals rests so decisively in the hands of State appropriations?

The controversy upon professional stages reflects the severity of experiencing profound shifts in economic controllers; scholars are inspired to recast their ethics to justify their new economic sponsor. Contention, for the academic community, takes the form of battling with words, just as other groups experiencing economic repercussions engage in their kinds of battles, e.g., Afro-Americans turning more and more to physical assaults upon the government, youth turning to acts of defiance, greater numbers of people "tuning out" through drugs, etc. Scholarly debate takes an ideological stance because basic ethical principles must be raised to challenge and justify the militarization of a State economy. The disputes before the professions are, however, mere shadow boxing, for the military takeover of society grinds forward, prepared to silence, eventually, open resistance—from scholars, blacks, students, businessmen, politicians, etc. And, eventually, we will come to see that the Social Myth has been reformulated so as to legitimate the militaristic, in place of the corporate, economy.

ENDNOTES

1. Alvin W. Gouldner argues this to be the proper interpretation intended by Max Weber when beseeching scholars to adhere to "value-neutrality." See Gouldner, "Anti-Minotaur: The Myth of a Value-Free Sociology," in *The New Sociology*, Irving Louis Horowitz, ed. (New York: Oxford University Press, 1964), pp. 199–200.
2. C. Wright Mills, *The Sociological Imagination* (New York: Oxford University Press, 1959), p. 97.
3. Thomas Cooper, *Lectures on the Principles of Political Economy* (1826), as quoted by Benjamin F. Wright, Jr., *Interpretations of Natural Law* (New York: Russell & Russell), 1962.
4. "The first master-symptom of revolution is the 'transfer of the allegiance of the intellectuals.'" Lyford P. Edwards, *The Natural History of Revolution* (Chicago: University of Chicago Press, 1927), p. 38.
5. See Eric Hoffer, *The Ordeal of Change*, especially Chapter 6 (New York: Harper & Row), 1966.
6. See William Appleman Williams, *The Contours of American History* (Chicago: Quadrangle Paperbacks), 1966.
7. See Richard W. Van Alstyne, *The Genesis of American Nationalism* (Waltham, Mass.: Blaisdell Publishing Co., 1970.
8. Quoted by Williams, *op cit.*, p. 295.
9. *Ibid.*, pp. 261–262.
10. "Sociology and the Rise of Corporate Capitalism," in *The Sociology of Sociology*, Larry T. Reynolds and Janice M. Reynolds, eds. (New York: David McKay, 1970), p. 69.
11. This emphasis upon rationality as a quality of bureaucracies rather than a process attributed to an individual is to be credited to Dusky Lee Smith as conveyed to me in conversations.
12. See the writings of Gabriel Kolko: *The Politics of War* (New York: Random House, 1968); *The Roots of American Foreign Policy* (Boston: Beacon Press, 1967); and *The Triumph of Conservatism* (New York: Free Press, 1963).
13. Thomas S. Szasz, *The Myth of Mental Illness* (New York: Dell Publishing Co., 1961), p. x.
14. *The Economic Basis of Politics*, compiled and annotated by William Beard (New York: Vintage Books, 1957), pp. 67–68.
15. Alfred L. Kroeber, *The Nature of Culture* (Chicago: University of Chicago Press, 1952), pp. 402 and 408.
16. Testimony of Thomas Schelling before the House Foreign Affairs Committee, January 27, 1966; *United States Policy Toward Asia*, Hearings before the Subcommittee on the Far East and the Pacific of the Committee on Foreign Affairs, House of Representatives. Washington, D.C.: Government Printing Office, 1966, p. 89; as quoted by Noam Chomsky, *American Power and the New Mandarins* (New York: Vintage Books, 1969), p. 239.

17. *Ibid.*, p. 337.
18. Quoted by William Appleman Williams in a review article, "Wilson," *New York Review of Books*, Vol. xvii, December 2, 1971, p. 4; emphasis supplied.
19. "The Cultural Contradiction," *New York Times*, October 27, 1970.
20. "The Multinational Corporation and the Nation-State," *New York Review of Books*, Vol. xv, February 11, 1971, pp. 20–25.
21. *Ibid.*, p. 22; emphasis supplied.
22. *Ibid.*, p. 23.
23. *Ibid.*, p. 25; emphasis supplied.
24. Professor Hermann Rahn, an internationally known physiologist, is so awed by his research funding from the Department of Defense that he dedicates one of his books, *Studies in Pulmonary Physiology*, to the Air Force; he sincerely promises to repeat his obsequious duty by dedicating a forthcoming book to the Navy for having provided him with additional fundings!
25. *The New Priesthood* (New York: Harper & Row, 1965), p. 85.
26. *New York Times*, December 31, 1970.
27. *Ibid.*, emphasis supplied.
28. *Ibid.*
29. Faculty members at Stanford University received a rather severe shock recently. Although 111 of their research projects were funded by the Department of Defense, they stated that it didn't matter where the money came from because they were conducting "basic research" or doing "pure science." "Radicals" had been charging that if the Department of Defense was financing the projects they must somehow or other be useful for the military. The Stanford Workshop on Political and Social Issues conferred with representatives of the Pentagon and found that *nothing is funded unless military applications are expected.* For example, a Stanford project entitled "Fundamental Investigations of Amorphous Semiconductors and Transition Metal Oxides" was funded by the Department of Defense because the Army believed it would aid the development of night-viewing devices, such as those now used by our military in Indochina and by our police at home. So much for the myths of objectivity, pure science, and basic research for projects funded by the military.—The editors.
30. *New York Times*, February 6, 1966.
31. *Ibid.*
32. C. Vann Woodward, *Tom Watson* (New York: Oxford University Press, 1963), p. 335.
33. Williams, *op. cit.*, p. 340.
34. *Ibid.*, p. 428.
35. Quoted by Robert Reinhold, "Social Science Gains Tied to Big Teams of Scholars," *New York Times*, March 16, 1971, p. 26.

James M. Henslin
Linda K. Henslin
Steven D. Keiser

27

Schooling for Social Stability:
Education in the Corporate Society

Education in our society is a major means of stabilizing our social system. Education regiments students into docility, socializes them into the values and ethics that serve our dominant economic order, and maintains the present social class and racial systems by systematically discriminating against some, while favoring others. We shall develop these points in detail.

Each society needs to pass its major values and orientations to the coming generation. Each society has a vested interest in maintaining its *Weltanschauung,* or orientation to the world, and its customary ways of doing things. Various techniques are developed in each society to accomplish these goals, and in industrialized societies they have become highly fused into a formal system of education.

This socialization function of education has long been recognized and has been the subject of discussion and sociological analysis for many years. In 1902 and 1905, for example, Emile Durkheim emphasized in his lectures at the Sorbonne that education was a primary socializer into major cultural values. Durkheim (1956:71) put the matter this way:

> Education is the influence exercised by adult generations on those not yet ready for social life. Its object is to arouse and to develop in the child a certain number of physical, intellectual, and moral states which are demanded of him by both the political society as a whole and the special milieu for which he is specifically destined.

As we focus on this socialization function of our formal educational system, we shall specifically examine how education in American soci-

This article was written for this volume and is printed by permission.

ety is a corollary of our economic and social class order. Contrary to popular assumption, the American educational system is not part of a pursuit of equality, but, rather, it is designed to maintain social inequality by reproducing the social class system and racial structure from one generation to the next and to meet the needs of employers for a disciplined and skilled labor force, one that is regimented for docility and that will support political stability. (Cf., Bowles 1975:38 ff. and Turner 1972:189 ff.)

TESTING AND TRACKING: PRESERVATION AND PREDESTINATION

In our present educational system, I.Q. tests and other standardized testing mechanisms are used to classify mass numbers of students. These test scores are regarded as an ultimate indicator of an individual's potential. On the basis of their performance on these tests, students become labeled as bright, normal, not so bright, and so forth. The assumption is that the students' potential has been adequately and fairly measured, and on this basis they are put into special classes and directed to specific programs that are supposedly designed to match their potential. This "tracking" exerts far reaching consequences on the students, as it destines them for "suitable" positions in life (Dewey 1962).

Tracking is by no means as objective as it is meant to be. It is, on the contrary, not objective at all. Tracking closely parallels social class lines. Lower class children score lower on standardized tests than do children from our middle and upper classes. Lower class children are consequently classified as being less intelligent. They are then reacted to by their teachers as they are perceived, with the consequence that lower class children are "tracked" into a program that destines them for subservient positions in life. Tracking has become a mechanism to maintain lower class children in the social class in which they were raised. Testing and tracking doom them to a life of poverty and to playing subservient roles in society—as it probably will continue to doom their children (Warner 1953; Lauter and Howe 1970).

Our educational tracking has the opposite effect on youngsters from middle and upper class homes. Those from more privileged backgrounds score higher on standardized tests and consequently are perceived as being more intelligent. They are then reacted to as though they were more intelligent. These expectations are fulfilled, and they perform better. Being tracked into a college preparatory course, they take classes that prepare them for entering the university, which in turn gains them entrance into professions and yields high financial security. Their performance on standardized tests destines them for the more elite positions in our society—as it probably will continue to destine their children.

Our standardized tests provide a formal basis for translating class-based factors into academic criteria that are used to separate students into two major groups—those destined for success and those destined for failure. Educational testing and tracking help stabilize our economic order by recruiting the "right" children to fill the technological and professional needs of our corporate society (Lauter and Howe 1970). By predestining students into particular social classes on the basis of their social class origins, our educational system preserves the status quo of the social system.

But aren't lower class children less intelligent than upper and middle class children? Don't our standardized tests demonstrate this? Certainly an educational system run by fair-minded persons knows what it is doing when it administers tests which have such far reaching consequences on the future lives of its students. It is this major question that we shall now examine.

TESTING BIAS: PROGRAMMING SUCCESS AND FAILURE

If lower class children are not less intelligent, how can their lower scores on standardized tests be explained? Can they be accounted for without making the assumption that they have less intelligence and abilities—those very things which the tests are supposedly measuring?

Standardized tests discriminate against students from lower social class backgrounds in a number of different ways. First of all, they place a premium on language skills, especially on reading ability, and most tests are speed tests which favor the good reader. While such criteria superficially appear to be objective, they are far from being so, for the lower class youngster does not begin school with the same preparation in paper and pencil skills as the child from the more privileged home. Rather than measuring intelligence or ability, these tests largely measure a background preparation that biases in favor of children from our higher social classes and discriminates against those from our lower social classes.

Lower class children are also less motivated to perform well on standardized tests. They come from homes where their parents have directly experienced the contradictions between the hard facts of life and the myth of the interrelationship of hard work and success. They have discovered by bitter experience that success and hard work seldom go together. Moreover, they pass these orientations on to their children. It is quite a different matter with children from middle and upper class homes. Their parents have experienced benefits from the educational system. They have learned skills and orientations in school that are directly related to the life situation in which they find themselves, and they pass this "school success motif" on to their children. Such major differences in orientation are also reflected in test scores. (Cf., Biehler 1971:358.)

The content of standardized tests also discriminates against children from the lower class. As these tests ordinarily portray a middle class world, they bias in favor of middle class children. For example, the following is a sample question from a standardized I.Q. test:

A symphony is to a composer as a book is to a _____.

> _____paper
> _____sculptor
> _____author
> _____musician
> _____man

Because middle class children are apt to be more familiar with the concepts of symphonies, composers, sculptors, and musicans than are children from the lower class, it is not surprising that they perform better on such tests (Turner 1972:206).

Consider the reverse. What if the following were a question on a standardized test? In what direction would it bias?

When the welfare worker comes, children should_____

> _____truthfully answer all questions
> _____keep their mouth shut
> _____run into the bedroom and hide
> _____lock the doors
> _____open the windows

Because lower class children are more likely to be familiar with welfare workers than are middle class children (to grossly understate the matter), they are apt to score higher on this question. They would be much more likely to give the second choice as the "correct" answer than would children who are unfamiliar with visits by welfare workers.

While this example makes the matter sound obvious, social class bias has not been obvious to test makers. This is probably because they come from a middle class world, and in their ethnocentricity they either have presumed that the middle class world is the world of experience for everyone or that the middle class world represents the correct standard by which all should be evaluated.

The social class bias of standardized testing includes asking children from backgrounds of poverty questions about writing checks when their parents have no bank account; and asking the color of jewels they have never seen, and perhaps have never heard of, since jewels are certainly not one of their major possessions (Henslin 1975:334). Consequently, most studies of school achievement find that family background and neighborhood are the major influence on a student's test scores (Coleman 1966; Jencks 1969).

More than paper and pencil skills, motivation, and middle class biases are involved in test results that show lesser ability for the lower social classes. Impoverishment of experiences can also lead to impoverishment in concept formation and to differences in intellectual development. Certain forms of impoverishment, as in the case of deprivation of sensory experiences during infancy, for example, can drastically affect intellectual development and may remain with an individual all his life. Such factors are also involved in test-taking, but they come a long way from accounting for social class discrepancies in test results. (Cf., Greene 1965.)

Because the minority groups of the United States are disproportionately members of the lower social classes, they also become systematically victimized by our testing and tracking. They are systematically tracked into programs that prepare them for subservient roles in society. All the above points concerning preparation, motivation, and social class testing bias also apply to American minority groups, but to see how testing and tracking specifically discriminate against minorities we can focus on the language of educational testing.

Standardized tests are given in standardized English. This obviously biases against people whose native tongue is other than English, as well as those who learn a form of English other than the middle class version of our language. When Spanish speaking children are given I.Q. tests in our schools, they actually take them in a foreign language. As would be the case if English speaking persons took an I.Q. test in Spanish, they are disproportionately classified as slow learners, and even as mentally retarded. On this basis, nine Chicano children who had been classified as mentally retarded brought suit against the State of California. When they were retested in Spanish, eight scored above the mentally retarded level. The resulting settlement provided for retesting 22,000 California Chicano children who had been declared mentally retarded on the basis of English language I.Q. tests. Part of this settlement also directed the state to seek ways to measure intelligence that are free of cultural bias (*The Brief*, February 1971).

The situation is similar with blacks. Although blacks learn English at home, it is a form of English which differs markedly from the standard English spoken in white middle class homes. It is not simply that blacks learn a different pronunciation of the English that is spoken by whites, but black English is in itself "a bona fide language system with its own rules of grammar, vocabulary, and structure" (Haskins and Butts 1973:40). Because our tests are standardized to the white middle class language and white middle class experience, minority groups are also consistently victimized by these tests (Henslin 1975: 335).

FINANCING THE FAVORED FEW

Educational funding is another major factor of our contemporary educational scene that operates to handicap lower class youngsters and those from minority groups. Our public schools are funded by a levy on personal property tax. Areas that have a higher assessed evaluation of personal property have greater funds available for the education of their children than do areas with a lower assessed evaluation. This means that if a school is located in an area of high property value, it has more money to spend. The more money it has to spend, the better trained and more experienced teachers it can afford to hire since it can offer larger salaries, the better facilities it can build, the more expensive textbooks it can purchase, the more specialized courses it can offer, the more guidance and counseling service it can make available, and so forth. Although there is much more to education than money, in our economically dominated society the more money a school district has the better education it can afford to buy.

Funding education by personal property taxes has a direct effect on both social class and race, working, as usual, to the distinct disadvantage of youngsters from the lower social classes and minority groups. It works like this. Those who have fled the inner cities are the whites. They have gone to the suburbs, from which they systematically exclude the poor and minorities. This has left a large proportion of poor and minorities in our inner cities. The inner cities have a much smaller personal property tax base from which to fund their educational systems. With their greater funds, the suburbs in general have developed superior school systems, and it is whites who almost exclusively benefit from this financial/geographical/social class/racial segregation. The poor and minorities are left with underfinanced inner city schools, with less experienced and undertrained teachers, deteriorating facilities, and so on. Not surprisingly, their education is markedly inferior.

THE EDUCATIONAL SYSTEM AS SOCIALIZER
INTO DOMINANT VALUES

The entire educational system of the United States is actually an institution that drills children into dominant cultural orientations (Henry 1965:283). Two of the major values in which it systematically instructs its pupils are conformity and competition.

Our schools are designed to crush intellectual creativity—to snuff out creativity before it can ignite ideas that would be upsetting to the dominant social order. Contrary to a belief still popular in some segments of our society, schools are by no means places for the stimulation of young minds. On the contrary, schools militantly socialize into stupidity. If a student begins to question the Great Truths of our society, teachers consistently react against the student to make him feel that he is stupid for questioning that which everyone knows is true. For example, if he questions the law of supply and demand, the Great Democratic Myth of the two-party system, the foundations of patriotism, the belief that there is "room at the top" toward which one should unswervingly strive, or the rightness of the profit motive in human relations, he is quickly put down and shut up. The creative thinker soon learns that he cannot doubt such Revealed and Self Evident Truths, but that he must accept them unquestioningly.

Creativity is the last thing that the directors of our educational system desire. Creative thinking carries with it the alarming potential for seriously disrupting the social system. To question the myths on which the social system is ideologically based is to threaten the foundations on which everything hangs together. It means to challenge the basis of the corporate state. Accordingly, students are systematically groomed for conformity of thought. Their creativity toward ideas is encouraged only after the creative thoughts surrounding an idea have been tamed to socially approved ends (Henry 1965:287–288).

For those at the top of our social order, the benefits of systematic socialization into conformity are manifold. Children are taught to accept things the way they find them. Our school system emphasizes that we are surrounded by a social system that represents virtue, that we are to hold private property sacrosanct, that the correct and logically appropriate duty of the citizenry is to obey authority, and that we are to peacefully take our place within the already existing scheme of social relations.

Training for conformity begins with the first day of school. Students learn to unquestioningly obey routines even when they make no sense to them. They learn how to properly sit, the correct intonations and phrasing for proper speaking, how to ask questions and to indicate needs by quietly raising their hands, and so forth. Kindergarten children learn that the teacher is the authority, and the authority is to be obeyed. Only then, they discover, are rewards given and the "business of learning" takes place (Gracey 1967). This process continues as students continue to traverse our educational system, being passed from one teacher to the next who officially sign their approval to the conformity-learning of the student.

The school system does more than transmit major cultural values. It also exploits dominant values in order to shape students into the type of people who fit the community that supports the schools. Students are taught to become punctual in order both to keep the school system running efficiently and to produce dependable future workers. Although the school system teaches the fundamental rhetoric of democracy, equality, and freedom, these virtues are ironically violated by the schools in their own treatment of students. Students have little or no choice in developing curricula for themselves; they must submit to a regimented 8 A.M. to 3 P.M. programming. Special sanctions are imposed on them that are applicable to no one else in the community; and they are generally totally subordinated to the demands of the school system. Only if they conform can they succeed. (Cf., Jencks and Riesman 1968; Friedenberg 1965.)

Ours is a pluralistic society. Many diverse ethnic and subcultural groups exist within the confines of a single nation. Each has developed its own basic approach to the world, its own system of values, its own orientations to what is worthwhile in life, and how to best approach life itself. The norms and customary ways of doing things belonging to our diverse subcultures are valuable in their own right, as they represent what groups of people have found meaningful for their own lives (Phenix 1969). In our educational system, however, the cultural integrity of our many subcultures is systematically denigrated and denied —with its overweening demand for conformance to major values, our educational system attempts to systematically erase subcultural differences, to blot out distinct cultural traits, and, in effect, to deny the validity of cultural diversity. All are to be like one another, and the model presented for all is dominated by the orientations of the middle class. Those who will not conform to these established norms which serve the ends of our highly competitive society are presumed not to have a legitimate basis for making demands on it (Friedenberg 1970; Friedman 1969).

Our society's basic "dog eat dog" economic orientation is also directly reflected by our educational system. When children enter school, they enter a competitive world that accurately mirrors the outside world. They learn to measure their own success by the failures of others, or, conversely, they learn to view themselves as failures when they measure their own abilities against the success of others. And, as we have just seen, the competitive cards are stacked for some and against others.

Educational competition is characterized by games, contests, and a reward/punishment system that pit student against student. Think back to your experiences in grade school. Remember how the children were encouraged to compete for teacher approval and attention. Teachers structure classroom participation and involvement in such a way that when the teacher asks questions eager students frantically wave their hands to be recognized so they can answer *before* anyone else. If a student answers incorrectly, snickers are heard around the classroom. Those who consistently give wrong answers are sometimes taunted by their classmates, that is, by their more successful competitors.

Among the most notorious competitive games in our elementary schools is the spelling bee. At the teacher's direction, children choose teams and compete against each other. Needless to say, those students who frequently misspell words are the last to be chosen for team membership. As the teams compete, one can win only if the other loses, and each team awaits the downfall of the other with anxious anticipation. Those who "go down" first know they have failed on the "easier" words, and they are conspicuously segregated from the participants. Consequently, this common competitive game is a systematic exercise in humiliation. (Cf., Henry 1965: 297 ff.)

Grades are perhaps the major competitive device used in our schools to instill obedience to authority and competition with one's peers. Although they are regularly given with the supposed intent of measuring "progress" and "achievements in learning," they are in reality a competitive ranking device. That they are an essential part of our educational contest system is demonstrated by their culmination in high school, with the public awarding of the Grand Prize, designating someone as "valedictorian." Room is also provided for the student who comes in second place; the runner-up in this contest of the absurd receives a consolation prize by being designated "salutatorian."

What are the consequences of such a strong emphasis on competition? Competition creates anxiety within children and engenders hostility between classmates. Children learn to ridicule and criticize each other's endeavors in order to make their own efforts appear better to the teacher (Henry 1965). In addition to fostering such negative emotions as fear and anxiety, instilling such negative attitudes as hostility, and encouraging such negative behaviors as ridiculing others, competition further reinforces the dominant cultural value of conformity. As they pursue the elusive goal of success, children find it safer to follow traditional paths rather than striking out in new directions. They learn to passively accept ascribed student roles and to follow the designated signposts that mark the path to educational success. The successful student sees no alternatives open to him, and his adherence to traditional normative expectations is virtually assured.

The basic competition in our educational system, however, is not the specific competition among students in an individual classroom. It is, rather, the competition among the social classes. The schools are the battlegrounds that our society has established for the young. Lower class children enter the competitive sphere of struggle and conflict on an unequal basis, and consequently, they have an unequal chance of success. Again, the dominant middle class value system of our schools serves to weed out the lower social classes. The middle class orientation of our schools rewards achievement in middle class values, with good grades and other rewards for participating in extracurricular activities being disproportionately handed out to children from middle class homes.

The game is rigged—consistently in favor of the same players.

COOLING OUT THE FAILURES

Although our schools can be a golden avenue of opportunity for those who succeed in them, they are also the arena in which many confront failure that condemns them to the more subservient positions in our society. How are those who "fail" handled so they do not become bitter revolutionaries intent on overthrowing the system that so brutally used them?

"Cooling out" is the process of adjusting victims to their loss (Goffman 1952). When someone has lost something that is valuable to him, it leads to intense frustration. This frustration and its accompanying anger are dangerous to society because they can be directed against the social system if the social system is identified as being responsible for the loss. But our educational system is insidiously effective, and many who fail within it, perhaps most, never even need to be cooled out. They learn early in grade school that they are stupid and that higher education is meant for others. They suffer miserably in school as they continue to be confronted year after year with more evidence of their failure, and they can hardly wait until they turn sixteen so they can leave for greener pastures. Such persons are relieved to end their educational miseries and need no cooling out.

For those who do need to be cooled out, however, a variety of techniques is used. The primary one makes use of the ideology of individualism. To socialize students into major cultural values means to teach them more values than conformity and competition, the two we analyzed above. Two other major values students consistently confront in our educational system are the ideologies of individualism and equal opportunity. They are taught that people make their own way to the top in a land of equal opportunity. Those who make it do so because of their own abilities, while those who do not make it do so because of a lack of ability or drive on their own part. They consequently learn to blame themselves for failure, rather than the system. It was not the educational system that was at fault, for it was freely offered. But it was the fault of the individual who failed to make proper use of that which society offered him. Individualism provides amazing stabilization for the maintenance of our social system, for it results in the system going unquestioned as the blame is put squarely on the individual who was himself conned by the system.

If this technique of cooling out fails to work, as it does only in a minority of cases, other techniques are put into effect. Counselors and teachers may point out to the person that he is really "better suited" for other tasks in life. He may be told that he will "be happier" doing something else. He might also be "gradually disengaged" from the educational system, perhaps being directed to alternate sources of education, such as vocational training (Clark 1960).

The individual may also be encouraged to blame his lack of success on tough luck, fate, and bad breaks. In one way or another, as he is cooled out, he is directed away from questioning the educational system itself, much less its relationship to maintaining the present class system and his subservient position within it. Above all, ignorance is used to help cool out the malcontent. Such information as this article contains, for example, will be studiously kept from him. Counselors and teachers themselves, in fact, do not like to think in terms of the information and concepts of this article as it casts serious doubts upon their own role in society. They generally prefer to remain ignorant of such things themselves, as it helps their own adjustment.

Finally, the malcontent-failure has the example before him of those from similar social class circumstances as his own who did "make it." This becomes incontrovertible evidence that the fault does lie with himself and not the system, for if they could make it, so could he. This evidence of those who "made it" is a powerful cooling out device, as it directly removes any accusatory finger that might point to the educational and social systems.

Having our educational system set up in such a way that some lower class youngsters do manage to be successful and are able to enter upper middle class positions serves as a pressure valve for our social system. In the final analysis, it may well be this pressure valve which has prevented revolutions in our country—as the most able, the most persistent, and the most conforming are able to rise above their social class circumstances (Jencks and Riesman 1968). And in such instances, the educational system is pointed to with pride as representing the gateway to golden opportunity freely open to all.

SUMMARY

Our present educational system well serves the vested interests of the wealthy and powerful controllers of our society. It instills dominant values and orientations that develop subservient workers who obediently carry out their assigned tasks. It recruits a managerial elite from those who demonstrate the greatest support for major cultural values, who, in turn, gain for themselves a vested interest in maintaining the social system as it is. It simultaneously instills a sense of inferiority in others, and warns the rest of society against them as troublesome and untrustworthy. In such ways, our educational system makes a vital contribution to both social mobility and social stratification, for as it recruits the "right kind" of people to get ahead, it makes certain that those who might subvert the system are left behind as a salutary moral lesson (Friedenberg 1965:49).

REFERENCES

Robert F. Biehler, *Psychology Applied to Teaching,* Boston: Houghton Mifflin Company, 1971.

Samuel Bowles, "Unequal Education and the Reproduction of the Social Division of Labor," in *Schooling in a Corporate Society: The Political Economy of Education in America,* Martin Carnoy, ed., New York: David McKay Company, Inc., 1975, pp. 38–66.

Burton R. Clark, "The 'Cooling-Out' Function of Higher Education," *American Journal of Sociology, 65,* May, 1960, pp. 569–576.

James S. Coleman *et al., Equality of Educational Opportunity,* Washington, D.C.: U.S. Government Printing Office, 1966.

John Dewey, "Mediocrity and Individuality," *New Republic, 33,* December 6, 1922, pp. 35–37.

―――, "Individuality, Equality and Superiority," *New Republic, 33,* December 13, 1922, pp. 61–63.

Emile Durkheim, *Education and Sociology,* Glencoe, Ill.: The Free Press, 1956.

Edgar Z. Friedenberg, "The Real Functions of Educational Testing," *Change Magazine, 2,* January/February, 1970, pp. 43–47.

Edgar Friedenberg, *Coming of Age in America,* New York: Random House, Inc., 1965.

Marjorie Friedman, "Public School: Melting Pot or What?" *Teacher's College Record, 70,* January, 1969, pp. 347–351.

Erving Goffman, "On Cooling the Mark Out: Some Aspects of Adaptation to Failure," *Psychiatry: Journal for the Study of Interpersonal Relations, 15,* 1952, pp. 451–463.

Harry L. Gracey, "Learning the Student Role: Kindergarten as Academic Boot Camp," in *Readings in Introductory Sociology,* Dennis H. Wrong and Harry L. Gracey, eds., New York: The Macmillan Company, 1967, pp. 288–299.

Maxine Greene, "The Teacher and the Negro Child," *The Educational Forum, 29,* March, 1965, pp. 275–280.

Jim Haskins and Hugh F. Butts, *The Psychology of Black Language,* New York: Barnes and Noble Books, 1973.

Jules Henry, *Culture Against Man,* New York: Vintage Books, 1965.

James M. Henslin, *Introducing Sociology: Toward Understanding Life in Society,* New York: The Free Press, 1975.

John Holt, *How Children Fail,* New York: Pitman Publishing Corporation, 1964.

Christopher Jencks, "A Reappraisal of the Most Controversial Educational Document of Our Time," *New York Times Magazine, 118,* August 10, 1969, pp. 12, 13, 34, 36, 38, 42, 44.

Christopher Jencks and David Reisman, *The Academic Revolution,* New York: Doubleday and Company, Inc., 1968.

Paul Lauter and Florence Howe, *The Conspiracy of the Young,* Mountain View, Ca.: World Publishing Company, 1970.

Philip H. Phenix, "The Moral Imperative in Contemporary American Education," *Perspectives on Education,* Winter 1969, pp. 6–13.

Jonathan H. Turner, *American Society: Problems of Structure,* New York: Harper & Row, Inc., 1972.

Lloyd W. Warner, *American Life: Dream and Reality,* Chicago: University of Chicago Press, 1953.

Carl Weinberg, "The Price of Competition," *Teacher's College Record, 67,* November, 1965, pp. 106–114.

James M. Henslin

28

The University as Factory

In our economic system, various schemes have been developed for measuring production and assessing the worth of workers. One such scheme is known in the factory as "piece work." The worker on piece work is paid on the basis of how much he produces. The administrative staff orders a "time study" of a particular machine, and on the basis of its evaluation of how many pieces (machined items) a worker can be expected to turn out during a shift, it sets a rate of pay. If a worker consistently produces less than the base amount, he is removed from the machine. If he produces the base amount, he is given base pay. If he produces over the base amount, an increment directly dependent upon the amount of his "overproduction" is added to his base pay. The goal, of course, is to increase the production of the worker and the machine. The more a worker produces on his shift, that is, the greater his "efficiency," the greater is his pay.

Education in the United States has increasingly become similar to the factory. After all, so this reasoning goes in some quarters, since the factory system has worked fantastically well in producing consumer items, why not use it in the university? With the dominance of the world of business and production in our society, it was only a matter of time, of course, before the factory model would be applied to education. When it is so applied, students are conceived as products, teachers as workers, and the administration as management. In the educational institution, the Board of Directors of the factory goes under such names as the Board of Trustees and the Board of Governors.

The difficulty the managerial elite confront in applying the factory model to education is that educators do not produce as easily measurable "products" as those produced in the factory. Certainly one can easily measure isolated bits of knowledge and the acquisition of skills. If this is what education were about, the application of the factory model

This article was written for this volume.

to education would not be too bad. With our technological state, we can, in fact, largely automate our schools and mostly do away with teachers in the production of bits of knowledge and specific skills. Machines can teach typing, computer programming, *facts* of history, and so forth.

Education, however, is at least theoretically a process of growth in awareness and conceptual development. To the degree that educational institutions are involved in such growth, educators are facilitators in this process of growing, becoming aware, and developing conceptually. If the university and other branches of formal education are supposed to develop creative thinking, new ways of conceptualizing, critical evaluations of orientations to the world of nature and the social world, and the evaluation and formation of contrasting theoretical schemes for ordering known data, these are a far cry from turning out factory products, each identical to the preceding. Such processes, moreover, cannot be measured easily.

The Board of Governors of our universities, however, are attempting to apply to the university the piece work and efficiency rating models of the factory. The men sitting on these boards (and across the nation the make-up of boards of trustees is almost exclusively male) are largely drawn from the world of business. They have little understanding of the educational process, but they do understand businesses and factories. Consequently, it is the model of the factory and business that they apply to education.

They are increasingly emphasizing concepts such as CHPs (Credit Hour Production) and FSRs (Faculty Student Ratios). Although the specific terms vary with the particular university-factory, the direction toward obtaining "efficiency ratings" is the same. As is usual in the American style of education, each student taking a course is given a specified number of credits for the course. This number becomes the basis for computing faculty efficiency ratings. One merely multiplies the number of students enrolled in an instructor's class by the number of credits each student is "earning." That number then becomes the instructor's Credit Hour Production for that class. CHPs can then be computed for each class an instructor teaches. They can then be added. If this total is divided into his salary, the instructor's share of the Unit Cost (UC) appears. It then becomes apparent that some professors are turning out their products at a cheaper Unit Cost than are other professors.

After introducing such concepts to the university, the next step is to apply them. If these factory-business concepts can be legitimated, a process they are now undergoing, greater centralized control over university instruction can then follow. Faculties with high Credit Hour Production and low Unit Costs can be rewarded with higher salaries, plusher offices, more secretarial help, and more graduate assistants—the usual amenities given instructional staff in the university. Such rewards can then be withheld from faculties with lower CHPs and higher UCs in order to induce change in their approach to education.

Using Credit Hour Production as the basis for allocating the university budget appears to be highly rational since it provides objective bases on which to decide salary increases, the hiring of additional staff, and so on. Those departments with fewer students per faculty member can be given less money, while departments with more students per faculty member can be allocated more money. Such an approach has a superficial ring of logic to it because its economic basis can so easily be demonstrated in black and white; and in our culture we are taught to look at things almost exclusively in economic terms.

When products are being produced for sale, such as in the factory, this approach to cost and budget allocation makes good sense. But it works out quite differently when the university becomes a factory. What is not recognized is that the same teaching techniques do not apply to all branches of knowledge. Those that are primarily skill acquisitions (i.e., "doing" courses) require less personal contact with students than those that highly emphasize conceptual formation (i.e., "thinking" courses). Courses in the "business division" of a university, for example, are able to function well with larger numbers of students per teacher, while courses in departments of philosophy are not.

When a department or faculty's budget is reduced, it ordinarily means reducing "support services," such as secretarial assistance and equipment items such as typewriters. Dedicated faculty can make up for such losses through increased efforts on their part, such as by providing their own typewriters and typing up their own tests. This is somewhat awkward at best, but it is more than this; it shortchanges the teaching of students. By wasting professional talent and time on secretarial skills, the instructor is denied involvement in the creative thought processes for which he was trained. This means that he is able to read fewer books and has less opportunities to discuss with his colleagues developing ideas in his academic area. This gives him less professional worth for his encounters with students, in and out of the classroom.

But how can one communicate the value of books and intellectual exchange to those whose reading is primarily limited to financial reports? Those whose world consists of cold calculations do not know what the university is about.[1] For such persons, such as those sitting on Boards of Governors, what is the loss of reading one less book on some esoteric area about which they have no understanding in the first place?

Decreased budgeting means far more for a department and the teaching process, however, than the loss of secretarial assistance and the misappropriation of faculty. Library resources are also part of the budget allocation. When CHPs are consistently applied, departments with more students per faculty member are also assigned more money for purchasing books and periodicals.

In one university where this procedure is in effect, the business department has an abundance of funds for library acquisitions, although it requires less library resources for its students. In this same university, students studying philosophy find that their university library is missing much of what they need, and they are forced to drive considerable distances to surreptitiously use the facilities of two neighboring universities. With its small allocation, this department of philosophy has a difficult time replacing missing volumes, not to speak of adding acquisitions to keep up with the development of its own discipline.

Certainly this approach to spending is not on the basis of what a faculty needs in order to teach. Accordingly, some might think it irrational. It is rationally consistent, however, with our basic cultural economic orientation. To assign money for library acquisitions on the basis of need smacks of communism or socialism, but to do so on the basis of Credit Hour *Production* is solidly in the mainstream of the capitalist tradition. This approach also is consistent with another aspect of capitalism: it is not what one produces that matters, but how efficiently one produces. In this case, it is not that elusive, ephemeral thing called knowledge that is being measured as the product, but accumulated hours of credit—something that is so easy to plug into the computer— that newly developed measuring machine of corporate capitalism.

More serious than all, however, is this: to apply the factory model to the university is to stifle creativity, something that has already become rare. Larger classes mean less time for probing ideas. Rather than being able to delve into the fires of controversy that contextually surround an idea, or to bring out its interrelationship with other ideas, or to elaborate on its rough edges that need further refinement, the teacher must present ideas as though they were finished products of knowledge that arose in an historical vacuum and burst on the social scene in finished form. The instructor becomes a machine that passes on a facade of knowledge in assembly-belt fashion. He becomes a mechanism to record more credits in the student transcript—for his job changes from educator to Credit Hour Producer.

The process is insidious, for it appears to be so rationally based. Its consequences, however, destroy education. Largely as a consequence of this growing emphasis on Credit Hour Production, a department in a university with which I am familiar has become known as the "Degree Mill." With only eighteen faculty members in their department, this degree factory has 367 graduate students, and in a single year has churned out 241 Masters in Science degrees. The modal grade for all students in this program is an A. The program makes money for the university, especially through its off campus offerings on military bases, where the students' fees more than pay the cost of the program. Each year thousands of dollars of students' fees are declared "residual," and the profits are divided between the "teaching" department and the President's office.

When in the early 1970s enrollments declined in our colleges and universities, administrators became alarmed. This gave further impetus to Credit Hour Production. Faculties were encouraged to look around and increase their enrollments under the guise of meeting "community needs." One ingenious faculty noticed that many housewives did not have much to do in the mornings except watch television. They are now offering a master's degree tailored for them, sometimes laughingly referred to as an HMBA, a Housewife's Master's in Business Administration, but more commonly known as a Ms. Bs.

Students are increasingly becoming aware that they are entering an educational factory when they enroll in the university. College degrees have become not indicators of intellectual achievement, but union cards. They are passports, at least in fair economic times, to better-paying jobs. As long as little work is required in class and little thinking is involved, they could care less what takes place in the classroom. Their goal is to garner credits, and at the end of the semester or quarter to receive another notice that for each course they have been enrolled in they have added an additional three or four hours to their accumulation. When they accumulate enough of these magical numbers, they receive their union card—sans learning, sans intellectual awakening, sans education.

The university-factory produces nonthinkers who will not question the status quo, the current social arrangements, the accepted ways of doing things. They will have been exposed to no contrary orientations, but will simply have been stamped: "Completed product; ready for insertion into desired location." The degrees granted will look the same as always and will contain the traditional wording, even with a few Latin phrases interspersed here and there, but the above will be a faithful translation of their diplomas and degrees.

The university as factory, however, well serves the interests of those who are economically dominant in our society. It is an excellent device for stabilizing our social order and protecting the privileged and politically powerful. It makes passive receptors of students and regularizes the transmission of sanitized ideas and isolated bits and pieces of factual knowledge. There is no battleground of ideas. Even the thought of the free exchange of ideas in the university is horrendous to the controllers of society, for there is no guarantee that *their* ideas will win. Such a thought is appalling to those in power, for they are firmly entrenched in positions of privilege and have much to lose if ideas that challenge the underpinnings of the capitalistic order were to prevail.

The wealthy and politically powerful controllers of our universities well know the dangers represented by the free exchange of ideas. The

Student Rebellion of '69 and '70 alarmed them to this potential. It cost the withdrawal of an incumbent President from his race to re-election, as well as the withdrawal of troops from Cambodia by his successor. The potential of dissident students forcing social change in a direction not desired by the powerful became readily apparent. Something had slipped out of place and had to be taken care of. The university as factory was not the consequence, for it was already long in process. But the process was incomplete and had to be augmented. Its complete augmentation represents the destruction of the university—although students still will be sitting in buildings and instructors still will be mouthing words.

I was in Germany during one period of the Great Rebellion, where on the wall of one of the buildings of the University of Heidelberg I saw painted graffiti that put this matter most succinctly. It read: *Universität = Monoversität = Conformität*. It could hardly have been expressed better: University = Monoversity = Conformity.

The American educational system always has functioned to dispell dissenting thought, to produce a disciplined work force, and to offer to selectively recruited students their passports to upper middle class positions. It always has stabilized the social system by offering limited mobility and serving as a safety valve on pressures that might otherwise become too great. But with the application of the factory model to the university, the subservience of education will be complete. Not only will it function for the benefit of those in economic control of our society, but it will also be using their own model in doing so.

ENDNOTE

1. I should say, rather, what the university *should* be about as this process of becoming factory has been going on for many years. Although Parsons College may have been an aberration of educational values, it was an epitome of factory-economic-business values, as well as an unfortunate harbinger.

Robert Cirino

29

A New Communication System— With Real Competition

The most vociferous critics of bias in the media propose for their solution the reinforcement of those aspects of the communication system that are most responsible for bias.

Nixon Administration spokesmen Clay Whitehead and Patrick Buchanan propose measures that would give local station managers—of both commercial and public stations—more power at the expense of the national networks. This sounds good until it is realized that local station managers are on the whole less courageous and more protective of the status-quo than their colleagues at the national level. To increase local control without at the same time changing the present commercial and public communication systems will merely allow fuller play for those coercive elements that account for most of the bias in the media—the pro-establishment station managers and their hired reporters, the need to make a profit, and the pressure from advertisers and the local power structure.

Edith Efron, author of *The News Twisters*, and economist Milton Freidman, along with other critics who claim the media are too liberal, have proposed the government get out of broadcasting completely and allow the "private property system" and "dollar vote" of the people to determine which information agencies and messages thrive or fail. We have just such a system in operation today—daily newspapers. But instead of a marketplace of ideas for the consumer most Americans are offered one conservatively oriented daily newspaper which uses its freedom to slant, distort and censor the news.

The "dollar vote" may insure a marketplace of transistor radios or pencils, but it does not and can not insure a fair marketplace of ideas in

Robert Cirino, "A New Communication System—With Real Competition," The Review of Southern California Journalism, *August, 1972, pp. 12–14. Reprinted by permission.*

the mass media any more than the popular vote can insure justice for individuals accused of crime. What if there are not enough customers to financially support a radical, very liberal or far-right daily newspaper, radio or television station? Does that mean then that their ideas should die out, and the public at large should not be equally exposed through the mass media to their information products?

It is apparent that the proposals for more local control over networks, elimination of government regulations and the extension of the private property media system will not eliminate bias or produce a marketplace of competing biases. They are clearly proposals designed to give conservatives even more control of mass media and favorable coverage than they at present enjoy.

Proposals by establishment liberals writing in the *Columbia Journalism Review, The Nation, New Republic* or *Progressive* are little better. They zealously defend the concepts of objectivity and fairness by insisting that they, as elites, can fairly edit and present other people's views for them. Assuming control over access and executive decision making are not relevant to achieving balance, their proposals are merely reforms such as press councils or calls to professional excellence. They favor alternative financing and an expansion of public broadcasting, but not the kind of expansion and change that would create a new system adequate for a democracy. Most are more fearful of government coercion than of the more subtle and less apparent coercion inherent in the present commercial and public systems. If all of their liberal reforms are accomplished the public will still be exposed to the same basic ownership, access and decision-making patterns that produce the present bias.

Very liberal or radical journalists admit their bias. They forsake the facade of objectivity and detachment that allows establishment journalists to cooperate with and contribute to mass media products. Instead of looking to corporations or the government to create a marketplace, they have set up their own alternate communication system with "underground" weeklies, radio stations and portable video networks. This plan has worked well in providing the left community an alternative media, but it hasn't worked to provide a marketplace of ideas for the over 90 per cent who still depend solely on the daily newspaper, radio and television.

In fact none of the proposals, whether from the conservatives, establishment liberals or radicals, offers an alternative that will provide a marketplace of ideas adequate for a democracy.

What we need, then, are proposals for a new communication system that will provide real competition as looked at from the consumer's vantage point. The basic premise of this system is the concept that fairness cannot be achieved nor censorship decisions eliminated by any one person or news agency. This can only be achieved when all basic viewpoints have a chance to present their own ideas with equal money, equal technology and equal artistic force. The end product, viewed as a total-ity, will thus be fair and uncensored for the consumer.

A second premise is that all viewpoints don't and will never have a chance to produce a message of equal artistic force within a commercial communication system. Some viewpoints will never have the necessary political power, money or advertising support to break into the mass media.

These two premises make imperative a vast governmental role in order to bring about an adequate system. No one has more precisely stated the people's and thus the government's right to be involved in the media than a Canadian Senate Committee on the mass media: "If government can legislate to insure a more diverse and antagonistic press, it is not interfering in freedom of the press; it is moving to protect a broader, more basic freedom: the freedom of information."

In view of the above, the Congress should immediately establish a new U.S. Broadcasting Corp. that avoids all the shortcomings of public broadcasting as it now exists—shortcomings that guarantee it will remain inadequate and even more afraid to dip into controversy than the commercial networks. At present, not only is public broadcasting woefully short of money, its structure is designed to prevent it from ever offering the public a marketplace of ideas.

First, the system is required by law to be "fair, objective and balanced." This prevents journalists from owning up to their own bias, and effectively keeps extremes at both ends of the spectrum from presenting their own viewpoints. What is left is a Pseudo marketplace with establishment liberals (mostly on the national level) at one extreme of the spectrum and the very conservative (mostly on the local level) at the other.

Second, local station managers are given a free hand to censor, if they find a program is too controversial they merely reject it. A significantly large number of local affiliates censored documentaries on China, Cuba, U.S. imperialism, Bobby Seale, and discrimination against black ex-convicts. Two of the five stations in Texas refused "Banks and the Poor" and at one time "Black Journal" was being refused by eight PBS affiliates in Alabama alone.

Third, the boards of directors at both the national and local level are made up not of journalists representing different viewpoints, but of businessmen, university presidents and station managers whose political ideas fall within what the establishment and Ford Foundation consider safe.

Fourth, whatever money public broadcasting receives has strings on it. Since funding is on a year-to-year basis, broadcast executives are responsive to subtle and direct Congressional or Administration intimidation. Corporate foundation money supposedly carries no strings, but can anyone expect too many hard-hitting programs depicting the foundations as tax shelters, establishment and CIA fronts, molders of elite thinking and covert directors of university research and purposes? For years the Ford Foundation with its nearly $200 million in contributions made the most important decisions regarding public television. One of its innovations was a "board of editors." Set up to evaluate programs, it in practice served as a board of censors.

Fifth, the system allows corporate advertising (or sponsorship as they like to call it) to have an effect on programming. Certain programs are more likely to be viewed by the public because some sponsor will pay for them; others are not presented or even imagined because there is no potential corporate sponsor.

To avoid these five shortcomings the new U.S. Broadcasting Corp. should establish four different and independent television-radio networks representing different viewpoints on the political spectrum: the "Very Liberal" for the radical and very liberal, "Liberal" for the moderate liberals and those just to the left of center, "Conservative" for the moderate conservatives and those just to the right of center, and "Very Conservative" for the very conservative and far right. Each network will have its own 13-man board of directors made up of five journalists, two artists, two laymen, two professors and two others all having the political viewpoints that the network is supposed to represent. A minimum of four board members on each network will be from minority groups. Initially such members will be chosen by a Senate committee after open hearings. These boards will in turn elect their own successors after open hearings, and elect three members each to serve on a 12-man board for the new U.S. Broadcasting Corp. as a whole. Congress will give to these four boards all allocation, editorial, hiring, programming and production powers. The Corporation's charter will be renewed by Congress every 10 years.

Funding for the networks will be on a permanent basis, equally divided among the four networks. The amount granted each network will be sufficient (close to $200 million per year) to enable it to artistically and technically compete with the commercial networks both in entertainment and public affairs programming. Funds will come from the federal budget plus special communication taxes on the profits of commercial broadcasters as well as on gross receipts of broadcast advertising, on gross receipts of long distance phone calls, on gross receipts of radio and television sales, on the trade price of any broadcast license, and on gross receipts of a national lottery when established.

At least 25 per cent of prime time for television, and prime time and commuter time for radio, will be devoted to public affairs. Minority artists and journalists serving each network will produce a minimum of 25 per cent of prime time programming. A bi-weekly radio and television program guide for the four networks will be sent to every American address.

Advertising and sponsorship will be prohibited. Any foundation, corporate or private grants to the national system will go, no strings attached, to a general fund to be used by all four networks. Private grants at the local level will be channeled to a statewide fund to be distributed equally to all state stations.

The Fairness Doctrine will not apply since the public will have the same access to all viewpoints being presented with equal force. The total mosaic of information products from all four networks over a period of time will be as balanced as any information product can be.

Since politicians will be prohibited from buying time, and the four networks prohibited from giving time to any group or politician, the Equal Time provision will not be needed. All political appearances will be under the editorial control of the networks in programs such as live coverage, debates, interviews or documentaries.

The Fairness Doctrine should still apply to commercial stations, and be interpreted to automatically cover any special interviews with politicians or ads that deal with controversial topics. A new amendment to the Equal Time provision would permit the purchase of a minimum of fifteen minutes of time on commercial stations by any politician or group, but no matter who pays for it the time would have to be divided equally among all candidates or viewpoints.

Frequencies on the AM band for all four networks should be made available in every radio market as soon as possible. If necessary, the FCC should make such space by refusing to renew the license of the station that is found to have least served the public interest. Until this is achieved, frequencies on the FM band should be allocated. Transmitters with sufficient power to serve each of the four U.S. time zones should be constructed. This will avoid the necessity of establishing thousands of separate radio stations.

Today three states have no public television, 86 of the top 198 television markets have no public TV station, and in some major cities where there is public television it is on the UHF band (which prevents reception by about 50 per cent of the homes). This situation should be remedied immediately by establishing a public television station in the 86 markets that now have none. The FCC should take actions to insure that all stations that are not now on the VHF band will be so within a three-year period. Where necessary, this can be done by refusing to renew the license of the VHF station that is found to have least served the public interest during the previous three years. The owners can be compensated with the market value of their station less the previously mentioned tax on the trade price of the license. The new U.S. Broadcasting Corp. should have its own satellite and computer system. Besides serving the four networks, its services could be rented to commercial networks to help fund the system.

All local public broadcasting stations should be funded by $1 to $2 million in federal funds each year depending on the size of the community served. This amount can be supplemented by state and local revenue.

The present membership of the board of directors for local public television stations should be changed so that each board will have twelve members: three members (one journalist, one artist and one layman) representing the viewpoint of each network. A minimum of one of the three will be a minority group member. Each network board will appoint the three members from a list of local applicants. As with the network and national board, the chairman will be elected by board members, the term will be five years and the board will select its successors after open hearings. Affiliates will be required to show whatever programs are produced by the networks which will be responsible for 75 per cent of prime-time programming. Affiliates are free to program for all other hours.

Each network will alternate every fourth night in having its programs shown over all local public television affiliates. In the case of presidential speeches all four networks will pool their personnel for that evening, each viewpoint provided with time for an immediate commentary. Each network can later offer an opposing viewpoint when its evening comes up within four days.

A federal law should require that every cable system allocate four channels for the public system so that in the future each can have its programs carried daily. This is in addition to a minimum of two channels set aside for public access. Besides production and programming for radio and television, each network will plan to produce a weekly magazine and daily newspaper for the time when cable transmission of such is feasible.

This is a minimum proposal consistent with a democratic society's need for a true marketplace of ideas. It is less than ideal for it leaves vested interests with a disproportionate advantage in controlling commercial broadcasting, daily newspapers and mass-circulation magazines. But it is a beginning that would for the first time allow the citizen to choose from among information products that are really competitive.

Truth is a powerful tool of persuasion. It often takes only a small amount of truth, widely spread, to topple the artistically created media fabrications and slow down the corporate pre-emption of American resources and feelings of patriotism. The new U.S. Broadcasting Corp. will at least allow that small amount of truth to get to the public through mass channels that will make it competitive. That's all any American wants—some real competition, not just on the athletic field or in the sale of transister radios, but where it counts.

Consequences of the Concentration of Economic and Political Power

This section pulls together many of the social problems analyzed in the preceding sections. We deal here with the causes underlying our major social problems. As has become apparent from our earlier selections, the basic cause is the current socio-economic structure of the United States. Economic power has become concentrated in the hands of a few, and those few use that power to pursue financial profit regardless of the consequences it brings to others. This section takes an overarching view of this central cause of our social problems. While doing so, we again focus on many of the specific problems we covered earlier. We also emphasize in this section the social problems of modern warfare, inflation, and recession.

In the opening selection, Greenberg documents the ascendancy of the modern corporation in American life. He analyzes not only the dominance of the corporation over other forms of the business enterprise but also the dominance of a relatively few corporations over others. We previously examined the dominance of oil corporations in the energy crisis. Now we focus on the dominant few in manufacturing, banking, insurance, merchandising, transportation, and the utilities. Greenberg dispels the ideological myths of competition and the "stockholder's democracy," where ownership and control are separated and there has supposedly been a movement away from profits to benefits for the public. Interlocking directorships of worldwide scope have led to concentrated control. Decision making has become increasingly centralized, gaining control over capital, resources, prices, and profits. This concentrated power has far reaching ramifications for the perpetuation of our major social problems, and daily affects the lives of each of us in vital ways.

Harrington then analyzes the inflation-recession cycle that is endemic to our economic system. He emphasizes that recession and depression are not accidents, but they are built into the structure of our economic system. In making this analysis, he covers the specific social problems of the food and energy crises, illustrating that they are not due to "natural" factors but are the consequence of the profit policies of our current economic orientation. He similarly indicates that social problems such as inflation, pollution, and our lack of rapid mass transit are not accidents, but are also products of our economic system.

The final tragic consequence of our current concentration of economic and political power on which we focus is that of militarization and war. A new power has emerged in the United States that overarches our contemporary capitalistic system—that of Pentagon control. With the ascendance of the Pentagon, as Melman analyzes in Article 32, we have a new major instrument in decision making, one that both unites the economic and political spheres of our society and threatens our remaining freedoms. This gargantuan power preempts our resources, manpower, materials, and industrial products. With its annual budget in excess of $100,000,000,000, it diverts about 10 percent of our total Gross National Product into militarization. In order to continuously expand its war machine, the Pentagon uses its concentrated power to successfully sell to Congress and the public alike myths under the name of defense.

Just as our other social problems are not accidents, but are part and parcel of our socio-economic system, so our war policies of death and destruction are not accidental. On the contrary, they are vital parts of our current economic system. As several contributors have emphasized, if it is to thrive corporate capitalism needs to expand. With our internal markets drying up, our industrialists have sought other efficient means of expending manufactured products. Warfare serves this purpose admirably, for warfare consumes economically. To destroy vast quantities of materials in a war means that those goods must be reordered and remanufactured. The whole process of reordering, retooling, and remanufacturing reaps huge profits for our industrialists. Accordingly, warfare has become an extremely profitable venture for those who manufacture the weapons of warfare. Since war is being used to maintain the growth of our economic system, continued warfare is the likely outcome of our present subservience to the ruling triumvirate of our economic-political-military leaders.

Note that in this final selection, Reynolds and Lundgren emphasize that our war in Southeast Asia was not simply a tragic mistake on the part of the United States, but it was an integral part of basic policies pursued for profit. They predict that as long as the complex of military-industrial-political leadership remains in control of our society, our warfare in Southeast Asia represents just one of a continuing series of similarly gruesome events which will be inflicted on the world. Because war maintains our corporate capitalists, they conclude that we can expect war to be maintained. The authors also analyze why this new parasitic imperialism feeds on small scale wars.

30

Edward S. Greenberg

The Dominance of
Corporate Capitalism

When thinking about business enterprise, Americans seem to carry with them the baggage of values and opinions connected to the "Ma and Pa" corner grocery store. Americans are prone to speak in similar free enterprise terms both about the small business of Adam Smith's classical models and the giants of American industry, such as the American Telephone and Telegraph Company and General Motors. Yet, from nearly every perspective, the corporation is a different breed of animal. In the eyes of the law, for instance, the corporation is a form of organization different from other forms of business enterprise. Of special importance are the following features: [1]

1. The corporation is considered a person with unlimited life span in the eyes of the law, and as a "person" it has the ability to buy and sell, sue and be sued, hire and fire, and so on. This gives it tremendous flexibility and continuity compared to other forms of business enterprise.
2. In the small proprietorship, the owner is liable to an unlimited extent for all business losses. He may be forced to sell home and possessions to settle business debts. The corporation, on the other hand, has the advantage of *limited liability*. No investor is liable for more than his initial investment, and as a result, the corporation is a more attractive investment than the single proprietorship or partnership. Limited liability allows the corporation to attract backers more easily and to accumulate capital. Limited liability is the basis for almost unlimited capital accumulation, and helps account for the staggering growth in the size of corporations. The growth is of such magnitude, in

From Edward S. Greenberg, Serving The Few. © *1974 by John Wiley & Sons, Inc. Reprinted by permission of John Wiley & Sons, Inc.*

fact, that in the relatively short span of a century and a half American society has been transformed from an economy of small businesses and widespread proprietorship, to one in which the bulk of economic activity is conducted by a relative handful of firms. Measured in terms of gross receipts, for instance, corporations account for about 80 percent of all business activity, though they comprise but 10 percent of all business firms. The growth of corporations has been so spectacular that there remains no doubt that today they dominate the American economy whether measured in terms of capital, production, investment, new products, consumer impact, or employment.[2]

It is difficult perhaps to grasp the magnitude of the modern corporation, to comprehend its size, concentration, and power, but Richard J. Barber helps us with this description:

"General Motor's yearly operating revenues exceed those of all but a dozen or so countries. Its sales receipts are greater than the combined general revenues of New York, New Jersey, Pennsylvania, Ohio, Delaware, and the six New England states. Its 1,300,000 stockholders are equal to the population of Washington, Baltimore or Houston. G.M. employees number well over 700,000 and work in 127 plants in the United States and forty-five countries spanning Europe, South Africa, North America and Australia. The total cash wages are more than twice the personal income of Ireland. G.M.'s federal corporate tax payments approach $2 billion, or enough to pay for all federal grants in fiscal year 1970 in the field of health research. The enormity of General Motors . . . should not be thought of as unique. Some 175 other manufacturing, merchandising and transportation companies now have annual sales of at least a billion dollars. One, rivaling GM—is Standard Oil of New Jersey. With more than a hundred thousand employees around the world . . . , a six-million ton tanker fleet . . . , and $17 billion in assets . . . , it can more easily be thought of as a nation than a commercial enterprise."[3]

This leads us to another observation about the modern corporate system, and that pertains to the existence of a giant sector within the corporate sector; an economy within an economy if you will. Students of the subject agree that concentration is not merely the story of the dominance of the corporation over other forms of business enterprise, but also the dominance of a relatively few corporations over all others. In 1962, for instance, out of 180,000 manufacturing corporations, the *one hundred* largest accounted for 55 percent of all net capital assets, and 58 percent of all after-tax profits.[4] In 1969, after-tax profits remained at 58 percent for the top 100 and almost 25 percent for the top 10.[5] Moreover, on most indicators, concentration has been increasing steadily for the past several decades.[6] ". . . The 100 largest firms in 1968 held a larger share of manufacturing assets than the 200 largest in 1950; the 200 largest in 1968 controlled as large a share as the 1000 largest in 1941."[7]

We gain a similar picture of concentration if we look at particular industries. Thus, in 1966, the *top four* firms in each industry accounted for the following percentages of all output.[8]

Aerospace	67%
Motor vehicles	79
Computers	63
Tires	71
Cigarettes	81
Soap detergent	72
Photographic equipment	67

Although we have focused on manufacturing, similar patterns of concentration hold for banking, insurance, merchandising, transportation, and utilities.[9] As of 1964, for instance, *one-tenth of one percent* of all commercial banks in the United States held 24 percent of all deposits. Concentration is even more dramatic in the field of trust management (and more important, because the power to invest trust accounts leads to influence in corporate decision making) where but 26 banks accounting for almost two-thirds of all trust assets. Finally, as few as 20 banks manage half of all private pension fund assets.[10]

Concentration is enhanced by the heavily interlocked nature of large business firms. Nominal competitors, for instance, usually have directors sitting on each other's boards of directors, raising the suspicion that competition is not the essence of their relationship. Interlock is further enhanced by the trust activities of banks, by trade associations, by the practice of price leadership and, occasionally, by outright collusion and conspiracy.

This description of corporate concentration would be incomplete without an appreciation of its worldwide scope. The American tourist soon learns that he can easily purchase a Coke, Kodak film, Standard gasoline, a Singer sewing machine, Tide detergent, and Ivory soap in almost any country in the nonsocialist world. The American and foreign businessman can purchase American computers, machine tools, heavy road equipment, tractors, and an infinite variety of other goods directly from American-owned subsidiaries in Europe, Latin America, Canada, or Asia. These mundane examples merely highlight the undisputed fact that American corporations control a good deal of the world's economy and that the expansion has not yet abated. As the French journalist J. J. Servan-Schreiber has so graphically put it: "Fifteen years from now the world's third greatest industrial power, just after the United States and Russia, may not be Europe, but American industry in Europe."[11] To take one example, it has been estimated by Servan-Schreiber that American firms will own 75 percent of all European science-based industry by 1980 and thus the most advanced sectors of European economies.

The worldwide scope of the American corporation is a phenomenon characteristic primarily of the largest firms. Only 16 percent of all American companies, for instance, owned almost 60 percent of total United States foreign investments in 1957. The top 100 firms, moreover, accounted for approximately 75 percent of all earnings on foreign investment.[12] Concentration in the foreign market, then, is even more extreme than in the United States.

Concentrated economic power in a relative handful of business enterprises has enormous implications for American economic life and, as we shall see later, for social and political life as well. Most obviously, these giant corporations have amassed sufficient power to allow them, in general, to tame and transcend dealings in the marketplace. Instead of the market system envisioned by Adam Smith, a system characterized by vigorous competition between many small firms, a new system has emerged on the American scene, one that economists term *oligopoly*. Oligopoly leads to private control of prices and profits, and thus wide discretion in the decision making power of corporate executives.[13] Oligopolistic power means that a few firms are able to control the marketplace, to deny entry to new firms, to control sources of raw materials, and to generate their own internal sources of capital for investment and expansion.

What has emerged is the fully integrated firm.[14] As described by economist John Kenneth Galbraith, the primary goal of the modern giant corporation is predictability, stability, the avoidance of risk, and results neither automatically nor ordinarily forthcoming in the marketplace. In order to reach predictability and stability in an industrial process that requires the mobilization of enormous resources of capital, equipment and technological talent, and manpower, the corporation attempts to stabilize its environment by the following methods:

1. Given its size and importance as a customer, it attempts to control the price of the raw materials it buys (think of the power that G.M. has over a supplier of automobile parts and accessories).
2. It may even own the sources of raw material (e.g., steel companies usually own the companies that extract iron ore; oil companies usually own the concession for the extraction of crude oil).

3. High profit margins allow the giant corporation to use its own funds for expansion and investment out of retained earnings, thus avoiding the necessity of outside financing.

4. Given its transcendence of the market place, it, in conjunction with other large sellers, attempts to set its own prices (usually through the process of price leadership but occasionally through collusion and conspiracy).

5. It attempts to persuade customers to buy what it produces at the price at which it wants to sell by advertising and salesmanship.

Through these mechanisms, the mature corporation attempts to stabilize its economic environment, and to guarantee to itself a substantial profit and steady growth. When it finds itself unable to accomplish such goals by itself, or in cooperation with other business enterprises, it often turns to the state for assistance.[15]

JUSTIFYING CORPORATE POWER

Americans have traditionally been uncomfortable in the face of great power. Popular opposition to centralized power has been a part of our heritage from at least the time of the American Revolution. Recall the strong antiexecutive tone to the state constitutions of the Articles of Confederation period and the rigid and complex provisions in the Constitution of 1789 designed to fragment governmental power. Americans have also it seems, been traditionally concerned about economic power as shown by the antirailroad campaigns of the agrarian populists and the antitrust activities of the Progressives. Periodic and ostentatious resurrection of antitrust activities by government suggests that Americans still hold to this set of values derived from an earlier era in our history. And yet, there is no denying that giant corporations, and concentrations of wealth exist and play a central role in our economic, social, and political life.

For corporate spokesmen, this vast concentration of power and its contradiction of traditional values offers no lasting problem, for while certainly acknowledging the corporation's size and power, they argue that the institution of the corporation has undergone such fundamental transformations that it is not only nonthreatening to the general public, but socially useful as well.

The basic argument may be stated as follows.

1. Ownership of corporations is now so widespread and diffused that the corporate system has become *democratized.* The entrance of millions of Americans into the stock market since the

end of World War II, has led to the development of what might be properly called "stockholder democracy."[16]

2. Unlike the early days of the "trusts," when the names of men like Rockefeller, Ford, Hanna, Harriman, and Stanford became a lasting part of the American vocabulary, corporations are now characterized by a separation of ownership and control. Modern corporations are run by professional managers, while owners have receded into the background.[17]

3. Professional managers and the technostructure that run the modern corporation have goals that differ from the earlier trust builders; namely, they have eschewed *profit* as their primary goal. Corporations, it is claimed, now hold to such goals as growth, steady but not maximum profit, and community service. Economist Karl Kaysen has, perhaps, somewhat facetiously, termed this new creature the "soulful corporation."[18]

4. Power is tamed and controlled because corporate management must balance a series of claims arising from its customers, its workers, its stockholders and the public at large. As one executive has said,
   "One no longer feels the obligation to take from labor for the benefit of capital, nor to take from the public for the benefit of both, but rather to administer wisely and fairly in the interest of all."[19]

The corporation has, it seems, undergone a fundamental transformation from an earlier day when the popular imagination likened the "trusts" to a grasping, greedy octopus. The question that we must address is whether claims for such a transformation square with reality. Is the justification of corporate economic power anything but mystification?

Let us turn our attention first to the claims for "stockholder democracy," a claim based on evidence of substantial increases in the number of Americans who own corporate stock. In the period 1952 to 1973, it is true, ownership expanded from 6.5 million persons to over 25 million. However, it is also undeniably true that most people buy and sell stock for the purpose of realizing either short-term or long-term profits, and hold no interest in the management of the corporation, annual symbolic meetings, complete with box lunches, notwithstanding. The constant refrain about 25 million stockholders must also contend with the fact that about 200 million other Americans own no stock at all. Finally, ownership among the people who own stock is severely concentrated. It remains true that a relative handful of people own most of the corporate stock sold to the public. One scholar estimated that the top one percent of all tax filers in 1960 owned 48 percent of all stock held by individuals.[20] Clearly the phrase "stockholder democracy" is a misnomer in the face of these facts. Stockholder "oligopoly" is perhaps more apt.

As for the separation of ownership and control, the Berle-Means hypothesis is not strongly supported by available evidence. Family ownership remains a reality in the American economy, as the names Ford, Rockefeller, Mellon, and DuPont suggest. *Fortune*, a magazine directed to business leaders, concluded after an extensive study that

> "*After more than two generations during which ownership has increasingly divorced from control it is assumed that all large U.S. corporations are owned by everybody and nobody and are run and ruled by bland organization men. The individual entrepreneur or family that holds onto the controlling interest and actively manages the affairs of a big company is regarded as a rare exception, as something of an anachronism. But a close look at the 500 largest industrial corporations does not substantiate such sweeping generalizations.*
>
> "*In approximately 150 companies on the current* Fortune *500 list, controlling ownership rests in the hands of an individual or of the members of a single family. . . . The evidence that 30 percent of the 500 largest industrials are clearly controlled by identifiable individuals, or by family groups, is something to ponder. It suggests that the demise of the traditional American proprietor has been slightly exaggerated and that the much advertised triumph of the organization is far from total.*[21]

The image of the independent managerial group painted by Berle and Means and, more recently, by John Kenneth Galbraith, must also be qualified in light of the extent of bank control of a significant number of corporations. Through their role as caretakers of trust accounts, accounts that were in excess of $600 billion in 1968,[22] and through their dominant position as executors of the nation's burgeoning pension funds, the largest banks have a significant impact on the shape of the American economy and in corporate decision making. Indeed, Congressman Patman's House Committee on Banking and Currency has reported that banks control at least five percent of the voting stock (the amount economists speculate is required for control of most large corporations) in 147 out of *Fortune's* top 500 corporations.[23] Moreover, the 49 top banks held, in 1968, 768 interlocking directorships with 286 of the top 500 industrial corporations.[24] Of the top 50 transportation companies, these banks held 73 interlocking directorships with 27. Among utilities, the story was much the same; banks held 86 directorships in 22 out of the 50 largest companies. Among the giant insurance companies, the top 49 banks held an average of five directorships per company.[25]

These figures suggest an economy that is dominated by a relatively few corporations and banks that are tightly bound together through interlocking directorships. When one combines the 30 percent of the top 500 industrial corporations controlled by family groups with the 30 percent that are controlled by financial institutions, it begins to appear that the description of dominance by professional corporate managers, with a set of unique, nonprofit motivations, has been slightly exaggerated, to say the least.

Beginning with Berle and Means in 1932, continued in the work of John Kenneth Galbraith, and filling the editorial and advertisement pages of various business publications like *Fortune, Barron's,* and *Business Week* is the image of the new corporate executive, an executive who despite the prodigious and awesome power at his command, practices self-restraint, community responsibility, and citizenship. He is a man that contributes to worthy charities, buys little league uniforms, is concerned with the welfare of the people that work for him and those that buy his products and, in the service of all of these goals, he eschews the pursuit of maximum profit. We are to believe that corporate power is held in trust for the community, that the interests of corporate management are similar to those of the public and that, consequently, there is nothing to fear from the concentrated power of corporate enterprise.

There remain, despite the claims, some imposing problems with this benign description. Basically, there is the assumption that since ownership and control are separated, the people who manage the corporation are freed from the need to pursue profit as a goal and consequently, can substitute goals that are more exalted and ennobling. However, we have already seen that approximately 60 percent of the top 500 industrial corporations are controlled either by family groups or banks. That leaves 40 percent to be accounted for and even in this remaining total, discussion of the decline of the profit motive is, at least, premature, because managers have a clear and vital stake in profits. "The managerial class is the largest single group in the stockholding population, and a greater proportion of this class owns stock than any other."[26] In fact, nearly one-half of all Americans owning more than $100,000 worth of stock are found in the managerial group. This group of men, one would assume, retains more than a minor interest in stock value, dividends, and profits. As Mr. Sheehan of *Fortune* remarked, "Chairman Frederic C. Donner . . . owns only 0.017 percent of G.M.'s outstanding stock, but it was worth about $3,917,000 recently. Chairman Lynn A. Townsend owns 0.117 percent of Chrysler, worth about $2,380,000. Their interest in the earnings of those investments is hardly an impersonal one."[27]

In fact, the Donner and Townsend examples are not atypical of corporate executives. One recent study showed that among the largest 94 corporations listed with the Securities and Exchange Commission the *average* chief executive received over $150,000 in salary, over

$23,000 in dividends, and held more than $650,000 in company stock.[28] To these data one can add everyday evidence from the news media: price fixing in the electrical industry; foot-dragging by the auto industry on the installation of safety devices; engineered fuel shortages by the major oil companies to force up prices; poor compliance with antipollution laws; the criminal negligence of mine companies with respect to mine safety,[29] and the shady practices of pharmaceutical manufacturers. One cannot help but suspect that *profit* remains the primary motive of big business.

Finally, the claim that separation of ownership and control leads to the decline of profit as a motive among big businessmen is exaggerated, because the demands of the market place compel managers to act very much like owners.[30] Long-term deviation from profit-maximizing behavior, for instance, would most likely lead to undervaluation of stock and to the transformation of a firm into a target for an outside takeover. It should be added, moreover, that without healthy profitability, the resource base for expansion and technological innovation upon which large firms depend would be absent. Where does all the preceding discussion lead? It suggests that the American economy is dominated by large corporations and financial institutions that are tightly interlocked and that are, despite the claims of their spokesmen to new sets of motivations, still moved primarily by the need to make private gains. It suggests that these enterprises, in the pursuit of profit, profoundly affect the lives of Americans without, in their turn, being much affected by public controls. It suggests also that the rationalizations made for corporate power in the face of traditional American fears of such concentration are not convincing.

ENDNOTES

1. See Harry M. Trebing, "Introduction," in *The Corporation in the American Economy.*
2. See Edward S. Mason, Ed., *The Corporation in Modern Society* (Cambridge: Harvard University Press, 1960) for a useful anthology on the subject.
3. *The American Corporation* (New York: Dutton, 1970), p. 20.
4. Walter F. Mueller, "Recent Changes in Industrial Concentration, and the Current Merger Movement," in *Hearings: Subcommittee on Antitrust and Monopoly of the Committee on the Judiciary, U.S. Senate, 88th Congress, 2nd Session* (Washington, D.C.: U.S. Government Printing Office, July 1964). Reprinted in Maurice Zeitlin, Ed., *American Society, Inc.: Studies of the Social Structure and Political Economy of the United States* (Chicago: Markham, 1970), p. 24. Note that the assets of the top 500 corporations

almost doubled from 1965 to 1972. See *Statistical Abstracts of the United States, 1973* (Washington, D.C.: U.S. Census Bureau, 1973), Table 777.

5. U.S. Department of Commerce. Survey of Current Business July 1970, Table 6–15.

6. Gardiner C. Means "Economic Concentration" in *Hearings: Subcommittee on Antitrust and Monopoly of the Committee on the Judiciary, U.S. Senate, 88th Congress, 2nd Session* (Washington, D.C.: U.S. Government Printing Office, July 1964), pp. 8–19. Reprinted in Zeitlin, *American Society, Inc.*

7. Daniel R. Fusfield, "The Rise of the Corporate State in America," *Journal of Economic Issues*, Vol. VI, No. 1 (March 1972).

8. Trebing, *The Corporation in the American Economy*, p. 4.

9. See Robert L. Heilbroner, *The Limits of American Capitalism* (New York: Harper Torchbooks, 1966), p. 11.

10. See the Patman Committee Staff Report for the Domestic Finance Subcommittee of the House Committee on Banking and Currency, 90th Congress, 2nd Session, *Commercial Banks and Their Trust Activities: Emerging Influence on the American Economy* (Washington, D.C.: U.S. Government Printing Office, July 1968). Reprinted in Zeitlin, *American Society, Inc.* Out of approximately 14,000 banks in the United States, the top *10* controlled more than one-fourth of all assets and deposits in 1972. See *Statistical Abstracts of the United States, 1973*, Table 708.

11. *The American Challenge* (New York: Avon Books, 1968), p. 3.

12. Howard J. Sherman, *Profits in the United States* (Ithaca: Cornell University Press, 1968). Reprinted in Zeitlin, *American Society, Inc.*, p. 44.

13. Gardiner Means, "The Administered Price Theory Reconfirmed," *American Economic Review* (June 1972).

14. See John Kenneth Galbraith, *The New Industrial State* (Boston: Houghton Mifflin, 1968) for a more complete description of the integrated, mature corporation.

15. A subject to be explored at length in the next chapter.

16. Michael D. Reagan, "What 17 Million Shareholders Share," in Trebing, *The Corporation in the American Economy.*

17. The classic statement of this position is Adolf A. Berle and Gardiner C. Means, *The Modern Corporation and Private Property* (New York: Harcourt, Brace & World, 1932). Galbraith borrows from this tradition in his *New Industrial State.*

18. *Ibid.* Also see Carl Kaysen, "The Social Significance of the Modern Corporation," *American Economic Review*, Vol. 47 (May 1957); and F. X. Sutton et al., *The American Business Creed* (Cambridge: Harvard University Press, 1956).

19. Quoted in Henry Kariel, *The Decline of American Pluralism* (Stanford: Stanford University Press, 1956).

20. Reagan, "What 17 Million Shareholders Share," p. 102.

21. Robert Sheehan, "Proprietors in the World of Big Business," *Fortune* (June 15, 1967), p. 179.

22. Barber, *The American Corporation*, p. 55.
23. Patman Staff Report, in Zeitlin, *American Society, Inc.*, p. 70.
24. *Ibid.*, p. 25.
25. *Ibid.*
26. Kolko, *Wealth and Power in America*, p. 67.
27. Sheehan, "Proprietors in the World of Big Business," p. 242.
28. Robert J. Larnes, "The Effect of Management-Control on the Profits of Large Corporations," in Zeitlin, *American Society Inc.*, p. 260.
29. Without exception, every mine disaster that has claimed human life over the past decade, including the tragedy at Framington, West Virginia, occurred at mines in which federal inspectors had repeatedly cited unsafe conditions but where, for reasons of profit, companies had not made necessary corrections.
30. Robert M. Solow, "The New Industrial State or Son of Affluence," *The Public Interest*, Vol. 9 (Fall 1967), pp. 100–108.

Michael Harrington

31

A New Crisis of Capitalism

The current inflation-recession is a crisis of the capitalist system.

At first glance, this proposition may seem absurd. It is all but universally agreed, Left, Right, and Center, that two of the most important causes of our present dismal plight are energy and food prices. But isn't it clear that the former is largely the result of the OPEC cartel and the latter a consequence of crop failure outside the United States (in turn, often caused by accidents of weather) and of growing global affluence? These things, it may be said, are hardly products of the American economic system.

One can make a slightly more plausible case for my opening assertion by pointing to the way in which Washington's policies promoted our disasters. Still, were Nixon's devaluation and Johnson's war in Vietnam expressions of some *structural* tendency within the system? Wouldn't it be more sensible to regard them as the judgments of fallible individuals rather than expressions of an underlying contradiction in capitalism?

Even though the argument against my thesis seems to have common sense on its side, I do not accept it. To explain why, it is first necessary to carefully circumscribe what is being said here. For exactly what one means in speaking of a "crisis of the capitalist system" is not immediately obvious.

Joseph Schumpeter was a profound conservative—the greatest of the century—and one of the few critics of Marx who troubled to read him carefully (and, more often than not, fairly). In his monumental *History of Economic Analysis*, he described a series of very important distinctions in Marx and thereby illuminated a point ignored, not simply by anti-Marxists, but by a surprising number of Marxists as well. It bears very much on an analysis of the inflation-recession of the 1970s.

Michael Harrington, "A New Crisis of Capitalism," Dissent, Winter 1975, pp. 5–10. Reprinted by permission.

Marx, as Schumpeter noted, carefully distinguished between the general institutional *conditions* permitting cyclical movements in the economy, the specific *causes* actually producing such a movement, and the *symptoms* accompanying this causation. The general "anarchy" of capitalist society was a condition of crisis but, since it persisted through good times and bad, not its cause. The latter, Schumpeter rightly holds, was to be found in Marx's analysis—in all of the historical specificity of each case—in the process of capitalist accumulation. Finally, the cyclical movements that resulted from these general conditions and particular causes did generate symptoms, such as the expansion or contraction of credit, which the simplifiers often mistakenly thought were basic to the whole process.

I would follow Marx's lead in developing an analysis of what is happening today. Therefore, when I say that the current crisis is a product of the capitalist system, I do not mean that it is inevitable, in the sense that the system had to function precisely as it actually did. That would be sterile reasoning, and I will leave it to the theologians of the Left who focus on general conditions and ignore immediate causes. Moreover, I believe that capitalism will probably be able to surmount this crisis, at least in America, within the confines of the system. I would only add that if this turns out to be the case—if the Left once again fails politically and programmatically to offer a workable, progressive alternative—then the people of this society, and of the world, are likely to pay a high price for such a "solution."

What, then, is left of my claim that the recession-inflation is a crisis of the system? *Not that its causation was preordained, but that it is a characteristic crisis of this kind of a society, one into which it is institutionally predisposed to blunder.* It could have acted otherwise (but then, those other options would have involved characteristically capitalist contradictions too, albeit different ones); but that it did not, and it brought us to this pass, is by no means an accident even if also not a fate.

If I am right, and such a capitalist crisis does exist, then there is a political corollary to my analysis that I will note but not argue here: that structural changes within the American economy are required if we are to find a tolerable way out of our current calamities.[1]

To return now to my central proposition: our crisis, including its food, energy, and governmental policy components, is characteristically capitalist.

FOOD

American agriculture, for a generation at least, has been the site of a "classic" Marxist crisis.

In the '30s, there were farmers who desperately wanted to till the soil, and there were millions of people with empty stomachs. The response was a governmental policy of planned scarcity. Our agricultural system had become "too" productive within the confines of a capitalist economy. The latter had become, quite literally, a "fetter" on production, and during a decade of hunger it was necessary to plow under fields and kill off animals in order to maintain income for the producers. Since the programs that accomplished this "solution" were geared to the subsidy of market farmers, they helped to drive tenant and subsistence farmers off the land. Thus the government promoted concentration in the fields and spent billions of taxpayers' funds aiding agribusiness and assaulting the small farmers.

These things, to be sure, did not *have* to be done in exactly this manner. The Brannan Plan, proposed by the liberals under Harry Truman, would have put all that acreage back into production, allowed food prices to reach a market level on the basis of abundance, and then would have subsidized farm income once the consumers had the advantage of cheaper prices. But even under this infinitely more enlightened procedure, the fundamental capitalist problem would have remained— there was "too much" productivity in a system that placed narrow structural limits upon consumption. The response, however, would not have been quite as irrational as the one that actually took place.

As the Joint Economic Committee pointed out in a 1972 Staff Study, the government paid farmers $5.2 billion in 1970, most of it for *not* growing crops—and the consumer paid an extra $4.5 billion because of the artificially jacked up high prices this planned and subsidized scarcity brought about. It cost roughly $10 billion that year for the United States to eat less and to produce less than it could have easily produced. There were, of course, hungry people, some of them eating cat food while all this was taking place, and there were starving men and women in the Third World. (To be fair, agribusiness discovered under Nixon that it could profit from Food Stamps and began to back the program that was rapidly expanded to meet some of the needs of the poor. Now, however, that speculative conditions on the world agricultural market are so favorable, one might expect the Farm Bureau, perhaps the most effective reactionary organization in the United States, to revert to type.)

All of this is far from ancient history. This insanity continued up to the eve of the current crisis, as a recent study of the National Farmer's Union documents. In 1972, the government paid to keep 62.1 million acres out of production; in 1973, when the handwriting on the wall might have been clear to all, it managed to idle some 19.5 million acres. Only in 1974, when the multi-billion dollar exporters discovered that they could make a killing on the world market, did we finally stop this policy of subsidizing scarcity.

The Farmers' Union summarizes the impact of Washington's actions between 1969 and 1973:

> An enormous volume of potential food production was sacrificed during these five years, which could have been used for providing adequate reserves and greatly expanded food aid shipments. Assuming yields of only two-thirds of the actual national average for the grain best-suited to the various lands held out of production, the five-year total would have reached the equivalent of 8,609 million bushels of wheat. This is nearly a billion bushels more than the actual total harvests of 7,668 million bushels of wheat in the U.S. during those five years.

So the equivalent of a five-year harvest of wheat, plus one billion extra bushels, was sacrificed at a cost of $15.5 billion. While we thus paid dearly in order *not to produce* 234.3 million metric tons of grain, we only shipped 32.7 million metric tons overseas under the Food for Peace Program. Even that latter figure is deceptive. Food for Peace, as the Farmers' Union points out, might better be called Food for War or Food for Politics. In 1973, 31 percent of the total went to Vietnam and Cambodia—and over half the total to military-related recipients.

While the American and the world poor were paying with malnutrition and starvation for our policy of planned and profitable scarcity, agribusiness, like every other capitalist sector, was busy trying to upgrade the diets of the affluent. This expresses another characteristic of present-day capitalistic society: *consumption, if profitable, is expanded without any thought of social consequence.* Barbara Ward estimates in a recent issue of the *Economist* that one-third of the world's increased demand for food over the last several years is a result of increased eating on the part of the affluent, and not of population growth. Roger Revelle of Harvard's Center of Population Studies tells us that the life expectancy of children in the developing countries is lowered by undernutrition while that of adults in developed countries is reduced by overnutrition.

In short, the food crisis is not a result of such "natural" factors as population, fertility, and the like (themselves social products)—but of corporate-governmental policies in the United States that saw our enormous agricultural productivity, not as a means of satisfying human needs at home and abroad, but as a source of profit.

ENERGY

So much has been written about the energy crisis that I need only summarize the rudiments of a socialist analysis. Since 1943 at least—when the United States used its power to secure the Saudi concession for

Standard Oil of California and Texaco—the government has followed corporate priorities in this area. Our vulnerability to OPEC pressure is not a result of a throw of the geological dice but a social and political outcome. Washington gave Big Oil a 100 percent tax write-off on levies paid to foreign governments (which was intended as a secret foreign aid program to conservative Arab powers when it was launched in 1950); there were depletion allowances and the "expensing" of intangible drilling costs, which add up to an investment tax credit of 50 percent; oil import quotas from the late '50s until the early '70s drained American resources at a high cost to the consumer and kept out cheap Arab oil without political strings; a federal highway program massively subsidized the private passenger car and effectively helped to destroy mass transit, the railroads, the central city, and thereby worsened the lot of the minorities and the poor; and so on.

In short, it took billions of governmental dollars spent in promoting corporate goals in order to engineer us into the wasteful, inefficient, and vulnerable energy economy in which we now find ourselves. At every point in this process, the decision-making was characteristically capitalist, i.e., motivated by the quest for profit rather than the common good.

ECONOMIC MANAGEMENT

The "Keynesian Revolution," which occurred in the wake of the Great Depression, is now much more ambiguous than it seemed to be during the euphoric days of New Economic triumphs in the mid-'60s. Here again, a specifically capitalist dynamic is at the center of the problem.

Keynes was, as he openly proclaimed toward the end of *The General Theory*, moderately conservative. He basically thought that private corporate initiative yielded the best result and he was a resolute enemy of "State Socialism" (as well as a middle-class snob). "I see no reason," he wrote, "to suppose that the existing system misemploys the factors of production which are in use. . . . It is in determining the volume, not the direction, of actual employment that the existing system has broken down."

This, it is now quite obvious, is wrong. Under conditions in which government has followed the Keynesian prescriptions to maintain investment, employment, and savings, the private corporations have availed themselves of the resultant prosperity to foul the environment, gull the consumer with ingeniously packaged pseudo-needs, and in general impose intolerable social costs upon the public while pursuing private gain.

All this is the familiar stuff of contemporary social criticism—some of the most brilliant instances of it have come from John Kenneth Galbraith—and it is routinely ignored by policy-makers. Now, however, a new problem has emerged from within the Keynesian synthesis. Like the issue of allocation, it is a product of the system itself.

To be fair, Keynes himself did not believe that mere monetary and fiscal management would create a full-employment equilibrium; we owe that happy thesis to his heirs. It would be necessary, Keynes said, for the government to socialize at least some investment; and he recognized that the success of his policies would result in an inflationary danger. The basic mechanism whereby this latter effect is produced is a part of the crisis of capitalism. For until Keynes developed a program that made it possible to deal with recession—i.e., after he had banished the idiocies of a conventional wisdom that taught governments how to deepen recessions in the name of fighting them—capitalism had a marvelously effective mechanism for dealing with inflation: depression.

Marx, as Schumpter rightly understood, had located the tendency toward crisis in the very process of capitalist accumulation. On an upswing, he argued, the workers' wages increased and they even managed to win a larger portion of the surplus value they had created. This, however, cut down on capitalist profit and, along with a number of other factors (e.g., production necessarily outrunning the effective demand of a market based on capitalist property relations), brought about a crisis of the system. In this context, the crash was functional, restoring the conditions for yet another round of capitalist expansion. In such a system, rationality asserted itself—as Marx commented wryly, "something like the law of gravity, when a house falls around your ears."

But how, then, is the system going to survive when one of its crucial mechanisms (recession and mass unemployment) must, in order to assure the very survival of any post-Keynesian government, be suppressed? Clearly there are whole series of options that can be used to deal with this problem, and during the last quarter-century some Western governments have employed them shrewdly. The general institutional conditions for a crisis were created the moment Keynes—or more precisely, the working-class, socialist, and (American) liberal movements—tinkered with the old, broken-down engine of *laisser faire*. But for reasons too varied and complex to describe here, the specific causation for such a downturn did not arise until quite recently. It took us about 30 years to get from Scylla to Charybdis, but we certainly have arrived.

There are two, contradictory theories that seek to demonstrate why these trends have matured in recent times. Both seem partly right.

It has been asserted by a fairly large number of economists (Michael Kalecki was the first, Galbraith the most prominent of the recent spokesmen of this view, and James O'Connor its advocate on the Marxist Left) that the new class structure of managed capitalism allows oligopolies to administer prices. Under these circumstances, when unions make demands, they are readily accepted since, it is said, they can simply be passed on to the consumers anyway. What seems wrong about this analysis is that it tends to equate "Big Labor" and "Big Business," even though there is no empirical evidence that the best-organized workers have improved their *relative* position in either the society or the working class itself. But it is quite right to emphasize that, in the post-Keynesian environment, the competitive forces that are supposed to drive prices down are not working. We have carefully deprived capitalism of one of its few virtues.

The second theory is more classically Marxist. It holds that the Keynesian-induced boom subverts the conditions of capitalist profitability by undermining discipline in the plant and by allowing wages to bite into corporate earnings. Raford Boddy and James Crotty, who argue this thesis succinctly in the October '74 *Monthly Review,* see a basic contradiction between full employment and high profits. The big corporations, they assert, cannot pass the wage increases on to the consumer, and the workers therefore gain on the bosses. I am disturbed by some of the aspects of this analysis: it is based on data, from the Federal Reserve Bank of St. Louis (a center of monetarism and conservatism), which were intended to show, as Boddy and Crotty themselves note, that wage and price controls worked against business. This, certainly, is not true. Second, the UAW Research Department has convincingly shown that, since 1970, prices have risen much faster than labor costs and "manufacturing workers are getting a substantially smaller share of the value of their output" than at any time since the Department of Commerce began to keep books on this ratio in 1947. Yet there is no question that big business *believes* the case to be as Boddy and Crotty describe it, and that is a powerful economic fact.

Indeed, this belief is at the very center of the current economic program of American capital. The Chase Manhattan Bank and the New York Stock Exchange have been claiming that profits are too low to provide the necessary financing for corporate expansion in the next period. They therefore want preferential treatment for profits while wages are held down. In this, they once again prove that the American bourgeoisie is our most (sometimes our only) class-conscious class. If the workers were as Marxist as the executives, socialism would probably have triumphed a generation ago.

In any case, my central point does not require that I pick and choose between the details of these competing theories. For both of them assert—and Chase Manhattan and the Stock Exchange concur in—that changes in the structure of the capitalist system are one of the reasons we find ourselves in our present situation. We have, thank God, abandoned the irrational rationality of periodic depressions as a way of reestablishing economic upsurge, but we have yet to find a substitute for depressions that will work *within* the system. And, though the thought would horrify Keynes, these events suggest that one look for a solution outside of the system.

As long as one accepts the corporate infrastructure as sound, the demand for discrimination in favor of profits does make a certain inane and antisocial sense. We have allowed the business sector to act as society's National Economic Planning Council, and it simply wants to utilize the funds to get on with the job. But what if we began to socialize investment, as Keynes proposed in a different context? What if we set up our own National Economic Policy Planning Council, run by the people instead of by the corporate rich?

These thoughts move in the direction of the "Policy and Program" article I am not writing in these pages. Right now, I simply want to reassert my main point. In the critical areas of food and energy, it is government policy in the service of private priorities that has brought us to our present condition; and in the area of government economic management itself, we are learning that capitalism tends to function poorly if we deny it the right periodically to rationalize itself at the expense of the millions. In each of these three cases, all of them prime sources of our recession-inflation, there is a characteristically capitalist process at work. Our plight was not exactly preordained by some systemic inevitability, and it is certainly not the result of a bourgeois plot. But it *is* a typical abomination of our antisocial economic system.

ENDNOTE

1.   I do not present the programmatic, political conclusions in this article because I have developed them extensively in an essay that will accompany a resolution I am submitting to the Second National Convention of the Democratic Socialist Organizing Committee in January. I also assume that every reader of DISSENT understands that in terms of immediate action, the democratic Left must support public employment programs for all who are laid off, redistributionist tax policies to finance them, and militant union action to permit organized workers to catch up with inflation.

Seymour Melman   **32**

Pentagon Capitalism

In the name of defense, and without announcement or debate, a basic alteration has been effected in the governing institutions of the United States. An industrial management has been installed in the federal government, under the Secretary of Defense, to control the nation's largest network of industrial enterprises. With the characteristic managerial propensity for extending its power, limited only by its allocated share of the national product, the new state-management combines peak economic, political, and military decision-making. Hitherto, this combination of powers in the same hands has been a feature of statist societies—communist, fascist, and others—where individual rights cannot constrain central rule.

This new institution of state-managerial control has been the result of actions undertaken for the declared purposes of adding to military power and economic efficiency and of reinforcing civilian, rather than professional, military rule. Its main characteristics are institutionally specific and therefore substantially independent of its chief of the moment. The effects of its operations are independent of the intention of its architects, and may even have been unforeseen by them.

The creation of the state-management marked the transformation of President Dwight Eisenhower's "military-industrial complex," a loose collaboration, mainly through market relations, of senior military officers, industrial managers, and legislators. Robert McNamara, under the direction of President John Kennedy, organized a formal central-management office to administer the military-industrial empire. The market is now a defined administrative control center that regulates tens of thousands of subordinate managers. . . . By the measure of the scope and scale of its decision-power, the new state-management is by far the largest and most important single management in the United

States. There are about 15,000 men to arrange work assignments to subordinate managers (contract negotiation), and 40,000 who oversee compliance of submanagers of subdivisions with the top management's rules. This is the largest industrial central administrative office in the United States—perhaps in the world.

The state-management has also become the most powerful decision-making unit in the United States government. Thereby, the federal government does not "serve" business or "regulate" business. For the new management is the largest of them all. Government *is* business. That is state capitalism.

The normal operation, including expansion, of the new state-management has been based upon preemption of a lion's share of federal tax revenue and of the nation's finite supply of technical manpower. This use of capital and skill has produced parasitic economic growth—military products which are not part of the level of living and which cannot be used for further production. All this, while the ability to defend the United States, to shield it from external attack, has diminished. . . .

In its beginning, the government of the United States was a political entity. The managing of economic and industrial activity was to be the province of private persons. This division of function was the grand design for American government and society, within which personal and political freedom could flourish alongside of rapid economic growth and technological progress. After 1960, this design was transformed. In the name of ensuring civilian control over the Department of Defense and of obtaining efficiencies of modern management, Secretary of Defense Robert McNamara redesigned the orgnization of his Department to include, within the office of the Secretary, a central administrative office. This was designed to control operations in thousands of subsidiary industrial enterprises undertaken on behalf of the Department of Defense. Modeled after the central administrative offices of multi-division industrial firms—such as the Ford Motor Company, the General Motors Corporation, and the General Electric Company—the new top management in the Department of Defense was designed to control the activities of subsidiary managements of firms producing, in 1968, $44 billion of goods and services for the Department of Defense.

By the measure of industrial activity governed from one central office, this new management in the Department of Defense is beyond compare the largest industrial management in the United States, perhaps in the world. Never before in American experience has there been such a combination of economic and political decision-power in the same hands. The senior officers of the new state-management are also senior political officers of the government of the United States. Thus, one consequence of the establishment of the new state-management has been the installation, within American society, of an institutional feature of a totalitarian system.

The original design of the American government was oriented toward safeguarding individual political freedom and economic liberties. These safeguards were abridged by the establishment of the new state-management in the Department of Defense. In order to perceive the abridgement of traditional liberties by the operation of the new managerial institution, one must focus on its functional performance. For the official titles of its units sound like just another government bureaucracy: Office of the Secretary of Defense, Defense Supply Agency, etc.

The new industrial management has been created in the name of defending America from its external enemies and preserving a way of life of a free society. It has long been understood, however, that one of the safeguards of individual liberty is the separation of roles of a citizen and of an employee. When an individual relates to the same person both as a citizen and as an employee, then the effect is such—regardless of intention—that the employer-government official has an unprecedented combination of decision-making power over the individual citizen-employee.

In the Soviet Union, the combination of top economic and political decision-power is a formal part of the organization and ideology of that society. In the United States, in contrast, the joining of the economic-managerial and top political power has been done in an unannounced and, in effect, covert fashion. In addition to the significance of the new state-management with respect to individual liberty in American society, the new organization is significant for its effects in preempting resources and committing the nation to the military operations that the new organization is designed to serve. Finally, the new power center is important because of the self-powered drive toward expansion that is built into the normal operation of an industrial management.

The preemption of resources take place because of the sheer size of the funds that are wielded by the Department of Defense. Its budget, amounting to over $80 billion in 1969, gives this organization and its industrial-management arm unequalled decision-power over manpower, materials, and industrial production capacity in the United States and abroad. It is, therefore, predictable that this organization will be able to get the people and other resources that it needs whenever it needs them, even if this requires outbidding other industries and other organizations —including other agencies of the federal and other governments.

Regardless of the individual avowals and commitments of the principal officers of the new industrial machine, it is necessarily the case that the increased competence of this organization contributes to the competence of the parent body—the Department of Defense. This competence is a war-making capability. Hence, the very efficiency and success of the new industrial-management, unavoidably and regardless of intention, enhances the war-making capability of the government of the

United States. As the war-making department accumulates diverse resources and planning capability, it is able to offer the President blueprint-stage options for responding to all manner of problem situations—while other government agencies look (and are) unready, understaffed, and underequipped. This increases the likelihood of recourse to "solutions" based upon military power.

Finally, the new government management, insofar as it shares the usual characteristics of industrial management, has a built-in propensity for expanding the scope and intensity of its operations—for this expansion is the hallmark of success in management. The chiefs of the new state-management, in order to be successful in their own eyes, strive to maintain and extend their decision-power—by enlarging their activities, the number of their employees, the size of the capital investments which they control, and by gaining control over more and more subsidiary managements. . . .

. . . Military-industrial complex means a loose, informally defined collection of firms producing military products, senior military officers, and members of the executive and legislative branches of the federal government—all of them united by the market relations of the military products network and having a common ideology as to the importance of maintaining or enlarging the armed forces of the United States and their role in American politics.

The miltary-industrial complex has as its central point an informality of relationships, as befits the market form which underpins its alliances. The understanding, therefore, is that the main interest groups concerned tend to move together, each of them motivated by its own special concerns, but with enough common ground to produce a mutually reinforcing effect. It is noteworthy that neither Eisenhower nor anyone else has suggested that there was a formal organization, or directorate, or executive committee of the military-industrial complex. The new industrial management in the federal government is, by contrast, clearly structured and formally organized, with all the paraphernalia of a formal, centrally managed organization, whose budget draws upon 10 percent of the Gross National Product of the richest nation in the world. . . .

Recently, two writers have developed theories of convergence between military industry and government. Better-known are the ideas of John Kenneth Galbraith, as formulated in his volume *The New Industrial State*. Galbraith states: "Increasingly, it will be recognized that the mature corporation, as it develops, becomes part of the larger administrative complex associated with the state. In time the line between the two will disappear." In this perspective, the major military-industrial firms, as part of the larger family of major enterprises, merges with governmental organization. But this theory does not specify which of the managerial groups involved becomes more important than the other. Indeed, one of the theoretical contributions of *The New Industrial State* is the idea of a "technostructure," a community of technically trained managers operating on behalf of enterprises, public and private, with their movements among these enterprises serving as a bond between public and private institutions. But the technostructure idea homogenizes the men of the managerial-industrial occupations on the basis of their skills and work tasks. This bypasses the fact that an accountant, for example, in the state-management participates in a power-wielding institution of incomparably greater scope than the management of any private firm. Being in the state-management amplifies the significance of his work tasks, which may be qualitatively undifferentiable from those in a private firm.

In a similar vein, a former economist for Boeing, Murray L. Weidenbaum (now Professor of Economics at Washington University), presented another convergence hypothesis before the American Economic Association in December, 1967. In Weidenbaum's view,

> The close, continuing relationship between the military establishment and the major companies serving the military establishment is changing the nature of both the public sector of the American economy and a large branch of American industry. To a substantial degree, the government is taking on the traditional role of the private entrepreneur while the companies are becoming less like other corporations and acquiring much of the characteristics of a government agency or arsenal. In a sense, the close, continuing relationship between the Department of Defense and its major suppliers is resulting in a convergence between the two, which is blurring and reducing much of the distinction between public and private activities in an important branch of the American economy.
> . . . .

SCOPE OF OPERATIONS OF THE STATE-MANAGEMENT

Since its formal organization after 1960 under Robert McNamara, the new state-industrial management has focused attention on military production, its organization and control. At the same time, many Americans, seeing the array of managerial and technical talent deployed in the state-management, have suggested that the same group could apply its talents to organize almost anything—housing, public health, and so forth. Some individuals in the state-management may very well choose to change their employment. Indeed, there has been a sustained turnover, especially in some of the more senior posts of the state-management. Such flexibility does not apply, however, to the organization as an institution. Military organization and military production have special value as a base for the power-extending operations of industrial management.

For a management seeking to enlarge its operations, the military sphere offers the unequaled opportunity to obtain virtually unlimited quantities of fresh capital from the Congress of the United States. This is so because of the "defense" use of this money; the name, Department of Defense, is itself helpful. (Would Congress and the public be equally compliant with a War Department?) Thereby, the state industrial management has an unmatched opportunity for extending its decision-power. . . .

The presumed function of the Department, as the name implies, is that of a Department of Defense—hence, the service to be performed is that of shielding the United States from outside physical attack. However since several countries have acquired nuclear weapons in quantity, defense—in the ordinarily understood sense of that word—is no longer possible. Instead, the United States is engaged in an operation called deterrence—an attempt to forestall a society-destroying war by sustained threat of nuclear counterattack. In September, 1967, Secretary of Defense McNamara discussed the nature of the relationship between the United States and its principal military rival, the Soviet Union:

> The blunt fact is then, that neither the United States nor the Soviet Union can attack the other without being destroyed in retaliation; nor can either of us obtain a first-strike capability in the foreseeable future. (From address to United Press International, San Francisco, September 18, 1967)

Deterrence is not defense. Deterrence is not a shield. Deterrence is an experiment in applied psychology. There is no scientific basis from which to forecast the probability of the success or failure of this experiment. Just imagine the difference in the public and Congressional attitudes with respect to lavish granting of funds if the name were not Department of Defense but Department of Deterrence. In many public addresses and reports, McNamara elaborated on ideas like "deterrence" or "assured destruction capability." At no point did he, or the President of the United States, say plainly to the American people that the nation could no longer be defended. The pre-nuclear promise of defense has sustained reality only in the title of the Department.

Instead of defense, the managers of the Department sell weapons-improvement programs to Congress and to the public. It is constantly implied that as you improve the parts, you improve the whole. Thus, weapons-systems programs are formulated and sold to the appropriate committees of the Congress and to the public on the promise that they are, in each instance, better than what had existed before. The M-16 rifle is thereby better than the M-1 rifle, because it fires more than 10 times as many shots per minute. Minuteman-3 is better than Minuteman-1, since it can carry a larger nuclear explosive and presumably have a greater capability for penetrating conceivable defensive systems. In nuclear as well as conventional weapons, technical improvement reaches a limit called overkill—meaning that, try though they may, even the United States state-management is unlikely to be able to kill more than once. Thus, technical improvement in the overkill range is militarily meaningless, but absolutely vital for sustaining the rule of the state-management over its military-industry empire. That is given first priority, in the name of defense. . . .

. . . The effects from giving priority to the military can be surmounted. This could be done in two ways: first, the drastic regrouping, under central control, of civilian production and other resources; or, second, changing the whole national priorities schedule away from military emphasis. Regrouping of industrial resources could mean, for example, the arbitrary conversion of two of the three major automobile firms, allowing the auto market to be supplied by the remaining firm. Thereby, an enormous block of industrial resources, manpower, and so forth, would be made available for other uses. This is technically conceivable, but it is not socially conceivable as long as the country wishes to have something other than a rigorously state-controlled economy and society. A garrison society, in which the state is empowered to dispose of resources at will, would be able to make this sort of regrouping. But such a regrouping of industrial resources under state control has not been acceptable to the American people except in a war crisis. Within the present political-economic framework, fresh resources for productive economic growth could only be made available by a basic change in national priorities. In detail, that would mean utilizing the federal public-responsibility budget of the nation for other than military priority purposes, which would necessarily involve a major reduction in the decision-power of the state-management. This is why the managers and apologists for the state-management are vigorous in maintaining the mythology of unlimited wealth, unlimited growth, and the absence of a priorities problem in American society. . . .

Even in the wealthiest economy, war expenditures change from economic stimulus to economic damage: first, when the military activity preempts production resources to a degree that limits the ability of the society to supply necessities such as shelter; second, when the military spending causes rapid price inflation, thereby depressing the level of living of all who live on limited incomes; and third, when price inflation disrupts the process of civilian capital investment which requires capability for predicting the worth of a nation's currency.

During the last years, there has been more than a beginning of an understanding that the nation does, in fact, have a priorities problem. But there has been hardly a beginning in preparing for the conversion of resources from military to civilian use. The official economic advisors of the federal government have repeatedly counseled that if there is sufficient advance planning, and the will in Washington to establish a clear set of priorities, then a transition from war to peace activity can be made without great upheaval (*The New York Times,* April 14, 1968). The point is precisely that until now, there has been no advance planning or a will in Washington to establish peace-time priorities, and the lack of will in this realm contrasts sharply with the clear will and the openhanded dedication of resources to the requirements of the state-managerial machine.

Many lines of evidence contribute to the conclusion that both recognition and denial of a national priorities problem cuts across conventional political lines. Support of the state-management and its functioning in the name of defense is independent not only of party, but also of personalities. The Kennedy administration was formally Democratic, but the architect of the present military machine, and its operating chief from 1961 to 1968, was a Republican, Robert McNamara. Support for the plans and the budgets of the state-management have come from both major parties in the Congress. At the same time, there has been a fair amount of turnover in the persons holding key posts at the top of the state-management.

Indeed, the very openness of operations of the state machine is one of its great sources of strength. Thus, no conspiracy, in the ordinary sense of the word, was required to get the American people to accept the myth of the missile gap and the subsequent major capital outlays for an overkill nuclear war program. The American people were sold on the myth and thought they were buying defense. Nor is a conspiracy required to secure fresh capital funds of unprecedented size for further expansion of the state-management. This is agreed to by a Congress and a public that has been taught to believe that all this activity is for defense and that it stimulates the economy of a society that can enjoy both guns and butter. In all of this, the controlling factor is not a political party or a single political theory, not a personality, not a conspiracy: the existence and normal operation of the Pentagon's management-institution dominates and gives continuity of direction.

The government of the United States now includes a self-expanding war machine that uses military power for diverse political operations and is based upon an industrial management that has priority claims to virtually unlimited capital funds from the federal budget. The state-management is economically parasitic, hence exploitative, in its relation to American society at home. The military-political operations of the Pentagon chieftains abroad, following the pattern of the Vietnam wars program, are parasitic there as well. To the older pattern of exploitative imperialism abroad, there is now added an institutional network that is parasitic at home. This combination is the new imperialism.

Larry T. Reynolds
Terry Lundgren

33

Corporate Capitalism
and Militarization

THE THESIS BRIEFLY STATED

The United States recently withdrew from an undeclared war in Vietnam. Although the conflict lasted well over a decade, a military victory was not achieved.[1] Yet, the United States, with the support of its militarily weaker allies, brought the Axis military behemoth to heel in less than six years. American military might has greatly increased since World War II; nevertheless, the United States has consistently failed to achieve a military victory over such powers as North Vietnam and North Korea, whose military strength pales in comparison to that of the 1940s Axis alliance. This essay addresses itself to this paradox by focusing on two key questions: 1) Why, since the end of World War II, has the United States been so regularly involved in warfare? and 2) Why do these involvements fail to result in military victories? While these appear here as two separate and distinct questions, to answer the first is to effectually answer the second.

Briefly stated, the answer to the first question is that the United States becomes militarily involved because the waging of war serves to maintain the American corporate capitalist system as it is presently organized. The currently dominant sector of the U.S. economy is composed of giant defense (or defense-related) industries. Such industries grow and increase their profits during periods of open hostility. Furthermore, a firm, self-serving commitment to the protection and growth of these military industries is the primary interest of the group C. Wright Mills termed *the power elite*.[2] In short, war is waged because it is both profitable for the power elite and necessary to maintain the defense industry form of corporate capitalism as the dominant structural feature

This article has appeared previously in other forms. See endnote 1.

of the American economy. To maintain the contemporary corporate state is to maintain the power elite. The answer to the second question, indeed, flows out of the answer to the first: U.S. forces do not attain military victories because it is not in the economic interest of those who own and control our defense and defense-related industries to do so.[3]

THE HISTORICAL BACKGROUND OF AMERICAN INVOLVEMENT IN SOUTHEAST ASIA

The remainder of this article deals with an analysis of America's most recent military involvement in Southeast Asia. It will be shown how the structural features of American society made this involvement not only profitable but also economically useful for the survival of our current form of economic organization. Before proceeding to such an analysis of American society, we shall provide a brief historical background by tracing the state of affairs in Southeast Asia from the French to the American involvement. Before World War II, those political units known today as Cambodia, Laos, North Vietnam, and South Vietnam were collectively referred to as Indochina. Practically speaking, this area came under French control in the year 1893. Initially, the Laotians and Cambodians had turned to France in seeking protection from Thailand (then Siam).[4] The Vietnamese, however, had resisted such "phony protection" from the very beginning.

Prior to the Second World War, Alexandre Varenne, ex-Governor General of Indochina, remarked, "It (Indochina) was not really a colony at all. It was an empire."[5] The reason Varenne conceived of Indochina as an empire can be readily gleaned from the following statement:

> Indochina was the third most important exporter of rice in the world and it also exported large quantities of rubber and corn. Its wealth was not only in agriculture, but also in minerals and timber; it had anthracite coal (most of which it exported) as well as iron ore, tin, manganese and wolfram (tungsten). And it was one of the few colonies in the French Empire to export more than it imported.[6]

Indochina's economic potential was realized fully as well by the United States as it was by the French. On February 12, 1950, a *New York Times* editorial stated:

> Indo-China is a prize worth a large gamble. In the north are exportable tin, tungsten, manganese, coal, lumber and rice: rubber, tea, pepper and hides. Even before World War II Indo-China yielded dividends estimated at $300 million per year.

The following year a State Department spokesman noted:

> We have only partially exploited Southeast Asia's resources. Nevertheless, Southeast Asia supplied 90% of the world's crude rubber, 60% of its tin, and 80% of its copra and coconut oil. It has sizable quantities of sugar, tea, coffee, tobacco, sisal, fruits, spices, natural resins and gums, petroleum, iron, oil and bauxite.[7]

With the French awareness of Indochina's vast economic potential, by 1938 foreign investments in Indochina were valued at almost $400,000,000; nearly 95 percent of these investments were French.[8]

Besides its economic potential, Southeast Asia is also strategically located. It is, as the old song says, on the road to Mandalay, and the Japanese lost no time in occupying it during World War II. There was brief French resistance, but as Paris was soon Vichy, the French in Southeast Asia technically became allies of the Japanese. The Vietnamese Nationalists, however, who had resisted the French in the 1920s and 1930s, put up stiff resistance to the Japanese. In May of 1941, several of these nationalist groups united under the leadership of Ho Chi Minh and the banner of "The League of Independence," more commonly called the Viet Minh.[9] The United States Office of Strategic Services assisted Ho Chi Minh and his group of nationalists. The Viet Minh fought the Japanese and Vichy French with the consequence that by August 18, 1945, the Vietnamese Nationalists controlled all key government posts.[10]

For the Viet Minh, however, this warfare represents a race against colonialism which they lost. British occupation forces arrived to accept the surrender of the Japanese authorities. They promptly used the Japanese and Vichy French to wrest control of Saigon away from their own "allies," the Viet Minh. By September 23, 1945, Saigon was once again in French hands. Disagreements between the French and Viet Minh culminated in war by December of 1946. After eight years of intense warfare, the French were defeated. An international conference was then held to determine the destiny of Vietnam in Geneva.

This conference divided Vietnam into two zones at the 17th parallel, ended the fighting, and set up the apparatus for the unification of Vietnam through free elections.[11] Little was ever done, however, to augment these Geneva Accords of 1954. Interestingly enough, two of the major powers concerned, the United States and the Chinese Peoples Republic, did not sign the agreement.

What was the United States doing with respect to Vietnam during this same period? Until February of 1950, when we recognized the French puppet government, the United States had more or less ignored

Vietnam. Then, on June 27, 1950, President Truman announced that he had "directed acceleration in the furnishing of military assistance to the forces of France and the associated States in Indochina and the dispatch of a military mission to provide close working relations with those forces."[12] American aid to France rapidly picked up; from 1950 to 1954, the United States gave the French military command in Vietnam $2.6 billion, approximately 80 percent of the cost of the war for that period.[13] Thus the United States actively participated in the military defeat of her former allies, the Viet Minh. We then cast about for a replace-to Bao Dai, the French puppet sovereign of Vietnam. Consequently, American policy centered on Ngo Dinh Diem.[14] By 1955, Diem was entrenched. We were now economically, politically, and militarily involved in Vietnam and in Southeast Asia.

ECONOMIC AND SOCIAL ANALYSIS OF OUR INVOLVEMENT IN SOUTHEAST ASIA

The time has come to explain in greater detail just why this initial U.S. involvement in Vietnam was the inevitable and expected consequence of the structure of American society—and why no military victory was achieved.

It should be noted at this point that the analysis here is cast along both economic and sociological lines, but these two forms of analysis overlap, for the economic argument merely augments the sociological one.

The basic assumption of the economic argument is that the maintenance of corporate capitalism depends upon the continual growth of the economic system. This need for growth is especially evident in the capital investment sector of our economy because of the nature of the relationship between investment and consumer expenditures in the system. Under such a system, as consumption increases, either new industries must emerge or existing industries must expand. Either course results in an increased demand for investment goods, with a concomitant production of those goods. These goods are highly durable, that is, they are slowly consumed (as with machines), and, being high priced, they reflect a considerable proportion of the economy's consumption expenditures.

Now let us examine the situation when the demand for such investment goods (machines, plants, etc.) levels off. Such a situation eliminates the need for new investment expenditures, except for those expenditures necessary to replenish existing equipment. Since the existing equipment is extremely durable, the replenishment expenditures will account for very little when compared to the original expenditures made when consumption was climbing. This situation results in the loss of considerable income for the investment goods industry, with the result that many businesses in this industry "go under." Included in this sector of industry is a considerable proportion of the total U.S. economy, a sector in which a high degree of wealth is concentrated.

As both the multiplier[15] and the accelerator[16] effects operate during expansion and recession of the economy, a leveling off of consumer expenditures results not only in a drastic decrease in income for the capital investment sector of the economy (due to the accelerator effect), but also in the removal of an even larger amount of wealth from the economy (due to the multiplier effect). One well known economist concludes: "It is now clear that a depression can set in just because consumption has stopped growing so rapidly, even if it has not dropped off absolutely, but only leveled off at a high level."[17]

Some economists argue that this analysis is invalid because it is couched in neoclassical terms. However, the same conclusion may be drawn by comparing the data available concerning investment, consumption, and measures of growth such as the Gross National Product. The conclusion is, of course, that continuous growth is necessary to prevent the collapse of the economic system.

Such economic growth almost always involves consumption. Consumption here refers to economic consumption, i.e., the permanent removal of economic goods from the marketplace. Thus, at any given point in time, dumping milk in the ocean, burying potatoes, or storing food surpluses may be viewed as consumption. Also included as consumption would be a shot-down fighter plane, expended ammunition, dropped bombs, and military aid.

Given that growth is a necessary condition for the viability of our current economic system, how may such growth occur? Clearly, the most obvious solution is to increase consumption. Assuming a relatively stable distribution of income,[18] various studies on the economy of abundance show that the consumer's ability to increase his marginal propensity to consume[19] is rapidly reaching the saturation point, where it is physically impossible to consume more present products. Planned obsolescence is one method of increasing consumption. The more rapid consumption of present products is useful because it involves less investment expenditures than the production and consumption of new types of goods.[20] Planned obsolescence, in the conventional sense of the term, has not been a total solution for increasing consumption because, for example, it is difficult to convince a housewife that her new washing machine should be built to last only six months. If planned obsolescence is expanded to include the commodities of war, however, the task of convincing the consumer is relatively easy. In this case the consumer is the government, of course, while the worker himself only purchases the products he makes to the extent that he pays taxes.

Traditionally, capitalism has embodied a "Say's Law" orientation, i.e., that supply tends to create its own demand. Although neoclassical economics has disproved the validity of this formulation, it has until recently retained at least a modicum of truth. Essentially, the factual element here is that the workers traditionally have constituted a large segment of the consumer market. The myth is still being perpetuated that production is designed to meet the needs of the "man in the street." If this were in fact the case, then population increases, coupled with the rise in real income over time, would be entirely sufficient to generate the necessary growth. The rate of population growth in the United States, however, is approaching replacement levels, i.e., zero population growth. Additionally, the highest rates of population increase are in precisely those segments of our population which have the least ability to consume, the lower classes. But these considerations are irrelevant to the structural shift in our society from *laissez-faire* capitalism to our current form of corporate capitalism, one dominated by the defense industries. Under corporate capitalism, consumption is predominately located in the governmental sphere, not in the workers. Since 1953, government spending has averaged about 36 percent of *total* national income, with the *largest single* expenditure being defense spending. Indeed, there is evidence that this percentage is increasing.[21]

The major contention of the sociological argument is the Millsian hypothesis of the existence of a power elite in American society. According to C. Wright Mills, this elite is composed of selected segments of the economic, political, and military orders. As Mills devotes a large portion of his book, *The Power Elite*, to describing the multi-bonded network of relations which exist with respect to the members of this clique, we need only spell out some of the implications of this "alliance" for American military involvement.

With respect to the role of the military sector of the power elite, the military assets in the United States are three times as great as the combined assets of United States Steel, Metropolitan Life, A. T. & T., General Motors, and Standard Oil. By the year 1960, $21 billion was being spent on military goods. About one-third of this amount was being divided among just ten of our corporations. Five of these corporations received a billion dollars or more apiece. Significantly, in the executive offices of these same corporations, sat 1,400 former military officers, 261 of whom were generals and officers of flag rank. One corporation alone, General Dynamics, had on its payroll 187 officers, twenty-seven generals and admirals, and the former secretary of the army.[22] Fifteen years later, we can note that these same favored corporations still receive the bear's share of the prime defense contract awards. They have grown tremendously in organizational size, and they have added many more former high ranking military officers to their payrolls.

By viewing the staggering sums of money spent on war arms and supplies, which are awarded in the form of contracts to corporations on whose boards of directors these high echelon officers sit (often the very ones making demands for such weaponry), we can see that giant industry and the top echelons of the United States military have formed an interlocking alliance. This interlocking alliance further consolidates their power and maximizes their profits. Even the "establishment sociologist" Morris Janowitz has stated:

> Within the defense contract industries . . . particularly aircraft, missiles, shipbuilding and to less extent, electronics . . . the presence of retired military officers is widespread and indicates a new type of interlocking between industry and the military establishment. All of the major aircraft and missile companies employ retired admirals and generals in key management posts; their duties involve both internal management and liaison in Washington. In June 1959, Senator Paul Douglas made public a list of 768 former military officers of the rank of colonel, naval captain and above who were in the employ of the 100 companies and their 153 subsidiaries which in the period from July 1, 1957, to June 30, 1958, received 74.2 percent of all military prime contract awards.[23]

The above described state of affairs has much in common with the situation which existed in Nazi Germany. Hitler himself had said that Germany must export or die, and war as a major form of market consumption gave national socialism economic growth and stability. In reference to Hitler's Germany, C. Wright Mills notes:

> In the trade policy, as well as in war; if we may so distinguish, the political and economic elites see eye to eye. Here there is an identity of interests and aims among the divisions of the ruling classes. The Nazi elite have further consolidated themselves, as have managers, by climbing, via political power, into the ownership of heavy industry.[24]

In the light of the foregoing descriptions of the current structure of American society, and especially of its economic institution, what can we conclude? Given 1) the basic economic tenet that in a capitalist economy continuous growth is necessary to prevent the collapse of that system; 2) the fact that defense and defense-related industries are the largest single sector of the current American economy; 3) that government spending is the largest single source of spending in the economy; and 4) that the largest single element of the national budget is defense spending; these premises, taken in conjunction with the cold war and nation-state cultural contexts, mean that warfare has become a major way of maintaining the economy, one which provides the most cultural justification and encounters the least structural resistance.[25] Tersely stated, war is the most feasible method through which to insure both the growth of the American economy and the maintenance of a defense industry based corporate system.

Notice that we do not endorse the extreme conspiracy theory, i.e., that the power elite always deliberately and rationally conspires to increase its holdings at the expense of the rest of society. Such a perspective is too naïve in its simplistic notions of the distribution of power and in its picture of human nature. We are suggesting, rather, that given the basic economic problem of the need of growth, to maintain corporate capitalism, the structural characteristics of American society result in militarization as a high probability solution.

WHY A "SMALL" WAR IN SOUTHEAST ASIA INSTEAD OF A LARGE ONE ELSEWHERE?

We have now discussed in some length just how the United States became involved in Southeast Asia and why a military victory was not attained. But the discussion to this point has not been sufficiently detailed. Other questions need to be raised in order to supplement the foregoing analysis. We need to ask such things as why a "small" war in Southeast Asia instead of a large one somewhere else? How is it that the defense industries reap such fantastically huge profits? Does the war provide "solutions" to domestic problems? Why is war preferred as a form of economic expansion rather than alternative mechanisms for promoting economic growth?

There are a number of reasons why defense industries realize disproportionate profits. One reason is that "defense industry" is a highly technological industry subject to high rates of technological "change." This change requires the retooling and redirection of the entire industry. This constantly justifies, or so we are told, "retooling" expenditures in addition to "normal" expenditures. New rationales have been developed recently which see "guerilla wars" as being so different from the type of war the economy is supposedly geared for, that the defense industries must now be completely retooled. When the government picks up the tab for such retooling and/or gives huge tax write-offs when such retooling is done, then the company affected has increased the size of its physical plant, updated its production equipment, and is guaranteed future contracts—all at no expense to itself. What lies ahead for such a company is something approximating "pure profit."

In spite of the immense wealth of the United States, millions of Americans live at the poverty level.[26] It is precisely for this reason that what we have referred to as the industrial-military complex is in reality the industrial-military-political complex. Members of the industrial-military combine and their protegés also sit in positions of power in the body politic. In this capacity, members of this triumvirate are in a position to 1) formally articulate the false need for increased arms through what members of the society take to be the "proper channels,"[27] 2) insure that the supply of arms for their self-created demand is handled by the corporate interests which they represent and of which they are part and parcel, and 3) "cool out the marks," that is, to placate and, in other ways, to con those millions who are forced to live at the poverty level because the industrial-military-political complex has taken control of American society and has twisted its institutional fabric into a hideous arsenal for a world economic empire. Because a seemingly effective way to "cool the mark out" is to convince him that a war is being fought to stop the spread of communism, coupled with there being reason to believe that members of the military-political-industrial complex sincerely feel that this is just what they are about, seem to present confirming evidence for Mills' power elite hypothesis. *Whether the power elite is consciously exploiting their fellow humans, or whether they feel that they are waging a "just" war to stop the spread of what they take to be a grotesque alien ideology, is totally irrelevant to the fact that corporate capitalism, when working at its best and in its healthiest form, demands increased growth (consumption) at all costs, lest the system fall apart.*

Actual war has a profit-increasing effect on defense and defense-related industries, whereas the threat of war is simply not as safe an economic bet. But large scale, all-out wars do not typically last long, and as a continuous war is needed for continuous growth, small wars are better from the capitalist's perspective. Thus, small scale wars become the more feasible structural alternative. But as the defense industries continue to grow, more wars are needed. Again, from the power elite's vantage point, several small wars are more economically advantageous than one large scale conflict. Large wars are wars which tend to be either won or lost, and won or lost in years and not in decades. The defense industries reap their profits in the fighting of wars—not in the winning or losing of them. Furthermore, war tends to maintain a steady or creeping inflation. Such inflation is supported by vested interests because it effectively reduces the cost of new and old investments. Thus, it is in the interest of the military-political-economic combine to maintain both inflation and war.

The foregoing arguments suggest that a decision to enter a war is fruitful from a purely political perspective on the domestic situation. The possibility of a war in Vietnam was studied and planned for many years before we entered it. Thus, the decision was made not only in terms of foreign interests, but also in terms of the domestic interests of those in power. Remember also that the Vietnamese-Cambodian-Laotian war was fought during a period of heightened concern over racism and poverty. The war provided certain "solutions" to these problems as well. The "solution" was, of course, to ignore them while contending that such issues would be dealt with in due course—as soon as the pressing business of the war was "taken care of." The original decision to enter the war in Vietnam left the way open for gradual escalation, and both Johnson and Nixon appeared to escalate at just those times when the problems of poverty and racism became most pressing.

WHY NOT OTHER ALTERNATIVES?

We might ask ourselves, are there feasible alternatives to war as mechanisms for fostering economic growth? Many alternatives have been proposed: 1) increases in public works projects such as the Works Progress Administration, 2) a redoubled effort at pollution control and environmentalism, and 3) more money pumped into the space program. Yet, each of these alternatives is proposed in a social vacuum. Each assumes that the defense and defense-related industries, and the power elite which supports these interests, are either nonexistent or that they would be willing to undergo whatever changes in their political and economic power positions are necessitated by the alternatives proposed. They assume that those who rule the welfare-warfare state are willing, if not eager, to take economic risks when warfare is a more certain economic bet. They would have us believe that the power elite feels that a bird or two in the bush is better than one in the hand. Simply stated, such alternatives are utopian.

Other alternatives likewise seem futile. We might buy new markets as we did in the case of Alaska, but this avenue is rapidly closing, if not shut, for the known exploitable markets are presently owned and not open for sale. We might annex new markets, though this, too, is rapidly dwindling as an alternative. Hawaii was probably our last successful annexation of a market.

Lastly, all of the above alternatives are truly utopian because they assume that economic growth can be delayed when to do so invites disaster. The fact is that *our economic system demands that profit be made on investment now.* There is no existing mechanism for delayed gratification on a societal level in capitalism as there is in socialism.

CONCLUSION

Let us consider now, given all the above assumptions and conclusions, just what type of war is most compatible with the current structure of American economy and the interests of its ruling class. First, from the viewpoint of the ruling class, it would be "best" to have a highly ideologically committed enemy who would fight for many years under poor conditions and destroy (consume) the products of American military production with all sorts of homemade and captured (consumed) weapons. Thus, tremendous demand is created for military production and expenditures. In short, the defense industry capitalists want a fairly small, drawn-out war which has little chance of resulting in a nuclear holocaust and yet is, at the same time, expensive. Second, an Asian war would be "nice" from the power elite's perspective because it has the fewest negative ethnic overtones. In other words, there is less domestic empathy for the Asians than there would be for the "enemy" if he were European. Hence, small but continuous Asian wars are not only sufficient, but from the ruling class perspective, they are ideal. And because they are "ideal," we may well expect to be continually engaged in a running series of such wars (declared or undeclared) for quite some time.

ADDENDUM

The major propositions in this article were developed in 1965. Now, these many years later, we have an opportunity to assess their validity. The war in Southeast Asia has ended without a military victory. Our economy is experiencing serious trouble. Growth is being barely maintained. It should be noted here that an aspect of short term growth, not explicated in our original analysis, occurs through the raising of real prices for economic goods via "shortages."

The question now is not *will* we become militarily involved, but *where* and *how soon* the involvement will occur. The United States recently agreed to sell Saudi Arabia $750 million worth of fighter planes, spare parts, training, etc. Kissinger is trying to negotiate peace between Israel and Egypt. Senior American military officers are considering the "feasibility" of seizing selected Middle East oil fields, and much more.[28] We suggest the Middle East as a high probability area for United States military involvement as such involvement fits our analysis quite well. The next possibility is the volatile Latin American countries. These are not idle speculations, for the United States has already started the war process in these places by providing military "advisers" and military aid. Unless unanticipated major structural changes occur, we can, undoubtedly, expect such continued military involvement.

ENDNOTES

1. This paper is a modified version of an article written in 1965 and published in the *Structuralist, 1*, (November, 1967): 64–74 (with J. V. Bunnell and E. M. Poston) and published with re-

visions in the First Edition of *Social Problems in American Society*, 1973, pp. 325–338, and in *Down to Earth Sociology*, James M. Henslin, ed., New York: The Free Press, 1972, pp. 363–374.

2. See C. Wright Mills, *The Power Elite* (New York: Oxford University Press, 1959).

3. Under colonial (laissez-faire) capitalism, wars were fought in the quest for empire (market). The motto of defense industry, corporate capitalism, on the other hand, is the old liberal cliché, "It's not whether you win or lose, but how you play the game," or as it reads in translation "profits are not maximized and shakey structures firmed by winning or losing wars but merely by fighting them." It does not appear to lose much in the translation.

4. See E. J. Hammer, *The Struggle for Indochina* (Stanford: Stanford University Press, 1954); pp. 11–13.

5. *Ibid.*, p. 11.

6. *Ibid.*, p. 13.

7. Quoted by Bertrand Russell in "Bertrand Russell's Appeal to the American Conscience on Vietnam," *National Guardian*, July 30, 1966.

8. Hammer, *op. cit.*, p. 14.

9. P. Warner, *The Last Confucian: Vietnam, Southeast Asia and the West* (Baltimore: Penguin Books, 1964); p. 46.

10. *Ibid.*, pp. 48–49.

11. R. Scheer, *How the United States Got Involved in Vietnam* (Santa Barbara: Center for the Study of Democratic Institutions, 1965), p. 16.

12. *Ibid.*, p. 10.

13. *Ibid.*, p. 10.

14. See Warner, *op. cit.*, pp. 105–106 and Scheer, *op. cit.*, p. 12.

15. The term "multiplier effect" is here used as it is defined by Paul Samuelson ". . . an increase in net investment will increase national income by a multiplied amount—by an amount greater than itself! . . . This amplified effect of investment on income is called the 'multiplier' doctrine; the word 'multiplier' itself is used for the numerical coefficient showing how great an increase in income results from each increase in such investment spending." See P. A. Samuelson, *Economics: An Introductory Analysis* (New York: McGraw-Hill, 1961), pp. 266–267.

16. Samuelson, commenting on the acceleration principle's tendency to cut both ways, as does the multiplier principle, notes that in periods of economic upswing the accelerator produces "a tremendous increase in investment spending as a result of a moderate increase in consumption sales." *Ibid.*, p. 297. Working in the reverse direction, if sales drop, or even level off, the acceleration principle operates in such a way that gross investment will drop altogether.

17. *Ibid.*, p. 297.

18. It has been shown that the distribution of income in the United States has been remarkably stable since 1910; indeed, such sta-

bility is a hallmark of corporate capitalism. See, for example, G. Kolko, 1962, *Wealth and Power in America.*

19. Samuelson defines marginal propensity to consume as ". . . extra amount that people will want to spend on consumption if given an extra dollar of income." *Ibid.,* p. 249.
20. See, for example, Vance Packard, *The Waste Makers* (New York: The David McKay Co., Inc., 1964).
21. G. Warren Nutter, "Where Are We Headed?", *The Wall Street Journal,* January 10, 1975, p. 8.
22. Russell, *op. cit.*
23. M. Janowitz, *The Professional Soldier* (New York: The Free Press, 1960); p. 376. By 1969, 2,072 retired military officers were employed by the largest hundred corporations, with half of them employed by the largest ten defense contractors. See Adam Garmolinsky, *The Military Establishment: Its Impact on American Society* (New York: Perennial Library, 1973), p. 73.
24. C. W. Mills, *Power, Politics and People* (New York: Ballantine Books, 1963); p. 175.
25. See "L.B.J.'s Budget and Its New Math," *Newsweek,* February 6, 1967; pp. 30–32.
26. See M. Harrington, *The Other America: Poverty in the United States* (New York: Penguin Books, 1962).
27. For an analysis of how this group presents false alternatives and uses scare tactics to increase military expenditures, see Seymour Melman, *Pentagon Capitalism,* New York: McGraw-Hill Book Company, 1972. The preceding selection in this volume is taken from Melman's book.
28. See any recent large circulation newspaper, for example, *The New York Times,* circa January, 1975.

Concluding Comments

James M. Henslin

34

Social Problems
and Systemic Origins

From the selections in this volume, it should be readily apparent that many sociologists and other social scientists are both concerned and pessimistic about the current state and direction of contemporary events in American society. Both concern and pessimism appear well founded, and I hope that these selections have communicated to the readers of this book at least part of the bases for such convictions. In this summary, I shall briefly pull together some of the major themes that have run through these selections.

Our social system is set up to maintain the wealthy in their positions of power and privilege. Although ours is one of the wealthiest countries in the world, we always have poverty. In spite of the vast technical and natural resources available to us that could well eliminate poverty if they were so applied, poverty remains. This is not accidental. Nor is there something about our poor that keeps them in poverty, although this is the myth that the controllers of our social order would have us believe because it focuses attention away from the social system onto individuals. But to concentrate on the oppressed, instead of the oppressors, does not get us to the root of the problem of poverty.

The simple truth is that people are poor because they are made poor. They are systemically discriminated against. That is, our social institutions are interrelated in such a way that certain classes of our people are kept from opportunities that might otherwise change their poverty state. Few people like to remain in poverty. Most find it a disgusting, loathsome, and humiliating experience that enshrouds their lives with uncertainty and anxiety. Most would readily choose a lifestyle that provided them security and material well-being—if, indeed, they had such a choice.

Yet poverty has become a way of life for millions of our citizens, in spite of the wealth about which Americans are so eager to boast. The poor who are lazy (and I only mention this because it is the most common myth put forward to account for poverty) are made lazy. Those who become indolent do not lose creative drive because they enjoy poverty, but because they find that whatever energies they direct to getting out from under the burden of poverty are uselessly deflected. They learn that they cannot get out of poverty by their own efforts because the deck is stacked against them. This realization drives them to despair and debilitates energies and ambitions.

The American educational system is an essential part of this stacked deck with which the poor are forced to play. School systems which the poor attend are underfinanced when compared with those of the wealthy. Their education is inferior. And with an inferior education, their opportunities are sharply curtailed. Their law-breaking activities are more likely to come to the attention of the police, as the police carry stereotypes which castigate the poor. The jobs open to them are the unskilled positions, which are low paying and from which they are quickly fired in times of economic crisis. They are systematically undercounted by the government, for they are of little consequence to those who count (pun intended). With the social system directed against them, they stay in poverty, as do their children.

In contrast, the social system is sharply biased in favor of those who already enjoy privilege. Children of the privileged attend the better schools and receive a superior education. The educational system selectively recruits them for the elite positions in our society through systematic testing that favors their backgrounds and orientations. Their law-breaking activities are less likely to come to the attention of the police, for white collar crime is more likely to be what they get involved in, and their corporate employers usually handle such matters more informally. If their activities are brought to the attention of the police, they are treated less harshly before the bar of justice, being more likely to receive suspended and reduced sentences—because they are the "right kind of people" who can be depended on to "go straight" after their "mistake."

Because American minority groups are more highly represented among the lower social classes than their numbers in the population, all of these factors operate to their disadvantage. The social class discrimination built into our social system works to keep a large proportion of American minorities in poverty. It maintains discrimination and poverty over generations. The "freedom" given to blacks during the Civil War was a myth, for without the opportunity to live as a free person, one cannot really be free—regardless what a piece of paper says. One can, of course, be free to live in poverty, but this is not even a freedom unless one is also free to *not* live in poverty. And this option has never been offered blacks—or Indians, or Chicanos, or Puerto Ricans.

The intolerance characterizing our society manifests itself in racial discrimination and prejudice. Persons whose skin color differs from the highly desired paleness of the Anglos are marked (literally!) for discriminatory treatment in such diverse areas as housing, education, employment, and jury duty. Mexican-Americans, blacks, Indians, and Orientals to perhaps a lesser degree, find themselves on the receiving end of a social system designed to exalt Anglo appearances, beliefs, values, and behavioral characteristics.

To look differently, to act differently, or to believe differently, is perilous in our society today. Such people are sometimes threatened or cajoled. At other times, they are imprisoned or killed; but for certain they find themselves in a system which brutalizes the individual, prevents the development of the "full person" with all of his or her potential, and systemically discriminates on the basis of ethnic or racial membership.

By "systemic," then, is meant that the various parts of the social system have built into them particular ways of acting and reacting. Structured into the institutions of our society is the discrimination minority groups face. This shows up in general tendencies or practices in hiring, firing, and promotion, to mention just the employment sector of our society. Other major social institutions reinforce or buttress these same practices. While the discrimination a particular member of a minority group faces may have many idiosyncratic aspects about it, general tendencies are built into our social institutions which guarantee discriminatory practices apart from the personal predilections of any particular individual. When discrimination is systemic, in other words, it is not merely the result of prejudicial action by individuals, although this is also involved, but it is built into the very institutions of the society.

Prejudiced individuals are themselves the product of such systemic discrimination: systemic or institutionalized discrimination produces people who are intolerant, people who believe that they and their ways are superior, and who believe that those who have less than themselves have less because they deserve it. Consequently, systemic discrimination brutalizes and dehumanizes those against whom the discrimination is directed. Once discrimination is built into a social system, discrimination and intolerance tend to perpetuate themselves. Their continuance does not depend upon the adventitious existence of individuals who believe the system should continue in a certain way. To abolish such discrimination is not a matter of changing the "hearts" of individuals, as many believe, but rather because this discrimination is systemic it would take either a thorough overhauling of the system itself or the replacement of the system with another.

The history of subservience of women goes back farther than any other single group in the world. They have been objects of discrimination in almost all cultures in almost all historical time. Men are biologically stronger, and they have systematically used their strength to sub-jugate women and make them obedient to their will and desires. Women have been the traditional captives of war, prizes to be brought home for domestic servitude. They have been possessions of men, who could do with them as they pleased. Only in the rare culture or society has this not been the case.

The situation for women in American society has been little differ-ent. There have been certain American trappings that have given the appearance of nonsubjugation, but they have been trappings only, decorations added that disguise the real situation. And women were fooled for centuries. They learned to believe the myth of masculine su-periority so forcefully taught by the dominant *Homo sapien* male— but no longer. Women are learning to throw off the yoke they have so uncomfortably worn. They are beginning to *demand* equality, and it is unlikely that they will take no for an answer. It is unlikely that they will ever again be content with the kitchen and bedroom, with houseclean-ing and church. The Küche, Kirche, and Kinder complex belongs to a bygone era, and it is doubtful that women shall ever again experience this type of subjugation in our society. Their freedom is certainly far from complete, but it is on the way.

Myths help maintain the social system and protect prevailing power relationships. These myths cover our eyes: we tend to see reality around us through the myths we are taught. Social myths help control a popu-lace by 1) directing attention to particular aspects of social life, 2) di-recting attention away from other aspects of society, and 3) providing a framework for interpreting what is experienced. By altering percep-tion, social myths make people more willing to accept the status quo and less inclined to demand social change.

Even the old find themselves on the receiving end of the discrimina-tion directed against those who represent disvalued commodities in American culture. They are forced out of their jobs by mandatory re-tirement laws, and contrary to the common myths they do not enter the peaceful, green pastures of leisure. They enter a period of cultural disengagement in which they are forced to withdraw from active par-ticipation in the labor market and in which they must also withdraw claim on what it means to be a vibrant, living, joyful human being. They enter a statusless period that is but a prelude to an uneasy death. And that is what we call retirement American style.

This is not much to look forward to after a lifetime of work. I do not suppose anyone relishes a fixed income with inflation cannibalizing the little one does have. But our social system is set up in such a way that even the old and sick and impoverished are systemically victimized.

At the root of systemic victimization in our society is our particular form of economy. We once had a form of economy known as *laissez-faire* capitalism. This literally meant a "hands off" policy by the government. Private enterprise was to be allowed to exercise its will because private enterprise represented the good of the citizens and country. We never had such an economic form, of course, except in American mythology, such as that perpetuated by our educational system. Some forms of capitalism always received government handouts in the form of land grants, government purchases, right of ways, and so on. These were the capitalists who had a voice in the power centers of state capitals and Washington.

They were used to their fullest. The "robber barons" of a bygone day garnered every public resource they could into their ever-expanding private storehouses. Fortunes were made, and passed on to the next generation. Wealth was accumulated. Businesses were added to businesses, until mighty corporations grew and industrial holdings multiplied. Interlocking directorships were developed to multiply power. And corporations became international in scope. Today these corporate elites direct a financial empire that stretches around the globe, with hardly a hamlet in the world not feeling their effect.

The basic motive for corporate being and corporate expansion is money—and the power and privilege that wealth brings. Like the robber barons of the past, today's corporate barons direct an empire. They, too, rape and pillage public resources for their own ends—but with experience has come a refinement that has made their greed somewhat more sophisticated for contemporary society. Only now, with worldwide outreach, they have gained a monopoly so broad in scope that they can control the marketing and pricing of basic commodities such as sugar, and resources such as coal. All is done in the name of profits, regardless of the consequence to others—and the consequences are serious indeed. The rape of resources and pillage for profits has resulted in a polluted world, a world whose parts are so precariously balanced that we do not know even at this moment whether or not our planet's life-support system has been irrevocably ruptured.

For our survival, it is not simply a matter of instituting a few controls over resource usage and allocation. It appears, rather, to be a matter of holding growth in check, not simply population growth, although that is a part of it, but also industrial growth. No longer can we permit urban sprawl and pride in a growing gross national product, for these represent losses. Such "gains" in standards of living are but ephemeral if they represent the destruction of the life-support system of this spaceship earth. Difficult but realistic choices that take the entire eco-system into account must be made.

But such choices directly contradict our basic economic orientation, and we have been so carefully schooled as to never doubt or question its basic premises. Those who are now in control of our society will not make such choices. And our other major social institutions remain subservient to the economic. Not only education, but also science and or-

ganized religion and the family serve the corporate elite. And under the
direction of the corporate elite, the course is clear: continuance on the
same path. For our corporate elite has been so schooled in profits that
they are blind to anything else.

With all the social problems facing us—those features of the "everyday life" of the corporate state such as pollution, discrimination, prejudice, sexism, racism, ageism, overpopulation, poverty, and war,—the
overarching one which makes the others pale by comparison, and
around which the others appear to revolve today, is that of the merged
interests of the industrial, political, and military sectors of our society.
This did not come suddenly upon us, as a generation ago FDR pointed
out the "grave menace" of the munitions industry in setting foreign
policy (*Congressional Quarterly Weekly Report, 1964,* 6, pp. 265–278).
As President Eisenhower left office, he warned us about the "unwarranted influence" of these coalescing interests. And the sociologist C.
Wright Mills analyzed the coming together of these three powerful social institutions and the implication for social control in our mass society. (Cf., *The Power Elite.*)

Those in power in American industry, politics, and the military
make decisions which have far-reaching consequences not only for us,
but also for people throughout the world. These leaders also have the
power to implement their decisions in order to attain their primary goal,
maintaining and consolidating their power. Industrial leaders want
greater wealth, and they bring pressure to bear upon those in politics
to help them gain and maintain this wealth, whether through import
duties or special tax write-offs. Industrial leaders who reap profits from
weapons production have the support of top leaders in the military, who
desire to increase their own power and prestige. This combined pressure
from the industrial and military sectors of our society has in many cases
made willing accomplices of our politicians. The longest war in the history of the United States, for example, was fought without even the
necessity of securing a declaration of war from Congress. Congress has
been shoved into the background in making the significant decisions
in our society, such as a war in which approximately 50,000 Americans
lost their lives and hundreds of thousands of North and South Vietnamese were ruthlessly slaughtered. Having been able to harness the
Pentagon war machine and having found "limited warfare" profitable,
what do deaths matter as long as they net profits? Profit is the name
of the game, and as far as our power elite is concerned, it is the only
game in town.

With the ascendancy of the military to the top power position, the
cooptation of the political sector, and the resultant Pentagon capitalism
which has come to dominate our society, the power elite appears to be
firmly entrenched in its supremacy.

The solution for change cannot and will not come from our corporate elite, nor from their allies in the political and military sectors. It is in their vested interest to maintain the social system as it is presently constituted. Nor will the solution come from the leaders of our other social institutions, as they have become the willing captives of the economic order while they play handmaiden to the corporate enterprise.

Where can the solution come from? And what is that solution?

There are no adequate answers to such pressing questions. It is much easier to point out problems and analyze their causes and consequences than it is to propose solutions, but I can indicate possibilities.

First, just as the solutions will not come from our present "leadership," so no little tinkering with our social system is going to solve our problems. Second, as indicated in this book, our social problems do not come about by individual actions, because of individual sentiments, or because of individuals. Rather, our social problems are endemic to our social system; that is, they are built into the social system that we now live under. They are part and parcel of that social system. Accordingly, the social system itself must be changed. To tinker with parts can at best ameliorate. According to the *systemic* analysis of social problems, the system itself is what is at fault.

With these two vital points, I can indicate that to solve our social problems, the direction for social change must come from other than our leadership elite, and the social change must center around a fundamental change of the social system itself. This means creating a new social system, the developing of a new social order, and instituting a new form of societal leadership. What that new social order will look like will have to be unveiled when and if such change takes place. Certainly for a more humane orientation, it must be one that is not captive to a favored few who control our social institutions for their own interests. Perhaps such changes will come when people see their common plight and no longer passively accept—perhaps.

If they do not, I see no way out of our current predicament. Without such change, I see, rather, the perpetuation of social control for the benefit of the few at the expense of the many—with the majority continuing to be blinded and hating those who differ from themselves as they fearfully maintain the only social order they know. But my vision may be blurred by working too closely with analyzing social problems. Perhaps there are alternative solutions that others will see. And perhaps those solutions will be put to work—hopefully for the good of humanity, and not for their exploitation and subjugation for the privileged few. That I know we have had enough of.

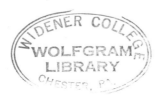

DATE DUE

DEC 0 5 2005			